PAGEANT OF THE POPES

By John Farrow

ILLUSTRATED BY JEAN CHARLOT

HOLY YEAR EDITION

NEW YORK

1950

Sheed & Ward

NIHIL OBSTAT:

    PATRICK J. DIGNAN, PH.D., CENSOR DEPUTATUS

IMPRIMATUR:

    ✠J. FRANCIS A. MC INTYRE, ARCHIEPISCOPUS ANGELORUM
    IN CALIFORNIA

la DECEMBRIS, 1949

SECOND EDITION • DESIGNED BY STEFAN SALTER

    FIRST PRINTING, SEPTEMBER, 1942
    SECOND PRINTING, OCTOBER, 1942
    THIRD PRINTING, NOVEMBER, 1942
    FOURTH PRINTING, JANUARY, 1943
    FIFTH PRINTING, SEPTEMBER, 1944
    SIXTH PRINTING, OCTOBER, 1945
    SEVENTH PRINTING, MARCH, 1947
    EIGHTH PRINTING, JANUARY, 1950

MANUFACTURED IN THE UNITED STATES OF AMERICA

BY KNICKERBOCKER PRINTING CORPORATION, NEW YORK

FOR MY WIFE

PREFACE

It was the late and great Archbishop of Los Angeles, the Most Reverend John J. Cantwell, who suggested that this book be written. He thought, and I agreed, that a one volume history of the "August Dynasty" might well serve to introduce the uninitiated into an enjoyment of the unhurried delights of Pastor and the rest of the great company of scholars. But because of the war and other circumstances it was rather slow to take form. My notes and research books were carried in many strange places. I can remember when, on anti-submarine patrol, I would grope my way to the bridge in the cold dark hours of the early watch and receive the cheerful greeting: "Well, have you finished another Pope?" Throughout it all Archbishop Cantwell kept me fortified, both by letter and in person, with his encouragement. I salute his memory.

I wish to thank Monsignor Patrick J. Dignan, Ph.D., who took time from his busy office of Archdiocesan School Superintendent to scan the manuscript for error. My gratitude is also due to the Reverend Thomas O'Toole of Los Angeles, the Reverend Edward J. Whelan and the Reverend Joseph J. Donovan of the Society of Jesus. They watched the development of the manuscript with sympathy and indeed it was Father Donovan who supplied the title. I also acknowledge the kindness of Mr. Elio Gasperetti, instructor at St. Basil's College, Stamford, Conn., whose careful eye and scholarship assisted in the revisions necessary for the Holy Year Edition.

The book is not shaped into chapters or parts. The Papal line has never been broken and for that reason my telling of the long drama is in a continuous narrative form rather than being divided into the more conventional pattern.

J. F.

St. Peter

IT WAS SEVEN WEEKS AND FOUR days since Christ had been nailed to the Cross. Fifty-three full days since the awful sentence that was so to change the course of mankind. A Procurator might brood in Herod's palace but his soldiery must patrol with watchful eye, for crowds of pilgrims were swarming upon Jerusalem eager to celebrate the Pentecostal rites, so ancient and significant to their race. On such a day, as the centurions well knew, the fires of nationalism could easily flare but as it happened there was no such trouble. Except by a few the tragedy of Calvary was either unknown or dimmed in the memory and a festive mood occupied the twisted streets. Rich harvests there must have been for the merchants and bazaars; and the clang of Roman arms, surely a minor note in all that Eastern tumult, continued to exact the usual respect although in the afternoon there was an incident which could not have escaped the attention of the patrol commanders. Around one narrow corner the flow of the mob had halted and the gay jostle and babble had faded as a man flanked by a small group of zealous-eyed companions began to speak. From his simple dress, the gnarl of his hands, the weathering of his face, one would judge him to be a laborer. He certainly was no known Doctor or richly fringed Pharisee yet he spoke, and with a strange authority, of God. And so eloquent was his faith, so convincing was his testimony that his haphazardly congregated audience, numbering between two and three thousand, did not jeer or scoff but listened with respect. It was the first sermon of Peter, the beginning of the Church on earth as an organized society, administered by men. A momentous event, this gathering on the crowded street, the commencement of a long story that has never yet sighted the horizon of finality, a story stained with blood and tears and woven with glory and shame, with triumph and disaster, but never obscured with the blanket of absolute defeat.

Although supernaturally inspired the new company was but of mortals and as such it was of course necessary to have authority vested in one person. Chosen was one well proven to have lived his full share of human weakness and folly. No unusual man, more righteous than his fellows, no pale blooded scholar, surfeited with learning, no ascetic celibate, ponderous with rectitude, had been the brawny fisherman when, in obedience to the divine command, he had stowed his nets and made fast the halyards of his small craft for a last time. Simon, born in the village of Bethsaida, had been his name; but the One whom he obeyed changed it to *Kīphā*, meaning in the Aramaic language, *Rock*, from which is derived PETER. "Thou art Peter (Kīphā) and upon this rock (Kīphā) I will build my church" were words that gave to the unlettered fisherman a precedence never to be questioned by his fellow Apostles and to him, after the departure of their Master, naturally fell the duty and dangerous honor of delivering the first public proclamation of the Christian Church.

Persecution of that Church is an accompanying theme from the beginning and it was not long before Peter and his friend John were summoned before the Jewish High Council and commanded to cease their activities. Their courageous reply was that they were bound to obey God rather than men. Death was then threatened and an end to their lives, prompt and cruel, would have undoubtedly been their lot if it had not been for the good offices of Gamaliel, a tolerant minded and highly respected doctor of laws, who advised his colleagues that: "If this counsel or this work be of men it will come to naught; but if it be of God, you cannot overthrow it." This plea served for the moment but the High Priests, wrapped in the obstinacy and jealousy of their own man-bestowed rank, remained unconvinced and eventually their bitterness resulted in the stoning to death of the deacon Stephen. Thus was enacted the first Christian martyrdom. To witness it, glowering satisfaction at the bloody sight, was a zealous young Pharisee, himself unknowingly doomed for a martyr's crown: he was named Saul, and was to be called Paul, when, upon changing his views, he became the great Apostle to the Gentiles.

The Church was born and it was in being but in those very first days it was not yet catholic. For long centuries their composite heritage of religion and race had been jealously guarded by the Jews. Conquered they might be, indemnities of gold and obeisance they might deliver but their blood remained undiluted, the Mosaic law undefiled. Gentiles might sometimes overwhelm and rule them but Gentiles also, according to the precious tradition, were to be considered unclean and unfit to worship in the synagogues. Therefore in that all-Jewish community of his fellow believers there was consternation when Peter, prompted by a vision and without even attempting any preliminary rites of racial adoption such as circumcision, baptized one Cornelius, a man of rank in the Roman Army of occupation. Without ostentation or elaborate ceremony the Gentile officer was touched by the Jewish fisherman with water, thus enacting with simplicity an event that proved to be of the highest historical importance, the act that marked the development of the Church into the international and inter-racial society which from that time on has offered participation to all, no matter of what race or rank. Many of the early Jewish Christians, or Nazarenes or Galileans as they were then called, were to show considerable hesitation before sharing what they had sincerely believed was their birthright of race. It was difficult for these members of the chosen people to realize that the common God of all, as St. Paul afterwards explained to the Athenians, "hath made of one blood all races of men."

It was inevitable that the new religion should spread to Rome.

All roads led to the seat of Imperial splendor, all things came there, for in truth it was the center of the known world. Roman rule and valor persisted everywhere and the measured tramp of the Legions was a sound as familiar to the Libyan plains as to the forests bordering the Rhine and Danube. There seemed to be no end to the mounting power of the Imperial City; and the Imperators themselves, in reality a sad succession of debauched murderers, not content with the glories of the purple, had even assumed the mantle of divinity. But in the administrative structure of the great city, which possessed an Empire there was one weakness. Many religions were practised, many gods were worshipped, but lacking was the sustaining influence of a true moral force. Thus it was an opportune time for the new faith, which at first was greeted by the Romans as a depraved and decadent sect sprung from the absurd religion of a conquered people. Actually there is no historical record to tell us when Christianity was first established in Rome, or who brought it there. It is supposed in some quarters that amongst those converted by the Pentecostal sermon there were Jewish pilgrims from Rome and that upon returning to their homes they formed a community of believers. Whether this was their founding or not, a group of Christians did exist to welcome Peter when he arrived to establish his headquarters in the second year of the reign of Claudius.

At the very fountain-head of temporal might and power the unarmed fisherman had come to preach a strange and new doctrine of a universal brotherhood. The humble Jew had come to give challenge to the code of the Emperors which said that men's consciences were, like their persons and properties, subject to the will of the State. Details of his life in the capital are not known. Licence in vice and a wild and ceaseless pursuit of pleasure in all forms was the fashion of the Roman populace; and that peculiar and arrogant characteristic of debauchees, exhibitionism, caused public scenes which could not but have saddened Peter who, when writing to the churches of Asia, sent greetings from "the Church that is in Babylon." It was an obvious comparison that makes very clear the opinion he held of his environment.

Tradition places his episcopate as having lasted a quarter century but this could not have meant actual residence. There was so much to do and the world was his parish. Many and laborious must have been the missionary excursions and the visitations to co-religionists in near and distant provinces. Some historians claim that he spent some seven years at Antioch, at that time a most flourishing center of Christian life. To Jerusalem it is certain he returned to preside over the First Council of the Church—a congregation of the Apostles which met to discuss the controversies that still attended the conversions of Gentiles, and which, owing to the inspired pleading of St. Paul, definitely decreed that excepting for a few restrictions such converts need not adopt or observe the Judaic conventions.

Upon Herod Agrippa, made King of the Jews by the Emperor Caligula, there falls the dark distinction of being the first monarch deliberately to single out the Christians for oppression. This had been in the year 42, the year the Apostles had dispersed to carry their faith to the world. At that time Peter had been imprisoned but had effected a miraculous escape. Twenty-two years later, however, a vastly more powerful prince than Herod was to turn the force of his malignity upon the new religion. The great conflagration of Rome in July of the year 64 was too immense a calamity to pass without somebody being blamed. The belief had swept through the city, perhaps with justification, that it was the latest crime of the Emperor Nero whose vicious appetites were notoriously without control or limit. As the mobs began to mutter he, in order to avert this suspicion, quickly turned the finger of accusation upon the Christians and in the orgy of bloodletting that followed it was his tortuous mind which devised new and elaborate ways not only for men to die, but their women and children too.

These helpless victims of a debauchee's lie and a rabble's fury perished both collectively and individually with what now seems an incredible heroism. The long centuries which separate their age from modern times are apt to endow their savage deaths with a perspective of unreality, but it should never be forgotten that the fierce fact of physical pain was no less then than it is today. The unlessening faith shown before lunging attacks of starved beasts, or in the awful agonies of the stake, or during the lingering tortures of crucifixion, produced an inevitable result. For every Christian who thus died a hundred were born.

During these massacres both Paul and Peter suffered martyrdom. Paul as a Roman citizen was given the "privilege" of being beheaded whereas his friend was sentenced to the ignominy of the cross. And when the end came, displaying a mood unlike that of earlier days, the fisherman was calm and serenely courageous, making but one plea of his executioners. He declared he was not worthy to die in the same manner as his Master and begged them to make the execution different by nailing him to the cross head downwards. The plea, it is said, was granted and so died Peter, the first of the pontiffs, in the year 67. Little is known of his immediate successors save their names, the approximate years of their terms, their common heritage of humble birth, and the fact, significant if unrecorded testimony, that during their time Christianity, despite all opposition, continued on its steady growth.

LINUS was the first to inherit Peter's mantle, officiating until the year 76. According to tradition he was not a Jew but an Italian from Tuscany. But Jew or not, as a Christian he must have grieved when during his time Jerusalem was razed by Roman troops under the command of Titus. He was succeeded by CLETUS (or *Anacletus*) who presided until 88. Throughout these years, because of the persistent menace of persecution, perhaps sometimes dormant but never absent, the administration of the Church was conducted with as much secrecy as can cloak the activities of any society which seeks new adherents; and despite the displeasure of the Imperial authorities the new doctrine was being carried by zealous missionaries throughout the known world, even as far as the mystery-shrouded regions of the Middle East. CLEMENT, who followed Cletus, had been a friend of Peter and Paul and it is in his time we can first clearly discern the workings and formations of ecclesiastical rank; the subjection of deacons and priests to the discipline of their bishops and these same bishops' acceptance of the authority of Peter's successors. The first known example of the exercise and acceptance of this authority was when Clement, in a firmly phrased letter, exerted his influence over ecclesiastical affairs in the distant city of Corinth, an act highly significant for living at Ephesus, much closer to Corinth than Rome, was one of the original Apostles, St. John.

In the sixth year of Clement's term the Emperor Domitian, who had assumed the title of Lord and God, commenced a new persecution. Much blood was again shed but this time it was not only slaves and obscure foreigners who perished. Many of the Roman aristocracy had by now been converted and they too showed they could uphold the Christian tradition of dying with fortitude and serenity. Domitian's severity was not confined only to the realm of religion and (in 97) he was to meet his own death at the hands of an assassin. Nevertheless the persecutions he had inaugurated were continued, although perhaps with less vigor, under the two year reign of the aged Nerva who succeeded him. Up to this time Clement by some means had eluded arrest but he was now seized and given the comparatively mild punishment of exile. Banishment, however, to him meant merely an excellent opportunity for missionary activities. He persisted and exercised his priestly functions even in the midst of the soldiery. Finally, after refusing to obey an Imperial order to render sacrifice to the gods, he, too, closed his life by dying for the Faith. Legend has it that he was hurled into the sea with a heavy weight fastened to his neck.

Evaristus now took the helm. Of him it is recorded that he was born in Bethlehem of Jewish parentage and that he founded the parochial system, dividing Rome into parishes. In the third year of his office he celebrated the hundredth year since the Birth of Christ. One full century since the Birth at Bethlehem and sixty-six years since Peter had preached the first sermon. To be a Christian still meant death but nevertheless the teachings of the Nazarene had spread to, and sometimes beyond, all corners of the huge Empire. Despite the terrors of persecution a disciplined priesthood was administering to a laity that was formed of many races and different tongues yet which was bound together with a unity stronger than the command of any Caesar, the bond of common faith. And it was about this time, this first turning of a century since the birth of its Founder, that the Church received the name by which it is now known. From the pen of the great bishop of Antioch, St. Ignatius, came the significant and historical words: Catholic Church.

Trajan was then the Roman Emperor. History has judged him to be an able ruler and possessed of high character. There is no doubt that under his rule the Empire prospered yet from the first he frowned upon the Christians, regarding them as misguided fanatics who were troublesome to the civic power and as such should be stamped out. This he endeavoured to do by giving impetus to the Third General Persecution amongst whose victims were St. Ignatius and St. Simeon of Jerusalem. The persecution failed in its objective and Trajan, conqueror of Dacia and brilliant soldier and administrator, was defeated. However, he allowed no feeling of chagrin to drive him into angry excesses. He continued to persecute but eventually showed less severity and at no time of his reign can it be claimed that his actions were characterized by the murderous brutality of his predecessors. Writing to his Legate, Pliny the Younger, who had appealed to him for instructions he said "They (the Christians) are not to be sought out, but if accused and convicted they must be punished." In other words he was leaving the matter entirely to the discretion of Pliny. Evaristus died during this reign in the year 105 and although the exact circumstances of his death are not known tradition counts him as one of the martyrs.

St. Alexander, a native Roman, came next, presiding until 115 when he was beheaded and his body buried in the catacombs. Little is known of him save that he is credited with the inauguration of the institution of holy water. Of his successor, Sixtus, we are told even less. He was a Roman; his rule lasted ten years and he was followed by Telesphorus, a Greek whose pontificate (to 136) was disturbed by a series of grave heresies. It is not within the province of this limited work to enter into descriptions of the formidably numerous heresies and schisms which have troubled the Church from its founding. A great number of volumes would be needed for such a task but in passing it can be said that time has proven that the results of schism have always been the same. Severed from the fount of their beginning they inevitably lose energy within themselves and so gradually perish.

Telesphorus was well equipped to use measures, both of authority and argument, necessary to combat the heresies of his day. Previous to his election his had been the meditative and strictly ordered life of a desert anchorite. Evidence of this early life of penance and fasting is discernible in his act of taking the old customs of Lent and molding them into one definite rule. The first Christian Apology was addressed to the Emperor in his time. This document, written by Quadratus, a disciple of the Apostles, aimed to explain the position of the Christians but it had no immediate effect. Christianity was still a crime against the State and as such was punishable by death. Hadrian had succeeded Trajan and, if anything, was even less severe than that ruler; nevertheless the law remained unaltered.

It is not difficult to understand the official Roman viewpoint. By this time the pattern of the Empire had apparently attained perfection. Never before had it, or any other country, been so prosperous or powerful. Yet the Christians proposed to effect a complete social change. They talked of the brotherhood of man and to the Emperors this theory was not only ridiculous and blasphemous, but treasonable as well.

Persecution continued and in one of the periodic raids Telesphorus was captured and despatched to his martyrdom. A few years before his death the Jews at Jerusalem made their final desperate rebellion against Roman rule and for a last time in history the ancient ram's-horn, the *Shofar*, called the Jewish people, as a nation, to arms. But, as Titus had ruthlessly suppressed their fathers only sixty-five years before, so did Hadrian again, destroying completely whatever had been left from or built since the first siege. The ancient city was now no more. Its residents were either killed or banished from the sight even of the ruins, upon which a Roman colony called Elia Capitolina was formed.

HYGINUS, of Greek birth, was the ninth Pope, presiding for about four years and principally remembered for his regulation of minor clerical orders. He was followed by PIUS and of him history tells nothing except the fact of his name and that his pontificate lasted from 140 to 155. After him came a Syrian, one ANICETUS, who ruled eleven years, during which time there arose the great argument with the Eastern Church as to the day which should be celebrated as Easter. In Rome it was the *Sunday following* the fourteenth Nisan (i.e. the fourteenth day after the March moon). In the East it was the actual day of the fourteenth Nisan. Polycarp, able Bishop of Smyrna, tried to urge the latter usage on Rome but Anicetus remained steadfast to the custom that had begun with Peter. Great controversy was waged between Bishop and Pope but the Pope did not make it a question of papal authority and the Bishop had the good sense not to suggest or cause a schismatic break. The argument was to continue until finally settled, in favour of the Western Church, at the Council of Nicaea in 325. And even after then we find the Celtic monks disputing the Easter question with the Roman missionaries in Britain. Other things there were besides this vexatious altercation that Anicetus found to disapprove of in ecclesiastical ranks. He accused his clergy of being over-considerate of their personal appearance, and in a series of regulations expressed his censure and wishes. As the Church had grown, so of course had the priesthood; and with such a quickly spreading organization, still forced to the shroud of secrecy, it was easy for unauthorized changes to creep into the liturgy, particularly when that liturgy was not yet recorded in written form. SOTER who succeeded Anicetus in 166 turned a vigilant eye on these errors and insisted on the correct and orthodox observance of all sacred customs. In searching for such abuses he came in contact with many of the poorer Christian communities and these, it is recorded, he made it a special mission to assist.

Marcus Aurelius the Philosopher was Emperor during this pontificate but despite his philosophy he displayed less tolerance than had been shown during the previous reigns. Persecution was intensified and remained so into the time of Pope ELEU-THERIUS who officiated for fifteen years. Both in Rome and in the provinces Christian blood ran freely and with terrible persistence. No resistance was offered but in this generation there were not lacking learned Christians who could utilize the potency of words, in the phrasing of philosophy which the Emperor so admired, and so defend their faith with logic as well as vigor and courage. But as far as Marcus Aurelius, and his son, the despicable Commodus, were concerned the Apologies bore no weight and the persecutions were continued. And with the same sequel as earlier times. Each martyrdom served as a beacon to attract droves of converts, the Church continued to grow, and the propaganda of the faith unceasingly went on. And sorely harassed as Pope Eleutherius must have been he yet found time to formulate plans for the conversion of such far-off places as Britain.

His successor was VICTOR, a strong willed man who did not hesitate to strike with the drastic weapon of excommunication when he deemed it necessary. He rightly pronounced this awful sentence against the apostate and schismatic Theodotus, and indeed he almost gave the same penalty to the entire Eastern Church over a dispute based on the old argument of the Easter date. However, Irenaeus, a Syrian theologian who became Bishop of Lyons in France, persuaded him to reconsider this action. Thus peace was made, with the Eastern bishops resolutely keeping to their own customs. Victor died in 199 and the third century of Christianity dawned with ZEPHYRINUS, a Roman of humble birth, as Pope. He was kind to sinners and generous to the poor but possessing little education he sought the advice in many matters of his friend, the deacon and ex-slave, Callistus. For this he was bitterly criticized by such writers as

Tertullian and the scholar-priest Hippolytus, both of whom at this period fell into heresy, becoming adherents of the harshly ascetic doctrine of Montanism. Their outcries fortunately did not serve to prevent the election of CALLISTUS after the death of Zephyrinus in 217. Able qualities of leadership soon justified the confidence of his friend and the decision of those who had chosen him. However, Hippolytus whose undeniable brilliance had won him a considerable following declared the election to have been false and then allowed his own disciples to bestow upon him the title of Head of the true Church. Thus for the first time we have an Anti-Pope. No salvo of excommunications from Callistus however followed this announcement. Indeed unlike some of his contemporaries who, immersed in the interpretation of the Gospel, were apt to forget the essence of Christian teachings, the Pope in this and many other matters exhibited a charity worthy of his office. He changed and modified the harsh penitential system and in one radical edict made known that adulterers, providing their remorse was sincere, were not to be refused absolution. This gesture of mercy drew the wrath of certain righteous doctors who had forgotten the famous admonition to those who would stone the Magdalen. "Where shall we post up this generous concession," asked the irate Tertullian, "on the doors of brothels?"

The pretensions of Hippolytus persisted after the death of Callistus, throughout the pontificate of URBAN (222-230), and into that of PONTIAN. For the first five years of this Pope's reign the struggle was bitter and grave for Hippolytus was a dangerously skilled antagonist. Then in a fresh outburst of persecution by an Emperor who took no trouble to differentiate between true or schismatic Christianity, both were banished to the Sardinian mines. In the stultifying confines of imprisonment antipathies are usually intensified into deadly hatred: less commonly a friendship is formed strong with understanding and loyalty. Happily it was the latter case with Pope and Anti-Pope. Hippolytus acknowledged his error and made a complete and unconditional submission to Pontian who without rancor received him back into the Church. Soon after, this new friendship was sealed with the bond of dual martyrdom.

When Pontian had been seized he had resigned his office and elected in his stead was ANTERUS who, however, died a few months later. The next Pope was FABIAN and he proved himself to be a capable executive, directing the Church through times that were turbulent not only for his co-religionists but for all under Roman rule. The barbarity of the peasant-born Emperor Maximin had thrown the Empire into excesses of disorder that were to endure for many reigns. Murder now seemed to be the usual instrument of accession to the honors of the purple and it was by this decidedly un-Christian method that Philip, sometimes known as the first Christian Emperor, achieved the Imperial station. Little is known of his conversion but once on the throne he seems to have been suitably remorseful of his former violences. In his reign and for the first time official tolerance was accorded Christians and to Pope Fabian was granted the right for ecclesiastical authorities to possess properties.

But the unfamiliar tranquillity was not to endure for long. In 249 Philip was dispossessed of his rank in the same bloody manner in which it had been acquired. Decius, his erstwhile lieutenant, was now hailed by the Legions, savage in their passions and so fickle in their loyalties, as Emperor. He was a man of severe nature who sincerely believed the salvation of the State could be only achieved by return to the pagan standards of ancient Rome and his temper towards the Church was quickly manifested in an edict which declared that death was to be the penalty for all who would not forsake Christianity. This savage decree was a challenge quickly accepted by Fabian who made gallant answer with his life. Nor did he die alone. With splendid celerity there was a rush of martyrs worthy of his heroic example. But this time too there were also found many who in the terror of the moment denied their faith. The easy years of non-persecution had produced "easy" Christians who preferred to live with the accusations of their consciences rather than to die before the sentences of the judges.

The Church was a public enough organization by now for Decius to have a thorough knowledge of its means of government. Without a Pope, he reasoned, the Christians would be without a centralized authority and so eventually would be bound to dissolve as an organized society. He set himself to prevent a new election after Fabian's execution and so vigilant were his officers that for a year the scheme was successful. But though no Pope was elected the administration of the Church went on uninterruptedly in the person of a Council of Presbyters who in defiance of the Emperor met and dwelt secretly in Rome. To this regency there came one Novatus from Africa with accusations of apostasy against the powerful Bishop of Carthage. This was Cyprian who, better to direct his clergy, had justifiably taken refuge from the civil power. Novatus had no success with the Council but he did find an ally in the clever but too ambitious priest Novatian who, as later events proved, harbored designs on the papacy.

Meanwhile there were problems other than the Christians to employ the attention of the Emperor. For the first time of any importance the Goths invaded the Empire and the Emperor was summoned to the Danube to head his soldiery. His absence from Rome was the signal for a papal election where the honor fell to the gentle-mannered CORNELIUS, a Roman of aristocratic antecedents. Quite naturally this choice found no favour with the envious Novatian who, embittered by his own lack of success, soon fell into schism, declaring loudly that Cornelius was at error in permitting penitent apostates to be granted forgiveness. As this was a question widely discussed in the Church at that time Cornelius with some wisdom called upon sixty bishops to journey to Rome and form a Council. This was in the autumn of 251 and the result was the condemnation of Novatian's propaganda, and the excommunication of him and his followers.

The net of the persecution now tightened around Pope Cornelius and he was sentenced to banishment and then, while still in exile, put to death. LUCIUS, named as his successor, was promptly sent to exile also. But instead of being executed he was ordered back to Rome at the direct command of a new Emperor, Valerian, the second successor of Decius. This ruler at first exhibited every sign of being tolerant and conciliatory. The Pope on his return was astonished to find openly professing members of his flock in favor at the Imperial Court and there were other evidences of official magnanimity to warm his heart. To the happy Pontiff, so recently a prisoner, it seemed as though a new era had commenced and he was never to suffer disillusionment for that same year, just twelve months after his election, he passed away peacefully; a death rare enough to merit mention in the history of the earlier Popes. He was followed by STEPHEN who, apparently anxious that no incident should stir Pagan ire and so start the persecution again, cautioned that the clergy should not wear ecclesiastical vestments, except inside the churches. A long argument with the Bishop of Carthage concerning the validity of baptism by heretics then engaged his attention. Stephen, who affirmed such baptisms as valid, finally made public throughout the Church a definite ruling on the subject which served to draw several other bishops into the fray. This altercation lasted three years and was interrupted, although not settled, by an alarming change in Valerian's attitude.

For the first time in history a Prince became suspicious and envious of the Church's material wealth. The moment was propitious. Disorder at the frontiers and a series of internal confusions had reduced the Imperial coffers to a near-emptiness. The growing strength of the Church, the increasing importance of the bishops, presented a target too conspicuous to escape the envy of a perturbed Emperor. Readily he listened to the calumnies and advice of an anti-Christian member of his court and soon there came an edict. Gatherings of Christians were forbidden and the bishops and clergy were ordered, under pain of death or exile, to render sacrifice to the Pagan gods. There followed the same brave sad sequel of the previous persecutions. The Pope perished in exile and a new crop of martyrs was made.

Terribly certain of martyrdom was he who would be chosen to head the faithful at such a hazardous time. SIXTUS II courageously accepted the fatal honour and soon after was beheaded upon his own throne. The lot of his successor, DIONYSIUS, was happier for once again an invasion of the Empire providentially caused a cessation of the persecution. The alarmed Valerian marched to a campaign which was to mean his defeat, his capture, and his death. To him came the most ignominious end that was to befall a Roman ruler. During his imprisonment he was used by his Persian conqueror as a human stool upon which to step to the saddle and after his death in these shameful circumstances his corpse was stuffed with straw and publicly exhibited as a trophy of his defeat. These formidable insults to the purple and to the prestige of Rome were lightly borne by his son, Gallienus, who in fact lost no time in changing the policies of his father, including, happily, the laws against the Christians. Nor for them was this change the mere benignity of a tolerant mind. Active restitutions for past damages were made, full privileges of citizenship were granted, and Church property was restored.

Again it seemed as though the clouds of persecution had been permanently relegated to the past, and with the horizon of the future clear, the jubilant Pontiff was now able to devote full energies to the internal affairs of the Church. During his lifetime the happy relationship of State and Church continued to exist and at his death (in 268) he left it as a legacy which was to prevail until near the close of the century, throughout the pontificates of his next three successors, who were respectively FELIX, EUTYCHIAN and CAIUS. These Popes successfully carried on the tradition of good administration. There was much to do, for the faith was spreading rapidly. Heresies were abundant but were met with wise discipline, and orthodoxy was protected. Bishoprics grew, both in numbers and size, and certain powers of authority were delegated to higher bishops who were termed Metropolitans. The Papal position did not suffer by these necessary acts of administration. On the contrary during this period the primacy of the Apostolic See was becoming a more accomplished and more regulated fact than ever before. As the age of concealment passed the dark caverns of the catacombs ceased to provide the only chapels for Rome. Churches were built, and splendidly, everywhere. The Church had finally emerged as a recognized and united Society, with too numerous and powerful a membership to invite, so many thought, aggressive restrictions again.

But the brightness of success is rarely unaccompanied by the shadows of jealousy. Swords may have been sheathed but pens were at work, producing a steady stream of ridicule and falsehood that in turn was kindling the rancor of resentment amongst that considerable part of the population who in earlier days had regarded the Christians as too insignificant a minority to excite any feeling save indifference or occasional pity. But indifference could not survive in the face of the mounting and obvious strength of the Church and as the end of the third century neared most Romans held one of two opinions; if not Christian, then anti-Christian. Such was the condition of affairs when in 296 the Roman MARCELLINUS became Pope, eleven years after the able Diocletian had reached the Imperial station which he was to occupy with undeniable brilliance until his abdication in 305. At the beginning of his reign Diocletian did not show any signs of bitterness towards the Christians. Combining exceptional talents of martial skill and civil administration, so rarely found united in one human brain, he set out to reorganize the government of the Empire, partitioning the vast territories into two portions, East and West, each to be governed separately by an Emperor who in turn was to be assisted by a sub-ruler. The East he chose for his own jurisdiction and for his chief lieutenant, with the august title of Caesar, he selected Galerius, an energetic product of the Legions, a barbarian who proved to be a true personification of the pagan standards he so assiduously followed. The hatred and contempt that this man held for the Christians, his utter incomprehension and warrior's disgust at their precepts of kindness and forgiveness, finally resulted in Diocletian's promulgating an edict against them.

Bitter and savage were the cruelties that followed for such was the discipline maintained by this ruler that any order issued by him was executed to the minutest detail, to the fullest extent of human endeavour. But human endeavour has its very definite limits; the skies of his domains were clouded by the smoke of burning churches, the streets of his cities were stained with the blood of new martyrs, the consciences of his magistrates were made heavy with unjust sentences, but never could the Christian spirit be obliterated. Pope Marcellinus perished during these outrages and the story of his death is as lost as his sacred books which were destroyed in the pagan fires. According to our tradition he apostasized at first, but repented after a few days and expiated his sin by the shedding of his blood.

Four years elapsed before another Bishop of Rome could be elected. This time it was MARCELLUS, who immediately and with courageous defiance set out to provide new places of worship for the churchless faithful. He died only one year after he had taken office (309) and was succeeded by EUSEBIUS whose death in exile occurred after a term of equal brevity. The reign of the next pontiff, MELCHIADES, of African birth, was dramatically made bright with triumph; for even the savage Galerius when on his deathbed, like so many other implacable enemies of the Church at the same solemn moment, was to beg for Christian prayers and forgiveness. Maximin, who succeeded him as Emperor of the East, did not allow this unexpected mood to soften his judgment which was vehemently anti-Christian. This tyrant in turn stoked the fires of the persecution to a renewed intensity which, however, was not to endure for long. The tide was soon to turn. But let us return to Diocletian.

Within a year of the publication of his infamous edict he, prompted by a philosophy none of which, alas, he showed in his treatment of the Christians, had astonished his subjects by divesting himself of his exalted rank and had retired to forget the turbulence of an Empire in the peace of a country garden. He who had controlled the destinies of millions of men was content to turn his energies to the nurturing of a few cabbages. After successfully regulating great territories he was satisfied to anticipate death, and to pass on his power and policies to his successors. But rarely do the plans of a despot run smoothly after he has quitted the scene. Divided rule was not for the Empire and Diocletian's successors were quick to learn that purple is a color that loses much of its glory when worn by more than one. Contemporary rulers soon became rival rulers and as ambitions clashed wars and confusions were born and from these struggles eventually came the incident which was to mark the turning for the Christians.

In the Autumn of 312 the new Emperor of the West, Constantine, a young leader who had inherited the virtue of a tolerant nature from a wise father marched his army across the Alps and was about to storm the gates of Rome. On the day before battle, alone with solemn thoughts that must haunt even the most confident of commanders at such a time, he says that he saw a vision. Brightly etched against the evening sky there shone a Cross and beneath it to dazzle his astonished eyes was the shimmering legend *In hoc signo vinces.*

"By this sign thou shalt conquer." These were startling words and were to inspire a startling decision: for to most Romans the Cross was still the repugnant symbol of a dishonorable death. Nevertheless Constantine had commanded that the fateful words were to be the motto of his troops. The next day he won his battle and with a memory unlike most Princes his gratitude was always to remain. A few months after this particular victory, along with his colleague of the West, Licinius, he not only announced freedom of worship for all but also promised restitution of properties to a dispossessed Christian clergy.

Joyfully Pope Melchiades bent to his altar as the Edict of Milan was issued. After three centuries a Christian was no longer to be considered a criminal because of his faith. Roman law had changed and in the reign of the thirty-second pope a new era had begun.

The very year of the Edict of Milan saw the first Council of the Church to be convened with full sanction of the secular authorities. But the occasion was not one for celebration: for no sooner had the sword of the persecutor been stayed than ominous and formidable dissensions within their own ranks began to threaten Christian unity. Melchiades was forced to convene a meeting of bishops. On arriving in Rome the clerics were saluted as persons of rank and honor and their pride and happiness can well be imagined, these veterans, all of whom had suffered and administered under the shadows of oppression. Even the building that was the scene of their meeting, and where they pronounced judgment against the Donatist heresy, was in itself a splendid sign of the Imperial magnanimity for it was a gift from Fausta, the wife of Constantine, to Melchiades who made it the papal residence. And as such the Lateran Palace remained until its destruction by fire ten centuries later.

Melchiades died in 314 and was followed by SYLVESTER who was troubled by the grave schism of Arius and who was also to witness, in 321, a brief renewal of persecution under the direction of Licinius. This erstwhile ally of Constantine became his bitter enemy and opposed all his policies including the tolerance guaranteed the Christians by the Edict of Milan. The struggle between the two Emperors was ended by the violent death of Licinius which left Constantine the undisputed and sole ruler of the Empire. His own generation was to add to his name the title Great and that memory of successive generations which is called posterity has endorsed the bestowal—so commonly offered by sycophantic subjects to a ruler and so quickly forgotten—as well deserved. Like all of human mould he had his weaknesses, his vanities, his cruelties, but there can be no denial of his magnitude as an administrator. Nothing less than heroic were his efforts to reorganize the Empire. And not the smallest of his achievements was the prodigious task involved in the transference of the Imperial Headquarters to the strategically situated city of Byzantium, afterwards, in his honor, called Constantinople. This shifting of the temporal power was to prove of immense consequence to the Papacy for notoriously the protection of a ruler is seldom without its drawbacks to the Church. The intrigue so inevitable to courts thrives on proximity and the long miles separating Rome and Constantinople were to prove healthy indeed for the Papacy.

A strange fact of Constantine's life is that despite his championship of, and his obvious faith in, Christianity he was not to receive actual baptism until shortly before his death in 337. And so strong had become the Arian heresy by this time that it was the Arian bishop, Eusebius, who officiated at the important function. Arianism had begun with the teachings of Arius, a priest of Alexander, who attacked the doctrine of the Trinity and declared the Son to be subordinate to the Father. The eloquence of this misguided theologian rapidly won many supporters including the powerful Bishop of Nicomedia, Eusebius, who became his ardent patron. By 325 the theological dispute was waxing with such fury that the puzzled Emperor, although not yet a baptized Christian, saw fit to take action as a protector of the faith. He called together the Council of Nicaea. Three hundred and fourteen distinguished Fathers of the Church met amidst elaborate ceremonies of Imperial hospitality. Pope Sylvester did not attend because of the infirmities of his advanced age but he sent as his Legate, Osius, the Bishop of Cordova, and Vitus and Vincent, two priests of Rome.

"I consider dissension in the Church more dreadful and more painful than any war," Constantine told the assembled Churchmen as he exhorted them to unity. The Council sat from May to August and the important outcome was the formation of what has been known since as the Nicene Creed: "We believe in only one God, the Father, Almighty, maker of all things visible and invisible; and in only one Lord, Jesus Christ, the Son of God, the sole-begotten of the Father, that is to say of the Father's substance, God of God, Light of Light, true God of true God; begotten not made, consubstantial with the Father, by whom all things were made; who for us men and for our salvation came down, became incarnate, became man, suffered, was raised again on the third day, ascended back to heaven and will come again to judge the living and the dead; and in the Holy Spirit. As for those who say 'There was a time when He did not exist; Before

He was begotten He did not exist; He was made from nothing as from another substance or essence; The Son of God is a created being, changeable, capable of alteration,' to such as these the Catholic Church says Anathema."

In addition to this avowal some twenty canons of Discipline were promulgated; including a decree that said no cleric should have living in his residence any woman who was not a relative. As yet celibacy for the clergy was not a law of the Church although it was a traditional custom dating from Apostolic times when St. Paul had said, "He that is without a wife is solicitous for things that belong to the Lord, how he may please God. But he that is with a wife, is solicitous for the things of the world, how he may please his wife: and he is divided. . . ." At the end of the third century the tradition thus prompted by the great Apostle had become an actual rule in Spain. But when Osius, the Legate, sought to make it a universal law at the Council he received vigorous opposition, mainly from one Bishop Paphnutius whose spirited protest marked the commencement of that difference of opinion and practice on the same subject which still exists between the Eastern and Western Churches. Paphnutius pleaded sympathy for those priests who had been married before ordination, declaring that they should not be separated from their wives. The majority of his listeners agreed and Osius was defeated.

Eleven years after the great Council Pope Sylvester died and he was succeeded by MARK, an able prelate, whose pontificate however did not extend a full year. JULIUS, a valiant preserver of orthodoxy, was then elected to the sacred office. This good man's calm judgment, his able custodianship of dogma, was to stand like a beacon over a stormy sea for in truth the bark of St. Peter was at this time in danger of being swamped by the treacherous seas of schism. To aid him was the brilliant hero bishop of Alexandria, Athanasius, who was well equipped both with faith and scholarship to carry on the desperate struggle with the dissenters.

It was an age of schism. Misguided theologians, sincere in

their beliefs but noisy in their errors, were offering many new interpretations of the faith. And there were not lacking bishops to support them, for in the ranks of the latter there was now a troublesome new class, opportunists who did not hesitate to use ecclesiastical office in the pursuance of doubtful schemes. At this time, before actual consecration, the selection of a bishop was still determined by the inhabitants of a vacant See. In theory this might seem to be an admirable practice but in truth it was dangerous; for now that the Church had the approval of the majority there were the inevitable aspirants, in many cases successful, to the episcopal office whose sole vocation was a hungry desire for temporal power. Rascals of this caliber whose artful conniving had won for them the confidence of a community did not hesitate to adopt innovations in dogma whenever it suited their convenience. So when the Emperor, because of an unhappy ignorance, showed favor to Arianism such consciences quickly and conveniently followed that path. But though the Arians held Constantinople, Rome remained firm and uncompromising. In matters of discipline the pontiffs might accommodate but when it came to dogma they were adamant, not deigning to answer argument with counter argument but content to guard their heritage of traditional faith and quick to pronounce against any who would seek to change that trust.

After the death of Constantine the rule of his domains had descended to his sons, one of whom, Constans, was loyal to Pope Julius. But when, in 350, this prince perished in battle the Empire was subjected to the dominance of his brother Constantinus who favoured the Arians and frowned at Rome. Julius courageously defied this tyrant's will until his death two years later. He was succeeded by LIBERIUS who continued the admirable tradition of courage and orthodoxy until he was arrested and brought before the Emperor who banished him to exile and appointed the Arian bishop Felix to usurp the Roman See. The latter has always been mistakenly referred to as "Felix II," which explains why the next legitimate pope to bear the name Felix is called the third.

"The laws of the Church are more important than residence in Rome," was the pontiff's answer to the Imperial sentence. He remained in exile two years and the circumstances of his return are clouded with historical dispute for many authorities have agreed that the harassed man, in the plight of his exile and in the weariness of his advanced age, did eventually sign his name to a document insufficiently explicit against Arian doctrine. Whether he did or not may be the subject of argument but what remains clear is that there is no evidence of any kind to prove he ever *taught,* or approved the teaching of, any part of the Arian philosophy which differed from the Catholic faith. On his return to Rome the Imperial arrogance dictated that he should share the Papal office with the illegally appointed Felix. This absurd and presumptuous decision was suitably received by the Roman populace who, when it was announced in the Circus, loudly chanted with vigorous logic, "One God, one Christ, one Bishop."

The successor of Liberius was DAMASUS who, immediately after his election in 366, had in his turn to deal with a schismatic usurper, the deacon Ursinus. This time, however, the pretender received no Imperial support. On the contrary, after inciting his misguided adherents to noisy disorders, he was ordered from Rome by an Emperor of different views, Valentinian I, who also decreed that henceforth his magistrates were not to exercise any authority over ecclesiastical or religious matters. Vastly different had been the attitude of Valentinian's immediate predecessor, Julian, who in a reign of only two years had earned for himself the ignominious appellation of *Apostate.* In vain this obstinate prince had tried to revive Paganism but Christianity had proved too strongly rooted in the public conscience to be crushed, or even stemmed. By giving a semblance of Church organization to Pagan practices he had endeavoured to win allegiance to the ancient cults but no matter what measures he took, sweetened though they were by bribes and fortified with threats, he met with scant success. His death actually found the Christians enjoying more unity than when he had commenced his rule and as the profane fires of the sacrificial altars he had inaugurated flickered miserably into oblivion the Cross was once again carried before the Legions. Imperial animosity towards Christianity proved fortunate in one way for orthodoxy. Schismatic bishops were no longer able, by court intrigue, to cause harm or win favor.

The pontificate of Damasus is studded with achievement. In his person were combined the talents of theologian and administrator, and in the warmth of his zeal and the fertility of his wisdom the power of the papacy became nurtured to a larger and well consolidated strength. In all fields his energy was manifested. Ardent missionaries journeyed to distant places. Eloquent legates harangued Councils and Synods. Churches were restored and built. And masons and architects, spurred by the papal patronage, labored diligently to preserve the catacombs. It was Damasus who fixed the canon of the Old and New Testaments and it was with his encouragement that St. Jerome, for a while his secretary, revised the earlier Latin version of the Bible. Schismatics were outmaneuvered and heresies were stemmed. It was only natural that the author of so many vigorous policies should become a target for the plots of those whom he had frustrated. And indeed some of his enemies succeeded in bringing charges even of adultery against his name. The Emperor listened to this calumny as did also a synod of forty-four bishops with the result that not only was the scandal rejected but the accusers suffered excommunication for their lies. Two years before Damasus died and in the sixteenth year of his jurisdiction splendid triumph came to him in the form of the famous Imperial Edict De fide Catholica, issued by Theodosius, which declared the official religion of the Roman State to be "that doctrine which St. Peter had preached and of which Damasus was supreme head." He was the first pope to refer to Rome as the "Apostolic See."

SIRICIUS came next and his reign, lasting fourteen years, was a successful and peaceful continuation of Damasus' policies, unmarred by any great crisis or disaster, but witnessing the unprecedented spectacle of an erring Emperor bowing before the anger of a prelate. The principals of this significant drama were the Emperor Theodosius and the patrician-born Ambrose, Archbishop of Milan. Theodosius, for the most part an amiable and astute prince, had proved second only to Constantine in the furtherance and protection of the Church but unfortunately his record became blotted with a bloody and unjust crime. At the town of Thessalonica several of his officers had been brutally murdered and in the exasperation of his grief the Emperor, not waiting for the tedious workings of justice to punish the actual miscreants, had impatiently caused the entire city to be put to the sword. After fury had subsided there came the agonies of remorse to disturb the unhappy ruler, who was possessed of some degree of conscience, if not of discipline. He admitted his sorrow, his guilt, his unhappiness, but such protestations were not enough to appease the wrath of the redoubtable Ambrose who halted the Imperial passage to his cathedral, refusing admittance to the sacred premises, unless Theodosius made a public confession of his sins. This, before the awed gaze of his court, the contrite Emperor agreed to do and so as the end of the fourth century neared we find the kneeling figure of a Caesar, stripped of the emblems of his exalted rank, petitioning for clemency, humbly accepting the stinging words of accusation, rebuke and sentence, and submitting unconditionally to the authority of one of his own subjects.

Siricius died in the autumn of 399 and elected to succeed him was ANASTASIUS, a pious and wise prelate whose term in the sacred office was only to endure two years. INNOCENT followed him and with vigor and firmness this pontiff was to rule until 417. In the first year of his reign the martyrdom of a Christian was enacted for the last time in the Roman amphitheater. Christians though they now professed to be, the Roman populace still relished and patronized the savage spectacle of gladiators killing one another in vicious combat. In protest against such displays of savagery, so incompatible with Christian thought, a monk named Telemachus hurled himself into the arena one day and separated the combatants. The anger of the blood-hungry mob was aroused and he was stoned to death but his heroic act was not in vain and his bruised corpse proved to be the poignant sermon which finally ended all such barbaric practices.

Innocent's reign witnessed the invasion and sacking of Rome (410) by the Goths who however showed unexpected respect both to the ecclesiastics and the places of worship. The strength of the greatest temporal power the world had ever known was now plainly on the ebb. The Church had built its organization on the structure of the Empire and it might have been expected that as this foundation weakened so too would the ecclesiastical fabric. But events proved otherwise. The Barbarians might defeat and overrun the Empire but the Church, with its inexhaustible patience, was to absorb the Barbarians. More than ever the name *Catholic* was to be proved and justified.

The authority of Innocent was exercised over both Eastern and Western Churches but of course, like his predecessors, there were not lacking dissenters to draw his attention, his judgment, and his ire. This latter emotion he did not hesitate to manifest against the Empress Eudoxia who with a presumption fostered by an intriguing prelate, Theophilus, Patriarch of Alexandria, had ordered the deposition of the saintly Bishop of Constantinople, St. John Chrysostom. ZOSIMUS, the next Pope, lived but a year after his installation. During this time he was mainly occupied in dealing with Pelagianism, a heresy which denied the doctrinal belief of original sin. After his death there was an irregular election which resulted in the assumption of the papal title by the Archdeacon Eulalius. However at the correctly conducted election an aged Roman priest, BONIFACE, a man of great charity and learning who was sincerely reluctant to accept the high office, was proclaimed to be the rightful Pope and this just decision was finally supported by the Emperor whose soldiery ejected Eulalius and his supporters from the Basilica where they had been obstinately installed for nearly four months. Boniface was never to display the weaknesses that would have been understandable in a man of his advanced years. He showed himself to be a firm disciplinarian, regulating and defining the powers of the hierarchy, and strengthening in general the primacy of the Holy See.

His successor, in 422, was a really great Pope, the gentle and dignified CELESTINE, a staunch friend and supporter of that greatest Doctor of the western Church, St. Augustine, who was living at this time and was to die in the same year as the Pope. The kindness of Celestine's character is shown in his letters to the Bishops of Vienne and Narbonne when he admonished them that absolution should not be denied truly repentant sinners who were on their deathbed. His wisdom is shown when he urges that laymen are not to be consecrated bishops, and that the system of a bishop being chosen merely by popular acclaim should be discontinued. Great wisdom this pointiff must have possessed and exercised to govern at such a time when there was so much distress both within and without the Church. The Barbarians were successfully invading the Empire and a strong array of heresies were gnawing at orthodoxy. Yet Celestine's reign is somehow characterized by an air of orderly administration and of happily wielded and accepted authority culminating in the triumph of his legates over the pretensions of the heretical Nestorius at the Council of Ephesus. And not least among his meritorious deeds was his despatch of St. Patrick to convert the peoples of Ireland, the planting of a seed that was to flower with such magnificent and immortal results.

After the death of this great man in 432, SIXTUS III was elected and consecrated to the Holy See on July 31st of the same year. He presided capably for eight years and during this time a signal honor was bestowed upon his clergy when from their ranks a deacon was selected by the Emperor to be his envoy in the settlement of a dispute between the military commander and the civil magistrate of Gaul. The Emperor's act was not misguided for in addition to the judicial and conciliatory talents that the chosen ecclesiastic displayed on this occasion he was a scholar possessed of all the virtues that are necessary for unselfish and sagacious leadership. His name was LEO and he was destined to achieve the papal station in 440. Like Damasus his achievements were to extend to all fields and to all places and like that able pontiff he ascended to the Sacred Office to be confronted with the gravest problems, both spiritual and temporal.

The Empire was now in the tempestuous throes of its uneasy decline and whilst wars and campaigns were being waged the essence of Christian philosophy could very easily have been lost. Schisms and heresies, some new, some old, were flourishing with alarming vigor. The perilous conditions demanded that a competent pilot should be at the pontifical helm and Leo proved magnificently equal to the occasion. He disciplined erring priests and unruly bishops with stern but just measures. He met rulers with a diplomacy that had no taint of sycophancy. He carried on a prodigious correspondence in letters that were masterpieces of lucid philosophy. Perhaps the most important act of Leo's reign was the convocation of the Council of Chalcedon in 451, which defined the Church's doctrinal stand on the two natures of Christ. Just two years before the Emperor Theodosius had called together a "council" at Ephesus to decide on that same question. Through his legate the pope had sent his now-famous *Tome* which explained clearly the Catholic teaching on the point at issue. But the assemblage at Ephesus was dominated by the see of Alexandria, once the bulwark of orthodoxy but now termed heretical. Leo's *Tome* was not allowed to be read and the papal legate, after having registered his protest, was driven from the premises under peril of life and limb. There then had come appeals to the Pope from Constantinople and Antioch against Alexandria's unjust usurpations. Leo, of course, denounced the gathering at Ephesus as "the Robber Council" and asked for another to be convened under more legal auspices. In 451, therefore, the largest gathering of bishops the Church has ever had at a council met at Chalcedon and confirmed Leo's declaration that Christ had both a divine and human nature. Egypt was lost to the Church but with this pronouncement the purity of the Faith and the reality of the Redemption were once more triumphant. There was one other unfortunate corollary to the council. The prelates of Constantinople introduced a canon claiming that their see was the second see of Christiandom because it was the Empire's new capital. Leo, perceiving the danger this idea might cause to the doctrine of Petrine supremacy, protested vigorously, as was to be expected. Nevertheless, this motion on the part of the Byzantines planted the seeds of the schism which was to come six centuries later.

The greatness of Leo's moral leadership was apparent in other ways. When the Huns were marching on to Rome it was he who went and, with an eloquence that succeeded where the might of the Legions had failed, persuaded their leader, Attila, to halt the ominous progress.

Three years later when the Barbarian hordes again approached the Eternal City it was the pontiff who once more emerged as the calm and resolute hero of the disaster. Anticipation of frightful rapine had brought chaos and confusion to the city long before the invaders attacked, and the excited populace, surrendering to the hysteria of terror, murdered the Emperor Maximus. When all authority of the temporal power had vanished Leo took control and it was he who heroically went out of the city and confronted Genseric, King of the Vandals. But this time the Barbarians, with their rich spoil directly ahead, were not to be thwarted. They did loot and sack Rome but even in this savage disorder Leo received from Genseric the merciful concession that those inhabitants of this city who showed no resistance would not be harmed, nor would the Churches be pillaged or fired.

Inspiring examples of Leo's piety and scholarship are extant in the form of ninety-six of his sermons and 143 of his famous letters. He died on the 10th Nov. 461, and his remains were suitably interred under the porticoes of St. Peter's. One of his trusted aides, HILARY, now became the Supreme Pastor and in a term that was not to last to a full seven years ecclesiastical discipline and definition occupied a great deal of his energies, particularly in Spain and Gaul when the hierarchy was being strengthened as the civil power became the more disorganized. This pope was also endowed with a trait common to most

Romans of rank, a keen appreciation of architectural beauties, and under his patronage the city became the richer by the addition of several new churches and oratories, also libraries, baths, and other public buildings.

After Hilary came SIMPLICIUS who was to witness the dramatic events that actually marked the ending of the Western Roman Empire. In 476 Odoacer, a Barbarian leader, dispossessed the Emperor Romulus Augustulus and was proclaimed King of Italy. Although Arian by persuasion, this newly created monarch showed no disposition to persecute the Church. On the contrary he displayed respect to the papacy and whilst he was the nominal ruler of Italy the power of the Church in temporal matters was growing. Meanwhile the powerful Sees of Constantinople and Antioch had been won by the Monophysite schismatics and when they secured the protection and patronage of an usurper of the Eastern purple, Basiliscus, their power and numbers mounted with a rapidity alarming to the pope, who fought them vigorously and with some measure of success. For when the rightful Emperor, Zeno, was restored to the throne of Byzantium he sent to Rome a Catholic confession of faith and a vow to support orthodoxy. This solemn promise however was not fulfilled and the bitter struggle continued on into the reign of the next pope, FELIX III who upon learning that Zeno was negotiating and indeed showing favor to the schismatics wrote: "Supreme power has been entrusted to you over world concerns, but it is your duty to leave ecclesiastical matters in the hands of those whom God has appointed to control them. You must leave the Church free to follow her own laws." After a pontificate of nearly nine years Felix died to be followed by GELASIUS who, strongly continuing the same policy, wrote to the Emperor: "There are two powers by which chiefly this world is ruled: the sacred authority of the priests is so much weightier, as they must render before the tribunal of God an account even for the Kings of man." The Bishop of Rome was now powerful enough to define and emphasize the limits of lay power to the highest representative of that authority.

His profound scholarship did not prevent Gelasius from displaying acumen in practical affairs. Revenues were regulated and properly divided and he became renowned as a builder of asylums and as a patron of the poor. Monks were his favorite companions and his private life was one of austerity, penance, and prayer. He was vigilant to abuses perpetrated by ecclesiastics, and canon law gained from his decrees. In 496 he was succeeded by ANASTASIUS II who in his short term of two years chose to adopt a more conciliatory attitude towards Constantinople. But this was an age in which orthodox theologians, jealous of tradition and apprehensive of the future, viewed with alarm and suspicion the relaxations of tolerance. His compromise in recognizing the validity of the Byzantine Patriarch's sacramental acts made for his own unpopularity and caused considerable dissension amongst the Roman Clergy.

After his death there was disorder. A Sardinian priest, SYMMACHUS, was validly called to the sacred office but there was also an illegal election, conducted by a minority group of the clergy who were, perhaps sincerely or perhaps because of bribes, of the Byzantine party. These individuals, with the sympathies of some of the Roman Senate, proclaimed the Archpresbyter Laurentius to be Pope. What might have become a scandalous deadlock was then solved by the arbitration of the Gothic King Theodoric who declared in favor of Symmachus. The anti-pope submitted to this logical decision but his supporters, although temporarily acquiescent, remained unconvinced and in a series of rebellious agitations, such as reviving the old discussion of the Easter date, continued to harass the true pontiff. In 501 their charges and complaints were formally placed before Theodoric who summoned the pope to answer them. But his services in giving an opinion in the validity of the papal elections were not to mean that he had a right to judge the actions of the successful candidate. Quite properly Symmachus refused to agree to such an indignity, but suggested that a synod be assembled to investigate the accusations of his enemies. A synod was called and the result was a victory for Symmachus; for the Fathers agreed that no earthly power had the right to pass judgment on the action of the real Vicar of Christ. The verdict was proclaimed amidst a series of stormy sessions and turbulent incidents for the incorrigible Byzantines still tried every method, including a savage but unsuccessful attack upon the life of Symmachus, to achieve their ends. Right had triumphed; and buoyed to a fresher strength perhaps by his victory, the Pope ploughed through his dangers and vexations and now found the time and means ably to pursue the duties of his office. Missions were despatched, churches founded, charities disbursed, and disputes adjudicated.

Peace enveloped the Holy See with accession of its next occupant, Hormisdas, in 514. A Roman aristocrat of great personal charm and blessed with the better diplomatic traits he won back many schismatic bishops to the Church without sacrificing the policies of his predecessors. While keeping good terms with King Theodoric he sent embassies to the Byzantine Emperor Anastasius who, while friendly, remained obdurately steadfast to the heretical party. But with Anastasius' successor, Justin, the pope won success and on the Holy Thursday of the year 519 a reunion, temporary though it proved to be, of the Roman and Greek Churches was celebrated with joy and pomp.

Not so serene was the lot of the next pontiff, John, a Tuscan, upon whom fell the ire of Theodoric. The new peace between Rome and Constantinople had alarmed that hitherto tolerant monarch and he received with anger the information that Justin was forcibly depriving of their civil rights those of his subjects who still remained staunch to their Arian beliefs. Theodoric, an Arian himself, called upon Pope John and told him he expected the same tolerance shown to his fellow believers in the East as he had exhibited to his Catholic subjects in the West. It was a dangerous situation for the Pope and he undertook to solve it by journeying to Constantinople, the first of his rank ever to do so, and conferring with Justin. He received a magnificent welcome and the tumultuous crowds of the Eastern metropolis had the wonder of witnessing their Emperor bow his proud and purple-clad person before the pontiff, humbly beseeching the honor of being crowned by the consecrated hands. The news of this triumphant reception of John by the persecutor of his co-religionists was conveyed back to Italy and only served to infuriate King Theodoric the more. Meanwhile John had conscientiously employed his influence successfully to stay the measures of oppression levelled against the Arians; but it was too much to expect that he, head of the Catholic Church, would plead that the large numbers of those former Arians, converted it was true by the Emperor's forceful actions, should revert to their former state of heresy.

With the echoes of Imperial homage still fresh in his memory John on his return to Rome was seized by Theodoric's officers and incarcerated. Being old and infirm he was unable to survive such adversity and so he soon perished in imprisonment. Nor was he the sole victim of the royal injustice. Two greatly respected men of Rome, the philosopher Boethius and his aged relative, Symmachus, were also arrested. Theodoric who for so long had withstood the temptations of despotism had finally succumbed to those excesses of suspicion and uncertainty which lead to tyranny. Jealously he watched over the machinations of the next papal election and there can be no doubt his powerful influence carried weight in the choice of that gathering. The pontiff announced was Felix IV who was consecrated Bishop of Rome on the 12th July, 526. The royal favor he had enjoyed as a candidate for the papal honors this pope now employed to the benefit of the Church without sacrificing the dignities or the responsibilities of his office.

When Theodoric died his successors, the minor Athalaric and his regent mother, maintained the same amicable relations between Prince and Pontiff and it was undoubtedly because of this friendship that a Royal Edict was issued confirming the rights and privileges of ecclesiastical courts. Under this law such courts were to be the sole judges of clerical conduct, even when an erring churchman violated the ordinary civil or criminal codes. Pope Felix seems to have feared a dominance of the Church by the Byzantine party and in order that such an event should not happen he, when aware death was approaching, conferred his own pallium on the age-bent shoulders of his friend the Archdeacon Boniface with a proclamation that here was his successor. Threats of excommunication against anyone who would dare to oppose his wishes were delivered with his pronouncement, and after his death in the latter part of 530 BONIFACE II took office. Here was the first pontiff of Germanic ancestry and his character and record, both as pope and priest, are that of a pious and charitable man. But the unprecedented method of his ascension to the papal rank found no favor with many of the Roman clergy who promptly met and pronounced one of their own number, Dioscorus, to be the real pope. What threatened to be a stubborn deadlock was solved, only twenty-two days later, by the death of the contender Dioscorus whereupon Boniface convened a synod which after deliberating on the validity of his claims delivered an assurance of their immediate and future obedience. Soon after he called together a second synod and proposed, and his proposal was accepted, that a constitution be formed which would give him also the right to select a successor. But the dangerous resolution was not destined for fulfillment. This was an age when the shame of simony was not uncommon and that the elevation to the supreme office of the Church should depend upon, and be subjected to, the weaknesses of any one man was abhorrent to the people. Such a storm of protest greeted the announcement that a third synod was hastily assembled and the constitution which he had so enthusiastically sponsored was burned publicly by the Pope himself. And when he died the man he had named, one Vigilius, was not elected as his successor. Instead, JOHN II, a priest of St. Clement's Basilica, was installed on the 22nd July 533. The first pope to change his name on accession he ruled for only two years but the next two pontiffs were to have reigns of even scantier duration. AGAPITUS, succeeding John, became the second pope to visit Constantinople and like the first his journey was because of a request from the King of Italy.

Justinian I now wore the Imperial diadem of the East and

with the glories of the past to inspire his considerable abilities he had set out to restore the Empire. The defeat of the Persians, the conquest of the Vandals in Africa, the ousting of the Gothic rulers of Italy, the re-arrangement and clarification of Roman Law, and a prodigious patronage of the arts were all part of a vast scheme which occupied his energies and followed his high ambitions for a reign that was to endure for more than three decades. When his troops were menacing Italy the Gothic King, Theodehad, besought the Pope, in the interests of peace, to intercede with him.

The Pope, escorted by five bishops and a suitable retinue, set out for Constantinople where he was received with all the niceties of Imperial courtesy. He made his plea but Justinian was not to be dissuaded from his dreams of a united Empire. However, the failure of this mission did not prevent the pontifical visit from achieving other important results. Owing to the powerful influence of the Empress Theodora, a woman of resolute purposes and dubious antecedents, a heretical bishop, Anthimos, had invalidly assumed the title and privileges of the Byzantine Patriarchate; a position which he occupied with little grace and no popularity. On representations from the disturbed clergy Agapitus ordered Anthimos to quit the patriarchal seat; whereupon the Empress, enraged at this affront to her protégé and to her will, and skillfully uniting the weapons of her position, cunning, and sex, persuaded her husband that Imperial commands and privileges were being rejected and denied by the pope. Thus incited to anger Justinian threatened Agapitus with banishment but the pontiff received his words with sadness and refusal to be awed by them.

"I came," he said, "to gaze upon a Christian Emperor Justinian. In his place I find a Diocletian whose threats, however, terrify me not." Such courage from an aged and unarmed man cooled Justinian's wrath and excited his admiration. He made a thorough investigation of the patriarchal pretender and finally agreed he be deposed. And while his defeated consort brooded sullenly, a dangerous mood for such a determined female, great rejoicing was manifested by the clergy and populace as Agapitus then consecrated to the Byzantine See a rightful occupant. But he did not live to see his triumph acclaimed in Rome. He died on the 22nd of April, 536, and his remains were conveyed back to the Eternal City where they were interred amidst scenes of veneration and sorrow. SILVERIUS was then elected. He was the son of Pope Hormisdas (who had been married before accepting the higher orders of the priesthood; a practice still permitted in the Greek Orthodox Church and in some of the Eastern rites in communion with the Holy See. Thus the same strange occurrence, the son of a pope achieving the same high rank as his father, could happen in modern times).

Silverius was elected and installed but the staunch fact was not an obstacle sufficiently important to deter the schemes of the Empress Theodora. Acutely aware that she had been successfully opposed by one pope, she was now inexorably determined to have a creature of her choice occupy the august station. The deacon Vigilius had accompanied Agapitus to Constantinople. He was the same Vigilius whom Pope Boniface II had proclaimed as his successor. That ill-received announcement had left a dangerous echo in his memory and the Empress found in him a willing and eager participator in her plans. He promised to give recognition to the heresy she favored, the Monophysite and to restore her ousted favourite to the honors of the Byzantine Patriarchate if she aided him to procure the tenancy of the Holy See. But what of the already elected Pope? The solution was simple and shameful. Justinian's armies had, under the brilliant leadership of Belisarius, successfully driven back the Goths and were now occupying Rome. Theodora's agents, with a display of forged letters, accused Pope Silverius of treasonably communicating with the Goths and by the commands of the Byzantine commander he was divested of the insignia of his exalted rank, thrust into rough garb of a monk, and exiled as a prisoner to an island where he soon perished. After an "election" conducted under the formidable and certainly not disinterested protection of Belisarius, VIGILIUS was finally enthroned, while at Constantinople Theodora enjoyed the stimulating tonic of triumph.

But her satisfaction was not destined for permanence. Vigilius, on his ascension to the papal rank, absolved himself of his promises to his benefactress and revealed that his policies were to be as orthodox as had been those of his predecessors. His pontificate, so irregularly gained, was never to bring him tranquillity and, in 544, he entered upon a serious disagreement with Justinian. The Emperor, not content with his many other activities, now saw fit to exercise his talents in the field of theology, a formidable pastime for one who so quickly could settle debate or emphasize opinion by a gesture to his soldiery. The bishops and clergy close to his court had readily subscribed to an edict issued by him which condemned the "Three Chapters" and by which he hoped to make peace with the Monophysites. The "Three Chapters" were the teachings of Theodore of Mopsuestia; the writings of Theodoret of Cyrus in favour of Nestorius and against St. Cyril and the Synod of Ephesus; and the letter of Ibas of Edessa to the Persian Bishop Maris. Undoubtedly there was heresy in the "Three Chapters" but endorsement by Vigilius of this condemnation might have seemed to mean his repudiation of the Council of Chalcedon—for Chalcedon had reinstated two of the authors in question when they had repudiated the Nestorian heresy. Besides all this was an encroachment by the Emperor and thus by the secular power on the prerogatives and duties of the Church. Vigilius demurred and hesitated but not so the Emperor. His soldiers seized the Pope and carried him to Constantinople where for seven years he was detained. These seven years are an unhappy story of his vacillations, his oppositions, and sometimes his submissions. His major submission came in 553 with regard to the Fifth Council, at which the "Three Chapters" were condemned. The condemnation was unjust, but Vigilius had considered it inopportune and it was under pressure that he acquiesced. The Emperor finally released him. But by this time the unfortunate pope was an old and broken man. He died before reaching Rome.

PELAGIUS, the next pope, suffered the sharpness of unpopularity during the first years of his jurisdiction because of the conciliatory attitude he adopted in negotiating with Justinian. But soon an abundance of good works and his energetic talents in preventing and healing schisms served to dispel antagonism. The savage conflict between the Goths and Justinian's troops had devastated Italy and the neglect of the harvests and the spoliation of towns had reduced the people to the direst depths of poverty. Pelagius, who came of a rich and noble Roman family, not only donated his entire personal fortune but performed other great feats of charity and well-merited was the title he bore when he died in 561: "Father of the poor and of his country."

Five months elapsed before his successor, JOHN III, could be consecrated. It took that time—and by now significantly there is no question about it—to receive the Emperor's confirmation and approval. Though this pope's reign lasted thirteen years little is known of it. Turbulent and war-torn was the period and the part played by the pontiff is best described on an inscription which still existed in the XV Century: "In the midst of straits he knew how to be bountiful, and feared not to be crushed amidst a tumbling world." Nearly a year went by before the Imperial confirmation arrived to sanction the installation of BENEDICT I and again it is the chaos of war, the ravaging of the Lombards, which obliterates the details of a pontificate that did not last five years. PELAGIUS II, a Goth, was then elected and— typical of the initiative he was always to display—he did not wait for Imperial confirmation. The effective blockade of Rome by the Lombards was a reason sufficient in his opinion to dispense with this irksome assumption of a right that the Emperor did not have; and after but a semblance of waiting he was consecrated and installed. The responsibility of temporal affairs as pertaining to the countryside surrounding Rome was now being forced upon the papacy. Appalling conditions bred by the marauding military finally induced Pelagius to appeal not only to Constantinople but to the Franks. To the Bishop of Auxerre he wrote: "We believe that it has been brought about by a special dispensation of Divine Providence, that the Frankish Princes should prefer the orthodox faith, like the Roman Emperors, in order that they may help this city, whence it took its rise. Persuade them with all earnestness to keep from any alliance with our most unspeakable enemies, the Lombards." To Constantinople he sent an able ecclesiastic, the deacon Gregory, who finally persuaded the Emperor, now Maurice, to answer the Pope's pleas with the despatch of a relief expedition. The many tasks involving the defense and well being of temporal Rome were not the only occupations of Pelagius II. He strove to preserve and improve hierarchial harmony and when certain bishops threatened to recede into one of the innumerable schisms of the period he wrote that they were doing so "for the sake of superfluous question"; a statement which, seen from the perspective of centuries, seems very true indeed.

Pestilence is a familiar aftermath of war and there was no exception to this sad rule when a temporary truce was finally made with the Lombards. As though to complete the depredations of the enemy a terrible plague descended upon Rome and perishing amidst the resultant horrors was the pontiff. The name of his successor is illustrious. Elected at a time when famine stalked the streets of Rome and when deathcarts, rumbling to their dreaded tasks, were the only traffic of those broad avenues GREGORY THE GREAT was destined to become one of the great popes and the Father of the Medieval Church. His ability combined with the fact of his patrician birth had secured for him the post of Prefect of Rome at the age of thirty. This honor he renounced and donating his estates to the monasteries he entered upon the austere life of a simple monk, following the rule of St. Benedict. But his talents were far too well known to permit of his being, as he wished, forgotten by the world. In the grievous times of 579 Pope Pelagius II ordered him from his seclusion, ordained him one of the Seven Deacons of Rome, and despatched him as his Nuncio to the Byzantine Court; a position he occupied with brilliance and, amidst the luxuries and artifices of that exotic assemblage, considerable personal distaste. Much more to his liking was his appointment on his return to Rome, as Abbot of St. Andrew's monastery. Here, under the fostering of his enthusiasm and knowledge, the monks acquired great fame for their piety, learning, and munificent charities. During this time he became imbued with a zeal to go to Britain and there assist in converting the Angles but when he commenced the missionary journey his path was blocked by the protesting citizens.

Such a man, already so popular, was inevitably marked for the papacy and, after the death of Pelagius II, he was elected as Pope amidst the unanimous acclamation of clergy and people. Dreading to take the high office and loath to leave the peace of the cloisters he wrote to the Emperor a letter of eloquent entreaty, beseeching him to withhold the official confirmation. But this measure failed; and finally he was seized by the people, conveyed to the Basilica of St. Peter's, and consecrated Pope. Once in office he not only rapidly fulfilled but soon exceeded the high expectations of his admirers. Banishing idlers and perquisite-holding laymen from the papal court he formed a highly efficient administrative body of hard working clerics, most of whom were monks. The papal estates, known as "St. Peter's Patrimony" and now constituting an area of some fifteen hundred square miles, were regulated so as to become a highly productive source of charity. To protect the peoples and revenues of these lands he was forced to the wielding of temporal power and the paternal significance of his title became splendidly realized when, unafraid of Imperial displeasure and exasperated with the dilatory methods of the Byzantine authorities, he sued for separate peace or, as the occasion demanded, made bold resistance against the Lombards. But it is in the conversion of the English that we find his greatest achievement. Though never able to go himself among the Anglo-Saxons, as he had wished, he made the evangelization of England his pet project.

This man, who so earnestly had desired the contemplative peace of a monk's life, was, by circumstances and responsibility, thrust to the position of a sovereign prince, to become a ruler of cities and provinces, a master of troops and fleets. "Gregory's exercise of his power was one of the great moments in the world's history," wrote one historian. "All over the Christian world he had taught men to look to the Pope as one who could make peace and ensure it." Nor was he ever to cease being the exemplary ecclesiastic either in private conduct or in the execution of his office. In an age when titles were a serious measure of a man's rank and pretensions, he chose for himself, and founded for his successors, the great phrase *"servus servorum Dei"* ("servant of the servants of God"). The Church of today carries the mark of his genius in her liturgy, music, and discipline. And his story is made all the brighter by reason of the ill-health he suffered throughout his pontificate which ended, to the sorrow of his people, on the 12th of March, 604.

The Middle Ages had begun, and the complete collapse of the Roman Empire in the West makes that commencement a chronicle of savagery, lawlessness, and ignorance. In the gloom of the century following Gregory's death no fewer than twenty men take their places in the succession of the papacy and none of them approached the stature of his magnitude. Their story is mainly a repetitious narrative of the preservation of hierarchical harmony, continuous struggle with the Byzantine Emperors and Patriarchs, and doctrinal controversy which revolves around the question of the number of wills in Christ. To the name of one the stigma of heresy is attached, to another the glory of martyrdom, and to a third the credit for convoking the Sixth Ecumenical Council. Forty or more years after the death of Honorius, actually a pious and saintly man, condemnation came, not for formal heresy, but because as one of his successors, Leo II, declared: "He did not extinguish at once the incipient flame of heretical error, as befitted Apostolic authority, but by his negligence nourished the same." The martyred pope was Martin I who, presiding at a council which antagonized the Emperor Constans II, was seized by troops and brought to Constantinople where at an outrageously unjust trial he was convicted of being a traitor and blasphemous usurper. A victim to the harsh treatment of his imprisonment he died—to become, despite the propaganda of the Emperor, an object of veneration and inspiration to the faithful. The doctrine for which he died was vindicated by Pope Agatho who called together a council at Constantinople in 681 which defined the doctrine of two wills—one human and one divine—functioning harmoniously in the person of Jesus; a pronouncement which was necessarily consequent upon that of Christ's dual nature. In continuity the pontiffs of the Seventh Century and the first years of the Eighth were: SABINIAN, 604-6, BONIFACE III, 607, BONIFACE IV, 608-15, DEUSDEDIT, 615-18, BONIFACE V, 619-25, HONORIUS, 625-38, SEVERINUS, 640, JOHN IV, 640-42, THEODORE, 642-49, MARTIN, 649-54, EUGENIUS, 654-57, VITALIAN, 657-72, ADEODATUS II, 672-76, DONUS, 676-78, AGATHO, 678-81, LEO II, 682-83, BENEDICT II, 684-85, JOHN V, 685-86, CONON, 686-87, SERGIUS, 687-701, JOHN VI, 701-5, JOHN VII, 705-7, SISINNIUS, 708, CONSTANTINE, 708-15.

The absence of individual genius in the recorded acts of the seventh century popes does not rob the Church of the credit due for the survival of the graces that made for the machinery of civilization. Private law had usurped public law but in the chaotic gloom that followed there was one brightness, the stabilizing influence of the monasteries. The monks had spread everywhere and not only were they zealously implanting and nourishing the truths of Christian philosophy but the network of monasteries was founding a structure that was to be the only hope for a social order of any kind. From the wild coasts of Ireland to the equally wild shores of Africa the monks labored and preached; their monasteries housing the principles of justice and the exercise of mercy. In an age when academies of learning were but ruined buildings and their uses the dimly remembered echoes of earlier generations the cloisters were alone open to the practice of the arts. Not that all these champions of the faith were scholars and philosophers. There was also the vast army of their sturdy brethren, bound by the same vows of service, who tilled the soil, hewed the wood, and performed the many other prodigious tasks of industry which made possible the formation and continuance of those communities which, in the seas of surrounding disorder, were self-supporting havens of peace, citadels of learning, and asylums of charity.

Christian monasticism had originated in the deserts of Egypt during the IVth Century when groups of ascetic hermits gathered to dwell under one rule. The movement in various forms spread rapidly throughout the Christian world. The great figure of its inauguration in the East was St. Basil; in the West, nearly two hundred years later—although it had existed there previously —St. Benedict. This founder of the great Order which was to be of such immense service to the papacy, and from whose ranks were to come over four thousand bishops, sixteen hundred archbishops, two hundred cardinals, twenty-eight popes, and five thousand saints, can best be judged by St. Benedict's description of the ideal abbot ". . . he must be chaste, sober, and merciful, ever preferring mercy to justice, that he himself may obtain mercy. Let him hate sin and love the brethren. And even in his corrections, let him act with prudence, and not go too far, lest while he seeketh too eagerly to scrape off the rust, the vessel be broken. And by this we do not mean that he should suffer vices to grow up; but that prudently and with charity he should cut them off, in the way he shall see best for each, as we have already said; and let him study rather to be loved than feared. Let him not be violent nor over anxious, not exacting nor obstinate, not jealous nor prone to suspicion, or else he will never be at rest. In all his commands, whether spiritual or temporal, let him be prudent and considerate. In the works which he imposeth, let him be discreet and moderate, bearing in mind the discretion of holy Jacob, when he said: 'If I cause my flocks to be overdriven, they will all perish in one day.' Taking, then, such testimonies as are borne by these and the like words to discretion, the mother of virtues, let him so temper all things, that the strong may have something to strive after, and the weak nothing at which to take alarm."

Such were the standards the monks had for their guidance when they set out to implant their faith throughout the world and such were the standards that were to keep the spirit of the Church alive when many princes and prelates, dazzled by the pomp of sovereign status, succumbed to the temptations of rank. These indeed were the standards so gloriously upheld by Gregory the Great. Benedictine wisdom shines in his letter to an abbot missionary in England. "Tell him," he wrote, referring to St. Augustine whom he had sent to convert England, "what I have long been considering in my own mind concerning the matter of the English people; to wit, that the temples of the idols in that nation ought not to be destroyed; but let the idols that are in them be destroyed; let water be consecrated and sprinkled in the said temples, let altars be erected, and relics placed there. For if those temples are well built, it is requisite that they be converted from the worship of devils to the service of the true God; that the nation, seeing that their temples are not destroyed may remove error from their hearts and, knowing and adoring the true God, may the more freely resort to the places to which they have been accustomed. And because they are used to slaughter many oxen in sacrifice to devils, some solemnity must be given them in exchange for this, as that on the day of the dedication, or the nativities of the holy martyrs, whose relics are there deposited, they should build themselves huts of the boughs of trees about those churches which have been turned to that use from being temples, and celebrate the solemnity with religious feasting, and no more offer animals to the devil, but kill cattle and glorify God in their feast, and return thanks to the Giver of all things for their abundance; to the end that, while some outward gratifications are retained, they the more easily consent to the inward joys. For there is no doubt that it is impossible to cut off everything at once from their rude natures; because he who endeavours to ascend to the highest place rises by degrees or steps, and not by leaps . . ."

The spirit of such men was to prove of immense aid to the Church. But in this, the VIIth Century, there also was born another influence which for centuries was to be a bitter and fiercely militant antagonist of Christianity. A theocratic state was welded in Arabia by one Mohammed who claimed to be a true Prophet of God. With fanatical zeal he propounded to his nomad listeners a religion that was a strange mixture of Judaism, Christianity, and Paganism.

"Four women I revere above all others," he said, "the sister of Moses, the Mother of Jesus, my wife Kadiza, and my daughter, Fatima."

His doctrine did not call for a definite priesthood although there were to be interpreters in the form of doctors and preachers. The real leaders were to be warriors, for it was by sword and conquest he proposed to spread his faith. "The sword," he declared, "is the key of heaven and hell; a drop of blood shed in the cause of God, a sigh spent in arms, is of more avail than two months of fasting or prayer: whosoever falls in battle, his sins are forgiven at the day of judgment, his wounds shall be resplendent as vermilion, and odoriferous as musk; and the loss of his limbs shall be supplied by the wings of angels and cherubim."

The visions such eloquence conjured dazzled his audiences and they became frenzied armies which, as they rushed rapturously to battle, chanted "There is but one God, and Mohammed is the Prophet of God." With astonishing swiftness the standards of Islam were implanted throughout Arabia; then, defeating the Byzantine legions, in Syria; and in Palestine, Egypt, and Persia. For a time the bulwark of Constantinople was avoided, but not so the fertile islands of the Mediterranean or the coasts of Northern Africa. Unafraid and feared, the indomitable Saracens marched and sailed and plundered and at the beginning of the Eighth Century they had landed in Spain and with determined eyes fixed on Gaul were triumphantly advancing to the Pyrenees. Such was the alarming progress of their conquests, achieved in less than a hundred years, when Pope GREGORY II succeeded Constantine I in 715.

The new pope had been papal librarian and he quickly showed he was not unworthy of the great name he carried. Realizing the menace of the Saracens he arranged the city for defense, rebuilding and manning the ancient walls to make them capable of withstanding a sustained siege. Occupation with the many details such a task must have necessitated did not prevent him from receiving and listening to a zealous monk from England, Winfred. Impressed with the latter's plans and abilities he made him a bishop with the new name of Boniface and despatched him to Germany where in his own generation the consecrated missionary was to achieve a magnificent and permanent success. Multitudes were converted. Scattered and disorganized Christians were brought back to discipline. Sees were apportioned and an organized hierarchy established.

But while this progress of the Church was being accomplished new troubles loomed again from the direction of Constantinople. Temporal power had, because of the Byzantine negligence, been forced upon the Popes but up to this time, because of a loyalty to the ancient Roman name, they still tendered a nominal allegiance to the distant Emperors. This gracious fealty had been, with monotonous repetition, singularly ill repaid by a succession, with few exceptions, of irresponsible tyrants who insisted upon intruding upon theological affairs; a province in which the Popes would brook no interference. Instead of affording Rome adequate and consistent military protection the Imperial troops had been used, as has been seen, several times in efforts to force submission in realms far beyond temporal boundaries. Such efforts had always failed. Nevertheless, not learning any lessons from the past, the Emperor of this time, Leo III, otherwise an able statesman, had seen fit to create the situation which was to sever the historic union between the Eternal City and the Byzantine capital. An Edict, signed by him and therefore the law, was issued condemning the veneration of images. A wave of indignation swept through the Empire as orders were received to put to axe and fire the sacred and revered statues of Christ, the pictures of His Mother, and the likenesses of the Saints. The Pope made immediate and vigorous protest. "If you send troops for the destruction of the images of St. Peter, look to it," he warned. The Emperor's answer was to order the deposition of the pontiff, who retorted with a sentence of excommunication. Troops were assembled and under the command of the Exarch Paul, marched to arrest the Pope.

The alarm was given in Rome and the citizens gathered at the walls to resist the invaders. Help arrived from an unexpected quarter. The Lombards, former aggressors against Rome, drove off the Exarch. These warlike people were now orthodox Catholics and their King, Luitprand, was quick, with a great display of devotion, to kneel before Gregory and to dedicate his sword and his crown at the Altar of St. Peter's. The Pope accepted the elaborate manifestations of friendship with a wary eye, knowing full well that the Lombards now possessed both North and South Italy and that "protection" from them would probably mean subjection and complete dominance. Far better a distant tyrant than a local despot, he reasoned: and so, frowning on attempted rebellions against Leo, he made truce and entered upon negotiations with the Exarch. But the Emperor continued to be obstinate and rashly hostile. And his terms were unbearable. The symbols of the Saviour were to be levelled to the ground, portraits of the Virgin were to be defaced, monuments of St. Peter were to be broken, and heavy indemnities were to be paid. These outrages he demanded. There could be no alternative for the Pope. Independence was forced upon him—and hovering by, staring eagerly at the walls of Rome, waiting for the prize they had for long past coveted, were the Lombards.

For Gregory II the situation was solved by death but for his successor, the Syrian-born GREGORY III, the anxious problem remained. Then opportunely enough came heartening news from Gaul. Not content with subjugating Spain the Saracens had with consummate daring invaded France and had marched victoriously as far as Tours. There they were met by a determined army headed by Charles Martel, leader of the Franks. The armies clashed and at first it seemed as though the Saracen story of triumph was not to be interrupted; but on the seventh day of the desperate battle the tide turned and the invaders were put to ignominious and bloody rout. The Cross had triumphed over the Crescent of Islam and all Christendom breathed the easier. It had been a momentous and decisive battle for without the genius of Charles Martel and the valor of his troops the Mohammedan march, unhalted, would have conquered all Europe, and, as Gibbon says "the Arabian fleet might well have sailed without a naval combat into the mouth of the Thames. Perhaps the interpretation of the Koran would now be taught in the schools of Oxford, and her pulpits might demonstrate to a circumcised people the sanctity and truth of the revelation of Mohammed."

To the Frankish hero the pope despatched an embassy which carried significantly symbolical gifts, the keys of the tombs of the Apostles. With courtesy and respect the busy soldier, still campaigning, received the papal envoys, accepted the gifts, assured the bearers of his friendliness to the donor, and to repay their visit sent an Ambassador, bearing the same sentiments, to Rome. More at this time he could not do, for war with both his northern neighbours and the Moors were keeping his energies and his armies fully occupied. But even his gesture of friendliness seems to have carried some emphasis in Italy. The Lombards, who had been warring in the vicinity of Ravenna, desisted and subsided into an uneasy and impermanent peace.

It is a glorious characteristic of Church history that at her most perilous times, when danger and crisis threaten to engulf the existence of the Holy See, the continuity of missionary activity is not interrupted. Conquerors might prowl the streets of Rome, marauders might sack and endanger the structure of St. Peter's, antagonisms and evils of a subtler variety might bring scandal and discord, those whom she has invested with extraordinary powers might betray their trust, but the work of her propagandists goes serenely and staunchly on. Defeat, either spiritual or temporal, might sometimes darken her story but always, somewhere in the distance, there is a new victory brightening that same eventful tale.

It was so at this time. While the pontiffs were worrying for their existence in Italy, Boniface was winning all Germany to the Church. In 737 he visited Rome and delivered a report of his astounding success, an imposing record of souls gained, of churches and monasteries built and endowed, of bishops consecrated and abbots installed. The great missionary now wanted to resign these activities, feeling they could be well sustained by those whom he had trained. He wished to commence again in newer and less pleasant fields but the Pope, gently refusing this request, conferred upon him the honors of increased authority and sent him back as Legate to deal with and rule the episcopacy he had created.

When Gregory III died he was succeeded by the popular deacon ZACHARY whose talents for persuasion and conciliation were certainly not the least amongst his many abilities. It was 741 and once again the Lombards, under the same clever King, Luitprand, were making ready to invade the Roman provinces. The papal ally, the Duke of Spoleto, had already shown his unreliability and the time and circumstances seemed propitious for the Lombard schemes. But, with the memory to inspire him of how Leo had stayed the Huns, Zachary did not wait for hostilities to commence. He went to meet the advancing King. Deeply impressed was the ambitious and warlike monarch with the courage, dignity and eloquence of the pontiff. And as he had once declared his friendship and orthodoxy to Gregory, so now he solemnly made the same assurances to Zachary. His troops were halted, and as further proof of the new cordiality four cities which in the past had been taken from the Romans were returned to their jurisdiction. It was a victory for the Pope's diplomacy; and that his influence with Luitprand was no temporary mood is evidenced a year later when the Lombards were determined to give battle at Ravenna to the Byzantine Exarch. The latter made frantic appeal to Rome. Once again Zachary spoke and once again the magic of his words brought peace where bloodshed had seemed inevitable. Soon after this incident Luitprand died and with his successor, Ratchis, the Pope was to have no difficulties. Persuasions against violence were not needed by this gentle prince who had so little taste for the ambitions and pleasures of this world that he eventually renounced his rank and, taking monastic vows, became a simple monk.

Even Constantinople seems to have capitulated to the charm of Zachary. The decree forbidding the worship of images was no longer enforced. Papal envoys were honourably received by the new Emperor and to supplement St. Peter's patrimony came a Byzantine gift, two Italian villages and the surrounding territories. Nor did distance stay the harmony. With the industrious Boniface acting as his Legate, discipline, without rebellion, was strengthened among the Frankish bishops and ecclesiastics. Pepin, worthy son of Charles Martel, was now the leader of the Franks and from him an embassy, consisting of Bishop Burkard of Wurzburg and his chaplain, came to Rome with an unprecedented and historic request.

Pepin wanted the Pope's approval to be crowned King of the Franks. For three generations his family had successfully led the Frankish peoples and had virtually exercised all the prerogatives of Kingship save the royal title itself, a privilege still vested in the insignificant descendants of Clovis. The last of this once proud but now debased family was Childeric III, an unhappy weakling whom Pepin without trouble or fear could have disposed of in any manner he wished. But instead of violence he wisely preferred to seek the sanction of a higher authority. Yet who was of a higher rank than a King? Who could wield the power of bestowing or transferring crowns? Pepin found his answer in the person of the Vicar of Christ. "Whosoever has the power is the King" was the Pope's decision. Childeric, unprotesting, was then tonsured and ushered from the turmoil of a world which despised him to the peace of a monastery where even if he was no longer a monarch he at least found honorable seclusion and a welcome tranquillity. And Pepin, kneeling in solemn ceremony before Boniface was, by authority of the Pope, consecrated King of the Franks.

After Zachary a priest was elected as Stephen II. He was never consecrated for he died four days later as the result of an apoplectic fit. The five-year reign of the next Pope, STEPHEN

III, who succeeded Stephen II in that same year, 752, was not to be as peaceful as Zachary's for once again the Lombards, with the ascension of a new King, Aistulf, were threatening to engulf Rome. Stephen tried to negotiate with Aistulf but the obstinate King insisted that Rome was to be his capital and that the papacy was to be under his temporal authority. The ancient city rose to arms at this arrogant challenge and the citizens swore to suffer death rather than to submit to an usurper. In desperation the pontiff, who had already sent envoys to beg assistance of Pepin, personally undertook the hazardous journey to Gaul. His arduous efforts and eloquent entreaties were not in vain. The Frankish King did not disappoint him, an army was sent across the Alps and quickly the Lombards made treaty to respect the papal dominions.

With gratitude in his heart and actions the happy pontiff then presided at a second coronation of Pepin, this time adding to the Kingly title the hereditary dignity of Patrician of Rome. But the perverse and stubborn Lombards were not yet dissuaded from their king's ambitions, for no sooner had the Frankish troops left Italy than once again they deployed throughout the papal territory. A second French expedition rewarded this treachery with the severe defeat it deserved and this time Pepin was determined his work should remain permanent. The protection of the Holy See which had been so neglected by the Eastern Emperors was now solemnly undertaken by him and its temporal sovereignty assured. Nor was it an empty honour for the warrior King in a magnanimous gesture placed on the tomb of St. Peter's the keys and deeds of some twenty-two towns and provinces which his troops had captured from the Lombards. The Papal States were now a fact. And thus, in the form of a gift, a tremendous burden of responsibility and complication was added to the Church.

A dangerous precedent dominated the next election when Stephen's brother, PAUL I, was chosen for succession. But happily, kinship with august rank and fraternal favors had neither magnified the pride, dwarfed the character, nor lessened the abilities of the new Pope. In the uneasy infancy of the newly acquired status of the Papal States, there were many vexations, both external and domestic, to give him sore distress. The very power that had made possible their being dwelt across the Alps; a distance far enough to allow hope to remain alive in the breasts of the resentful Lombards. Still brooding in sullen defeat these incorrigible people never neglected an opportunity to harass the unfortunate Romans. Each time a new prince succeeded to their leadership he was haunted by the ambitious and unfulfilled dreams of his fathers. Desiderius was now their King and he proposed to the Byzantine Emperor that they should form a military alliance to crush the papal sovereignty and regime and divide the lost territories. Once again the power of Pepin's name was invoked by the anxious Romans and the scheme failed. But the ten years of his reign were a series of ceaseless worries for the Pope, a train of negotiations, threats and treaties, punctuated by appeals for Frankish intervention. Within Rome itself the pontiff was forced to be a martinet and to exercise with drastic measures a severe authority. Abuse of privilege and of rank was now common in both civil and ecclesiastical circles. There were all the machinations of politics, the maneuverings of diplomacy which accompany the responsibilities of temporal power, the intrigues inevitable to human nature when rich prizes are to be gained. And there were rich prizes. New territories to be governed and revenues to be collected. Then too, there was the greatest of all prizes, the papal office itself, this supreme rank that could create kings or depose them. Such a prize could not fail to attract the stratagems and plots of the unscrupulous. In 767 when Paul was stricken to his deathbed the solemnity that should have enveloped Rome at such a time was broken by an unruly and bloody seizure of the Lateran by Toto, the villainous and unprincipled Duke of Nepi. It was his soldiers who kept the death watch and no sooner had the pontiff expired than their rude shouts proclaimed as next Pope one of their own number, the Duke's brother, Constantine. A bishop was compelled to ordain the soldier there and then and a few days later the rascal was put through a ceremony of consecration.

But the outrage was not allowed to stand. Another powerful noble, Prince Christopher, who had been close to the persons and confidences of the last pontiffs and who was bitterly opposed to Toto, fled and enlisted the support of the Lombards, always ready on any pretext to march on Rome. By guile and not by battle they secured an easy and prompt entrance to the City. Toto suffered immediate death, but for Constantine, discovered cringing in a chapel, it was not so easy. His punishment began with the slow destruction of his eyes by hot branding-irons.

The disorder and scandal were slow to cease. When Christopher arrived in Rome he discovered that during the tumult the Lombards had announced a pope of their own choosing. This was an aged and bewildered Abbot named Philip but before he could be consecrated, Christopher, who was as ambitious as Toto, had him thrust back to his monastery and at the same time announced the invalidity of both his and Constantine's election. All Rome, prelates and clergy, nobles and citizens, now gathered in the forum and unanimously voted for Christopher's candidate, STEPHEN IV, a pious and learned monk but undoubtedly subjected to the determined will of his sponsor. One of his first acts was to convene a Council before which the unfortunate eyeless Constantine was dragged, berated, and sentenced to life imprisonment in a monastery cell. And to prevent the recurrence of a similar crime a law was enacted declaring that in future the papal elections were to be confined to the ecclesiastical province. The Bishop of Rome had always been chosen, not by the whole Church, but by the church in Rome; up to this point the Roman laity had had some kind of say in the matter. This new decree of the year 769 reduced their part to acclamation only.

This same year had witnessed the accession of Pepin's sons, Charlemagne and Carloman, to the joint occupancy of the Frankish throne. Carloman was to die within a few years, leaving Charlemagne possessor of a title which was to change from King to Emperor. To him, Desiderius, the Lombard King, now turned, realizing that if his ambitions in Italy were to be achieved he must first gain the friendship of the Franks. A match was arranged between his daughter and Charlemagne. When the news arrived in Rome there was consternation and apprehension. The Pope protested vigorously and with good reason for not only might the new alliance endanger the independence of the Holy See but it was alleged that Charlemagne had contracted a previous wife whom he was divorcing with celerity but not with validity. So declared the canonists. But pontifical opposition did not prevent the solemnization of the new marriage. It was however doomed to an early failure and soon an annulment was declared because of the sterility of the Frankish princess.

Stephen was only to officiate for three years and the last year was marked with as much violence as had characterized the first. In 771 Desiderius, exercising his privileges as a Christian pilgrim, but carefully escorted by his troops, journeyed to Rome to perform his devotional duties at the tomb of the Apostles. But Prince Christopher, whose will was still law to the Pope, was alarmed and fortified the city against him. Then followed a rapid succession of incidents as astounding as they were shameful. There were revolt and treachery amongst the Romans, weary of the injustices and presumptions of Christopher and his equally arrogant son, Sergius. Even the Pope, perhaps swayed by the same emotions, made no effort to protect or defend in any way his ex-patron when, at the conclusion of the disgraceful episode, both Christopher and Sergius were seized by the Lombard executioners and subjected to the same dreadful punishment as had been given Constantine. Their eyes were torn out and then they were hurled to the dungeons. Stephen meekly submitted to the protection of the Lombard king from whom death liberated him on the 3rd of February, 772.

Of an entirely different mould was ADRIAN I. Here was a pontiff who did not permit patronage from any man: friendship and assistance perhaps, but never the indignities that had so ignominiously clouded the previous pontificate. A patrician by birth and a churchman by sincere vocation he ruled splendidly for nearly twenty-four years, a term of office not to be equalled by any of his successors until ten centuries later. On his accession he quickly restored order to the Roman scene. Lombardian intrigues were rejected, their agents expelled, and in preparation for their certain revenge the fearless pope, determined to make fierce resistance against anyone who would encroach upon his independence, formed a militia of his own. Desiderius, with his schemes facing ruin but now the possessor of a formidably superior army, lost no time in accepting the challenge. His hosts advanced on Rome, ruthlessly and thoroughly ravaging the countryside. Adrian had already sent messages to Charlemagne but that warrior was engaged in one of his bitter wars with the Saxons and there seemed little chance, so the Lombards thought, of his intervention. He did send pleas for peace and they were not only ignored, but Desiderius, construing them as weaknesses, began to plot. After all Italy was subdued to his rule, he would force the Pope to proclaim Charlemagne's nephews the legal Frankish Kings. With lesser opponents perhaps these lofty dreams might have had some chance of fulfillment; but fortunately Charlemagne and Adrian were of a superior breed. Not only was one a great soldier prince and the other a splendid pope, but they were friends. And by rare and happy circumstance their harmony was never to be disturbed by the rivalries which could so easily have been born of their individual greatness.

Displaying the consummate skill of his military genius Charlemagne marched his troops across the Alps with surprising swiftness and after attacking and defeating the Lombards at Verona, surrounded their chagrined ruler in his own capital. Leaving his generals to continue with the irksome task of siege he pressed on to Rome, arriving in time to celebrate the festival of Easter. Acclamations and, significantly, Imperial honors greeted his entrance to the city but the wise prince preferred to enter as a pilgrim. On his knees he made his way up the steps of St. Peter's while a huge choir of monks chanted *"Benedictus qui venit in nomine Domini."* The jubilant pontiff raised him to his feet and embraced him as a son and as a saviour. Devotional duties of Holy Week took precedence over temporal affairs, but in a few days all Rome was elated to learn that in similar ceremony and by deed Charlemagne had renewed the *Donation* of Pepin. Added to the papal domains now were the island of Corsica, the provinces of Venice, Parma, and Istria, and the duchies of Spoleto and Benevento. A few months after this superb generosity the indefatigable warrior, taking to the field again, decisively defeated Desiderius and took for himself the Kingship of the Lombard people. It seemed as though all menace to Roman security had been dissipated. But in fact, obscured beneath the friendship of Charlemagne and Adrian, the ancient city and its provinces had actually become, as time was to prove, a vassal state to the Frankish power.

Adrian's ability was not limited to temporal fields. Sovereignty of Rome at this seemingly triumphant hour did not cause a neglect of his duties as Supreme Pastor of the Church. An ardent patron of the missionaries he also took vigorous measures to fight the nascent heresy of Adoptionism. Harmony with the Eastern Church was another of his interests and in 787 at the Seventh General Council, held at Nicaea, it was his Legates who interpreted the Papal principles concerning the veneration of images. When on the Christmas day of the year 795, amidst exhibitions of universal grief and regret, he died, it was his lifelong friend Charlemagne who sadly inscribed the appropriate epitaph: "Here the Father of the Church, the Glory of Rome, the illustrious author Adrian, the blessed Pope lies buried. Born of noble parents, he was still nobler by his virtues. . . . I join our names together: Adrian and Charles; I the king, you the father. . . . With the Saints of God may your dear soul be in peace."

The very day of Adrian's funeral saw the election of a new pope, LEO III. Such unseemly haste was not without its consequences for although Leo had, and was to keep, the support of the all-powerful Charlemagne there existed in Rome a faction bitterly and dangerously hostile. The conspiracies of these malcontents finally had results in the form of a sudden and murderous attack on the person of the pontiff while he was walking, unprotected by guards, in an ecclesiastical procession. The unfortunate Pope was seized by the ruffians, beaten into insensibility, mutilated, and dragged to a monastery cell where his attackers then attempted to gouge his eyes and tear out his tongue. Wound him grievously they did, but not to their hopes. Both sight and speech were regained and he lived to evade the vigilance of his captors. Gathering together a small band of supporters he hastened to the court of Charlemagne who received him with consideration and sympathy. This latter emotion took practical expression in the form of an armed expedition to escort the Pope back to Rome where he was received with every manifestation of joy by the citizens.

Ferreted from their hiding places his enemies would have probably suffered quick reward for their villainies but the pontiff insisted that their accusations against him should be heard first. A court of bishops and doctors was convened and Charlemagne, deeming such an event important enough to warrant his presence, hurried to Rome to make his second visit. After hearing the testimony the judicial clerics decided, and it was sound law, that they had not the power nor would they dare, even at the Pope's own behest, "to judge the Apostolic See, which is the head of all the Church of God." To this decision the Emperor gave his hearty assent whereupon the Pope voluntarily declared on oath that he was innocent of all the charges levelled at him. His accusers and would-be assassins were then sentenced to die but Leo, with the mercy of his station and the magnanimity of his victory, intervened and their punishment was changed to exile. The dramatic scene was not to be the only eventful incident of Charlemagne's visit. A few days later it was Christmas and while the King was kneeling at his devotions in St. Peter's the Pope suddenly placed a gold crown on his head and a purple cloak across his shoulders. The surprised monarch then heard the wild acclamation of the people who joined in the thunderous chant of the choir, "Long life and victory to Charles, the most pious Augustus, crowned by God, the great and pacific Emperor of the Romans."

Once again there was an Emperor of the West and the vast territories that were united by his valor and fortune now marked the beginning of what was known as the Holy Roman Empire, that idealistic scheme which could never arrive at perfection because of the imperfection which exists in all men. But on that Christmas day of 800 it seemed a magnificent plan; the temporal power of a united Christendom invested in a powerful prince who swore to uphold and protect but not interfere with the authority or offices of the Church. It seemed a magnificent plan but in it no provision was made for the very human emotions of greed and ambition which for centuries to come both princes and churchmen were to display in the usurpation of each other's provinces.

Nor was this projected spiritual and temporal empire founded on true Christian principles. Devotion and faith perhaps, but in many cases only a nominal allegiance was paid to the teachings of the divine Founder. Many of the evils, if not the tenets, of paganism were still discernible in the life of the period. Even the great champion of Christendom, Charlemagne, in many instances showed a singular disregard for the proprieties and virtues of his undeniable faith. In war he notoriously displayed little mercy and in matrimony, with equal fame, he had no constancy. The imperial couch was a changing scene to a long succession of consorts, some of whom he married and divorced but many of whom he did not deign to trouble with the pretence of any dubious ceremony. And along with his protection of the Church there also grew, despite the loud condemnations of the true clerics, the evil influences of lay investiture; that pernicious system which made bishops out of soldiers and *vice versa*. By Charlemagne's orders the sacrament of baptism was many times enforced by the sword and other abuses of the time can well be illustrated by the fact that the Emperor's own daughter, Bertha, was the mistress of Angibert, Abbot of St. Regnier and one of her father's most trusted friends and admirers.

In 814 the Emperor died and almost immediately the absence of his powerful influence was shown by revolt in Rome. This time however Leo needed no external aid to quell the conspirators, who were soon defeated and their ringleaders executed. These harsh but necessary measures shocked Charlemagne's son, known to history as Louis the Mild, who had succeeded his great father but who had not learnt that the sternest of actions are often times necessary to the discipline which is essential to wise government. Although possessed of the same laudable aims as had directed the policies of his father, Louis unfortunately was not blessed with the same genius for administration. On accession to power the conscientious and considerate prince had reformed the court which was the seat of his inheritance, banishing to their monasteries those worldly ecclesiastics who had been such boon companions of his father and ordering other clerics of similar sort to divest themselves of such unpriestly attire as spurs and swords. To the real and hardworking warriors of the Church he gave unstinted assistance and with sympathy he listened to the monks who would have him help the conditions of the serfs. There is no doubt that mercy and charity characterized the every action of this good man; but in an age where violence seemed necessary for survival these virtues became the weaknesses which spelled the ruination of his father's mighty plans.

Louis was not crowned by Leo, for that pontiff soon died. He was succeeded by STEPHEN V, a Roman of good family, whose pontificate only lasted six months. During this time he journeyed to Rheims and there, after assuring Louis of the friendship and loyalty of Rome, he ceremoniously invested both the Emperor and his wife with the golden circlets that were the symbols of their rank. The next Pope was PASCHAL I who was gloomily aware that Louis lacked the strength so necessary to keep the unwieldy bulk of the Empire intact. Already there were signs of anarchy and even the Imperial sons and nephews played at plot and intrigue. With Rome apparently a subject state to the Emperor, events might soon place a tyrant or villain as feudal lord and "protector" of the ancient city. Charlemagne and Louis had displayed nought but generosity and respect to the Romans, but their successors might reveal entirely different policies, so the new Pope, with foresight and with firmness, hastened to formulate a written pact which would guarantee the papal sovereignty and forbid lay intrusion into ecclesiastical affairs. Through his ambassadors the Emperor agreed to these measures in a document which is extant, *Pactum Ludovicianum,* but at the papal court there were high officials who for the furtherance of their own dark intrigues tried in every way to wreck the treaty. They failed and so savage was the feeling against them and their treacheries that the infuriated supporters of the Pope first captured, then blinded and killed their leaders. Once again the gentle Louis was shocked and this time he sent an embassy to make investigation. Paschal, under a solemn and voluntary oath, declared he had had nothing to do with the bloody deed but at the same time he invoked the privileges of his sovereignty and refused to allow the Imperial envoys to apprehend the perpetrators, stating that the murdered officials had been guilty of treason and deserved their end.

A gentler side of his nature was revealed when, on turning from political problems, he was magnificently hospitable to crowds of orthodox Catholics, monks and laity, who were fleeing from Greece before the persecution of the current Byzantine tyrant, now Leo the Armenian. Paschal erected hospices and monasteries and opened the gates wide to the needy and he also was responsible for the founding and restoration of many other important buildings throughout Rome. From splendid evidence still existing his name can be included in that large and illustrious company of pontiffs who, in addition to those other virtues which made certain their claim for posterity, are remembered as assiduous patrons of the arts.

The pro-Frankish party in Rome, consisting mostly of conniving nobles who had favors to gain at the Imperial Court, was very much in evidence at the next papal election in 824 and despite an open violation of the law of 769 it was their influence which brought the pontifical honors to EUGENIUS II. Such dubious support was not however to cast the shadows of dishonor over the acts of the new Pope. He was only to reign three years but in that short time his record is sweetly that of a humble, pious, and learned prelate. Valiantly he strove to bring harmony to the factions that were now so dangerously exciting Rome, and emerging from the maneuverings of all concerned was a new concordat between the Franks and the Papacy. But in the interest of peace it would seem the Pope sacrificed some of the hardly won rights of his office for there is no doubt the Franks were favored in the new agreement: and although the independence of the Church was still guaranteed in lofty terms it is significant that once again the laity, the powerful Roman nobles, were to be allowed to take part in the papal elections. This mistake did not prevent Eugene from being alarmed at the evil effects of lay investiture. He called sixty-two bishops to Rome and from this meeting thirty-eight decrees of ecclesiastical discipline were issued. Illiterate clerics were to be suspended, new schools established, and doctors of learning were to dwell with bishops.

During the late summer of the next year Eugenius died and the selection of VALENTINE as Pope was due entirely to the support of the nobles, now acting in their legal rights. Valentine only survived his election six weeks and the same clique who had voted for him were responsible for the choice of GREGORY IV. But several months elapsed before there was an official installation, for again it seems a pope should await the Imperial sanction before taking office. Although supported by a united nobility the new pontiff was no villain and before his election, as Cardinal-priest of the Basilica of St. Mark, his life had been characterized by dignity and ability. But the magnitude of the problems which were plunging the Empire into chaotic gloom left him bewildered and often inadequate. During his time the Imperial princes twice went to war against their father and once when the Pope went to end such a disgraceful situation he was seized by one of the sons and it was made to appear he was a party to the shameful rebellion. Such, indeed, became the Emperor Louis' opinion and for a time he viewed the Pope with distrust and anger, an attitude which would have served him far better if it

had been employed in the direction of his bellicose and mutinous offspring. This suspicious and hostile spirit was absorbed by
some of the bishops who were attached to the Imperial Court
and on one occasion they were presumptuous enough rudely to
refuse a papal summons. To them Gregory administered a dignified and fitting rebuke. "You must not forget," he wrote, "that
the government of souls which belongs to the Sovereign Pontiff
is higher than the imperial power which is only temporal."

Louis was finally convinced of the Pope's loyalty but his many
attempts to bring peace to the unruly family were never successful. The unhappy Emperor died in 840 and his sons, who
had shown such a lack of filial devotion, now hastened to display
an even greater absence of fraternal affection. Their armies followed the clashings of their mean ambitions and at the battle
of Fontenoy it is estimated no fewer than 100,000 of their misguided followers perished. In reality this huge slaughter marked
the end of Frankish power but the immediate outcome was a
treaty between the three brothers, dividing the already disrupted
Empire among them. Charles the Bald took France and Louis
the German received everything east of Lothair's portion which,
along with a few provinces of Gaul, was Italy.

This kingdom was in sad disorder. The bloody rivalries of the
Imperial family had been a pattern closely followed by petty
tyrants and minor princes, and the tranquillity of good government was rapidly becoming something to exist only in memories
of old men or in the prayers of good women. The alert Saracens
had landed and taken possession of Sicily and from their ranks
savage gangs of mercenaries had been foolishly imported to enforce the claims of aspirants to the duchy of Benevento. The
Pope was well aware of these dangers and he knew that there
was now no Prince powerful enough or willing to come to his
immediate assistance if Rome was invaded. The power of
Charlemagne's name had been dissipated by his descendants and
with foreboding the pontiff set out to prepare the city for defense; but even while he frantically superintended the construction of fortifications it is interesting to note that the work of the

Church continued on its determined way. Saracens might be a near and fearful menace to Rome but that did not prevent Scandinavia from being given the faith and St. Anscar, Apostle of the North, was sent the pallium and the authority of legate to the Swedes, Danes, and Slavs. Across the seas to the Archbishop of Canterbury and over the long roads to Salzburg and Grado, went the same coveted symbol, along with lengthy missives of advice and guidance.

Shame stained the three years of the next Pope, the aged and gout-stricken SERGIUS II. Turmoil had marked his election. When his name was announced there was an angry roar from an indignant and disappointed populace who had hoped for their own candidate, the deacon John. But mutinous incidents which might have developed into grave revolt were quickly and effectively suppressed by Sergius' henchmen and while the luckless John was whisked away to the obscurity of a monastery cell the new pontiff was, behind the swords of his friends, validly consecrated and safely installed. From this unholy beginning his policies, if his actions can be dignified by such a name, seemed to have had an anti-Frankish tinge. He ignored the custom of obtaining Imperial sanction, an oversight not overlooked and quickly resented by Lothair who sent an army, headed by his son, the future Emperor Louis, to demand explanation. In Rome long discussions and fervent protestations of amity greeted the prince and that supreme flattery which might have dazzled a stronger and older head was now employed. With pomp and solemnity the Pope placed the golden circlet of kingship upon the brow of the royal scion while the Frankish soldiers, with ebullient loyalty, and the clerics, with sound discretion, roared approval.

The real power behind this and every other act of the Pope was his brother, Benedict, an unscrupulous domineering ruffian who had received episcopal honors but not grace with the family's advent to the papacy. This blackguard, without any pretense of reticence or shame, inaugurated a regime of unbridled simony. Benefices, sees, honors of any kind, were put on sale at the

Lateran and the Pope made no protest. Indeed he offered nought but condonation and, while his brother dominated and plundered, the pontiff's main interest in life seemed to be the exercise of a gluttonous appetite at the delights of the table. The supreme disaster of this calamitous reign was reached when, in August of 846, a large Saracen fleet anchored off the mouth of the Tiber and discharged thousands of Arab warriors, fierce and hungry for plunder. They landed and easily overcame the defences of Ostia. With daring and insolence the invaders swept up to Rome where fortunately the stout walls, built so honestly by more honorable generations, proved sufficient obstacle to the audacious attack. But the Basilicas of St. Peter and St. Paul were unprotected and so with an exultation doubly inspired by religious fanaticism and prospects of rich loot the raiders flung themselves upon the sacred places. The tombs and temples of the Apostles were plundered and profaned to the savage chant of "There is but one God, and Mohammed is the Prophet of God."

The conscience of Christendom could not remain indifferent to such an insult to its spiritual capital. The autumn rains drove the invaders back to their ships but Lothair also sent an expedition which expelled them from Benevento and, under Imperial stimulus, a subsidy was arranged to build fortifications around the Basilicas. Pope Sergius died about this time and perhaps because of his unhonored memory or perhaps because of the distress and peril of the moment there were no disgraceful intrigues to mar the election of Leo IV. This man sincerely had no wish to be Pope but the unanimous acclamations of both clergy and laity forced him to accept the responsibilities. He ruled for eight years with firmness, initiative and discretion; setting his temporal government a goal which was a triple objective: adequate defences for Rome, independence of the Church from secular domination, and the abolition of simony. The first he achieved with an elaborate building program which was financed partly from the subsidy advanced by the Frankish King, and partly from taxes levied throughout the Papal States. Fifteen of the towers that were an integral part of the city's massive bulwarks were entirely rebuilt and staunch walls were erected for the first time around the Vatican hill. Four years elapsed before the hard working Pope was content to call the new fortified area finished and then a grateful people insisted it should, in his honor, be called the Leonine City. And while busy with engineers and excavations he manipulated the more delicate instrument of diplomacy to such advantage that he won sufficient assistance from the maritime States of Naples, Amalfi, and Gaeta, all Byzantine vassals, to congregate a strong fleet which, with the help of a provident storm, was able to destroy the ships of the audacious Saracens when they again ventured to approach the Tiber.

In the reign of such a Pope multitudes of pilgrims flocked to Rome to pay tribute and to receive the pontifical blessing and amongst them was the young Anglo-Saxon, Alfred, afterwards called by an adoring nation, the Great, and his father, Ethelwulf. That the pontiff was impressed by the young prince's virtues is shown by the fact that he adopted him as his godson and also placed the circlet of consecrated gold on Alfred's head, thus making him the first and only English King ever crowned in Rome.

Leo IV was shocked and grieved at the disgraceful life led by many of the bishops of his time and in order to combat such evils he held two synods in Rome. At one of these gatherings it is noteworthy that anathema was pronounced against usury. Already the Church was viewing with alarm and endeavoring to check the growth of a pernicious system which in time was to develop into a gigantic and unwieldy and unjust law of economics.

The disgust with which the Frankish monarch, Lothair, had viewed the misdeeds of Sergius II changed to alarm when he became aware of Leo's vigorous and independent policies. Lothair had assumed the Imperial title with his portion of the Empire and he harbored exalted ideas of playing the same role in history as had his great forebear, Charlemagne. Perhaps if he had been blessed by the same genius his plans might have been better received by the wise Leo, who steadfastly fought to keep

LEO IV

St. Leo IV (847-855)

the papacy free of Frankish intrigues and schemes. After several rebuffs from the pope, Lothair resorted to a fresh stratagem. He began to prepare for the next papal election, certain his wait would not be long for Leo was an old man. For his tool in the ghoulish plot he chose a willing and clever priest named Anastasius who, dazzled by such lofty patronage, was certain that with a strong display of the Imperial power he could control, in his own favor, the election following the Pope's death. But Leo also thought of the future and in a clever move ordered Anastasius to leave Lothair's court and return to Rome. Reluctant to submit to certain discipline the priest refused whereupon the Pope, after several warnings, solemnly pronounced a sentence of excommunication not only upon Anastasius, but also any who should ever dare to support that luckless intriguer at a papal election.

Leo died shortly after this pronouncement and elected as his successor was BENEDICT III. But the Emperor, still harboring confidence in his plan, announced he would not sanction the appointment. This news he sent along with his candidate, the excommunicated but still optimistic Anastasius, and a large military escort which on arrival in Rome promptly arrested Benedict. Anastasius was installed in the papal palace by force of arms but the clergy courageously refused to countenance such a flagrant and shameful violation of Church law and when the Roman populace with anger and indignation supported the churchmen the Emperor's envoys wisely escorted the legitimate Pope back to his honors and the papal pretender was made abbot of St. Maria in Trastevere.

Benedict died in 858 but before progressing with the papal continuity some mention should be made of the "Popess Joan," a female who is supposed to have occupied the Holy See at this period. The fantastic legend makes its appearance four hundred years later and at various times has been given great circulation by enthusiastic enemies of the papacy. It makes a colorful story but historians, even those most critical of the Church, unite in denying credence to such a weird libel. The story is that she ruled for two years—and between the reigns that history, by irre-futable documentary evidence, assigns to Leo IV and Bene-dict III! The former died on the 17th of July 855 and as has been seen Benedict succeeded him almost immediately. The Emperor Lothair died during the September of the same year and in the two months his reign coincided with that of the new Pope a coin was minted bearing both his likeness and Benedict's. This is one of the briefest of the many proofs that give the lie to the absurd story.

Louis, son of Lothair, succeeded to his father's throne and policies but was resolved that although he would dominate the election of a Pope he would employ more subtle methods than had his father. So when Benedict died he sent no ambassadors but he himself hastened to Rome and there is no doubt that it was his astutely wielded influence which was responsible for the selection of NICHOLAS I, a priest with a reputation for piety, eloquence, and learning. Nor was this reputation to be altered by the acquisition of the Fisherman's Ring. Although he had been supported by the Emperor, he quickly made known that he would not suffer interference with his duties either as spiritual leader or temporal sovereign. Of course Louis must have been disappointed at the very definite failure of his scheme but such was the logic of the Pope's honesty and the charm of his manner that at first there was no antagonism between the two. Indeed there were manifestations of great friendship and whenever they met the Emperor accorded the pontiff the same kindly respect and deference a well-mannered son shows a father. Nicholas accepted such courtesy with the graciousness it merited but when the time came he did not hesitate to give rebuke when it too was needed. Disagreement eventually occurred and reached such proportions that during the winter of 863 Imperial soldiery besieged Rome and for two days kept the pontiff a prisoner, without food, in St. Peter's. The quarrel was because the Em-peror's nephew, Lothair II, King of Lorraine, had divorced his wife to marry his mistress. With a firmness that would allow of no compromise Nicholas declared the divorce to be invalid and ordered Lothair to return to his lawful wife. The thwarted King and his imperial uncle employed every argument, from threats of force to the opinions of dishonest prelates, to change the Pope's decision but he remained adamant. And at unscrupulous ecclesiastics—including such important figures as the Arch-bishops of Cologne and Treves—who, untrue to their vows, were submissive to the Emperor, he levelled sentences of deposition.

It was part of his wise policy to keep a vigilant eye and employ strict discipline, whenever possible, against the irregularities per-petrated by powerful clerics who, in the formation of the feudal system, were assuming sovereign status as temporal rulers. The incompetences of Charlemagne's descendants had broken the Empire into portions loosely held by the titular monarchs and in reality a shifting disorder of territories ranging in size from kingdoms to fortified villages. Each had his army and most deliv-ered tribute of some kind to a superior power and in turn ex-tracted vassal homages from weaker neighbours. The lords of such principalities wielded absolute power within their own boundaries and often these rulers, by the circumstances of ac-cumulated property, were prince-bishops of rich sees or abbots of large monasteries. Allegiance to Rome could be very irksome to prelates of this type, many of whom were products of the system of lay investiture, and indeed with a weaker man occupy-ing the pontifical office this allegiance might have become neg-ligible. But Nicholas resolutely demanded observance of the rights due to the Holy See. When the powerful Archbishop of Rheims deposed a bishop, then imprisoned him for appealing to Rome, the Pope quickly annulled the sentence and reinstated the victim. Even more drastic was his treatment of another im-portant prelate, the Archbishop of Ravenna, whom, despite spirited protestations from the Emperor, he actually excom-municated for misgovernment.

To the East, his attention was directed by the injustices of the Eastern Emperor, Michael III, who, at the instigation of his debauched patrician uncle, Caesar Bardas, had, it was sup-posed, brutally deposed and exiled the Patriarch of Constantinople, Ignatius. But there are arguments for a possible thesis that St. Ignatius resigned voluntarily because of strained relations with Bardas. At any rate, Nicholas, after investigation, espoused the cause of the saintly Ignatius and called upon the Eastern bishops not to tender allegiance to the individual who, as he saw it, had usurped the Patriarchal throne. This was Photius, a scholar of famed but misguided brilliance, whose transference from the lay state through all the degrees of priesthood had been accomplished in six days! He seems to have been the popular choice in the synod of 861, which followed the descent of St. Ignatius from the see, and, presuming the latter actually did resign, Photius may indeed have been a legitimate patriarch. At the synod the papal legatees had, in fact, raised no objection to the accession of Photius, but Nicholas refused to recognize one whose office had been assumed under such equivocal conditions. Tension increased when the new occupant of the Byzantine see would not acknowledge the Pope's claim to direct patriarchal jurisdiction over those Catholics of the Byzantine rite dwelling in Calabria, Sicily, and Illyricum, and when newly-converted Bulgaria, under pressure from Constantinople, accepted the Byzantine, rather than the Roman rite.

In the unseemly quarrel that now commenced, studded wtih anathemas, charges and threats, can be discerned the seeds of the great Schism between East and West. Although in the past the Byzantines had often differed with Rome on matters of discipline and had even gone as far as schism, never did fracture leave such a deep scar as that made by Photius. Misdirecting his remarkable erudition along the channels of ambition, he declared the Latins to have fallen into error because (1) they fasted on Saturdays, (2) they did not begin Lent till Ash Wednesday instead of three days earlier, as in the East, (3) they did not allow priests to be married, (4) they had added the *filioque* to the creed. With deplorable effrontery he then "excommunicated" the Pope and all orthodox Catholics, saying they were "forerunners of apostasy, servants of Antichrist who deserve a thousand deaths, liars, fighters against God." A sudden and violent shifting of Emperors in Constantinople deprived, but only temporarily, the audacious malcontent of support and he was ejected from the Patriarchate. This was in the September of the year 867 and Pope Nicholas concluded his splendid reign two months later.

The next to take his place in the unending procession was ADRIAN II, a priest of venerable age and high character who had twice before refused the high station and whose final acceptance was to bring him tragedy. Before taking orders he had been married and to this union had been born a daughter. With his elevation to the papacy there was now created a situation which presented enormous and tempting possibilities to the ambitious. That the daughter of a Pope was a prize of the highest value in the matrimonial lists did not escape the attention of the wily Anastasius, the same who as the persistent papal candidate had been so vigorously rejected by the Roman people. Together with his equally ambitious father, the aged Ursenius (who also was possessed of episcopal rank), he plotted to make his brother, Eleutherius, the husband of Adrian's daughter. Alliance with such a family did not appeal to the Pope who rejected the proposal, saying that marriage with another suitor had previously been arranged. On receiving this rebuff Eleutherius grew so enraged that he seized both the Pope's daughter and her mother and fled from Rome. A marriage ceremony was then forced upon the unhappy girl but this outrage was only a preliminary crime to the vicious brutality of her murder which, together with that of her mother, occurred soon after. This wickedness did not pass unavenged. Eleutherius was apprehended, and put to death. Ursenius fled from Rome and shortly after died; but Anastasius managed to convince an assemblage of clergy and even the angry and grief stricken pontiff that he was innocent of any participation in the crime.

In 872 Adrian died and he was followed by JOHN VIII whose reign of a decade was also one of violence and bloodshed. Problems of all kinds and from all directions came to harass him. The death of Louis II had left the title of Emperor sought by two claimants, his uncles, Louis the German and Charles the Bald who ruled France. The Pope, sadly in need of a strong secular power to regulate the disorders of Italy, endorsed the claims of the French prince and crowned him in Rome on the Christmas day of 875. But this act failed to bring the desired troops across the Alps and only served to inflame the slighted aspirant to a more determined bellicosity. Armies marched and men died to settle the Imperial contest. In two years both rivals were dead themselves; but the violent altercations were continued by their heirs, intoxicated by the same dangerous dreams of the purple. Meanwhile the Saracens were again in Italy and their ships were once more sighted beating off the mouth of the Tiber. Throughout this entire pontificate the Mohammedans were to constitute a menace to the distressed Pope who wrote "our coasts have been plundered, and the Saracens are as much at home in Fundi and Terracina as in Africa. . . . If all the trees in the forest were turned into tongues they could not describe the ravages of these impious pagans. The devout people of God are destroyed by a continual slaughter; he, who escapes the fire and the sword, is carried a captive into exile. Cities, castles and villages are utterly wasted and without an inhabitant. The bishops are wandering about in beggary, or fly to Rome as the only place of refuge."

To keep such a refuge adequately protected John tried desperately to awaken the consciences of the warring kings and plundering nobles but it was in vain. Occupied in suicidal struggles they refused to unite against the common enemy and finally the pontiff as defender of Rome was obliged to assume the unecclesiastical duties of both General and Admiral. After fortifying Rome he assembled a fleet and went to sea, patrolling the coast until Saracen pirates were sighted. With courage and skill he then engaged and dispersed them off the promontory of Circe. Physical danger was no novelty to this gallant Pope. Once indeed Lambert, the duke of Spoleto, invaded Rome and made the Pope prisoner, seeking to get pontifical allegiance to the cause of Carloman of Bavaria, an aspirant to the Imperial title. Pope John managed to flee to France where he implored the aid of Louis the Stammerer. (Aptly does the title of this Prince and his contemporaries, Charles the Fat and Charles the Simple, describe the level to which the House of Charlemagne had fallen.) No protection for Rome was received in France by John and in 880 he was forced to accept the Bavarian as Emperor.

Assistance for his temporal domain was not the only task to engage the attention of this busy Pope; his energies were manifested in Spain where the intricate business of creating a metropolitan was accomplished and laws against sacrilege emphasized; the distant Archbishop of Canterbury received encouragement and consolation and the young English King Alfred was given advice. Within the walls of the city he so zealously sought to guard, problems and vexations came in the form of a discontented fraction of the aristocracy who sought to hinder his every move. There he fought with habitual vigor, finally expelling from Rome their leader, Formosus, bishop of Porto, who, to escape a heavier punishment, solemnly promised he would never again venture within sight of the city. This was the vow from a man destined himself to occupy the papal throne thirteen years later! Over three hundred letters of anathema were produced by the tireless energies of John VIII and the violence that had so characterized his reign persisted even to his deathbed. Even a peaceful exit from this world was denied to this active man. He was poisoned and then, while he was still writhing with agonies incited by the drug, his impatient murderers smashed his skull with a hammer. This crime was ascribed to conspirators belonging to his household, relatives or servants who desired treasure. Many Popes had been martyred before but this was the first to be assassinated.

Formosus, bishop of Porto, was permitted to return to Rome by the new Pope, MARINUS, who as bishop of Caere was the first of episcopal rank to be elected to the Chair of Peter. Marinus did not live to see whether his action in absolving Formosus was wise or not for he died about a year after his election. He was succeeded by ADRIAN III whose reign of almost

equal brevity witnessed the re-establishment of a strong and mis-
chievous faction in Rome headed by the tenacious Formosus.
In the summer of 885 the Pope died near Modena while journeying to negotiate with Charles the Fat, the unpopular and inadequate possessor of the Imperial station. There was a rapid
scurrying in Rome when the news arrived but Formosus and his
allies could and did easily shape the results of the election. The
choice was STEPHEN VI who soon was confronted by a problem
of magnitude, whom to recognize as the rightful Emperor. For
with the death of Charles the Fat three princes rose to claim the
now almost meaningless title: Arnulf, king of Germany, Berengar,
ruler of Italy, and Guido, duke of Spoleto. The first two princes
were of the Charlemagne line and tradition but Guido was possessed of the Lombard spirit which regarded the temporal sovereignty of the Pope with contempt and jealousy. Berengar and
Guido met in battle and when the latter was victorious he
marched on Rome and without any gestures of obeisance or
council commanded the Pope, as his vassal, to proclaim him
Emperor. This was done. But soon after the unhappy Stephen
was relieved of any further humiliations by death. The hardy
survivor of many turbulent intrigues, FORMOSUS, was elected to
occupy the sacred position. The guile which had characterized
and clouded his earlier history was now manifested by an attitude of eager submissiveness to Guido while secretly urgent
entreaties were despatched to the German King. Still yearning
to be called Emperor, the northern prince, Arnulf, was not
unmindful of the Pope's pleas and before his commands and
under his leadership his troops turned towards Rome. But before
such an objective could be reached many obstacles had to be
overcome and while the northerners were maneuvering and
campaigning through the seasons and distances Guido died,
leaving in power an equally hostile son, Lambert.

With profound duplicity the Pope, employing all the ceremonial paraphernalia of a solemn coronation, crowned the young
duke and pronounced him Emperor. Meanwhile Arnulf neared
Rome and Lambert, carrying his new crown, hastily retired to

defend it behind the fortifications of his native Spoleto where with rage and chagrin he learnt that the deceitful pontiff had with jubilance conducted a second coronation and now hailed Arnulf as Emperor and deliverer of Rome. The victorious German turned his attention to Spoleto but before his triumph could be concluded by the annihilation of the enemy he was stricken with paralysis. His alarmed soldiers, suddenly bereft of able leadership, decided not to continue the campaign and, carrying their prostrate monarch on a litter, returned across the Alps, leaving Rome to the mercy of the angry Lambert. At this time, deeply grieved and disappointed at the miscarriage of his plans, Formosus died, but even the tomb, as events will show, was not to save his body from the vengeance of Lambert. Elected to succeed him was BONIFACE VI but a fortnight later this Pope also died and a candidate of the Spoletan party, STEPHEN VII, was installed in the Lateran.

At last Lambert was free to do as he pleased in Rome and before the promptings of his mother, Agiltrude, a woman of implacable will and terrible passions, and with the consent of the new Pope, there was enacted a dreadful drama of revenge. The decaying body of Formosus was disinterred and once again dressed in the gorgeous robes of a presiding Pontiff. Before the gloating eyes of Agiltrude the corpse was propped upon a throne around which a conscienceless assemblage of clergy took their places and went through the motions of a trial. A defender and prosecutor played their parts in the awful farce and a judgment was pronounced which declared the pontificate of Formosus to have been invalid. All his acts were annulled and all ordinations performed by him were announced to be false and illegal. This decision, as will be seen, was to make many innocent clerics bewildered and angry, particularly when they were deprived, on this pretext, of benefices and offices. The horror of the barbaric incident was concluded by a series of degrading insults to the corpse. Richly embroidered vestments were torn from the rotting flesh and the fingers which had been used for consecration were chopped from the right hand. The unsightly remains of the dead and degraded Pope were then cast, unblessed and dishonored, into the Tiber where, secretly, a monk with the assistance of some hired fishermen, rescued them and interred them decently in a burial ground. The Pope who condoned such savagery was himself to be a victim of violence. The annulment of the Formosan ordinations had deprived many of their offices and consequently in the ranks of the clergy there was a strong and discontented faction inimical in every way to the Pope. In the August of 897, before he had reigned a year, he was seized, chained to a couch, and then strangled to death.

Murder was no longer unfamiliar to the papal station, and the vile acts of this time marked the symbolical commencement of an era which was to persist for a century and a half and which was to shroud the papacy with gloom and shame. The Chair of Peter became the prize of tyrants and brigands and a throne fouled by fierce tides of crime and licentiousness. Nevertheless the destined succession continued steadily on, perhaps polluted by but always outliving the schemes of despots and villains. The five months following the murder of Stephen VII saw the accession and deaths of two pontiffs, ROMANUS and THEODORUS II. The latter in his brief reign once again exhumed the abused corpse of Formosus and removed it with suitable ceremony to an appropriate and honored resting place. A decree was then issued—and there was great excitement along the streets of the city as the citizens read it—that the ordinations of Formosus were, despite previous edicts, to be considered valid. Two militant factions were now struggling bitterly for supremacy in Rome, the Formosans and the anti-Formosans, and at the death of Theodorus both parties promptly and emphatically named a Pope. The Formosans declared in favor of a Benedictine, JOHN IX, whilst their antagonists chose one Sergius. Intervention was needed to prevent a deadlock and it came in the person of the Emperor and his much disputed right of sanction. Strangely enough he was well disposed to John and this favor Pope John repaid by assembling a Synod which declared against the pretensions of the Emperor's rival, Berengar, and formulated a law to the effect that in future a pope-elect was not to be consecrated except in the presence of Imperial envoys. Such gestures must not be construed as mere sycophancy but as measures to restore the order so sadly lacking in Rome for the past decade. In many ways John strove, though not successfully for his obstacles were almost insurmountable, to introduce reforms and abolish abuses. Laws were passed to make impossible a repetition of the ghastly barbarism of Formosus' "trial" and the victims of the decrees accompanying that infamous act were now helped and reinstated. Sympathy was extended to the Slavs of Moravia who complained of the harsh attitude of the German bishops. John gave them their own hierarchy, consisting of a metropolitan and three bishops. In time much good might have come from his reign as he had the support of Lambert but unfortunately death came both to Pope and Emperor before the pontificate had lasted two years.

The war that was now the usual aftermath to a monarch's death was the unstable scene for the accession of BENEDICT IV. It was the last year of the ninth century and two princes, Berengar and Louis of Provence, were contending for Lambert's place. The Imperial crown was now merely a reminder of the glories of the past but nevertheless it was a token desired by the feudal war lords and whichever of them had an army strong enough to force the gates of Rome promptly demanded the bauble from the hands of the Pope. Thus the golden circlet had become a trophy of temporary martial skill and fortune rather than a consecrated symbol of a vast and solemn responsibility. Louis was crowned by Benedict but that the honor carried no great significance is illustrated when the new Emperor was soon captured by his rival who burnt out his eyes and banished him from Italy. In 903 Benedict died and was succeeded by LEO V whose story fits admirably into the tumultuous pattern of the period for he was seized by a worldly cleric named Christopher who, supported by armed followers, now claimed the high station. These pretensions were short lived for in his turn Christopher was ejected from the papal throne by a usurper and

marched to a prison. SERGIUS III, a member of the original anti-
Formosan party, was then called Pope and his first act is said to
have been to order the execution of Leo V and Christopher!

But although he carried the titular glory of the august office
Sergius was never to be the real ruler of Rome. That power was
vested in Theodora, a woman with no morals but many ambitions. She was the wife of Theophylact who from the spoils of
public office had accumulated the greatest wealth possessed by
any individual in the Papal States. The fruits of an evil union
were two daughters, Theodora the Younger and Marozia who,
according to some writers of the period, strengthened the bonds
between her mother and the Pope by acting as his mistress.

This regime brought not only sorrow to sincere priests but
also confusion for, continuing with the rancor of the old quarrel,
Sergius emphatically upheld the annulments of the Formosan
consecrations and took the further steps of declaring invalid the
ordinations of John IX and Benedict IV. A Council was convened and there were the usual anathemas, degradations, and re-
ordinations. The Apostolic Succession seemed in jeopardy and
Canon Law in danger of contradiction. There is little brightness
to record in the dismal and disgraceful reign of this servile Pope;
but fittingly established at this time was the famous monastery
of Cluny which eventually was to cradle papal reforms. Another
of the few acts which can be said to be allied with decency was
the handsome restoration of the Lateran Basilica. Sergius died in
911 and his sponsor, the house of Theophylact, installed two
popes in rapid succession, ANASTASIUS III and LANDO. Neither
of the two left any deep mark in history. And that the papal
election and office was completely controlled by the notorious
family was shown by the installation of the next pontif, JOHN X,
who according to some writers was the paramour of Theodora.
Whether this was true or not he undoubtedly owed his elevation to her determined support. He was a man who might well
have attracted the unhealthy attentions of such an unscrupulous
female for he had a will to match her own high spirit and he
was endowed with a sense of bravado that in a time when the

sword was the principal instrument of society had won for him considerable reputation as a warrior. This prowess was not belied when in the third year of his pontificate he congregated the armies of neighboring princes and repelled a Saracen invasion. Nor was he content merely to direct the plans of battle; this martial ecclesiastic marched with his troops and sword in hand led the final victorious charge, putting the Mohammedans completely to rout. Such a man could not remain a mere puppet on the papal throne and the stirrings of his initiative were made known by legates, carrying the pontifical authority, journeying to and treating with distant princes. In 915 he bestowed the Imperial crown on Berengar and when that ruler, conforming to the unfailing habit of the time, was murdered nine years later the Pope proposed that the purple should go to Hugh of Burgundy.

By this time Theodora and her complacent husband had gone to their splendid tombs but their malignant influence remained in the person of their equally predatory and immoral daughter, Marozia. The attempted independence of the Pope was an affront to this audacious creature who was now in the full bloom of womanhood. Thirty-four years old and a widow she was rich and popular, and the leader of the most powerful and organized party in Rome. At her command there was rebellion in the Lateran and Petrus, prefect of Rome and brother of John, was slaughtered in front of the Pope who was then dragged away and soon after, in the chill darkness of an obscure dungeon, had life obliterated by the slow horrors of suffocation.

The papal throne was now the uncontested property of Marozia and in the three years following the murder of John X two men of her choice, LEO VI and STEPHEN VIII, made their dim entrances and exits upon the unpleasant scene. Then once again a selection was necessary and this time the calculating gaze of the odious widow fell upon her own son. The machinery of a controlled election moved agreeably and in 931 JOHN XI was consecrated to the See of Rome. To augment her power his mother then married Hugh of Pavia, King of Italy for the past five years. With splendor the ceremony was performed by her son in Rome but it was the act which was her downfall for the lavish nuptials were dourly watched by another son, Alberic, who considered the power and riches of his infamous grand-parents far too great an inheritance to be jeopardized by the acquisition of an ambitious stepfather. The youth, for he was still that, displaying the dark genius of his blood, organized a skillful piece of treachery, imprisoned his mother and forced Hugh to flee from Rome.

With arrogance, courage, and ability, he assumed absolute rule of the Papal States and there was no protest from his elder brother, the Pope, who soon after, in the year 935, was saved further humiliation by death. By violence Alberic had gained his position and it was by force he was to maintain it for the next twenty years. In all justice to his memory it can be written that his reign did bring order to the temporal power and some benefits to the religious life of Rome. After his brother's death four popes were installed under his patronage: Leo VII, Stephen IX, Marinus II and Agapitus II. They seemed to have been suitably decent and pious men, perhaps not over-endowed with that sometimes troublesome talent, initiative, but attending to their duties and never conflicting with the policies of their sponsor who, with the benignity of a successful despot, treated them with good will.

Vices attract the pens of narrators more readily than do deeds of virtue and it is certainly true that the audiences of historical authors turn with greater interest to the crimes of villains than to the acts of saints. Much has been written of the evil church-men of this age and too little attention has been given to the less colorful exploits of their purer contemporaries. "The preser-vation of ancient learning," says the historian Hallam in his celebrated work on the Middle Ages, "must be ascribed to the establishment of Christianity. Religion alone made a bridge, as it were, across the chaos, and has linked the two periods of ancient and modern civilization . . . The sole hope for literature de-pended upon the Latin language, which these circumstances in the prevailing religious system conspired to maintain: The Papal supremacy, the monastic institution, and the use of a Latin liturgy."

Despite the great scandals of simony which undeniably caused every principle of Christian morality to be violated by tonsured scoundrels, there was a great army of the faithful whose institutions were "centers of light, restoring, maintaining, and raising the standard of cultivation, preserving some sort of elementary education, spreading useful arts, multiplying and storing books, and keeping before the eyes of the world the spectacle and example of a social backbone." These are the words of H. G. Wells, an author who certainly cannot be accused of any prejudice in favour of ecclesiastics. He continues, describing the activities of the Benedictine monks, ". . . a system of patches and fibres of enlightenment in what might otherwise have been a wholly chaotic world. Closely associated with the Benedictine monasteries were the schools that grew presently into medieval universities. The schools of the Roman world had been altogether swept away in the general social breakdown. There was a time when very few priests in Britain or Gaul could read the Gospel or their service books. Only gradually was teaching restored to the world. But when it was restored, it came back not as the duty work of a learned slave, but as the religious service of a special class of devoted men . . . We must remember that through all those ages, leaving profound consequences, but leaving no conspicuous records upon the historian's page, countless men and women were touched by that Spirit of Jesus which still lived and lives at the core of Christianity." A man of this type who did leave his imprint in history and who lived in Alberic's reign was St. Odo of Cluny who had considerable influence on the dictator's actions. Unfortunately the great abbot died in 942 and therefore was not present to prevent the circumstances that were to give the Lateran the atmosphere of a brothel.

Like many other great rulers the weakness of Alberic was manifested in the ambitions he held for his son, Octavian. Not content that his heir should inherit his own vast riches and power he desired the youth should also be Pope! Perhaps he reasoned that the House of Theophylact, with one of its own offspring occupying the supreme office, might escape a just retribution for having plundered the patrimonies of St. Peter. In 954, on his deathbed, he made his friends and henchmen swear they would vote for Octavian at the next papal election. This event came with the decease of Agapitus and on the 16th December, 955, Octavian, changing his name to JOHN XII, was declared to be the successor of St. Peter. The new Pope was only sixteen years of age but the sole evidence he was to give of youth was a sturdy capacity for all forms of dissipation and wickedness. A wild profligacy now became the tempo of the papal court and sacrilege was the rule. The fervent prayers and agonized moans of horrified monks were drowned by the mad noises of obscene orgies as the duties of the altar were supplanted by the pleasures of the flesh. A stable was the background for an ordination. Bishoprics were sold to whoever would purchase them. And the Pope was heard to drink a gay toast to the devil. Not one virtue did the young villain have to substantiate his priesthood and neither was he possessed, although he thought otherwise, of any talents that might have qualified him as a statesman or warrior. The Papal States, so long kept inviolate by the genius of his father, were now invaded by Berengar, King of Italy, and his son, Adalbert. To repel them John was forced to appeal to another of his father's enemies, the German king, Otto.

His pleas were heeded. Otto, who was both gallant and great, marched to Rome where he was received with sighs of relief and shouts of gratitude. The Pope crowned him Emperor, and the splendid memories of Charlemagne and Gregory were invoked as the northern prince swore that he would maintain the integrity of the papal independence while the pontiff for his part solemnly vowed on the body of St. Peter that he would have no further connection with Berengar or Adalbert. Otto left to give battle to these princes and while he was besieging the father at Monte Leone John, now thinking his benefactor to be of too stern a calibre, with a rare and foolish treachery commenced negotiations with the son. The surprised Adalbert came to Rome but so too did Otto who, justly enraged at the base deception being played upon him, wheeled his columns and deployed to the city. John and Adalbert fled and the Germans were now masters of the capital of Christendom. Everywhere the northern eyes turned they were affronted with scandalous evidences of the Pope's crimes. A council was convened and after deliberation fifty bishops, both German and Italian, called upon the Pope to come and defend himself against accusations of sacrilege, simony, perjury, murder, adultery and incest. To this summons the irresponsible youth, now safely ensconced at Tivoli, replied in an ungrammatical Latin message, "We hear that you mean to elect a new Pope. If you do, in the name of Almighty God I excommunicate you, and forbid you to ordain or say Mass."

It was a vexatious question that troubled the Imperial ecclesiastics for they had no procedure to guide or authority to support them. Unfortunately, their decision was uncanonical and created fresh complications. They passed a sentence of deposition against John and elected the Chief Secretary of the Papal States, a layman named Leo, to be his successor. These measures were greeted with hostility by the majority of the Roman citizens who, suspicious of German domination and jealous of traditional rights, were of the opinion that no power on earth could depose a Pope and then place a layman on his throne. Angry mutterings along the streets swelled into roars of protest and defiance as crowds eddied and a rebellion flared. It was suppressed by the irritated Otto at the cost of considerable bloodshed; but later, when the siege of Berengar called for his presence and troops, the angry Romans rose again and this time they were successful. The anti-Pope was driven from the Lateran and the disreputable John was welcomed back as a hero. That he had learned no lessons from his experience was rapidly manifested by his conduct. With barbaric cruelty revenge was wreaked upon those of his antagonists who were unlucky enough not to have escaped.

One prelate had his right arm struck off, another was publicly scourged, and a third high official lost his ears and nose. Once again debauchery stained the Lateran but only for three months was the pollution to endure. John XII breathed his last in the month of May, 964, and even the circumstances of the death of this inglorious and despicable man were not free from a disgraceful shadow for it was the popular belief that he died at the hands of a wronged husband. The only happy fact to emerge from his dreadful reign, and it is remarkable, is that amongst the innumerable villainies perpetuated by the consecrated miscreant there was never any pronouncement against any of the dogmas or moral teachings of the Church.

Without any mention of Otto's protégé, the Anti-Pope Leo VIII, who was still alive, the next election brought forth the person of BENEDICT V, a deacon with a reputation for piety and learning. But he had little opportunity to exercise his virtues, for the determined Emperor marched back to Rome and blockaded the walls until the starved inhabitants made a dishonorable surrender. The defenseless Benedict was handed to the Germans who, in a gesture magnanimous in an age of murder, sent him beyond the Alps to Hamburg where he remained in the kindly custody of the local Archbishop until his death a year later. Before his removal he seemed, either by force or by his own volition, to have relinquished his title to the papacy in favor of his rival Leo. Presuming that his acquiescence in this was voluntary, then Leo would have a valid claim to be listed as his successor. LEO VIII has in fact been placed on the papal list but only conditionally because the historical facts surrounding his ascension are not clear. Leo descended to the grave about the same time as Benedict did. Otto, in an effort to make peace with those Romans who were bitterly antagonistic, encouraged the election of JOHN XIII, scion of the House of Theophylact and a cousin of John XII. But even though he had been drawn from their own ranks, the fact that he was the Emperor's choice was sufficient to make the new Pope unpopular in Rome. A pontiff could not be tolerated who wrote of "the magnanimous exploits of the Emperor Otto" and the moment his patron withdrew he was assaulted and imprisoned, first in the Castle of Sant' Angelo and then behind battlements at Campagna. But John was of a breed that met desperation with resource and he managed to effect an escape and flee to a refuge at Capua. Otto heard the news and once again his troops descended on Rome. The Christmas of 966 saw both Pope and Emperor back in the city and effecting awful revenge. The twelve Tribunes were hanged, the corpse of the Prefectus Urbis was dragged from the tomb and quartered, and another high official was dangled by his hair from a tall statue, then flogged to unconsciousness. It was the discipline of the age, unquestioned by witnesses, and expected by the vanquished.

John's gratitude to Otto was never to falter. In 967 he crowned his son, also named Otto, and a few years later married him to the Byzantine princess Theophano. The support of the Emperor enabled him to devote time to ecclesiastical affairs and his seal rapidly became familiar to distant bishops as he convened synods, settled disputes, and granted privileges to churches and convents throughout Europe. But he was not fated to rule long and in the September of 972 his obituary was read to the congregations of Rome. The deacon, BENEDICT VI was, with the consent of Otto, consecrated in the January of the next year. Unfortunately for him, however, Otto died soon after, and immediately there was an uprising in Rome headed by the late Pope's brother, Crescentius. Benedict was imprisoned and when word arrived that the new Emperor, Otto II, was sending envoys to the city the unfortunate Pope, as too eloquent an evidence, was strangled in his cell. Crescentius then had his accomplice, the deacon Franco, placed on the pontifical throne with the title of Boniface VII. Within thirty days the representatives of the Emperor arrived in Rome, vowing justice but Boniface eluded them, fleeing to Constantinople and taking the contents of the Vatican treasury with him. BENEDICT VII, formerly bishop of Sutri, was now elevated to the hazardous honours. The party sympathetic to Crescentius, that is to say a small clique of selfish nobles, would have deposed him if they dared but the thought of Imperial troops was a sufficient foundation for his throne. One year less than a decade he presided and it proved an era of reform. Simony was checked and monasticism was given the impetus of his encouragement. In 983 he died and his successor was his chancellor, JOHN XIV, an astute and kindly prelate.

With the aid of this Pope the Emperor hoped further to pacify and unite Europe but death intervened to disrupt the dream and the end of the year saw the new Pope singing the Imperial requiem instead of sharing a worthy ambition. The heart of the pontiff must indeed have been heavy with both sadness and apprehension on that day as he chanted the final words of farewell and peace over the corpse of his patron. The death of the papal protector meant the end of protection. The heir to the purple was only three years old and when the princeling was conveyed back to Germany John did not have to wait long. Crescentius had sent word to the anti-Pope, Boniface VII, who, accompanied by an army which he had procured from the Byzantines by promises of concessions, now invaded Rome. What was expected by John then happened. He was thrown into a dungeon where four months later he perished, it is alleged, of hunger and ill treatment.

At last Crescentius and Boniface could boast that their conspiracies were successful. But as heavy-handed masters of Rome their ill-gotten triumph was not long endured: for death struck often now and within the twelvemonth both had been stricken from the earthly scene. At the funeral of the hated Boniface the fury of the mob seethed beyond control and his corpse was stripped and subjected to unmentionable insults before being flung, naked and abused, beneath the statue of Marcus Aurelius then standing in the Lateran piazza.

Bearing the same name as his father the son of Crescentius now attempted to play the same dangerous role in the Roman drama. He intimidated the nobles of the city into a semblance of unity and it was this influence which swayed the next election to JOHN XV who was consecrated to the Holy See in the September of 985. He ruled for eleven years and despite the irksome pretensions of his sponsors his pontificate was one of worthy accomplishment. He was the first Pope to preside at a formal canonization for up to this time the solemn process had been accomplished by bishops or synods. The Saint so announced, in a Bull dated 5 Feb. 993, was Bishop Ulrich of Augsburg. Many monasteries and convents were the recipients of this Pope's consideration and kindness and his influence brought peace between King Aethelred of England and Duke Richard of Normandy. When the founder of a new French dynasty, Hugh Capet, almost led his people into schism because of his despotic action in supplanting the Archbishop of Rheims, it was the well advised legates of John who finally healed the breach. Peace between all was his laudable aim and with this resolution in mind he achieved the difficult position of keeping friendly relations with the German Court without giving offense to Crescentius. The time was now approaching when young Otto III must come to Rome and receive the symbol of his inherited rank for like his father and grandfather the boy Emperor dreamed of a restored Empire and high expectations were held for him. In 996 while Crescentius watched with sullen but impotent jealousy he began the journey south to receive his crown. His way was made slow by the repeated homages of vassal princes and prelates and before he reached his destination John XV was in his tomb.

With the ordered tramp of German soldiers ringing along their roads the Roman faction dared not obtrude their own choice at the next election but with ostentation they deceitfully petitioned Otto to exercise his birthright and present a candidate. This he did in the person of his cousin and great friend Bruno who after the formalities of installation assumed the dignity as GREGORY V. He was the first Pope of German birth and his first act as pontiff was to place the crown on his kinsman's head. The past activities of Crescentius were too pronounced to be overlooked and he was put on trial and found guilty of many misdeeds but the new Pope, in the charity of his own good fortune, begged that the Roman should be pardoned and released. It was done and Gregory was soon to rue it. With his cousin apparently safely installed the young Emperor now set out for Germany where the Slavonians were giving trouble at his boundaries. No sooner was he a safe distance from Rome than agitators in the employ of the ignoble Crescentius disturbed the streets with cries of "Freedom." Mobs congregated, were excited to indignation over supposed injustices, and Gregory was forced to flee. He found refuge at Pavia and from there delivered a sentence of excommunication against his ungrateful enemy who retorted by proclaiming a new Pope with the style of John XVI. Such a situation could not endure and in the Spring of 998 Otto having defeated the Slavs brought his cousin to Rome again. This time there could be no mercy and the vengeance was terrible. To the hoarse commands of Teuton captains heavy swords rose and fell and the heads of Crescentius and twelve of his friends rolled in the dust. Their mutilated bodies were then hung by their feet from gibbets on Monte Mario. The unfortunate anti-Pope received a different punishment; his nose and ears were slit, his eyes and tongue gouged out, and then, so tortured, his bleeding body was dragged through the streets for the amusement of the mob. When, with incredible adherence to life, he survived this treatment he was chained to the floor of a cell at Fulda.

Even yet the obstinate Romans were not subdued and though armies were lacking there remained subtler weapons. The wearisome narrative of bloodshed and violence must continue and as the last year of the tenth century ebbed it was stained by the murder of another Pope as Gregory succumbed in the convulsions of poison.

Disillusionment was mixed with his sorrow as the tearful Otto knelt beside the prostrate body. Gone now were the lofty dreams born of his idealism wherein youth, in the form of his cousin and himself, were to bring an era of harmony and hope to a united Empire. He realized that the next Pope must be a man not only of virtue but of worldly wisdom, one who could with equal clarity discern the deeds of saints or the plots of villains.

With such thoughts in mind it was only natural that the Emperor should turn to his ex-teacher, Gerbert, Archbishop of Ravenna, for here was a prelate familiar with the intrigues of courts and yet a scholar of such ability as in an age of almost universal ignorance had earned for him a reputation for necromancy. The prodigious education of this remarkable man had begun in a Benedictine monastery at Aurillac, then schools in Spain and Italy and finally at Rheims had fed a genius which excelled with an equal facility in the arts of literature, music, mathematics, and astronomy. At a time when bishoprics were reserved almost entirely for the kin of kings and nobles he had fought his way up from a humble birth to a position where the ailing Archbishop of Rheims had nominated him as his successor. Hugh Capet, King of France, had in turn objected, approved, and objected again, to this move, and there had been trouble for some years but now the Emperor, the boy whom he had dazzled with the glories of Charlemagne's dreams, was offering him the highest position of all. He accepted and was consecrated Pope with the style of SYLVESTER II. Fervour, ability, and severity characterized his efforts at reforming the clergy. "Sylvester, Bishop, Servant of the Servants of God," he wrote to one unruly bishop. "Be not astonished that you do not find at the head of our letter either greeting or apostolic benediction. Bearing the name of bishop, you have, by your misdeeds, ceased to be a man. If fidelity lifts a man up to God, treachery brings him down to the level of brutes." Schools were founded and favoured under his rule for he knew well the value of learning. "The just man liveth by faith" was his message to another prelate "but it is meet to join knowledge thereto." Kings received from him favors or rebukes as the occasion demanded. Stephen, ruler of Hungary, received the hereditary title of "Apostolic Majesty" but to the French King went a sentence of penance for his transgression of the matrimonial law.

Otto established residence in Rome and together he and the Pope talked of the future and of Charlemagne. The great dream would be realized and across the splendid conversations a prophecy of the Crusades would flit for Sylvester's vision was not confined to boundaries and he had plans to liberate the Holy Sepulchre. But before any such schemes could be attempted Rome itself would have to be tamed for neither the learning and charm of the Pope, nor the force of the Emperor, had yet thawed the chill hostility of the Romans. The turbulent Marozian blood ran strong in two rival factions, headed by John Crescentius, son of the executed Patrician, and his cousins the Counts of Tusculum. Neither branch of the tempestuous and greedy family was lacking the ancestral ambitions, avarices, or audacity, and Otto was forced to give battle to their defiance at Tivoli. Finally even the gates of his palace in Rome were not inviolate against their insults and under such conditions it became increasingly evident to the young Prince that his plans would never grow to success. A melancholia gradually replaced his hopes and, abandoning his bright majestic mirages, he took to prayers and almsgiving and talked of entering a monastery. His spirit was gone and he died, only twenty-two years old, in the early Spring of 1003. The Marozian clan crowded nearer as the royal corpse was anointed by the sad Sylvester before being dispatched across the Alps to its resting place alongside the great Charlemagne. The Pope was grief stricken but in three months he too was dead, and against these deaths, so close together, some historians have levelled suspicion and hinted of murder.

The Imperial title passed to Henry, duke of Bavaria, whose own troubles were to prevent him from coming to Italy for eleven years. John Crescentius, outwitting his cousins, assumed control of Rome and his influence secured the election of the next three popes. JOHN XVII, who because "JOHN XVI" was an antipope, should actually be JOHN XVI, lived only six months after his consecration. Then came JOHN XVIII (or JOHN XVII), simple and pious, who devoted himself to bringing harmony to ecclesiastical affairs and whose soothing influence seems to have won Constantinople; for again the papal name appeared on the diptychs of that Church. He was an earnest patron of the monastic institutions and indeed, preferring the simpler life, he abdicated in 1009 to enter the cloisters of St. Paul's near Rome. SERGIUS IV, who was the son of a Roman cobbler, was of the same mold as his predecessor and after earning a splendid reputation as a friend of the poor he died in the May of 1012.

Just a few weeks previous to his own death he had celebrated the funeral mass of his patron, John Crescentius, and then the stage was set for another unedifying contest as the Count of Tusculum presented one of his sons, Theophylact, as a candidate for the papacy. The Crescentii did not agree with their cousins and announced as their own choice a certain Gregory. Both branches of the ancient family could support their opinions by private armies and each conducted a separate election. Two Popes claimed the title and while the Crescentii held the city, the Tusculans prowled the provinces. It was an insufferable deadlock and the only way to solve it was by appeal to other authority. Henry II was now safely ensconced and once again couriers sped north to enlist Imperial support and sympathy. Henry, a wise and good ruler, gave his decision in favor of Theophylact who as Pope took the name of BENEDICT VIII. Victory for the Tusculans meant that the pretensions of Gregory were soon to be abandoned and the new Pope was left unhindered to his responsibilities. Although he owed his elevation to the efforts of his father he quickly proved it was to be his own will which would govern his policies. Peace in Italy and reform throughout the Church were the immediate goals of a vigorous energy.

In the Spring of 1014 Henry, defeating some troublesome clans en route, came to receive his crown and with it the Pope presented a significant and symbolical gift, a jewelled orb upon which was attached a cross. The Emperor passed the costly bauble to the monks at Cluny but the hint was not lost; for with his aid, now tendered, Benedict was able to mass an army and completely defeat a Saracen force which had landed at Luni in Maremma. They were the best of friends and the Pope did not resent Henry's interest in ecclesiastical matters for the Emperor, no less than himself, was distressed at the sad discipline of the clergy and was desirous of ending a sorry state of affairs. Clerical incontinence was an all too familiar evil and with a view of stamping it out an important synod, held under both Imperial and Papal auspices, was convened at Pavia in 1022. This meeting was successful but the exalted partners had greater plans and talked of instituting a great reform throughout all Christendom. It was a laudable but tremendous scheme and careful preparation was needed for the morass of opposition was large and all encompassing. How could simony be abolished when it was the revenue of powerful rulers and how could a married clergy be purged back to chastity when wives dwelt openly and contentedly in many an episcopal palace? Undaunted the Pope and the Emperor set to work but the world was large and their time was short. Two years after Pavia both men, and, alas, their schemes with them, were in their graves.

While Benedict had occupied his time with lofty projects the mundane affairs of the Papal States had been directed by his brother, Romanus, who as he quickly changed from lay to clerical state managed the next election with such dexterity that he was declared Pope with the name of JOHN XIX. With him came a revival of the old abuses and simony flourished again. He held lavish court and with generous gifts, in the manner of the ancient Caesars, kept the good-will of the Roman mobs and with magnificent hospitality entertained Kings or their Ambassadors. Pageantry and splendor enveloped the ancient city when the new Emperor, Conrad, accompanied by two Kings, Canute of England and Rudolph of Burgundy, arrived for the Imperial coronation in 1027. Sorely taxed were the papal coffers by extravagances; and when envoys, laden with valuable presents and richer promises, arrived from the Byzantine Emperor, Basil II, with suggestions that the Pope should agree that the rule of all the Oriental Churches be under Constantinople, John was inclined to give his sanction. The proposals had been made in secret but somehow the news leaked out and an uproar came from the clergy. One alarmed Abbot wrote "It is a wholly unjustifiable presumption on the part of the Greeks to have claimed the privilege which, it is said, they wished to obtain from you. We beseech you to show greater firmness in correcting abuses and maintaining discipline in the bosom of the Catholic and Apostolic Church." The gifts were hastily rejected and in Constantinople the frustrated Basil had the papal name again erased from the diptychs of the churches. John seems to have been the first pope to have granted indulgences in return for alms bestowed; but offsetting this revenue he abolished the taxes that hitherto under the guise of customs duties had been levied on Danish and English pilgrims. He called together several synods but their fruit was unimportant. Verbose decisions were made concerning the precedence of powerful prelates whilst the splendid ambitions of his dead brother were forgotten.

But although scandals continued and grew and remained unchided from the Lateran the domestic bliss of many a cleric was now being disturbed by the sudden appearance outside his windows of stern-eyed and loud-voiced monks who did not allow any similarity of calling to stifle their accusations or horror. These good men were militantly on the march and at Cluny was their inspiration in a succession of Abbots renowned for virtue and austerity. That these influences as yet counted for little in Rome was evidenced by the selection of the next Pope, BENEDICT IX. His name had been Theophylact and he was the nephew of his two predecessors so it can be seen that the Tusculans were still in control. Various historians have claimed Benedict's age at his election to have been anywhere from ten to twenty. Whatever it was does not matter; for he soon proved himself as capable in crime as any veteran of vice and to be as lacking in discretion as the most foolish of adolescents. Together with his brother Gregory, who bore the rank of Prefect, the youthful bandit inflicted on Rome a series of misconducts until in angry desperation the citizens allowed themselves to be incited by his family rivals, the Crescentii, into a revolt which at first seemed successful. Benedict was driven from Rome and the opposite party declared a new Pope in the person of Sylvester III who had been John, Bishop of Sabina. But the Tusculans were quick to rally and soon their troops expelled the usurper and restored the capricious young villain to the Lateran.

Their loyalty was repaid only four months later by the supreme simony of all time—the papal office was sold! For a large amount of money Benedict resigned and attempted to convey the Apostolic Succession to John Gratian, Archpriest of the church of St. John at the Latin Gate. Here was a situation to stun canonists for there was no law to vitiate such a transaction. Actually the practical minded citizens of Rome sighed with relief at the new accession for John Gratian, now taking the name of GREGORY VI, was a pious and good man who, along with many others, had been appalled and shocked by the misdeeds of Benedict. Disdaining such means, so common to the age, as the dagger or poison he had resorted to gold to remove the criminal presence before further chaos ensued. Once installed he began reform and to assist he called from his monastery a zealous and clever Benedictine named Hildebrand. Their labors were promptly obstructed by the reappearance of the anti-Pope Sylvester who backed by the Crescentii loudly called upon the faithful to deliver homage to him as the true Pope. To complicate matters further Benedict whose word was as doubtful as his morals decided to revoke his resignation and, surrounded by Tusculan retainers, loftily announced that of course his had been the only valid consecration. The truly pious gathered in alarm around Gregory and begged him as their only hope for order to stay firm.

This he did and thus three Popes, each guarded by his soldiery, held court in a city whose lawless streets were now not thoroughfares but skirmishing grounds for ruffians and brigands. It was the year 1045 and once again history was repeated as a German Emperor, now Henry III, marched south to take command and bring discipline to the Roman scene. With alacrity Gregory accepted the Emperor's suggestion to convene a synod and at Sutri the Fathers assembled against a background of German spears. Sylvester was quickly judged, deposed, and conveyed to a monastery. Attention turned to Gregory who gracefully admitting his own consecration to have been a "shameful and demoniacal heresy" witnessed with signature a decree of his invalidity and was then, accompanied by his faithful secretary Hildebrand, taken to Germany as a state prisoner. Benedict was now ordered to appear and answer for his crimes. And when he refused to attend or recognize the authority of the synod and retreated to wait and brood behind the impregnable walls of the family fortress at Tusculum he was, amidst the solemnity of a ceremonial at St. Peter's, ordered deposed. To the dismay of the jealous Romans who, no matter how villainous a native-born pontiff might be, could seldom stomach the idea of a foreigner, the German bishop, Suidger of Bamberg, now took possession of the Sacred Chair as CLEMENT II. His first act was to crown his Emperor and Empress and sullenly the Roman nobles and their retinues thronged to St. Peter's to listen while northern accents echoed about the High Altar.

In the same dangerous mood the same audience watched Clement give his farewell blessing to Henry as the latter departed for Germany. The Pope was left with a bodyguard of his countrymen; tall, yellow-haired men who had no liking for the prospects of an exile to be spent amidst the sultriness of the approaching Italian summer. These simple northerners were skilled and faithful warriors but fidelity and adept sword play were to prove equally useless against the devices of Roman cunning. From his bulwarked fastness the waiting Benedict watched and commanded, and soon the German Pope was writhing in the tortures of a fatal and obscure poison. Flanked by the troops of the Marquis of Tuscany Benedict swept into Rome, drove out the small German garrison, and once again held possession of the Lateran. There he remained until, nine months later, the Emperor, who had been busy elsewhere, was able to send an expedition sufficiently large to dislodge him. Accompanying this army was the Bishop of Brixen who proudly took the title of Pope DAMASUS II; an appellation with which he was fated never to become familiar. His sentence was already written in the resentful glare of the mobs that his bodyguards were

thrusting back with stern commands and bared steel. Despite
the most elaborate precautions—German swords were waved at
every passing shadow near the papal residence and in the kitchens the most intricate care was taken against poison—he was
dead within three weeks and an unsurprised Roman clergy were
solemnly arranging his funeral. The Emperor received the news
with an anger that stiffened his determination. A German must
preside as Pontiff.

This time his choice fell on the royal born Bruno, Bishop of
Toul. Rome would be no novelty for this pious and courageous
cleric who had been there as a simple pilgrim and also as a commander of cavalry with the Emperor Conrad's expedition in
1027. Soldier prelates were no rarity in the Middle Ages but
Bruno was also possessed of the talents which made for a successful diplomat. Before accepting the dangerous honor he insisted the Roman clergy should be unanimous in the approval of
him and when he made his journey south he took as his advisor
the monk named Hildebrand, the same who had been the
assistant and friend of John Gratian. Guided by the monk's
wisdom Bruno did not enter Rome with the pomp of a great
prelate or the splendor of a German prince but instead came as
an ordinary pilgrim, barefooted and humble alike in garment
and manner. The lack of display did not rob but rather enhanced
his imposing appearance for he was a tall, straight-backed, fair-
haired man of vigorous middle age. Nor were his companions
vain and quarrelsome nobles. They were devout churchmen and
the Romans, displaying less surliness than was their wont,
offered no objections when his new name was announced as
being Leo IX. That his humility was no subterfuge was evidenced throughout the term of this third German pontiff. The
influence of Cluny chastened the Lateran atmosphere and with
Hildebrand at his elbow Leo, employing a thoroughness born of
military skill and experience, set out to convey the spirit of
reform throughout the Church. He ruled five years and was
incessantly busy; for in addition to those enormous ecclesiastical
problems his ambitions challenged there were to annoy him the

temporal affairs of the Papal States which were in a deplorable condition. And there was war too. The depredations of the Normans in southern Italy, in 1053, forced him to engage them but his troops were outnumbered and, despite great valor, defeated. But not their General. He was taken prisoner and in one of those incidents, bright with honor and kindness and so rare in history, the Normans impressed by the virtues and station of the illustrious captive, fell on their knees and declared themselves to be henceforth his soldiers.

Never dormant were his energies against the seemingly insurmountable and gigantic evils of simony and lay investiture. A series of councils were convened and directed against corrupt clergy and their decrees were conveyed in person by the Pope himself in journeys that took him throughout Germany and on to Rheims where he met "Spaniards, Bretons, Franks, Irish and the English." He charmed and swayed and directed the actions of their rulers; forbidding the marriage of William (soon to be the Conqueror) to Matilda of Flanders but sending friendly letters to Edward the Confessor of England (whose piety produced a generosity that resulted in the erection of Westminster Abbey). Hungary's monarch asked for advice, and to Rome begging for the soothing words of absolution came the King of Scotland, Macbeth, the same whom Shakespeare was to immortalize. But this heavy traffic with Western royalties did not awe the then reigning Patriarch of Constantinople. This man was Michael Cerularius, a politically minded prelate with exalted ambitions of placing his see on a level of equality of that of Rome. Reviving the teaching of Photius, he chose at this time to declare all Latin Catholics to be heretics and persuaded the weak-willed Emperor Constantine to back him up. Latin Churches in the East were closed and their bewildered and frightened congregations hastily made report to Rome. As the altercation was carried to its height Leo was seized by a serious illness and, his exhausted frame offering no resistance, he died amidst a general and sincere lamentation during the April of 1054. But his will persisted from the grave and on the July following, his legates the Cardinals Humbert and Frederick, in whom he had invested full authority, formally excommunicated the Byzantine Patriarch and all who remained his adherents. Despite popular misconception, the breach of 1054, though never healed, was not really definitive. For a long time afterwards, there were continuous essays at reunion, originating sometimes from the West, sometimes from the East. Not until 1472, after many unfortunate centuries of growing hatred was the split to become almost irreparable.

For almost a year after Leo's death there was no Pope. The mood of Rome grew heavy with unrest and anxiety and it was only the delicate diplomacy of Hildebrand that stayed hot tempers from breeding rash actions. It was his caution which restrained the impulsive Roman nobles from staging hasty "elections" before the Emperor had chance to nominate a German candidate. There were not lacking many who declared that the wise monk himself should be Pope but the very virtues which excited their admiration were the same that made him hastily and emphatically discourage their proposals. Personal ambitions played little part in Hildebrand's actions and with history to guide him he saw that in the interests of peace a German should occupy the Papal throne. With rare unselfishness he set out to win the goodwill of the Romans for Gebhard, Bishop of Eichstatt, and in September at Mainz the Emperor met a Roman delegation and it was agreed Gebhard should be Pope. To their surprise their choice refused to accept the honor unless—and here again we discern the hand of Hildebrand—the Emperor guaranteed to restore the duchies of Spoleto and Camerino and also to send troops sufficient to repel the Norman invasions. This last condition was not easy for the German ruler to grant; for now, to bar his soldiers from access to Italy, were the newly consolidated territories of the war-like and hostile Godfrey of Lorraine who had strengthened his position and augmented his power by marrying the widow of the Marquis of Tuscany. The negotiations continued for months but finally the Emperor acceded to Gebhard's demands—something he most certainly would not have done with an Italian candidate—and the new Pope was formally installed in Rome on the 17th day of April 1055. VICTOR II was the name he chose and he kept it bright with zeal and honor in a pontificate that endured for the next two years and which continued the policies of Leo and the plans of Hildebrand.

A year after his election Victor was summoned to the death bed of the Emperor and against that gloomy and dramatic background he was, at the dying sovereign's request, made guardian of the six year old princeling, Henry IV, and appointed Regent of Germany. The Emperor died and the Pope was left with heavy responsibilities. He met them well. First he safeguarded the Imperial succession by solemnly crowning and enthroning the Boy-Emperor, then he transferred the regency to the child's mother who was surrounded by a court of loyal and strong vassals. His attention now turned to Godfrey of Lorraine, the late Emperor's enemy, who might be expected to cause trouble. The Pope journeyed south, met this Prince and won him to peace. Alas, he was not destined to enjoy the sweets of his triumph for long. In the hot midsummer of the following year he died suddenly whilst settling a dispute between the bishops of Arenno and Siena.

Who was to be the next Pope? The present Emperor was but a child and his office controlled by an unambitious woman. The German shadow rested but lightly on Rome where there was a sudden stirring amongst old families. Swords were counted as Crescentii and Tusculans took hope again and had it not been for the capable actions of the resolute and incorruptible Hildebrand there would undoubtedly have been a repetition of the old regime of anarchy. Once again we read of his discouraging his own enthusiastic supporters and swinging their allegiance to a candidate who could steady the Papal throne with the support of a powerful prince and who at the same time would bring no disgrace to the high station. His choice was Cardinal Frederick, cousin of Pope Leo IX, and brother of Godfrey of Lorraine, now the strongest ruler in Italy. Despite his high birth Frederick had proved by long service his ability as a cleric. He had been the Papal librarian, and it was he, along with Cardinal Humbert, who had headed the historic embassy to Constantinople at the end of Leo IX's reign. He assumed the style of STEPHEN X and was consecrated during the August of 1057.

One of his first acts was to dispatch Hildebrand on a mission that had a dual purpose; he was to visit the German court and win the good will of the Emperor-Regent, and he was then to campaign throughout Germany and France on a crusade against the stubborn evils of simony. Reform was still the determined Papal goal but some comprehension of the obstacles greeting the efforts of the reformers can be gleaned from the events which now took place. With Hildebrand across the Alps and only eight months after Stephen's installation the Papal throne became empty again. Some said it was poison, and whether the whispers were true or not the dying Pope was sufficiently apprehensive of what might happen after his death to beg, with his last breath, that there should be no election until after the return of Hildebrand. He died and his wishes were ignored. The suspicion that his end bore the stain of murder was strengthened by the unseemly haste with which the old factions now moved to present their candidates. The Counts of Tusculum were, by a great show of arms and liberal donations of liquor to the fickle mobs, successful with their protégé John Mincius, Bishop of Villetri, who now took the highly significant name of Benedict X. And, while such worthy prelates as Cardinals Humbert and Peter Damien publicly and courageously but fruitlessly voiced objections, he was installed on the fifth of April 1058.

Unhappy and miserable must have been the mood of the absent Hildebrand when the news reached him. A puppet Pope had been proclaimed to the world and Tusculan soldiers, with the firm tread of possessors, were striding the streets of Rome. But, unhappy as he was at these facts, Hildebrand was neither daunted nor intimidated. Despair at the seeming collapse of his reforms was no brake to his energies. Rather it acted as a spur to his indomitable will for resourcefully he turned to the German court and successfully pleaded for support. The aid of Godfrey of Lorraine was also won and so with a mixed army behind him the zealous monk marched on Rome. At Sutri, under his auspices, an election was held and chosen to bear the supreme but dangerous honor was Gerard, Bishop of Florence. Rome was then invaded and the Tusculan dispossessed. The anti-Pope fled and Gerard was canonically installed amidst the cheers of the relieved citizens. This Pope took the name of NICHOLAS II and ruled well until his death eighteen months later. The most important act of his reign was the promulgation of a new electoral law. Guarding against the abuses which had preceded his own elevation Nicholas assembled some hundred and thirteen important prelates who formulated the *Constitution on the Election of the Sovereign Pontiff* which amongst other resolutions, provided that: The election is to take place in Rome, but if for some reason it cannot be held there, the electors may repair elsewhere. The candidate must be a member of the Roman clergy, if there is a suitable one; if not, the electors must look elsewhere for one. The Cardinal-bishops, that is, the bishops of certain Sees close to Rome, take the lead by choosing a candidate after which the other Cardinals are called in to vote. The rest of the Roman clergy and people are then given the opportunity to express their consent by acclamation. King Henry of Germany, the future Emperor, and those of his successors who shall have obtained this privilege personally from the Apostolic See, shall be asked to confirm the election.

It is important to grasp what the Cardinals were and why they chose the Bishop of Rome. From the late fifth century the term was applied to the senior priest of each of the Churches of the city of Rome, also to the deacons in charge of the seven regions into which for various administrative purposes Rome was divided, and later to the bishops of the Sees adjacent to Rome. The Cardinals really were in that sense the local clergy of Rome, to whom it naturally fell to elect the Bishop of Rome. Later the title of Cardinal was given to distinguished Churchmen resident in various parts of the world. With the title, they were made titular priests of this or that Roman church, thus members of the clergy of Rome. It is as such that these foreign Cardinals too take part in the election of the Bishop of Rome. A Cardinal is called Cardinal Bishop, Cardinal Priest or Cardinal Deacon according to the See near Rome or church in Rome to which he is appointed.

The new law was a determined effort of the Church to free the Papal elections from lay influences; a fact instantly perceived by both the German court and interested Italian factions. There was a loud outcry from these sources and it seemed perhaps that the new regulations had rashly deprived the Papacy of all temporal protection, and therefore it would be at the mercy of and subject to the whims of any tyrant who might wish to invade Rome. But Hildebrand had foreseen this situation and guided by him the Pope made a treaty with those Normans who were strongly ensconced in their own colony in southern Italy. In return for various privileges of recognition their Duke, Richard Guiscard, promised to provide an army of protection for the Holy See and to guarantee the freedom of the Papal elections. When the news of the treaty was made known the anti-Pope Benedict who had been persisting in his claims while hiding in one of the Tusculan retreats now made his formal submission to the real Pope. Nicholas died in the summer of 1061 at Florence and as Hildebrand assembled the Cardinal-bishops to select his successor a curious thing happened. The Roman nobles, frustrated in their schemes and prevented from violence by the presence of the Normans, sent emissaries to the German court where they had no trouble in arousing indignation and resentment at the exercise of the new electoral law. But while the smooth-tongued Italians were inciting the suspicions of the credulous and often foolish Empress Regent the Cardinals at Rome, free from temporal influences, quickly and unanimously elected the austere Bishop of Lucca, Anselm, who became Pope ALEXANDER II.

The news, as the constitution provided, was then sent to Germany where it was received with scorn and anger. Indeed, the royal widow, firmly convinced that the Imperial prerogatives had been encroached upon, assembled a group of intimidated and political-minded churchmen who obediently declared a new pontiff in the person of the Bishop of Parma. This man, by no accident, was the candidate advanced by the Italian nobility; and when the boy Emperor, Henry IV, under the prompting of his mother and amidst the smiles of the Italians, ratified the "election," he took the name of Honorius II. An army escorted his person and pretensions to Rome and it appeared for a while as though success was with him. His troops defeated the Normans and took possession of St. Peter's. Dismal indeed was the outlook for Alexander until help came from Godfrey of Lorraine who was jealous of German intrusion in Italy. Finally the sad spectacle of two claimants attempting to administer the Church was solved by the seizure from the Empress of the Imperial Regency by the Archbishop of Cologne. This stern prelate, Hanno by name, with his German prejudices, had little sympathy for the Norman alliance with the Papacy but there could be no doubt as to the legitimacy of Alexander's election. At the suggestion of Peter Damien, Hanno convened a general council which after deliberation acknowledged the true Pope and condemned the contender. Thus ended the stormy circumstances that arose from the first effort to exercise the new electoral regulations.

The troubles of inauguration did not prevent the twelve year pontificate of Alexander II from becoming a splendid record of unremitting reform and courage. The Pope was well endowed with this latter virtue and fearlessly he deposed powerful ecclesiastics who had the protection of rulers but had acquired their rank by simoniacal means.

When the young Emperor on reaching manhood showed disposition to be a libertine he was suitably reproved and his request for a divorce sternly rejected. To William, Duke of Normandy, a Prince of far different nature, about to embark on his historic invasion of England, he sent, as a token of his regard, a consecrated banner. Harold, William's enemy, had accepted the authority of Stigand, Archbishop of Canterbury, who was regarded by Rome as being a schismatic; for, after receiving the pallium from Benedict X, this prelate had never since bowed to the rule of the lawful Pope.

Standing by and serving Alexander during his twelve-year term with the same genius and fidelity he had given the previous pontiffs was Hildebrand, now Chancellor of the Apostolic See. For twenty years the inspired monk had been the outstanding figure in the ecclesiastical world. Physically he was puny and sickly, small of stature and wan of face, but the frailness of a vessel is not indicative of the strength of its contents. To that august station which he had so assiduously avoided he had helped direct far healthier men than himself and had outlived them all. Some men in history have been given the title of king-maker but the humble monk was even more than that, and when Pope Alexander died on the twenty-first of April 1073, it must have been with heavy heart that his friend Hildebrand pondered on the problem of succession as he labored over the burial arrangements. But for the people and clergy of Rome there was no problem. For them there was only one candidate and as the Chancellor turned from Alexander's tomb on the day of the funeral he was startled and horrified to hear on every side a steady chant "Let Hildebrand be Pope!" "Blessed Peter has chosen Hildebrand!" "Let Hildebrand be Pope!"

There could be no evasion this time. Both clergy and people were overwhelmingly insistent and the Cardinals voted accordingly. The reluctant Hildebrand, who up to this time had deemed himself worthy only to hold the minor orders of the priesthood, was fully ordained and a few weeks later consecrated Bishop of Rome. He took the name of GREGORY VII and following the directions of the electoral regulations he hastened to inform the profligate Henry IV of his elevation. In this same communication he warned the young Emperor, whose court was fast becoming infamous as a market for simony, that his policy would be even more stern than had been those of his prede-cessors. It was a bold letter but Henry seemed to bear no resentment and answered as a dutiful son, admitting error and swearing repentance.

The new Pope surveyed his problems and found them many and grave. Past popes had issued decrees of reform and the monastic elements had worked unceasingly but that which they opposed remained undislodged and undefeated. Two years after his election found the depressed Pontiff writing to his friend, Hugh, Abbot of Cluny: "Wherever I turn my eyes—to the west, to the north, to the south—I find everywhere Bishops who have obtained their office in an irregular way, whose lives and conversation are strangely at variance with their sacred calling; who go through their duties not for the love of Christ but for motives of worldly gain. There are no longer Princes who set God's honor before their own selfish ends, or who allow justice to stand in the way of their ambitions. . ."

Beyond the scenes of these vexations he had lofty plans for once again uniting Christendom by restoring peace between the Eastern and Western Churches and he also harbored ambitions to commence a crusade and free from the Mohammedan yoke the site of the Holy Sepulchre. But beyond the preliminary stages of the splendid schemes he could not advance because of the evils that flourished so near to Rome, evils that kept his wits and energies occupied to their fullest capacity. Finally he saw that it was useless to thunder against erring ecclesiastics when they had the protection and encouragement of rulers. There was only one weapon that he could use effectively against the latter class and that was the sentence of excommunication. This he promised to do whilst addressing a Roman synod in 1075: "Whoever in the future receives a bishopric or an abbacy from the hands of a layman, shall not be regarded as a bishop or an abbot. Similarly if an Emperor, a duke, a marquis, or a count dares to confer an investiture in connection with a bishopric or any other ecclesiastical office, he shall be cut off from the communion of Blessed Peter."

These ideas are embodied more fully in a document known as the *Dictatus Papae*, often ascribed to Gregory but representing clearly his opinions whether actually written by him or not. In it was written that the Pope alone had the power to instate or depose bishops or transfer them to other sees (with or without their appeal), that no council could be called without the Pope's consent, that his legate had the precedence over all bishops in a council even though he might be inferior in orders, and that the Roman church was free from error in doctrine so that no one who disagreed with it could be considered Catholic. As for the Pope's relationship with temporal rulers, the *Dictatus* declared that he was above all princes and that he had the right to depose unjust rulers, including emperors, and absolve their subjects from allegiance to them. Though some of these propositions are to be taken merely as the personal opinions of Gregory VII rather than as doctrines of the Church, it must be borne in mind that Gregory was sincerely convinced of the validity of all of them and was willing to act on that conviction when he thought a question of right and wrong was involved.

Such views were received in Germany with sullenness and opposition by a well-beneficed and incontinent clergy and with rage by Henry, who chose to regard it as a direct insult to the Imperial Majesty of his person. There was no mistaking the direct words of rebuke for there was only one Emperor and despite his previous letter, so filial and submissive to the Pope, he deemed the practice of lay investiture to be one of his inherited privileges. We have already seen this matter of investiture as troubling the Popes. It had become very much the custom within the Empire that on the death of a bishop or abbot, the Emperor should appoint his successor and bestow on him the ring and staff of office. It was obviously unfitting that the lay power should appoint to spiritual office, yet one can see the Emperor's point of view. Bishops of important sees (more so in the Empire than in the rest of Christendom) and the abbots of rich monasteries were of a necessity great temporal lords. In the feudal system their territories were of vital economic and military importance. It was unthinkable, reasoned Henry, for the bestowal of such powerful offices not to be vested in him who was the highest temporal authority. To counter the threat of excommunication he invoked at Worms a convention of German bishops, all of whom were linked by feudal ties, and most of whom were married. Their defence in this respect was that the laws enjoining celibacy had no basis in scriptural teachings. They quoted St. Paul that "It is better to marry than to burn" and "It behooveth therefore a bishop to be blameless, the husband of one wife." Clergy of this type declared they were men, not the angels that Gregory's standards required, and to emphasize their opinion they treated his legates with open and oft times dangerous hostility. With such a spirit animating high prelates revolt against Rome flared fiercely and spread quickly. The Archbishop of Rouen whilst trying to enforce celibacy among his clergy was stoned and forced to flee, while the Abbot of Pontoise was for the same reason hurled into prison and threatened with death. Such was the respect shown to Gregory's commands! But not even content with this brand of lawlessness the Emperor's churchmen at Worms brought a series of absurd and outrageous charges against the Pontiff and then proceeded to "depose" him. To Gregory came a preposterous message: "Henry, king, not by usurpation but by the will of God, to Hildebrand who is no longer pope but a false monk. Having been condemned by the sentence of our bishops and by our sentence, vacate the place which you have usurped."

At the Lateran Gregory calmly read the outrageous missive to the assembled Roman clergy and the next morning made his effective reply: "Hearken, O Blessed Peter. . . . In thy place, and by thy favor, God has given me authority to bind and to loose upon earth. Wherefore, filled with this confidence, for the honor and defence of thy Church, in the name of God Almighty, by thy power and thy authority, I deprive Henry the king, son of Henry the Emperor, who with unheard of pride has risen against thy Church, of all authority in the kingdom of the Teutons and in Italy. I release all Christians from their oaths of fidelity sworn to him or that they shall swear to him. I forbid

any person to do him any of the service due to kings. . . .
I bind him with the chain of anathema. . . ."

The sentence was as formidable as it was unprecedented and
it served its purpose well. The potent words from the Vatican
were to defeat the presumptuous monarch far more quickly and
more completely than any army would have done. In the dangerously balanced feudal structure that was Germany, the Papal
decree was an excellent and timely pretext for secession by many
of the Imperial vassals who already were disgusted with a corrupt
reign. Tumult and dissension swept through the land like fire
through dry timber and even those Churchmen who had behaved so basely at Worms now quickly changed their minds and
policies. Suddenly the alarmed Henry found himself without
friends or allies, without authority or even a court, and surrounded by menacing princes who threatened to depose him.

It was obvious that there was only one person who could save
him his precarious position and to that source of mercy, the Pope
whom he had so lately and so arrogantly reviled, he now turned.
Although it was harsh winter he commenced the arduous journey south, accompanied only by his wife and child and one
servant. His goal was the castle of Canossa where Gregory was in
residence as the guest of Mathilde, Countess of Tuscany. The
once proud Emperor arrived outside the walls of the fortress on
the morning of January 25, 1077. There he sought entrance not
as a consecrated monarch but as a penitent pilgrim, barefooted,
clad wretchedly, speaking lowly, and weeping copiously. For
three days his tears fell in the snow and his wails drifted up to
the turreted battlements. Perhaps he was playing the hypocrite.
Later events certainly support that theory and Gregory, with his
vast understanding of human nature, must have allowed such
suspicion to visit his mind. But Gregory was also a priest and
the charity of his vocation triumphed over the cynicism which
might have been expected of so astute a diplomatist. Finally he
succumbed to the entreaties and re-admitted the wailing sovereign to the communion of the Church. Absolution was given
on condition that Henry should, on his return to Germany,

perform no act of Government until he had appeared before and appeased a Diet of those princes who had harbored charges against him.

The papal act of mercy was ill received in Germany and Henry's return was viewed with well founded suspicion. Surely enough he broke his pledges and avoided the Diet. These exasperated princes considered such duplicity to be abdication and elected Duke Rudolph of Swabia to his place. But another party, swayed by extravagant promises, rallied to the sovereign and soon a savage civil war was in progress. Gregory was forced to remain neutral and his efforts to effect a peace only served to make him unpopular with both sides. Eventually the persistent villainies of Henry made further papal neutrality impossible and the sentence of excommunication was once again pronounced. This time Henry was not intimidated. In the civil war his troops were gathering victory after victory and this circumstance was sufficient to ensure him of the good will of those odious and conscienceless feudatory churchmen who once before had so brazenly supported his antipapal scheme. At Brixen, in 1080, these creatures assembled and with a great showing of the pomp of their rank but with little evidence of honor they announced that henceforth Guilbert, the excommunicated and simoniacal Archbishop of Ravenna, was to be called Pope under the title of Clement III. The fortunes of war continued to favor Henry. His rival, Rudolph, was defeated and mortally wounded and the Emperor, who had never forgotten the humiliation of Canossa, prepared his revenge. His triumphant armies began the long march south to storm Rome and capture the Pope. But it was three years before they finally forced entrance to the city and by that time the pontiff was behind the impregnable walls of Saint Angelo. With a typical and blatant treachery Henry now tried to negotiate, even promising to deliver as a prisoner his protégé, the anti-pope, if his demands were met. For answer came a reaffirmation of his sentence of excommunication. Angrily he turned back to Rome and there solaced his disappointment by having his puppet crown him Emperor. But not for long was the royal criminal to enjoy the city for to avenge the Pope came the Norman, Robert Guiscard, with six thousand knights and thirty thousand foot soldiers, many of whom were Saracens. Henry fled and the rescuers took possession, bringing back Gregory in triumphant procession.

Once again the Pope held the Lateran but it was only to be for a brief and unhappy tenure. Fighting soon broke out between the Roman citizens and the hot blooded Normans. Cavalry charged the streets and ancient residences were put to the torch. Rapine and bloodshed plunged the city into chaos and the unhappy pontiff was forced to retreat to a monastery. The peace so long denied to him then approached. In the pangs of his constant illness and disappointments he had often cried, "Lord, take me away from this world. Make no long delay." At last his wishes were heeded and on the 25th May, 1085, the frail and pain-wracked frame reached its final exhaustion. Near his death the great champion wrote: "I have loved justice and hated iniquity, therefore, I die in exile." And one of his Cardinals wrote back in splendid answer, "In exile, Holy Father, thou canst not die; *behold I have given thee the heathen for thine inheritance and the uttermost parts of the earth for thy possession.*"

It was a full year before the fancies of the Cardinals could unite in a choice of his successor and it was with considerable reluctance that VICTOR III took the honor. His name had been Desiderius and he was noble by birth and nature. When, as a young man he had announced his vocation for a monastic career his family had shown violent opposition. But the cloisters did not hide his ability as a scholar or leader and for thirty successful years he presided as Abbot of Monte Cassino. The world outside his walls held no allure for him and it was with trepidation that he finally bowed to persuasion and accepted the tiara. When the pretender Clement III promptly contested his election and appeared outside Rome with an army of mercenaries, the new pontiff sped back to his monastery with a celerity that evidenced little regret. These events happened quietly, for Victor was an old and sick man and only survived his installation by four months.

A friend of Gregory VII and recommended by Pope Victor was their successor URBAN II. He was French by birth and was the unanimous selection of the Cardinals. His given name was Odo and his record as an ecclesiastic was brilliant. While still in his thirties he had achieved the position of Archdeacon of Rheims but this honour he had renounced to bury himself as a monk at Cluny. At the monastery his talents were recognized and employed and he became Prior. But neither peace nor security was to be his lot and from the contemplative life Pope Gregory summoned him to be Cardinal Bishop of Ostia. Six months elapsed after Victor's death before he was elected. He was then Pope but he was also a bishop denied his See. A strong force of Imperial soldiery held Rome and "Clement III" paraded schism at St. Peter's. The affairs of the Papacy were in a truly lamentable state and because of the absence, during the past few years, of a strong and guiding hand, most of the gains won so valiantly by Gregory had been lost. Had Urban been a lesser man an "arrangement" would probably have been made with Henry IV but fortunately compromise was not his way and, as if to give challenge and allow of no intrigues, he reiterated the sentence of excommunication against the Emperor. German troops plundered afresh in Italy after this latest hurt to their master's pride and Urban was forced to the south and Norman protection; but gradually favor returned to sweeten his destiny as a series of disasters afflicted the papal antagonist. Troubles were coming to the pugnacious Emperor from unexpected sources, avenues indeed upon which he would find it difficult to unloosen his usual savageries. His favorite son, Conrad, weary of the shame and sycophancy and evil of his father's court, had deserted that sad scene and had joined forces with the proven and good friend of several Popes, the Countess Mathilde and her new husband Guelf of Bavaria. With their support and Urban's approval the German prince was crowned King of Italy at Milan. Meanwhile Henry's second wife chose to deliver an impassioned account of her grievances and his sins before a synod of sympathetic churchmen and while the Emperor's mind was occupied by his misfortunes an apathy seems to have incapacitated his warriors. The anti-Pope fled from Rome and to Urban came a torrent of sudden power. The papal dominions were enlarged and from all sides the papal authority was sought.

To the country of his birth, seven years after his election, the pontiff proceeded with the confidence of a victor. Acting truly as a Father of Kings he rebuked and chastised on his own soil the wretched Philip, King of France, whose only evidence of strength was the tenacity or obstinacy he displayed in adhering to a scandalous and adulterous union with the Countess Bertrada of Anjou. But while in France the Pope delivered a speech far more important both in content and result than a rebuke to a monarch. It was at Clermont where, before a Council of several hundred prelates and thousands of clergy and laymen, he delivered a plea for united Christendom, a holy unity which would liberate the precious Shrine of the Holy Sepulchre, a Christendom which would defeat and throw off the shameful yoke of oppression. He spoke well, his theme was magnificent, and the moment was propitious. "Altars are profaned and broken, Christians tortured, women violated. . . . Who will avenge these wrongs? On you rests this duty, on you. . . . That which above all other thoughts should stir you most is the Holy Sepulchre of the Savior and the Holy Places, ravaged and profaned by an impure race. Valiant soldiers, descendants of those who never knew defeat, make your way to the Holy Sepulchre and tear the Holy Land from the grasp of this abominable nation."

His audience wept and groaned in sympathy and with the vast sorrow and deep anger a mighty enthusiasm was born. Their Pope was not the first to tell them of Jerusalem's plight. There had been rumors, for always, despite insult and hardship, there had been pilgrims. And lately, travelling throughout Europe, stirring city and hamlet alike to compassion and indignation had been a returned pilgrim, a holy hermit, Peter of Amiens, who made it his vocation to tell of Christian disgraces and Turkish profanities. "Who will avenge these wrongs?" cried the Pope

with all the power of a flaming conscience. "On you rests this
duty . . . on you!"

"God wills it!" shouted his audience in wild excitement. "God
wills it." The First Crusade was born but its story cannot be
told in these pages. It is a history, like most narrative of human
endeavor, of shame and honor, of pain and ecstasy. More even
than the beginning of a gigantic adventure it marked the definite
formation of a great Christian confederation. Princes and peasants alike were enthralled again to the Christian spirit by its
splendid ideals and before its enthusiasm chivalry took form,
feuds ceased, and schisms wilted. Three years after Urban's
speech at Clermont, Godfrey de Bouillon set up his standard,
splendid and poignant, scarlet and white, at Jerusalem. In Rome
the joy this triumph brought was subdued by the solemnity of a
Pope's Requiem. Urban II was dead.

The next pope was PASCAL II. Like Urban he had been a
monk of Cluny and like him he had been called from the
cloisters to be made a Cardinal. His name was Ranieri and he
was a Tuscan of good family but was perhaps too mild in manner
and temperament for an age when strength was the measure of
achievement. Compared to the gigantic difficulties which had
confronted Gregory and Urban at the beginning of their reigns
his lot seemed far easier. The anti-Pope Clement died and was
succeeded in his imposture by another clerical rebel, Theodoric,
but such opponents, before the mounting impetus of the newly
awakened Crusading spirit, had the ineffectuality of passing
shadows. The annoyances of Henry IV were also losing much of
their former potency although opposition from that direction
never ceased. Between the Emperor and the new Pope the
familiar routine of excommunication and attack was continued
and any hopes for a reconciliation were killed when, in 1104,
Prince Henry, his youngest son, rose in revolt and was supported by the Pope. A vile and cruel conflict ensued between the
unnatural antagonists and finally the obstinate old Emperor succumbed to his age and broken spirit. Embittered and disillusioned he went to his lonely tomb without the solace of either

Church or filial affection. Henry V was the new Emperor and there was as little change in his policies as there was in his name, despite the fact of Pascal's having befriended him at a critical moment. Charlemagne's story, ever a dangerous dream to princes, swam dizzily in his head as with the thunder of thirty thousand horses about him he smote most of Italy to subjection. He was no fool and when he received the Pope's legate at Sutri he was flanked not only by soldiers but by lawyers as well. He had come, he said, to settle for all time the question of his inheritance. His sovereignty would be naught if he had not the right of investiture. Bishops were temporal lords and as such the power of their selection must rest in his hands, as it had in practice, so argued his advocates, since the time of Charles the Great. Except by investiture how could the holders of the huge land-owning abbeys, the rich cathedrals, be controlled? Two thirds of his kingly inheritance, Germany, he claimed was owned by the clerics and if they were appointed not by him but by Rome then his Kingship was but an empty name. His lawyers rested on their arguments while his cavalry contemptuously possessed the roads.

At Rome the harassed Pope took refuge in his prayers and then made a startling proposal. If the Emperor would abandon his claims of investiture he in turn would give up all temporal possessions of the Church. The immensity of this proposition staggered Europe. The wealth of the Church, accumulated over the centuries, was something almost beyond reckoning. And how would the clergy live? "On alms" was the Pope's simple answer.

He was saint or fool. Romans preferred to think the latter and when Henry arrived at the city to seal the bargain by a great coronation ceremony there was a loud uproar and sudden revolt. The German soldiery broke before the sudden fury and the Emperor was forced to retreat but with him he took Pascal and some of his court as prisoners. Meanwhile protests against the papal proposal rose to enormous proportions, for by a stroke of the pen the pontiff had essayed to change not only the status of the Church but the entire feudal system. It could not be done and this he soon and sadly realized. But the Emperor pressed his arguments and his despondent prisoner, weary and worn, perhaps with the lack of interest of a disillusioned idealist, made a gesture of assent. Gleefully Henry announced a concordat. At last the eternal question was settled. Market place and abbey, castle and hut, all Christendom stirred with excitement to learn the Pope had agreed that the rights of episcopal investiture should be vested in the secular power. Then shock changed to wrath. The unfortunate Pascal, miserably aware he had given away the precious rights so valiantly preserved by his predecessors, waited nervously at the Lateran as a flood of indignant messages poured in from all Europe. No epithet was left unuttered but he seems to have accepted all abuse with humility and chagrin. "I confess I failed," he said, "and I ask you to pray God to forgive me." Foreseeing the general indignation Henry, in the same unfortunate concordat, had extracted a promise from him never to invoke the retaliation of excommunication. Angrily the Fathers ignored this prompted vow and by their own authority severed the Imperial schemer from the sacred privileges. Life for the unhappy Pope now became a series of hurried exits from, and uncertain entrances to, Rome, dependent upon the maraudings of Henry. His dignity became less and less until even his Cardinals treated him with contempt. Continually he was committing the mistakes of the weak; making explanation and apology. "I am dust and ashes," he would weep, "Anathema, anathema to the unrighteous decree."

God gave him rest in 1118 and another Cardinal monk John Coniula took his place as GELASIUS II. The election was held in a Roman monastery and the mood of a brief term was set as once again the city was plunged in anarchy. Factions fought along the streets and daggers flashed in shadows and instead of receiving the respectful salute of the faithful, the new pope was seized by a lawless noble, Cenzio Frangipani, whose ruffians trod the Pope with their spurs before flinging him to a cell. But conscience was not entirely dead in Rome and to the rescue came the nobleman Pierleone who, supported by armed citizens, saw to it that the Pope was returned and installed in his residence with dignity. But civil conflict, bloody and violent, continued to shame the city. Once again the Frangipani managed to capture the sixty year old man, who once again escaped. Scant evidence of majesty, tranquillity, or reverence marked the papal existence at this period. The Roman scene was too violent a tapestry for an ecclesiastical background, so Gelasius sped to France where he was received with appreciation and hospitality. But the privations had been too many and broken in health he retired to Cluny where, one year after his election, he breathed his last.

The growing strength of medieval France is reflected in the choice and story of the next Pope. The Cardinals who elected him were only six in number, members of the loyal little court who had accompanied Gelasius from Rome. Guy, Archbishop of Vienne and a scholar of royal blood, took the name of CALLISTUS II. A younger son of the Count of Burgundy he never allowed this relationship to pervert his conscience. Nor did Henry of Germany intend any sympathy of blood should change his determined course. An anti-pope still received his subsidy and, with the help of bribes and German arms, had found residence at Rome. Callistus decided to clarify his position before a Council at Rheims. Here, after attempts to make peace with the Emperor had failed, anathema was once again pronounced. But efforts with other monarchs were not so fruitless. Harmony was restored between Henry I of England and Louis VI of France. Confidence and dignity returned to the papal station as the Pope's ability communicated itself through the channels of the Church. The Latin nations lined behind him and in Germany sympathies turned from the Emperor. Within a year Callistus was able to venture to his rightful see and inheritance. Loyal Normans captured the anti-Pope who quickly acknowledged error before being carried off to a monastery.

With dejection but with sagacity too the Emperor realized that events were being born of a mind that could not be seduced by trickery, perverted by bribes, or over-awed by threats. He made overtures for a peace and as the Pope had the same desire a meeting was arranged. A treaty was discussed and finally Henry, now older and wiser, conceded that the Church should be free in selecting her prelates. The Pope for his part consented that episcopal installations could be graced by the Imperial presence so long as there was no influence either by intimidation or simony. As a further gesture to temporal power it was agreed the monarch should ceremoniously touch a bishop elect with his sceptre to show that the temporalities of the see were subject to him.

The Concordat of Worms was a practical solution to a bitter and vexatious quarrel and it was in principle a victory for the Church. In the future it might often be violated and most grievously, but the pattern, the rule had been set. The Church was to select her own. During the following Lent, the initiative of Callistus was shown again when for the first time an Ecumenical Council, the ninth of its kind, was held in the West. Three hundred prelates assembled at the Lateran not only to discuss the new Concordat but to review the general conduct and discipline of the Church. Mourret, the historian, writes that the gathering proclaimed no new dogma "nor any new disciplinary law, but all the progress made by the Church in the course of the preceding centuries was confirmed, defined and sanctioned. The Concordat of Worms was read and amended: twenty-two canons were published. Simony was condemned afresh, likewise clerical concubinage, the encroachment of laymen in ecclesiastical affairs, forbidden marriages, infraction of the Truce of God, debasement of the coinage, violation of the oath to take arms against the infidel and outrages committed on pilgrims. Regulations were drawn up to control the relations of monks with their bishop, and also for a number of special questions."

Within a year both signers of the Concordat were in their tombs and a discord of the usual Roman species was marring the selection of a new pope as opposing factions regulated and declared a choice. Two men claimed the title but the deadlock was not to be for long. The Pierleone family thrust the honours to their candidate, Cardinal Tommaso Buccapecci, and called him Celestine II, but at the height of his ceremonial installation the Frangipani clan crowded forward and tearing off the robes of office forced him to mutter a resignation. Their choice was now declared Pope with the name of HONORIUS II. He was Cardinal Lamberto Scannabecchi, Bishop of Ostia, Archdeacon of Bologna, and a canon of the Lateran. Despite the circumstances surrounding such a debut he was an able churchman and doubts as to the validity of his authority were settled when, soon after his "election," his rival died and a more canonical procedure was enacted. He had been a friend of three popes, Pascal, Gelasius, and Callistus, and was thoroughly acquainted with the machinery of their policies. A test of the prudence and lessons learned from these associations came soon after his inauguration. Two princes, Frederick of Hohenstaufen, and Lothair, duke of Saxony, were seeking the succession to the recently deceased and childless Henry V. The Pope threw the weight of his support to Lothair but first obtained a promise that this prince would adhere to the spirit of the Concordat of Worms. He exchanged embassies with the Byzantine Emperor and let his approval seal the sovereignty of Baldwin II, third monarch of the Latin kingdom of Jerusalem. A disagreement between the French bishops and Louis VI employed his diplomacy and won him the goodwill of the French King. From England came the Archbishops of York and Canterbury, both claiming the primacy of their country. By compromise and with satisfaction to the disputants the Pope smoothed their trouble. York was to bow to Canterbury in his capacity of Legate.

But one man at least gave little approval to his actions and that one man, St. Bernard of Clairvaux, far more than anyone else was the outstanding churchman of the age. For nigh forty years the stern monk was, with his brilliant sermons and splendid example, a dominating figure of the Church. Austere and fearless he made it his vocation not only to serve God himself but also to bring reform to those who had professed the same solemn vow. He preached so well of the mystical delights of monasticism that regiments of men, married and single, rushed to the cloisters. In a barren Burgundian valley he was a leading member of the early community of Clairvaux which was rapidly becoming a model of true asceticism. Piety, penance, simplicity, humility and manual labor were the rules of these austere men known as Cistercians and forerunners of the Trappists, who with vigor and with honesty tried to follow the ideals of St. Benedict at a time when many monasteries of his name had grown not only rich in tradition but also in purse and correspondingly lax in discipline. The fame of the monk Bernard spread far and wide, and much more than any pomp-surrounded prelate he became recognized as the vocal conscience and defender of the Church. He was quick to ferret out heresy and evil-doing in high places and he was never afraid to hurl accusation or pronouncement at prince or prelate. He preached the Second Crusade and when a few years before this event, he thought the Pope was wrong in supporting Louis VI against the French bishops, he lost no time about stating his views in a pungent and severe missive to the pontiff.

The lot of Honorius was not to be happy as the end of his reign approached. The insolent bandits who were the feudal lords of Italy were in a particularly active, even for them, state of anarchy and because of their aggressions townships, forced to fortification, were enjoying a species of republican self-government. The Pope whose diplomatic efforts had been successful in distant places found, as his health failed, that his influence was weak in and about Rome so, fatigued and disconsolate, he retreated to a monastery to die. The deathbed was circled by the Frangipani crowd who clustered close, not so much to mourn as to ensure succession for their protégé, the Cardinal Gregory, who after a quickly staged election, took the name of INNOCENT II. But all the Cardinals had not been consulted and three hours later a group of these, chagrined and angry, and under the patronage of the Pierleone family, elected Cardinal Peter Pierleone who announced his name to be Anacletus II. Who was the validly elected pontiff? Innocent had to flee Rome for the city was under the control of the powerful Pierleone family although their scion was notoriously unfit for the high station. Doubtless his sorry reputation was one of the reasons which made the distant but powerful Bernard give his support to Innocent, for at the Monk's behest all France welcomed the latter as true Pope and recognition came too, so strong was Bernard's influence, from the Churches of England, Germany, Castille, and Aragon. But to offset these loyalties the wily Pierleone effected a truce with the fickle Frangipani; thus the Pope's position in his own see was shamefully precarious and not until the Emperor Lothair invaded Italy was the Pope able to visit the city. Even then it was to be for a brief time and not until the anti-pope died in 1139 was his residence secure at the Lateran. A "Victor IV" succeeded to the claims of Anacletus but he was no match for the oratory and devices of St. Bernard and he soon submitted to Innocent. Among the many clerical visitors to Innocent's court was St. Malachy O'More, Bishop of Armagh, to whom has been attributed authorship of the "Prophecies," a work supposed to predict the destinies and persons of future popes.

The joys of tranquillity and hospitality came finally to soothe this Pope's life. In 1138, fully recognized by all, he was able to assemble in Rome the tenth Ecumenical Council, the second to be held at the Lateran. Nearly a thousand prelates journeyed from near and far to be present at this event where the delivery of the usual decrees against simony, clerical incontinency, and the rest, were enlivened by spirited discussions on the evils of usury and the use of the crossbow in war. Dimly the Church was glimpsing into the future, trying to prepare for that day when unlimited armaments and an economic system based on usury were to bring the world to madness, fury, and waste.

The belated peace of Innocent's reign proved to be but temporary when a quarrel with Louis VII, the usual quarrel over the right of episcopal investiture, brought forth from the Pope a prompt interdict upon all the regions of France which should be graced by the monarch's presence. It seemed impossible for temporal rulers to adhere to their promises concerning the appointments of prelates, and indeed when those prelates were vassals who controlled territories and towns it is easy to understand, in those feudal times, the problems, temptations and fears of princes. Just before his death, which occurred on September 24, 1143, the Pope was forced to employ force against elements in the City who, cloaking nefarious schemes behind high sounding phrases, tried to revive the forms of the ancient Republic. Their designs failed and were, apparently, forgotten as Guido, Cardinal-priest of St. Mark, became Pope CELESTINE II at an election which strangely enough was harmonious and unanimous; the first time in four score years that such a gathering was unshadowed by violence. Unfortunately, the happy circumstances did not bring a long life to the new Pope. His reign only lasted five months and during that short time his principal act was to raise the interdict against the French King. At Lisieux the ever alert Bernard heard of this concession to a monarch with uneasiness, but any suspicion of weakness he might have harbored about the Pope must have disappeared when Celestine gave sharp rebuke and broke off relations with the churlish King Roger of Sicily. This Norman leader had sponsored the antipope "Victor IV" but had since made a species of peace with Innocent, forcing his own terms by a great display of arms but at the same time, with suspicious ostentation, declaring his willingness to swear fealty to the Pope. Celestine examined and did not like the conditions of such a truce and declared his mind, but death intervened to prevent his further participation in the matter.

LUCIUS II, formerly the Cardinal Gerardo Caccianimici, legate to Germany, began his term in predicament. King Roger menaced him from without, while in the city the malcontents of Innocent's reign revived their party and their ambitions in the form, so nostalgic to Roman mind and tradition, of the Senate. With arrogance and with the vehemence of newly assumed authority this group pronounced that they alone should control the temporal policies. Lucius was quick to seek aid from the only possible person, the King of Germany. He pleaded with an eloquence and passion born of necessity yet his pleas were in vain, and in desperation he was forced to an action necessarily repugnant to his calling, office and inclinations, but good to his memory. He became the active leader of his troops, a warrior-priest, exhorting and leading his men to action, inspiring them both by his prayers and his courage. Alas, the odds against him were too great and in this unfamiliar martial role he was unsuccessful against both King Roger and the Republican Romans. His gallantry brought him wounds which in turn brought death and so he perished during the February of 1145.

On the day of his death the new Pope, a Cistercian named Paganelli, was elected and took the title of EUGENIUS III. The rapidity with which the choice was made both angered and outwitted the Republicans who, not content with the usurpation of temporalities, had intended to set their own candidate upon the papal throne. Before their sinister displeasure Eugenius was forced to flee the city and seek refuge at Viterbo. Meanwhile, the news of his election continued to amaze Europe for news it was that a simple monk, without the sponsorship of faction or prince and known only for his piety, should be chosen as Pope. Even his former patron Bernard professed surprise and doubt. "You have involved in cares and thrown among the multitudes of men one who had fled from both," he wrote chidingly to the Cardinals. "Was there no wise and experienced person among you more fitted for such things? It seems absurd indeed that a humble and ill-kempt man should be taken to preside over kings, to govern bishops, to dispose realms and empires."

Despite the gloomy forebodings and despite his unworldliness Eugenius met his problems with sound judgment and serene courage. The temporal claims of his office were of little importance to the tonsured monk who always was, despite exalted rank, to set the routine of life by the frugalities and discipline of his Order. His obvious sincerity and goodness, the complete absence from his character of predatory traits or revengeful instincts, did not fail to have effect with the Romans. Perhaps this had been the purpose of the Cardinals when, so unexpectedly, they had chosen him. Almost everybody wanted peace, and peace there undoubtedly would have been, if it had not been for the incorrigible, eloquent ex-priest, Arnold of Brescia, who mingled errors in dogma and his visions of government with a bitter resentment and a burning hatred of hierarchical control. The gentle, truly Christian spirit of Eugenius was no match for the apostate's continual conspiracy and once again a Pope was forced to leave his See. The traditional path of his predecessors was followed and in France he was received with the proper honors by Louis VII and, of course, Bernard. The wide dreams and restless energies of the latter were at this time occupied with the plans for the Second Crusade. The Pope gave his assent and before a great gathering on the last day of March, 1146, Bernard expounded his project, a giant scheme of attack, against *all* the encroaching enemies of Christendom; Saracens, Moors, and Pagans. The spell of his oratory, the high ideals of his purpose, had the desired effect and thousands swarmed forward to take the Cross.

Once again all Europe reverberated with enthusiasm and by Christmas, as warriors prepared and their women saddened, even the Emperor Conrad III had declared his support and willingness, for such a cause, to make allies of former rivals and enemies of distant nations. Seventy thousand men gathered together and began to march. The Second Crusade was a fact but from the commencement failure was its story as bad organization, poor leadership, jealousies and the resultant treacheries, did their fatal work. Routed and defeated, disillusioned and despondent, the remnants of the Christian armies straggled back with spirits so damped that even the fiery Bernard could not revive or inflame the martial ardor again. And while the great monk reproached and urged, the Pope, a far gentler man and with little taste for military excursions, returned to Rome where, it had been promised, he would be unmolested. He intended to confine his endeavors to matters of a purely ecclesiastical province but his very presence in the city was a disturbance to Arnold of Brescia, a disturbance sufficient to set professional inciters of opinion at work. Murmurs, deliberate in intent and direction, became the uncontrolled roars of jostling mobs. The streets echoed with rebellious slogans and from the windows of their fortified palaces scions of the ancient houses and factions smiled cynically and drew their swords. Wearily the unfortunate Pope left Rome again and for him it was a last time. He died at Tivoli and in death he was not alone; for soon after the monks were praying for the soul of Bernard.

The Emperor Conrad had preceded both churchmen to the grave and in the person of his successor, his nephew Frederick Barbarossa, came a determined opposer of the papal interests. Events seemed to favor him in the selection of ANASTASIUS IV, the former Cardinal Conrad. A nephew of Honorius II, this pope was too old and infirm to offer anything save complacency to the encroachments of Frederick. Emboldened by his initial violations of the Corcordat of Worms and spurred by an intoxi-cating dream of rising to the rank and deeds of Charlemagne the prince gathered his armies and prepared to march on Italy. Once there he would bend the feeble wearer of the tiara to his will and then the glory of a united all-embracing Empire, beneath his rule, would be a fact. So ran his dreams but by the time he set foot on Italian territories Anastasius had died and there was a new pope, a man not weak but stern and obstinate, the austere ADRIAN IV, the first and only pontiff of English birth.

The solemnly handsome and pious Adrian was born Nicholas Breakspear and was of obscure parentage. A taste for scholarship had taken him from his native land and a natural talent for leadership had brought him rank in the Church. He had risen to be Abbot of the monastery of St. Rufus near Avignon, and there his reputation as a wise administrator and fearless reformer had reached the ears of Eugenius III who summoned him from the cloisters and despatched him as his Legate to Scandinavia. There the austere Englishman quickly effected a greatly needed hierarchical reorganization and brought satisfactory solutions to many hitherto thorny problems. He was a success and rapidly was recognized as such; grateful peoples called him "The Good Cardinal" and "The Apostle of the North." His return to Rome coincided with the death of Anastasius and the approaching menace of Frederick Barbarossa; and with the city itself once again being disturbed by the indefatigable Arnold of Brescia, his virtues and abilities were too obvious to be overlooked by the papal electors. Following his installation there came quick challenge to his powers of decision and initiative as the Senate, realizing that there was now a pope who would suffer no infringement on his sovereignty, made ready for the usual revolt with the usual ominous preparations. Adrian did not retreat before their threats but instead acted promptly and drastically, threatening to put the entire city under interdict. It was a strong and unusual sentence for Rome, and faced with deprivation of the Mass and with a closing of the churches the revolutionaries knew they could hold no army together. Their opposition weakened to ineffectuality and their leader, the chagrined Arnold, was forced, in his turn, to flee.

With Rome subdued but in danger as the savage armies of Frederick, spreading desolation and terror, came nearer the Pope went to confront the Emperor. They met at Nepi and from the beginning there was a clash of wills. The Pope, weak in temporal force though he was, showed no signs in his proud bearing of the anxious suppliant or the timid conciliator. He was Pope and as such he let be known, he expected the due obeisance of all Christians, be they kings or beggars. He was fearless but certainly some of his cardinals must have experienced a dark moment when, surrounded by the fierce panorama of German soldiery, he turned his back to the Emperor and refused to treat with him until the traditional act of homage—the holding of the Pope's stirrup while he dismounted—had been performed. But courage, perhaps, was one language that could impress the warrior monarch; and after a few days of brooding he consented to do the act of homage and in return it was arranged he should receive his crown from the Pope's hand at Rome. Thus, it seemed, thanks to the Pope's bravery and diplomacy, the city was to be spared the German brutalities and barbarities. But, spurred by Arnold, a group of the Republicans came to try and make terms with Frederick in the name of the Senate. Their pretensions or opinions did not impress one who considered himself to be a Caesar. He surveyed them with contempt and pointing to his bodyguard thundered: "These are my Patricians of Rome, this is my perpetual Senate. And I am your Sovereign." Such a viewpoint necessarily meant the end for Arnold. He was captured and delivered to the authorities at Rome where he was tried as a traitor and executed.

Frederick received his coronation at St. Peter's but, try as he could, the Pope was unable to prevent bloodshed. The arrogance of the invaders, the hot Roman temper, always suspicious and resentful of foreign intrusion, were ingredients which when thrust together could not make for anything save conflict. Once again massacre, fear, and torment were the routine of the city when suddenly to favor the Romans an unexpected ally came in the form of malarial fever. Frederick withdrew in haste as the epidemic attacked with an effectiveness far more terrible than any human endeavor; but his retreat caused no cessation to the turbulence and intrigue of the Romans. With a rare strength Adrian remained resolute in his judgment and steadfast in his principles yet sometimes he could not but be despondent. "I wish I had never left England," he confided to one prelate, "or had lived out my life quietly in the cloisters of St. Rufus; but I dared not refuse this difficult path, for it was the Lord's bidding. . . . He has put me between the hammer and the anvil. . . ." In a strategical sense he was indeed between hammer and anvil. Though he did not deny the titular claims of Frederick, the violence of the Germans had convinced him that their actions in Italy must be controlled, so he negotiated a treaty with King William, the Norman ruler of Sicily and an erstwhile enemy who in the past had usurped certain papal possessions and in doing so had incurred excommunication. The sentence was now withdrawn and William was recognized as duke of Apulia,

Naples, Salerno, and Capua while for his part the Norman acknowledged himself to be a papal vassal and so bound to pay homage with gold and, when necessary, provide armed protection for Rome.

As was to be expected the new alliance met no favor in the eyes of Frederick and at a diet held at Besançon during the October of 1157 relations grew more strained when Cardinal Bandinelli, the Papal legate, told the Emperor not to forget that it was the Church which had given him "the signal favor of the crown." In the translation of his speech the word *beneficium* was given as *fief* whereupon there was a tremendous outcry from the German barons who did not admit to their Emperor's being a vassal of any man or power. So intense was their fury that had it not been for the personal intervention of Frederick the Legate would have suffered bodily harm. He was a man of rare courage and standing his ground he defiantly asked his irate audience: "From whom then does the Emperor hold the Empire if not from the Pope?"

The next spring witnessed another German invasion of Italy. Frederick was out to prove that his title of Emperor was a true one and all towns and provinces must admit his ownership. With clarity and with alarm Adrian could see the Imperial intention of making the Pope, as ruler of Rome, submit to being an Imperial vassal. It was a dangerous situation. Discussions and maneuvering began but not until the next year, when Milan revolted against German domination, did the conflict become an open war between Emperor and Pope. The latter supported the Milanese while Frederick declared his position as to Rome. "If I, Emperor of the Roman Empire, have no rights in Rome I have no rights anywhere." The reply to his claims was a sentence of excommunication delivered from Anagni. It was the first salvo of the Church in what was to be a long and bitter struggle and it was a fit exit from the earthly scene of an energetic pope to whom, at this critical time, death now came.

By bribe and by threat Frederick now tried to sway the favor of the Cardinals to a candidate of his liking but only three were influenced, the rest voted for Cardinal Bandinelli who became ALEXANDER III. Promptly—and at his behest—the three hirelings of the Emperor now put up an anti-pope, "Victor IV." When Alexander's electors reminded Frederick that as Roman Emperor he should uphold and protect a validly elected pontiff, he with neat hypocrisy, concurred but suggested that inasmuch as there seemed to be dispute and doubt the claimants should present their cases before a Council. Such a suggestion from this despot was a command and soon some fifty Italian and German churchmen were gathered in a convention which was more like a martial review than a clerical assemblage as the Imperial troops crowded the sidelines and applauded lustily the message of their master who, with conceit and presumption, shouted he had a "right to call a Council as Emperor. It is well known that Constantine, Theodosius, Justinian, Charlemagne and others called Councils and I am their successor." Intoxicated by his own speech he then addressed his puppet, the pretender, as the true pope and referred to Alexander, who was at Anagni, as a Cardinal. The farce was continued and the Council announced their "judgment" to be in favor of Victor. But the circumstances of their shameful decision were too well known to carry any authority. Carthusian and Cistercian monks made it a mission to travel throughout Europe, informing all, in high and low status, of Frederick's misguided activities with the result that nobody except those in the Imperial power or employ would give recognition to the anti-pope no matter how much his royal master schemed or threatened. When Victor died Frederick appointed "Pascal III"; and when he died a "Callistus III" appeared for a brief time; and, when death struck once again an "Innocent III" accepted the false tiara. Meanwhile, pursued and harassed though he might be, the real Pope successfully carried on the complex affairs of his office. At times he was forced, in his need for aid against Frederick, to seek the sympathy of other monarchs and because of this reason he at first supported Henry II of England in that king's quarrel with Thomas à'Becket. But when the great tragedy of the latter was acted to its full the pontiff lost no time in admitting his error and in pronouncing punishment against Henry; and, two years later, it was he who presided at the canonization of the murdered Archbishop.

With all his might, and even though his military successes were many, Frederick was slowly discovering he could perhaps hinder but could not own the papacy. During one of his marauding expeditions he stormed St. Peter's and with his soldiers cut a bloody path to the High Altar where, against the desecrated background, his puppet anti-pope placed a crown upon his head and bade an unheeding Christendom to accept him at his own valuation. But it was all in vain. His attacks, no matter how violent or massive they were, had as much effect as a sword wielded against a running stream.

In 1176, for a fourth time, he invaded Italy but this time his former victims, united by the Pope's diplomacy, were prepared and were able to offer fierce resistance. Milan was avenged at Ancona, and at Legnano the Teutons, losing all semblance of order, ceased to be an army before the determined onslaught of the Lombards. The surprised and humiliated Emperor left the battlefield a fugitive like the commonest and most unskilled of his soldiers. A truce was in order but it took a year before his pride would allow him to relinquish his ambitions. Finally, after many negotiations there came the sweet moment of triumph for Alexander. At Venice, now rising to its greatest, the page escorted the Pope from the flagship of the Sicilian fleet to St. Mark's in magnificent procession. It seemed as though the world had come to pay tribute to the pontiff and share his victory. Envoys of England and France, Sicily, Spain and the Free Cities walked with Prince-bishops and mitred Abbots. Nobles, citizens, soldiers, and mariners jostled shoulders with monks from everywhere who eyed with wonder and perhaps with distaste the luxuriousness of the crowd. Gems and gold were in profusion and so were rich stuffs, velvets of deep color, scarlet and gold and wine, and damasks and silks and laces. Splendid St. Mark's was a fitting frame for the vivid pageantry and for the solemn drama which was its purpose. Enthroned, the Pope waited while the Emperor made his long approach through the staring court, his pride conscious of every eye upon him. Before the papal chair he bent his knee and tears were seen in Alexander's eyes as with a mercy worthy of his rank he bestowed upon the humiliated monarch the kiss of peace. Legend has it that at the moment he knelt Frederick whispered "Not to thee, but to Peter." And the Pope's gentle reply was: "To me as to Peter."

Two years later Alexander, in full and proper possession of Rome, crowned his triumphs by assembling a thousand prelates for the Third Lateran Council. From this assemblage came the law that at a papal election a two-third's majority of the cardinals would suffice to secure a choice and it is to be noted that the distinction made, in this matter of electing a pope, between Cardinal Bishops and other Cardinals is not in the new law. Ten years more than the allotted span had been granted Alexander. In his long life he had endured hardship, sorrow, and pain but he had also experienced victory and before him the claimant of Charlemagne's title had admitted subjection. Now, once again, the pendulum of fortune swung to an opposite extreme. With the Germans quelled, the Republicans of Rome began their usual noise and the Pope, aware of his years and with energies near exhaustion, was compelled to leave the city because of the whims of its rabble. Death came quickly to remove his heartbreak during the August of 1181. To assume his burden the cardinals appointed another old man, Lucius III, ex-monk and cardinal. This good priest tried to make peace with the Roman malcontents but would not compromise the principles of his office; so after a precarious sojourn at the Lateran he left the city and never returned. His character, mild and pious but not aggressive, was an invitation to the brooding Frederick who, using the lessons taught by past errors, betrothed his son Henry to Constance of Sicily thus leaving the papacy virtually unprotected and deprived of a former ally.

The most positive act of Pope Lucius was the establishment

of a form of Episcopal inquisition which was levelled at all
heresies and in particular at the followers of Peter Waldo, an
ex-banker of Lyons. This man, pious and earnest like so many
other founders of heresies, had felt an urge for a more literal
adherence to the Divine teachings. Preaching a dream of universal poverty he attracted many adherents who with zeal discarded worldly possessions and connections and swore to live by
alms and fasting and prayer. At the commencement of this movement there was no ecclesiastical disapproval but when fervor
developed into fanaticism and when the conceit of self-righteous-
ness begot dangerous errors of intolerance in the form of anti-
sacramentarian criticisms then anathema was considered necessary.

Lucius III died at Verona on November 25, 1185, and on
that same day the cardinals hastily gave their favor to a scion of
the Crivelli family, Uberto, Archbishop of Milan. He selected
the name of URBAN III and almost immediately was in conflict
with Frederick, for the machinations of the latter were rapidly
gaining success. The second month after Urban's election saw
the Emperor's son, Henry, married, as he had so astutely
planned, to Constance of Sicily. Gradually the lord of Germany
had won control of Sicily and Naples and at the royal wedding
his son was crowned King of Lombardy by the Patriarch of
Aquileia. The situation was grave indeed for Pope Urban but he
unhesitatingly showed his lack of fear or intimidation by two
immediate acts of firm opposition. He excommunicated the
obliging Patriarch and declared against Frederick's candidate for
the See of Treves. Enraged and thwarted, Frederick ordered his
son to leave his bride and lead an army upon the Papal State.

Quickly the undaunted Pope prepared a sentence of excommunication against the aggressor but the frightened citizens of
Verona, at this time the papal refuge, begged it might not be
delivered from their city. Urban journeyed to Ferrara; there at
this critical moment he died and it was there he was buried, a
pope who had never occupied Rome. Another old man succeeded
him as GREGORY VIII. He was Albert de Mora. As Cardinal of

St. Laurence in Lucina he had been known for a gentle and conciliatory nature and perhaps it was this reputation that won for him the favor of the worried electors. His reign was only to last two months but in that short time a new field had attracted the ambitions and energies of Frederick. Jerusalem had been conquered by the Saracens and their leader, the Kurdish warrior Saladin, was achieving success after success against the Christian knights who by constant quarrelling in their own ranks were well equipped for defeat. A new Crusade, the Third, was proclaimed by Pope Gregory and encouraged by his successor; and a seven-years' truce was declared—although never fulfilled—between Christian princes. Leaving his able son Henry to act as regent the restless Frederick marched on to the Holy Land—and to his death, for he perished by drowning while fording the swollen waters of the River Salef in Asia Minor. He was not the only prince of first rank to embark on this Crusade. There was Philip Augustus of France and Richard the Lion Hearted of England and, perhaps because of their wretched rivalries, Jerusalem remained undelivered and multitudes died miserably and in vain. If Frederick, with his will of iron and fierce determination, had not gulped his death in the muddy current of a distant river, the story, the sad bitter story of disaster by sword and by plague and by treachery too, might have had a different ending.

Henry VI inherited the stern nature of his father, the same severities and abilities, the same high ambitions. To stand in his way was the new Pope, CLEMENT III, who had been Paolo Scolari, Bishop of Palestrina and a Roman by birth. He was possessed of great diplomatic skill and at the beginning of his reign, without compromise of principle or rights, he managed to evade an open break with the prince whilst most of his energies were devoted to the encouragement of the Crusade and the negotiation of a treaty with the Roman Senate. Perhaps the latter was not a very satisfactory pact for while it was agreed that the pontiff should be recognized as the city's temporal lord much of the practical administrative machinery remained in the control of the Senate. Nevertheless, a pope once again sat in the Lateran. For three busy years he ruled and his diplomatic skill was manifested even in far-away Scotland where he freed the episcopacy of that country from the jurisdiction of the metropolitan see of York. But despite the most skilful employment of the diplomat's science it was inevitable that a break should come between him and Frederick's son, for the prince, carefully consolidating the schemes and accomplishments of his father, was relentlessly forcing the papacy, as a temporal power, to an isolated and pitifully defenceless position. There was only one chance to break the cunning encirclement. Henry's marriage with Constance had given him claim to the throne of Sicily but when her father died the claim was disputed by Tancred, an illegitimate descendant of the Norman kings and many Sicilians, fearful of the Imperial domination, supported him. So, too, did Pope Clement.

Promptly Henry accepted the challenge and, marshalling his armies, began the march through Italy. Clement died at this time and to inherit his burden the Cardinal Giacinto Boris was chosen, an Orsini who took the name of CELESTINE III. When Henry appeared at the gates of Rome with his vast army the new but aged pontiff had no recourse but to crown him Emperor. Not so easy was Henry's path elsewhere. Defeat was his destiny at Naples where, before the desperate fury of patriots, his fleet was destroyed and his army scattered. A grave illness sapped his own strength and he was forced to retire. In the bloody disorder of the retreat his wife Constance was seized and held as hostage by his opponent Tancred. In Germany there was trouble with Henry of Brunswick but this was finally solved by the marriage of that prince with the Imperial niece: not for nought was Henry the son of Frederick. Displaying the same fierce persistence and resourcefulness as his parent he gathered fresh armies, financed mainly from the moneys gained by the ransom of Richard the Lion Hearted, and hastened back to Italy. Meanwhile Pope Celestine had interceded with Tancred and had begged him to release Constance. This was done but there was no halt to the German march, so grimly the Sicilians prepared for defence. Twice before had Death opportunely removed antagonists to the will of Henry and his father. Now, for a third time, there was the same macabre assistance; for Tancred died, leaving as a successor a mere child. Bereft of a real leader the Sicilians were nothing before Henry's fury, and by sword and by flame he exacted terrible vengeance.

It was ferocity, but it was a ferocity that followed a plan. Henry lived to fulfill the same ambitions that had stirred his father. He would be Master of the World, and the Empire must be the property of his heirs. He would unite the West, he would subjugate the East, and he would free the Holy Land. He would take rank with Charlemagne and Constantine and by force and threat of force he set out to make facts of his visions. His soldiers marched, his agents informed, and below the Imperial insignia and by the Imperial authority, in city and in village and along country roads, men were killed, burned, and tortured to bring substance to a dream. All Europe groaned beneath a common tyranny and the pontiff, now ninety years of age, could not but have been alarmed when Henry ordered, for it was an order, that the papal authority should secure his son's intended inheritance. The royal infant, Frederick, was only two years old but Henry proposed that the pope should bestow the crown and so ensure the succession. Celestine demurred, but before the Emperor's wrath was translated to measures of revenge, death, surely no part of his plans for he was still a young man, intervened. Vainly struggling in the throes of fever he died, his dreams unrealized, his visions to become a jest upon the lips of those whom he would have conquered. It was the August of 1197 and six months later Pope Celestine also went to his grave. He had been the 174th pontiff.

13th Cent.

The new pope was INNOCENT III, who had been Cardinal Lothair Conti, a nephew of Clement III. He was but thirty-six and had written a book *On the Contempt of the World*. He was vigorous and able, good and clever, a right man at a most critical period for the coming of the XIIIth century was a time when the feudal structure, so indispensable, apparently, to the framework of the Church, was weakening before the formations of nationalism. The temporal power of the papacy was negligible and there was a growing disrespect for its spiritual mission. The writings of Aristotle had been rediscovered and, with all the errors accumulated by centuries of Persian, Armenian, and Arabian translators as yet unpurged, were being avidly studied, though not quite understood, by scholars throughout Europe. St. Thomas Aquinas, the great interpreter of Plato's student, had not yet appeared and error and doubt were in profusion. Men were seeking logic and reason in all things, groping even at the stars to find by astronomy an astrological rule for life. With the learned engaged in such practices it was small wonder that necromancy flourished and charlatans abounded. There were the grave errors of fanatics, too. Preaching a religious revolt and wandering from town to town were bands of misguided zealots who, shocked by the state of the world and in particular by the loose living of certain rich prelates, refused to believe that sacramental powers could be invested in unfit hands.

The horizon was not entirely dark. There was now no all-powerful Barbarossa seeking to dominate the papacy and in fact the son of Henry, Frederick, was committed by the widow Constance to the guardianship of the pontiff. Perhaps it was but the obvious anxious gesture of a worried mother to ensure a consecrated crown for her son but it was an act that also made Innocent, as regent, the ruler of Sicily. It was a gift, an opportunity, which was not dissipated. As suzerain of Sicily he was able by treaty and by alliance to ensure the independence of the Papal States and thus to remove the menace of German domination. He soon became the real ruler of Italy and his influence came to be felt at every court in Europe. There was disagreement in Germany between the electoral princes as to who should take the Imperial mantle, Otto of Brunswick or Duke Philip of Swabia. The Pope unhesitatingly declared in favor of Otto and named him Emperor whereupon the princes complained that the pontiff was interfering with their electoral privileges. His answer was that while it was true theirs was the right to elect a king it was his duty, as Pope, to judge upon the fitness of any candidate to the title of Emperor of the Holy Roman Empire. "Princely power," he said, "is exercised over earthly things, priestly power over heavenly things. One rules the body, the other governs the soul. Hence, the priesthood is as much superior to royalty as the soul is to the body."

Eventually Otto received his crown in Rome and soon after, with base ingratitude, violated his oath and attempted to follow the anti-papal policies of the previous Emperors. He was promptly excommunicated by Innocent and deposed by the German Princes. Innocent followed the same lofty program as Gregory VII. He demanded and received universal allegiance, the papal dignity grew and no monarch could escape, if the occasion demanded, from the sting of his ire or the lash of his chastisement. The scandals of princes were no longer protected by the complacency of private chaplains, for few courts were exempt from the cold scrutiny of this strong Pope. The kingdoms of Philip Augustus of France and Alphonse IV of Leon were placed under the dreaded penalty of interdict until their rulers conformed with the marriage laws of the Church. To the adulterous French king he wrote: "The Holy See cannot leave persecuted women without defence; the dignity of a king does not dispense you from your duties as a Christian." He curbed the invalid venturings of the English King John when that notorious ruler schemed against the appointment of Cardinal Langton to the See of Canterbury. His judgment as arbitrator was accepted in the selection of the rulers of Hungary, Poland, and Norway. He united the Kings of Castile, Aragon, and Navarre in a crusade which led to the defeat of the Moors in Spain; but unfortunately another crusade, the Fourth Crusade to the Holy Land, which he sponsored in 1202, did not have the same success. The expedition set out with the same laudable objective which inspired all such campaigns but because of the usual bad leadership plus the connivings of the wily Venetians, who had other purposes than the liberation of the Holy Places, the cavalcade was diverted to Constantinople instead of the Saracen strong-holds. The Christianity of the City did not save it from the greed and cruelty that was now unleashed. The Byzantine Emperor was murdered, the Patriarch evicted, altars profaned and churches looted! "The Latins," Innocent wrote angrily to one of his Cardinals, "have given example only of perversity and works of darkness. No wonder the Greeks regard them as dogs. These soldiers of Christ are drenched in blood."

Violence might be deplored but it was the habit of the time. That is the only excuse that can be advanced for the great massacres which in the name of the true religion took place in the south of France where large sections of the population were falling under the influence of Albigensianism, a heretical doctrine which taught amongst other errors that there could be no resurrection of the body and that the sacraments, including that of marriage, were sinful. More Christian methods to combat such evils were utilized by the good friar St. Dominic, founder of the great Order which carries his name. Another similarly minded saint of this period, whose simple but burning piety and great goodness resulted in the founding of an order, is St. Francis of Assisi. Once again holy men, pledged to the service of God in its most austere form, were on the march, begging from the rich and giving to the poor, nursing the sick and chiding the wicked, fearlessly preaching against the vicious profligacies and gross laxities of those in high places. In 1215, one year before he died, Innocent assembled the Fourth Ecumenical Council of the Lateran. For eighteen months he had prepared the event and an immense gathering of prelates justified his hopes. Seventy-one patriarchs and archbishops, four hundred and twelve bishops, and nine hundred abbots and priors came to Rome and from their discussions seventy canons were promulgated. Here was pronounced that famous law which imposed upon all Catholics the obligation of annual confession and communion and here was given the doctrinal definition of transubstantiation.

Innocent's successor, HONORIUS III, was elected by "compromise." Two cardinals, with the consent of their colleagues, made the decision at Perugia just two days after the death of Innocent and their choice rested upon the cardinal-priest of SS John and Paul, Cencio Savelli. He was an old man, well over eighty, and to be his opponent in the apparently endless struggle that surrounded the temporal claims of the papacy was a prince just emerging from adolescence, Frederick II. With the acquisition of maturity the erstwhile papal ward was developing the traits so tenacious to the Barbarossa blood, the same driving impulses which had governed his father and grandfather. He was a handsome youth, tall, blue-eyed, well-formed and possessed of a rare intelligence. Unfortunately, however, the ceaseless flattering attendant to his station and an abundance of evil influences had perverted his natural faculties and had resulted in a spirit of cynicism and scepticism which were reflected in his every act. He lived more like an Eastern potentate than a Christian king and his court became a scene of Arabic splendor and luxury including the maintenance of a large harem. "One day," says the historian Bonnefon, "he had a man thrust into a barrel which was then hermetically sealed, in order to prove that when the victim should at length be suffocated and the lid removed, no such thing as a soul would wing its way to heaven."

Honorius, continuing then along the same path as Innocent, put the seal of his approval upon St. Dominic's Friars Preacher and a few years later bestowed the same favor upon the Friars Minor of St. Francis. In Palestine the rule of the Carmelite Friars also received papal confirmation and in that same country, with hopes no less than those of his predecessor, the Pope yearned to set free the Holy Places. He preached a crusade but his words seemed only to breed a base deception on the part of Frederick for, realizing that with the Pope's support his plans to dominate all Italy would be the easier, the perfidious prince promised solemnly that if he were consecrated Emperor he would form and lead a crusade. The Pope accepted the bargain and in 1220 put the diadem upon the royal head. The following year was supposed to witness the despatch of the promised expedition against the Saracen but neither that year nor any other before his death, in 1227, was Honorius to have his wishes fulfilled.

The next pope was, at his election, almost as old as Honorius had been but he was far more vigorous and displayed rapidity in decision and action. He was Cardinal Ugolino Conti, a kinsman of Innocent III, and a staunch friend to the newly formed Franciscans. With the tiara he became GREGORY IX and one of his first acts was to excommunicate Frederick. It could not have been otherwise for typical of the Emperor's temper was the statement which has, at times, been attributed to him: "That the world has been deceived by three impostors: Jesus Christ, Moses and Mahomet; that two of these died in honor; the third, Jesus Christ, was hanged on a tree; that those are fools who aver that God, the omnipotent Creator of the world, was born of a virgin; and that man ought to believe nothing but what he can understand and prove by reason!"

Yet, blasphemer though he was, the sceptical prince gained success where a nobler knighthood failed. He did not lead a crusade but nevertheless he made peace with the Saracens and added King of Jerusalem to his title. Not by force of arms but because of his adept diplomacy a treaty with the Sultan of Egypt was made and the Holy Places were once again opened to the devout. Mahommedans living in the vicinity were to remain subjects of their Sultan and allowed free practice of their own religion. After this feat and laden with easy promises, Frederick, seeking to dominate by wile, negotiated an uneasy peace with Pope Gregory. It did not endure. It could not for, like the policy of his forbears, his unwavering design was to suppress the power of the papacy. His easy promises were soon broken and he embarked upon a savage and clever campaign to divorce the allegiance of Christian princes from the pope. While his couriers intrigued in near and distant courts other agents proclaimed that the Church should be reformed and returned to primitive austerity. In Rome, always so fertile in plots, he fomented trouble amongst the factions and throughout Italy any noble intrepid enough to support the pontiff became a target for his anger.

He declared no pope had the power to excommunicate him and in 1240 when the alarmed Gregory sought to convene a General Council of the Church the Imperial troops intercepted over a hundred English and French prelates and held them prisoner. This was an outrage that the King of France, regardless of a treaty with Frederick, could not ignore and because of his strong representations the churchmen were released.

Gregory died soon after this incident. Like many of his predecessors he had not neglected, despite struggles with rulers, the ecclesiastical province of his stewardship. He sought to heighten the standard of learning amongst the clergy and in his time authoritative decisions were made on questions of discipline. The years between 1225 and 1240 saw the establishment of the Inquisition and the association with that institution of the Dominicans.

A sinister reputation has grown to surround their efforts and particularly in Spain (some two or three centuries later) were there to be dark tales of cruelty and torture; but in Spain the civil power intruded strongly upon Church administration. As to this first institution by Gregory IX, it is to be noted that the Emperor Frederick II had already made heresy punishable by burning. Why did so irreligious a man as Frederick II decree that heretics should die by fire? Not in the interests of religion certainly. The answer seems to lie in the special nature of the heretics against which Emperor and Pope alike were striving. We have already seen some of the doctrines of the Albigensians (or Catharists). Their teachings, especially on the sinfulness of procreation, were liable to destroy the social order and it was in the defense of the social order that Frederick moved against them. It is possible, though not certain, that the Pope established the Inquisition as a check to Frederick and an assertion of the Church's right to decide who was or was not a heretic. What is quite certain is that both rulers and populace acted against the Catharists before the Church herself. As to the Church courts thus set up, there were, of course, abuses, but has there ever been any organization devised by man which has not seen error? The

Inquisition was actually a system of ecclesiastical courts inaugurated to detect heresy. Once detected, and persisting in his error,
a heretic was delivered to the civil courts for punishment. Heresy
was regarded in the same manner as high treason might be regarded in modern times and in those days torture and death were
sentences common to many crimes. Leniency in criminal codes
is of very modern origin. The days of Botany Bay are not far
distant. The gallows and the gibbet had heavy trade and for
slight cause in the England of a century and a half ago.

The Cardinals had difficulties in the selection of a new pope.
They were twelve in number. Two were prisoners of Frederick
and the other ten made their decisions under the "protection" of
the Orsini family. Two months elapsed before a choice was
announced. It was the Cardinal Godfrey Castiglione, an aged
Cistercian monk, and he chose to be called CELESTINE IV; but
before he could be enthroned he died. Two years passed before
his successor was named for there was deadlock and coercion,
confusion and intrigue. Most of the Cardinals, in order to preserve some degree of independence, had retreated to Anagni.
There they refused to make a decision until Frederick released
those Cardinals whom he held captive and ordered his troops
from the Roman vicinity. Finally, because of the efforts of King
Louis of France, Frederick agreed to their terms and soon after,
on June 25, 1243, Cardinal Sinibaldo Freschi was elected and
named INNOCENT IV. He was a Genoese nobleman and had
been a friend of the Emperor which was perhaps a factor to
influence the Cardinals, so weary of the seemingly perpetual
struggle, in making their choice. If so, they were doomed to
disappointment. "My friendship with a cardinal is possible," the
Emperor is reputed to have said, "with a pope, never." It is understandable why the two should have been friends. The new
pope was no gentle cleric with a yielding nature. He was as ruthless, when occasion demanded, as his new adversary and as harsh
in his terms. Negotiations were begun between the two soon
after the papal election. Frederick was quick to make his usual
promises, with a great display of obeisance and deference but

at the same time moving his troops in such a manner as to make the Pope his prisoner. Innocent was too alert for the manoeuvres to suceed. Dressed as a knight he escaped from Rome to Genoa where after a favorable reception from the people of that port he embarked for France.

These were strange times, patterned violently with tragedy and crime but with saintliness too, for it was the age that produced St. Thomas Aquinas, St. Dominic, St. Francis and the rest of a great company, this age that saw the most depraved of criminals, often as not wearing a mitre or crown, exercising their villainies in all directions. Anarchy was collapsing the Empire and was threatening the Church. Heresies in every land were rampant and the Pope was forced from his own city. Genghis Khan was on the march and his Mongols having conquered most of Asia, had driven deep into Europe. Rich abbots defied richer bishops while barefooted monks preached and prayed and fasted and gave hospitality to all who came to their doors. It was a miserable era in many ways yet not without glory. High chivalry, founded on Christian ideals, was practiced even though the most abominable cruelties were countenanced. These were the days indeed when the Vicar of Christ and the inheritors of Charlemagne's crown sorely needed each other's support but they were antagonists and fought and conspired while the entire fabric of Europe was rent with strife.

At Lyons Innocent convened a General Council where not only was excommunication levelled against the Emperor but with solemn ceremonial a sentence of deposition was pronounced. At this gathering a new Crusade, the Seventh, was also called, for Frederick's insecure treaty with the Sultan of Egypt had been broken and Jerusalem was once again held by the Mahommedans. The only monarch to heed the call was the good French king, Louis IX. He departed for the Holy Land during the summer of 1248 but the campaign, lasting six years, was doomed to failure and Louis suffered the shame not only of defeat but of capture. Eventually, he was released at the cost of a huge ransom. Meanwhile, without his active assistance, Innocent, although secure at Lyons, was forced to employ every resource in order to obtain finances for his fight against the Emperor. Special tithes were levied and loud were the protests against them. In England the Bishop of Lincoln wrote a burning letter on the subject; for English bishops were being forced to pay as much as £40,000 upon succeeding to their Sees.

As has been seen death to either a Pope or an Emperor sometimes brought a shifting of sorts in the long drama of their relationship, if not a complete end to the bitter struggle. The time came for Frederick to die and he succumbed to fever at Fiorento just before the Christmas of 1250. He who had been so avowedly sceptical turned to his religion eagerly when the end came, making his final confession and receiving absolution through the ministrations of the Archbishop of Palermo. He begged that his son Conrad IV should succeed him with papal approval; but the Pope, who had pronounced a sentence of deposition against him refused now to recognize his son as rightful heir to the diadem and gave his recognition and support to the claims of Count William of Holland. At the same time Innocent proposed that Charles of Anjou, brother of his benefactor, King Louis, should occupy the kingdom of Sicily. If this plan succeeded the Papal States would no longer be faced with the danger of a united power surrounding them.

But Charles of Anjou refused as did the brother of Henry III of England, and in a somewhat desperate move Innocent then offered the bait to Conrad's brother, Manfred, an illegitimate son of Frederick who was of a nature not content to accept the limitations of his birth. The high drama took another turn with the death of Conrad who left as heir his infant son, Conradin, and who on his deathbed made a bold diplomatic gesture in naming Innocent, rejector of his claims, as guardian of his son. Out of the tangle wrought by this latest circumstance loomed one clear fact. Innocent, without any princes' support, was suddenly, as Regent, the temporal lord of Sicily as well as the Papal States. It was a situation not accepted gracefully by his erstwhile candidate, Manfred. A quarrel was born and Manfred turned to those Saracens who had been his father's friends. His appeals were not rejected and an able army was soon pledged to his cause. It was an army which roundly defeated the papal troops and before the resourceful Innocent, who would never accept defeat, could turn the tide of fortune, death suddenly came to him at Naples on the 7th December, 1254. Charges of nepotism, cruelty, treachery, and unscrupulousness have been levelled against his memory. Nevertheless, his record as a pope must be recognized as that of an able and determined administrator. Occupied though he was with his wars against temporal encroachments his vigor was also reflected in missionary fields. In his time, as one of his biographers writes: "The Holy See had survived one of the most terrible crises it had ever faced, thanks to the *sangfroid,* the decision and incomparable tenacity of this great pope." In an age when papal authority was being questioned in every quarter he brought it strength by his clear definition of canon law, his courageous decisions, and his indomitable will to enforce those decisions.

The lot of the papacy was not so fortunate under the uncertain guidance of his successor who also was his kinsman, Cardinal Rinaldo Conti, ALEXANDER IV. The election was held at Naples and controlled by the Conti family yet the new pope was no evil conspirator nor is there evidence to believe he had other than distaste for his new role. He had been a good cleric, a friend of the Franciscans, and able enough in the rule of a diocese. But it was not enough, for with all Christendom suddenly made his responsibility, his energies, his initiative seemed to disappear. In a vain effort to follow the policies of Innocent he hawked the Sicilian crown to the English Edmund of Lancaster. The price was to be the assumption of the debts of the Papal States and an army was to be provided to carry on the fight against Manfred, who was gaining victory after victory. The bargain was made but the months, even years, passed and no help came from England for in truth that island kingdom was too occupied with internal affairs to permit of adventurings in distant lands. And England's king had been the only ruler even to listen sympathetically to the Pope's plight. All others were too busy with their own miserable quarrels. In vain Pope Alexander pleaded and begged and threatened while Manfred possessed all Italy, crowning himself, in 1258, King of Sicily and Palermo and laughing, as had his father, at the anathema that came from the despairing Pope. Even the satisfaction of voicing the sentence from Rome was denied the unhappy Alexander for there, without a strong hand to control them, the factions were at war again and the pontiff had been forced to flee to Viterbo where he died on May 25, 1261.

There were only eight cardinals to decide as to who should be the next pope yet it took them three months before a decision was made and it is probable the time would have been even longer had not the Patriarch of Jerusalem come to Viterbo, the scene of the conclave. His manifest ability was a solution to the deadlock and so Jacques Pantaleon, son of a French cobbler, became Pope URBAN IV. To erase that condition which had, in a manner, been responsible for his own election he promptly named fourteen new cardinals. Most of them were French and thus sown were those seeds of discord which were to cause so much trouble in the future. Urban was never to occupy Rome but, resembling Innocent IV in his determination, he established a court at Orvieto and from there behind the remnants of a defeated army he directed steady opposition to Manfred. With England still unable to help, the Sicilian crown was once again offered to Charles of Anjou. Manfred countered by having himself elected Patrician of Rome but other factions in that unruly city had paid the same honor, so dubious now, to the French prince. The resultant confusion and violence made even the papal retreat at Orvieto insecure and Urban went to Perugia. Again it must be emphasized that even in the midst of personal dangers and struggles a pope did not neglect that large province which was his ecclesiastical interest. His envoys were not only busy at the courts of Christendom but also in the abbeys and in the palaces of distant prelates. A truce, after much negotiation, was made with Michael Palaeologus, the Byzantine Emperor who had driven the Latin dynasty from Constantinople and in the year the Pope died, 1264, he instituted, for the whole Church, the feast of Corpus Christi.

Four months passed before the cardinals could agree and again it was a Frenchman who won their choice. He was Guy de Gros, CLEMENT IV, a cardinal of noble birth who at the time of his election could count but ten years as a cleric. He had been a married layman, a father of two daughters, and had sought the ecclesiastical life only after the death of his wife. Despite the fact of parenthood and in an age when nepotism was the rule rather than the exception Clement never, either before or after his acceptance of the tiara, allowed his family to sway favor or judgment in the execution of his office. He was not unequipped for the great position and, brief though his career as a churchman had been, it shone with achievement. He had been the Archbishop of the great See of Narbonne and had acted as the papal legate to England. When a layman he had been an adviser to the French King but neither the wisdom accumulated by his long experience as an accomplished administrator nor the stern piety that was his sincere vocation was able to bring success or harmony to his pontificate. He dreamed of inaugurating a Crusade and negotiated with the kings of England and France for this purpose but his end was to come before they were brought to action. No aid could be expected from Germany for that region was chaotic with a general and seemingly endless anarchy. War still despoiled Italy with Charles of Anjou gradually emerging as the victor and revealing himself to be a tyrant of no mean scope with each new success. At the battle of Benevento, February, 1266, he defeated and killed his rival Manfred and furthered his triumphs by crushing a revolt which was led by the young Conradin. The Pope had recognized Charles as King of Sicily and as Senator of Rome but his support seems to have borne little influence when against his wishes and spirited objections Conradin, not yet seventeen years old, who had been taken prisoner, was put to death. The Pope lamented the evil deed but it was done; and so perished the grandson of Frederick II, the last of the Hohen-staufen, the bewildered scion of a haughty dynasty which had thought an Empire its property for evermore, the final heir of that proud House which had promised to subjugate the papacy but which was to achieve naught save quick extinction, stained by murder.

Clement never occupied Rome and for the most part his three years as pope were spent at Perugia although at the time of his death, on the 29th November, 1268, he was in residence at Viterbo. There were only fifteen cardinals to select his successor but not for three years was one chosen. This interregnum, one of the longest vacancies recorded in the story of the Roman See, was due to the intense rivalry between the French and Italian cardinals. It was finally agreed that the selection should be made by "compromise" and so, as in the case of Honorius III, a small number of cardinals was entrusted with the decisive powers. Their favor, guided, it is said, by the influence of the great Franciscan cardinal, St. Bonaventure, fell to the archdeacon of Liege, Theobald Visconti who was at this time in Palestine, serving as Papal legate with the Crusaders. On receiving the news Visconti hurriedly received the orders of priesthood which he had not previously held and journeyed on to Viterbo and then to Rome. There he was consecrated on the 27th March, 1272, and there he was proclaimed Pope GREGORY X. The task he set himself was herculean for he proposed to resuscitate the Empire, to bring the Byzantines back to the papal fold, to free Palestine, and to pacify Rome. Four days after his installation he gave notice that in two years' time a general council of the Church would be convened at Lyons. Thus prelates and canonists both near and far had ample time for preparation and travel.

With princes Gregory seemed to have the fortunate touch. Even the difficult Charles of Anjou appeared to have no wish other than to please him and sought the ceremonial privilege of holding the Pope's stirrup when he mounted and the honor of serving his masses. His arbitration was welcomed in the selection of the candidates for the Imperial honor and his judgment gave the diadem to Rudolf, Count of Hapsburg. Thus the Great Interregnum was ended and the Holy Roman Empire once again had a recognized leader, albeit his power was far less than those former wearers of the purple who had been so formidable in both their animosities and friendships to the papacy. With the Greek emperor Michael VIII Palaeologus, Gregory's negotiations were blessed with equal good fortune. The Byzantines sorely needed protection from the Turks and to get it were apparently willing to shed their prejudices against the Holy See. At least this was the will of their Emperor who, after silencing the patriarch Joseph I by imprisoning him in a secluded monastery, dispatched more agreeable churchmen to represent him at Lyons. Over fifteen hundred prelates came to form the Council and before them the Byzantine envoys professed submission and with elaborate ceremony the schism of the East was pronounced to be at an end. But ceremony born of political expediency is a poor foundation for matters involving faith and within eight years the frail union was ended and the schism was in being once again.

St. Bonaventure played a leading part at the gathering where amongst the measures adopted—not without protest from some prelates—it was resolved that a tax consisting of a tenth of all ecclesiastical revenues for the next ten years should be imposed to finance the Holy War. In order to prevent long and dangerous vacancies of the Holy See rules were formulated, such as the drastic curtailment of food after three days, with a view to hastening the decision of cardinals in conclave. Other decrees were aimed to control new religious orders and it was at this Council that Avignon was given to the papacy in return for the forfeit of certain rights in Provence. The result of Gregory's wide interests and zeal was inevitable. His strength became overtaxed and instead of resting after the Council he journeyed to Lausanne where he made treaty with the new Emperor, Rudolf. From there he went to Milan and then to Drezzo when suddenly an illness overwhelmed him and so weakened was his condition because of overwork that he succumbed immediately. Thus passed an able pope. Three great contemporary champions of the church, St. Louis, St. Thomas, and St. Bonaventure, had preceded him to the grave and there seemed nobody of similar stature on the horizon. Who then was to perpetuate the ideals and precepts of medieval Christianity, that thing which had eclipsed the greatness of the Roman Empire? And which now, by the relentless process called progress, was undeniably, despite the vastness of its structure and the glory of its ideals, faced with decline.

The legislation governing conclaves which Gregory had sponsored resulted in a new pope very quickly. INNOCENT V, formerly known as Peter of Tarentaise, was a Frenchman and a Dominican scholar of great repute who, in addition to his learning, had experience as an administrator for he had been both Archbishop of Lyons and Cardinal-Bishop of Ostia. On the assumption of his office his energies were immediately occupied by efforts at peacemaking, efforts that were directed to the realms of both religion and politics. He saw that the unity of the Greeks and the Latins as proclaimed at Lyons was on a precarious basis and he set out to try and strengthen the frail union. Charles of Anjou did not welcome the pretensions of the new Emperor, Rudolf of Hapsburg, and a quarrel seemed likely in that direction which Innocent resolved to prevent. He was only fifty years old but suddenly death, caused by a rapid fever, halted his activities after a pontificate of only five months. Brief though his term had been that of his successor, the Italian Cardinal Ottobuono Fieschi, POPE ADRIAN V, was even briefer for this pope only survived his election by five weeks. He resided and died at Viterbo and the most important feature of his reign was the fact that, attributing his own ill health to hardships suffered whilst in conclave, he suspended those regulations which had been made at Lyons and which had been formulated to prevent time-wasting deadlock.

Deadlock then was at the next conclave but after a month it was broken because of the ugly mood of the townspeople of Viterbo who, rioting outside the quarters of the congregated cardinals, made it emphatically known that they were resolved there should be no long vacancy again. Neither a Frenchman nor an Italian was chosen this time although there was little doubt that the new pope, JOHN XXI was supported by the Italian faction. He was a native of Portugal and had been both friend and physician to Gregory X whom he had accompanied to the Council of Lyons. He seems to have been an able man of many parts for in addition to his skill in the science of medicine he was a philosophical author of repute and as a churchman he had been Archbishop of Braga and later cardinal-priest of Frascati. He was in his middle fifties when elected and possessing splendid health and vigor he energetically embarked upon a programme which was modeled upon the wide policies of his patron, Gregory X. His representatives left for Constantinople in an effort to stimulate and strengthen the supposed union of the Eastern and Latin churches, while others of his legates worked strenuously to keep a state of peace between the Emperor Rudolf and the still truculent Charles of Anjou. In England Edward I was reminded that certain taxes promised to the papacy had been in arrears for over fifty years and at Viterbo envoys from the Khan of Tartary received sympathetic attention. Because of this visit, Franciscan missionaries were soon after sent to China and Persia. The country of the pope's birth, Portugal, also felt his influence with the improvement of certain ecclesiastical conditions. Because of his magnificent health and because of his great energy it was thought on all sides that the reign of Pope John would be both long and fruitful but only eight months after his installation he died of injuries received when scaffolding collapsed in the library of the papal palace which he was rebuilding at Viterbo.

For six months the Cardinals deliberated before the name of the Cardinal Gaetano Orsini, a member of the powerful Roman family, was given. This was a distinct rebuff to Charles of Anjou who was seeking the tiara for a candidate of his liking and patronage. The new pope was called NICHOLAS III and although his career, under eight pontiffs, as a high ranking cleric had been without reproach it was now sullied by frank and unrestrained nepotism as to the Orsini brood went a steady flow of rich benefices, high offices, and special privileges. Of the six cardinals he created three were of his family and the weak explanation was that he desired to clean Rome of all alien influences. Highly apprehensive of the French he tried strenuously to combat the intrigues of Charles of Anjou and from that ruler was taken the dignity of the Roman Senatorship whilst to Charles' enemy, the Emperor Rudolf, who extravagantly made fervent confirmation of all former Imperial promises and grants to the Holy See, went special expressions and tokens of approval.

The affection Nicholas held for Rome had one advantage: for while workmen swarmed busily, making repairs and additions to the Lateran and Vatican palaces, the papal purse was opened still further to finance a programme which brought wide beauty and ornament to the entire city. Outside this sphere however his plans had little success and when he died of apoplexy at Viterbo during the summer of 1280 the alert Charles of Anjou was on hand, determined this time that his will should sway the opinions of the conclave. His machinations succeeded but not with ease for again six months of dispute and deadlock passed before a pope was made. He was Simon de Brion and he took the name of MARTIN IV (actually he was but the second Martin but chose to be called the fourth to avoid confusion with the Popes Marinus). He was a Frenchman and a cardinal-priest and was without any doubt under the complete domination of the now triumphant Charles to whom victory brought neither temperance in judgment nor moderation in action. Once again this prince gave to himself the titular glory of being called Senator of Rome although the city was too dangerous a residence either for himself or for his pope who was installed at Orvieto where he awaited such directions as he received with quick obedience and smooth docility. As the previous pontiff had given to his family, so now the favours were poured, without stint or discretion, to the French. And punishments, under the same solemn authority, were delivered against all who dared to oppose the whims of King Charles. Excommunication was the quick lot of the Eastern Emperor for the alleged violation of those convenient promises made at the Council of Lyons; and similar sentences came flood-like but unheeded when in Sicily there was a revolt against the tyranny of the French and when, after a bloody massacre of the intruders by the dangerous tempered Sicilians, they proclaimed the rightful monarch to be, not Charles, but Peter of Arragon, son-in-law of Manfred. Before he could fully cope with these circumstances Charles died on January 7, 1285 and the pope followed him a few months later. During their last days and whilst calamity was in Sicily all pretence of the Eastern Church's being in communion with the Latin was completely dissipated by the new Emperor of the East, Andronicus II, who upon succeeding to his throne broke all former pacts with Rome and restored those Byzantine prelates, including the Patriarch of Constantinople, who had been ousted by Michael.

Pope Martin had died on the 25th of March 1285 and within a week the cardinals, gathered in hasty conclave at Perugia, selected a Roman, Giacomo Savelli, Cardinal deacon and papal prefect of Tuscany, to be his successor. No great deeds could have been expected of him by his electors for he was five years beyond the normal span and so infirm that he was forced to celebrate mass sitting down. HONORIUS IV was the style he chose and leaving Perugia after his election he was able to take up residence in Rome. His reign lasted two years and during that time he proved to be a notable patron of the Mendicant Orders and the universities, particularly that of Paris which was his Alma Mater and where he caused to be established the teaching of Oriental languages so as to make easier the relations of the Church with the Eastern peoples.

The next pope was an Italian also but not until six wasteful months of dispute after the death of Honorius was his name announced. He was NICHOLAS IV and while of humble origin was General of the Franciscans and had been known as the Cardinal Jerome Masci of Ascoli. In the sphere of missionary and educational activities his endeavours met with success. The universities of Montpelier, Lisbon, and Gratz in Styria were founded in his reign and in Pekin Franciscan fathers threw open the doors of their chapel and displayed the solemn pageantry of the Mass and its mysteries to the wondering natives. In other fields however Pope Nicholas had not the same happy success. He was closely, too closely, associated with the Colonna family and faction and perhaps it was they, possessed and driven by the familiar Roman appetite, who influenced his actions in the fields of diplomacy. Two of them he had created cardinals, another was made Count of the Romagna, and a fourth became Roman Senator. With the approval of these friends the papal endorsement was given to Charles, the son of the late Charles of Anjou, as Sicilian monarch but in reality it was James of Aragon who was to hold that unstable throne. The Pope opposed the nominee of the Emperor Rudolf for the crown of Hungary and put forward his own candidate but the fierce-willed Hungarians would have none of either and selected their own ruler, Prince Andrew, who was so invested and from then on clung staunchly to his throne.

In vain Nicholas threatened punishment. The papal displeasure seemed to mean little to the temporal ruler now, and if further proof was needed of waning authority and influence there came the news of the fall of Acre, a final and complete Saracen victory in the Holy Land. Despite the desperate efforts of the pontiff no new crusade was undertaken. He tried to outfit a fleet and muster an army but except for some interest in England the princes of Christendom remained lethargic to his entreaties and Palestine was forced to remain Mohammedan property until six centuries later. The year following this calamitous event witnessed the death of Nicholas on April 4th, 1292, but not until two years and three months had passed was there another pope. The most vigorous action was needed to unify Christendom but the response of the cardinals was an unsavoury and disgraceful exhibition of procrastination and intrigue. The scene of the Conclave shifted from Rome to Perugia and as the first year of vacancy passed, then the second, it appeared that the quarrelsome and often base schemes of the jealous and obstinate prelates would never be guided by high purpose or be cemented with unanimity.

One of the older cardinals, an Orsini, finally proposed the measure which was adopted to end the disagreeable situation. It was his idea that the electoral gaze should be directed beyond the College of Cardinals and someone be found who was free from the prejudices of factions or the favour of princes. The suggestion was received by his colleagues with approval and when the name of Peter of Morone was advanced the applause continued for Peter of Morone was an eighty-year-old peasant-born hermit renowned for virtue and piety. He had started his monastic life as a Benedictine but in time had sought an even more austere existence by forming a community known as the Benedictine Celestines on Monte Morone. To this place three cardinals deputized by their comrades journeyed and made known their decision. The consternation which replaced the usual placidity of the monastery can well be imagined. Peter was terrified and retreating to his cell tearfully set forth that his age, his infirmities, his ignorance of the world, could not allow of acceptance. But the cardinals were firm and their suave arguments made so solemn and awesome by the authority of the Conclave overwhelmed the protestations of the trembling monk and eventually convinced him that a refusal of their entreaties would be a rejection of Divine Will. Thus convinced that the new role was a duty of his vocation he ventured forth from the walls which had been the boundaries of his world for so long and was led, the centre of a noisy and triumphant assemblage, to Aguila. Here he was crowned and given the name of CELES-TINE V.

Once again there was a pope and he was truly good and pious and humble but unfortunately these simple virtues do not in themselves constitute that talent which is demanded in a leader. Celestine was not only innocent of wickedness but he was also ignorant of its forms and devices. Truly Christian, he

Boniface VIII (1294-1303)

was willing to accept any man for the values he professed and for what he seemed to be. When Charles II of Naples, who was as astute and ambitious as his late parent, held the papal stirrup and was sweetly submissive with the downcast eyes of a true penitent the Pope was enchanted. Thinking he had found a true friend, wise in the art of government and high of principle, he accepted with sighs of gratitude and relief the advice of the wily monarch. Royal wishes soon became papal proclamations and under such auspices twelve new cardinals were made (with the French outnumbering the Italians). Favours and benefices were lavished upon those who held the King's good will and who in the presence of the pontiff were suitably correct in the outward forms of devotion. Under such conditions the papal court became a place of mockery and tragic mummery and when realization came to the startled pontiff he retreated to a cell, hastily improvised in the papal palace, where he sought a solution to his troubles by fasting, prayer, and mortification. Then, after consulting canonists, he announced he would abdicate "because of my lowliness, my desire for a more perfect life, my great age and infirmities, my inexperience and ignorance of the world's affairs." (He was one of the six pontiffs who have ended their reigns by resignation. The others were Marcellinus, Liberius, Benedict IX, Gregory VI, and Gregory XII.)

The Sacred College decided that the abdication was valid and within twelve days proclaimed a successor. Apparently a sharp lesson had been taught for the new pope, BONIFACE VIII, who, by the way, ought more properly to be called Boniface VII since "Boniface VII" was not a legitimate pope, was the former Cardinal Benedetto Gaetani and certainly no recluse, ignorant of the ways of the world. He was a canonist of skill and a diplomat who as legate had exercised his wits at the courts of Sicily, France and England. Although born at Anagni and related to three previous pontiffs, he was sprung of an ancient and noble family which had its roots in Spain. The University of Paris had bestowed upon him a distinguished degree and that he was no mean diplomat was shown by the fact of his election

being approved by both the Orsini and Colonna and Charles of
Naples. Accusation has been made that it was his ambition
which planted the idea of abdication in the mind of his predecessor but this charge is untrue. Celestine, well aware of the
confusions bred by his inability, determined his own destiny.
Perhaps the calumny against Boniface was born of the confine-
ment, after his election, of the sorrowing and miserable ex-
pontiff. This apparently drastic measure was the only course
open; for the dangers to the new reign of the simple Celestine
being at large and subject to the control of any adventurer can
readily be seen. The old man was placed in a castle near Anagni
where he is reputed to have said "I wished for nothing in the
world but a cell, and a cell they have given me." And it was
there and in such a mood that he expired, ten months after his
abdication from a pontificate which had lasted five months.

In almost every way Boniface differed from Celestine. He
was strong and confident, proud of his noble lineage and proud
of his august rank. He enjoyed and expected the splendours due
to a temporal ruler and it was with magnificence that he received
the tiara. Rome was the scene of this ceremony for following
his election he had come to the City to escape the dangerous
proximity of Charles of Naples. Well indeed that he was self
confident. That quality was needed in the man who faced his
problems, for they were many and large and complicated. The
Eastern Church had resumed its schism, the Holy Land was
lost and war raged in every direction, between Naples and Sicily,
Castile and Aragon, France and England and with the latter
nation also fighting the Scots. In Germany Albert of Austria
had drawn the sword against Adolph of Nassau whilst in Rome
of course there were the usual altercations between the usual
factions. Dissension was even disturbing the domestic unity of
these clans. The Colonna were quarreling and this quarrel was
to bring the new pontiff much trouble and to contribute to the
failure that was to darken his reign. For disaster, no less than
that which had confronted the simple and pious Celestine, was
to be the lot of this pope who had been selected for his great

skill in law and for his great knowledge of worldly matters. He knew and accepted his problems and at first met them without hesitation and with strong action. His plan was to make practical that elusive structure which had been the ideal of the Holy Roman Empire and all rulers and all states were to be subject in spiritual matters to the authority of the Holy See. This was, briefly, the basis of his famous bull, *Unam Sanctam,* issued in 1302. It brought forth violent opposition from Philip of France for in truth the life and properties of the Church were so tightly woven into the fabric of society that divorce from the temporalities was impracticable and indeed unthinkable. The new bull, so interpreted the French king along with many of his royal colleagues, merely meant that all princes and rulers should be vassals not only of the spiritual head of Christendom but also of the temporal ruler of Rome.

From the commencement of his reign Boniface had incurred the wrath of Philip. France and England were at war and the kings of both countries were paying their armies and fleets with monies appropriated from ecclesiastical revenues. To impose peace the Pope, after lighter protestations had been ignored, issued the bull *Clericis Laicos* which prohibited, under penalty of excommunication, any layman from taxing or annexing Church revenues. So far, so good. But promptly Philip countered by making a law which, by preventing the export of gold and other negotiable things under certain conditions, hindered the transit of the normal and periodical dues from the Church in France to the Holy See. At this stage of the quarrel Boniface, employing the devices he had learned as legate, adopted a policy of compromise and withdrew some of the demands he had made with such vigour and haughtiness. It was an unfortunate move, fatal to his aims, for compromise is a highly delicate and dangerous business which can easily degenerate to appeasement instead of equity and justice. The same mistake was made in his relations with Edward I of England. First the drastic *Clericis Laicos,* followed by a compromise, then another rupture because Boniface, on the ground that Scotland was an ancient fief of the Holy See, emphatically declared the English king should refer any rights he claimed over that country to Rome. But again his assertiveness proved temporary for in order to enlist the support of Edward against Philip he changed his policy and withdrew his demands.

As it proved, the struggle between Boniface and the French king was never to end and was to reach the extremes of invective and indignity on both sides. To assist Philip came those Colonna, including two cardinals, whom the Pope had sided against in their family quarrel. It was a powerful alliance and was responsible for a council in France which declared Boniface's election to be invalid and levelled a long list of accusations, including heresy, simony, and murder, against his name. In an epistle, contemptuous and libellous, Philip referred to the pontiff as "Your Supreme Foolishness" and called upon him to vacate the Holy See. These insults were not the end. There were greater to come, yet there was but meagre defence rallied for this pope who had launched his reign so auspiciously. The friendships that were cradled in his magnificence were as unstable as his dreams. Despite his errors he had brought to Rome prosperity and gain but the gratitude of the citizens was small. Under his seal, in 1300, there had been the Holy Jubilee and to the great celebration, splendidly organized by him, had come a vast gathering of pilgrims from all parts of Europe. He had caused to be founded the University of Rome and the city gained liberal proof of his lavish patronage of the arts. Nevertheless as his enemies became triumphant the city, adhering to its traditional fickleness, could not be trusted to afford him safe asylum. He retired, as had other popes in similar circumstances, to Anagni where utilizing his considerable skill as a canonist he prepared a bull of excommunication and deposition against Philip. Before it was issued however a gang of mercenaries, led by Guillaume de Nogaret and Sciarra Colonna, stormed the papal retreat. They found Boniface deserted by his attendants but gloriously unafraid. He had donned the formal insignia of his office and was seated on his throne. "Here is my head," he said, "I, a Catholic, lawful Pontiff and Vicar of Christ, desire to die for the faith of Christ and His Church."

With singular brutality, for he was now in his eighty-sixth year, he was thrown into a prison cell whence after three days he was liberated by the indignant townspeople but only to be captured again. This time it was the Orsini who held him. They called it a rescue and conveyed him back to Rome with a show of respect but he was their prisoner. It was the final humiliation and one he did not survive, for he died on the 11th of October, 1303. Broken-hearted and unhonoured went the once proud man whose worldliness was to have been the cure for the errors born of the inexperience of the saintly Celestine.

To Boniface we owe one important institution, however, namely, the Holy Year pilgrimage. Having got wind of a tradition popular among the common people that there was a special indulgence to be gained from a pilgrimage to Rome at the opening year of each century, he resolved to translate this popular credence into actuality. On February 22, 1300, therefore, he proclaimed a great Jubilee year, retroactive to Christmas of 1299, in which a special plenary indulgence was to be granted those faithful who would undertake a pilgrimage to Rome and visit the basilicas of St. Peter and St. Paul. He further stipulated that the Jubilee was to be repeated at the beginning of each new century. This is the direct origin of our Holy Year. Clement VI later shortened the interval between Holy Years to fifty years and, later still, Sixtus IV shortened it further to twenty-five.

Eleven days after Boniface's death there was the election of the Cardinal Nicholas Bocrasini, BENEDICT XI, an Italian and an ex-General of the Dominicans, who had also served extensively as a legate. For the sake of desperately needed peace he made treaty with Philip although to his credit he refused to lift the censures against those villains, friends of the French king though they were, who had maltreated and insulted his predecessor at Anagni. Benedict was a good man and he essayed peace and reform in all directions but unfortunately for his plans his reign was brief. The dark temper of the Romans caused him to move to Perugia where he died, by poison according to rumour, during the summer following his election. So great was the hatred Philip bore for Boniface that he had urged that a General Council be convened to pass judgment on the supposed misdeeds of that pope. This Benedict, despite his desire for conciliation, refused. Soon after came his sudden death and then, gathering like clouds around his tomb, came the rumours of foul play.

The time now comes when the march of the great drama shifts to Avignon. Rome had reached the extremes of degradation and despair. Its broken thoroughfares were, for the most part, the uncontested property, filth-littered and unsightly, of starved mongrels and lawless wretches. Those houses which remained occupied were fortified and barricaded and if their owners were not bandits they were forced to a fierce self-reliant code which rendered possible their survival amongst bandits. Benedict had died at Perugia and it was there the Cardinals chose the next pope. The election was long and only after eleven months was a name announced. It was the Cardinal Bertrand de Goth, ex-Vicar General of Lyons and Archbishop of Bordeaux, and his election was obviously a triumph for the French faction in general and in particular King Philip and those of the Colonna who were his allies. The new pope took the name of CLEMENT V and for his installation he went, not to Rome, but to Lyons where with great pomp and surrounded by the elated French cardinals he was given the tiara. There was never any attempt on his part to visit Rome after his election and after a few years spent at various residences in France he finally chose a permanent home, a Dominican monastery by the banks of the placid Rhone, at Avignon where the papacy was to remain for nearly three quarters of a century. Most historians unite in seeing it as a grievous sojourn and many words have been written of the resultant evils and mistakes, although little, as Pastor remarks, has been said of the successful missionary activities of the Avignon popes.

Clement V was unaggressive and admittedly a servant of

French interests, nevertheless under his patronage great progress was made in the propagation of the faith. India, Abyssinia, Nubia, Egypt and Morocco saw his missionaries, and in his time the metropolitan see of Pekin was established with a Franciscan, John of Montecorvino, as the first Archbishop and seven fellow-members of his order as his suffragans. Clement owed his election to the French king and probably had, before that circumstance, entered upon some sort of an agreement with him; yet twice, and importantly, he displayed both opposition and principle against the royal will. Revenge and cupidity still haunted the dark dreams of Philip, revenge against Boniface whose memory he still wished to have stained by official condemnation, and a cupidity which was stirred by the rich possessions of the Order of the Knights Templars. The pope showed complaisance in most matters, cardinals were created at Philip's whim and the same reason caused new decrees to be issued and existing ones to be annulled. But he would not lift the ban of excommunication against the assailants of Boniface nor would he, as Philip wished, arbitrarily suppress the Knights Templars. Finally both matters, as was canonically correct, were referred to a General Council, the Fifteenth, which Clement convoked at Vienne in 1312 and which was attended by one hundred and fourteen prelates. The charges against Boniface were reviewed and, despite the powerful menace of Philip, rejected; but the Knights Templars fared less well and the order was given for their dissolution. It was an order which fitted so well with the schemes of Philip that he did not wait for it and by the time of its publication many of the Knights in France had already perished at the stake, their property confiscated.

The Order of the Knights Templars was a religious organization, with a strong military flavouring, which had been founded early in the twelfth century with the object of defending Jerusalem. The three vows of religion—poverty, chastity and obedience—were undertaken by the Knights, and skill in the military art was required as were also certain genealogical qualifications. Over 20,000 members of the Order had perished in battle in less

than two centuries. Great properties were accumulated and such
an organization, rich and armed, claiming indeed at certain times
the prerogatives of a sovereign power, could not but be an affront
to a monarch of the calibre of Philip. Heresy and sacrilege and
the practice of unnatural lust was his cry and soon the loathsome glare of the dreaded stake was visible against the sky of
many a city and castle as confessions, before the processes of
rack and screw, came quick and bountiful. The nature of these
admissions can be gauged by that of the Grand Master Molay
who swore that on his entrance to the Order "he was made to
deny Christ and spit upon the crucifix, and that, by his command, the same was done by postulants who were received by
him after he became the Grand Master."

Despite the fact of Avignon and the ugly nature of King
Philip, the Italians were resolved the next pope should not be
French. After Clement's death in 1314 the strife between the
cardinals was bitter. The election was held on French soil and
the majority of the twenty-four electors were of that nationality.
But the Italians were stubborn and two years went by before
Clement's successor was chosen. He was a sixty-seven-year-old
French Cardinal, James d'Euse who thus became Pope as JOHN
XXII. He was the son of a shoemaker and had a reputation for
austerity and good judgment, learning and administrative ability,
and he was of such unprepossessing appearance that no writer
of his day neglects to mention his extraordinary ugliness. He
was the most energetic of the Avignon popes and during his
reign, lasting some eighteen years, he issued sixty thousand
official documents. His first acts were aimed at securing the
success of his faction and to the despair and anger of the Italians
seven more Frenchmen were created cardinals. During the long
interval which passed before he became pope death struck at
both Philip and his son Louis. Another Philip became the new
French king but royal enmity against the papacy now was to
shift from France to Germany as Louis of Bavaria, whose claims
to the Imperial title were not accepted promptly enough by John,
made alliance with the notorious and excommunicated Sciarra

CLEMENT V

Clement V (1305-1314)

Colonna and took upon himself the protection of all those antagonistic to the pontiff. Prominent amongst the latter were the
Spirituals or *Fraticelli,* a fanatical division of the Franciscans,
and another group sprung from the same Order who were just
as troublesome because they were no less sincere. Both of these
parties or sects had been seduced to heresy because of impracticable dreams of a return to the austerities of primitive Christianity. Supported by theologians from their ranks and in connivance
with the wily Colonna, Louis with insolence and arrogance
called for a General Council to depose the pope. Nor was this
the end of his effrontery. At Rome his accomplice, Sciarra
Colonna, enacted the farce of creating an anti-pope, one Peter
Rainalducci, who assumed the style of "Nicholas V." It was too
much even for the Romans who ever ready for violence rose in
angry riot and within three days put the anti-pope to flight.
Eventually he made full submission to John who treated him
with mercy and consideration.

Throughout this considerable reign controversy mounted concerning the relations of Church and State. Criticism and doubt
were everywhere, and throughout all Christendom there was an
epidemic of charges and counter-charges of heresy. Even the
pontiff himself was not to escape this stigma for in one of his
sermons he declared the Beatific Vision was held from the dead
until the Last Judgment. There was an immediate storm of
protest from the theologians and the harassed pope pointed out
that his statement was a private opinion and not a dogmatic
definition. But the uproar was not abated until, at the request
of the University of Paris, he made a public profession of orthodoxy, saying that "the Saints are in heaven, where they see God
face to face."

John continued that policy of Clement which had given
sturdy encouragement to the foreign missions, and Tartary and
Turkestan were invaded by zealous monks whilst the established
missions of Africa, Persia, and India were enlarged. Universities
also profited by his interest and in 1321 he even gave some
substance to the dream that never could really have been absent

from the ambitions of a pope of those times. A crusade, very small but a fact, was formed and, consisting of a fleet of galleys, gained a few victories over the Turks. John's private life was void of scandal for he adhered, as much as his many administrative duties would allow, to the strict regime of a simple monk. His great fault was an unswerving belief that the papacy should remain in France. Of the close on thirty cardinals he created twenty-three were French, three were Italian, and one a Spaniard. Such a majority at least obviated any chance of a long interregnum and when he died, on 4th December, 1334, his successor, BENEDICT XII, was chosen and installed within two weeks. The votes of the conclave had at first gone to the Cardinal of Porto, much to the delight of the Italians, but he was a determined man who refused to give guarantee that the Curia would remain at Avignon. The choice then went to one who, although a good man and probably sincere in his every action, could be depended upon to take the advice of his faction. Indeed, after becoming pope, he made two attempts to go to Rome but each time he was thwarted, without any real opposition on his part, by the French cardinals. Finally he abandoned all such wishes and as though to express his viewpoint he wholeheartedly set about building the palace which was intended for the permanent papal residence. The tranquillity of the Avignon landscape quickly vanished as a swarm of busy artisans built palaces not only for the Pope but for each of his cardinals and their retinues. There was the construction necessary to house and feed and defend the great army required of any administrative centre. Soldiers and priests, clerks and bureaucrats, lawyers and merchants, beggars and lackeys, jostled and shouted through thoroughfares that were no longer peaceful country lanes.

The man who was the centre of this new activity had begun his ecclesiastical career as a Cistercian monk and the influence was never to leave him. Perhaps he lacked the strength of will and ambitions of a successful ruler but this did not prevent him from the exercise of those simple virtues which make for a good man. He was gentle in manner and sincerely religious. He tried to make peace between France and England and in fact one of the reasons given for his failure to visit Rome was that his presence was required in France because of this aim. To his see however he sent gifts for the poor and money to repair the churches. Embassies passed between him and Louis of Bavaria but the interdict remained. The practice of nepotism was an especial object of his dislike and he made every effort to eradicate it. Before wearing the tiara his name had been James Fournier but no kinsman came to flaunt it at the papal court. "A pope should be like Melchisedec," he said, "without father, or mother or genealogy."

This statement did not influence his successor, CLEMENT VI, for out of a creation of twenty-five cardinals, most of whom were French, twelve were drawn from his own family which was powerful and noble. His name had been Pierre Roger and he had worn the Benedictine habit although it could not be said that his life was ever restrained to the monastic pattern. High birth and influence combined with intelligence and eloquence had previously won for him the rich sees of Arras, Sens, and Rouen. Luxury and splendour had always characterized his career as a high prelate and the acquisition of the tiara was an opportunity he did not neglect to indulge these traits further. The papal court became the scene of lavish hospitality although to his credit it is recorded that his extravagances were equalled and always accompanied by deeds of charity. The funds accumulated by the economies and administration of the previous reigns were now dispensed with an open hand. "Our predecessors," he is reputed to have said, "did not know how to be pope." That he firmly believed the home of the papacy should remain in France is shown by his purchasing, from the Queen of Naples, the sovereignty of Avignon. The price paid was 80,000 gold florins. The death in Italy of Robert of Anjou had enabled the Romans to bring some sort of peace to their city and they had formed a none too strong democratic government, consisting of thirteen members, which sent an embassy to Avignon in an attempt to persuade the pontiff that he should return to Rome.

Clement listened to their entreaties with sympathy and although he refused the request he did, as a measure to bring some prosperity back to the ravaged city, give his support and encouragement for an official Jubilee to be held in Rome at the turn of the half century.

In Germany Louis of Bavaria was losing his sway and in 1346 several of the more powerful princes suggested that the Imperial title should be given to Charles of Bohemia. Clement agreed and thus to Avignon came Charles where with splendid ceremony he held the papal stirrup and received confirmation of an empty title. Trouble with Louis was averted by the death of that prince during the following year whilst boar hunting. The real ruler of Rome at this time was a young and ambitious man, named Cola di Rienzi, who had met Clement as a member of the visiting Roman mission. Upon his return he had defeated the factions, already conspiring again, and it seemed, for a few hopeful years, that he might achieve his aim of reviving the ancient unity and harmony. But his success was fleeting and the intoxication of being Master of Rome, even though briefly and insecurely, was to whirl him quickly to ruin and to a violent death.

The greatest virtue possessed by Clement VI was his charity. This took on proportions equal to his usual sense of the magnificent, with the energetic measures he used to abate the miseries that followed in the wake of the Black Plague which devastated all Europe during his reign. Another aftermath of the dreaded epidemic was a wave of anti-semitism, for fanatics were hysterically accusing the Jews of spreading the disease by poisoning wells. The aptly name Pope fought the libel with vigour and announced that the Jews were under his protection. Consequently, at his death on the 6th December, 1352, there was not only the prescribed mourning in Christian churches but there was also sorrow in the synagogues of Israel.

A different figure took his place. The cardinals, with the extravagances of Clement affecting their own revenues, had found the memory of the sombre and economical John XXII to be most agreeable. They scrutinized their ranks for a man of

similar quality and found him in the person of the cardinal-
bishop of Ostia, Stephen Aubert, who upon receiving their
favour took the name of INNOCENT VI. Whilst gathered together
at this Conclave their Eminences also formed a pact to the effect
that in future a pope should rely upon the guidance of the
Sacred College in such matters as the disposal of the higher
revenues, the appointment of new cardinals, and similar important affairs. The first act of the new pope was to cause the
nullification of this agreement. That he did it so forthrightly
was a tribute both to his perception and to his courage and that
there was no great manifestation of discontent from its originators was proof of his diplomacy. Highly dangerous indeed would
it have been for a pope to transfer such authority from his own
province to what would have become, if so endowed, an autocratic and entirely independent body. The supporters of Innocent VI were not disappointed in either his economies or reforms.
With the help of his friend, the General of the Carthusians, drastic changes came to Avignon and a gloom descended upon the
companions of the late pope as court life was diminished sharply
and courtiers scattered and a great throng of absentee prelates
sent back to their sees and benefices. The latter act however
did but emphasize the sad truth of the pontiff's being absent
from his own see. Rome still remained unvisited by its bishop
and outside the borders of France resentment was gradually
mounting with the belief that the pope was entirely under
French influence. Furthermore, protection from such a source
was held with scant respect: for France, weakened by war with
England, was in poor position to defend anybody and when
gangs of mercenaries hovered in sinister proximity to Avignon
the Pope was forced to avert attack by resort to his coffers.
Another affront was a proclamation, known as the *Golden Bull,*
issued by the Emperor Charles which stated that henceforth the
bestowal of the Imperial title would be decided by seven Electors; the lay fiefs of Bohemia, Saxony, Brandenburg, and the
Palatinate; and the three archbishops of Mainz, Treves, and
Cologne. The coronation of Charles, with the full approval of

the Pope who sent his legate to officiate, had been held at Rome in 1335 and the *Golden Bull* came a year later. Ruling Rome at this time was a firm-handed Spanish prelate, actually more of a soldier than a churchman, Cardinal Giles de Albornoz who, after the collapse of the Rienzi regime had been sent to the city by the pontiff. The resolute methods employed by this warrior cleric had restored some semblance of order and were in fact to clear the way for a return of the papacy.

When it came time again to choose a new pope the conclave looked beyond itself and selected the Benedictine Abbot of St. Victor's monastery at Marseilles, William de Grimoard, who chose to be called URBAN V because, as he said, "all the popes called Urban have been Saints." He was a holy man, a patron of many missions and universities including that of Oxford, who valiantly tried to solve problems and stem circumstances that were now too great, it appeared, to be vanquished by any one man. Five years after his election which had occurred in 1362 he even, against strenuous opposition from all who surrounded him, went to Rome where he was greeted with joy. The news spread quickly throughout Europe and was received with pleasure everywhere outside the boundaries of French influence. The Emperor Charles came to meet him and protestations of amity and cooperation were exchanged. The Emperor of the East, John V. Palaeologus, made the long journey from Constantinople and Urban received him graciously on the steps of St. Peter's. The Byzantine ruler swore he was not in schism but perhaps his oath may have been influenced by the fact that he had come for aid against the ever pressing Turks.

Military assistance was a commodity Urban could not afford anyone. Indeed his own safety was at times insecure in turbulent Italy and both he and his court looked with longing eyes and an increasing nostalgia back to Avignon. In Rome they felt as aliens in an alien land and the sullen hostility of the factions, ever present even though in temporary retreat behind family walls, did but heighten the impression. Albornoz, able protector of the papal interests, had died and everywhere the French attendants of the pope were greeted with hisses and insults. At length preparations were made for a return to Avignon and the fact was reluctantly announced. Cries of protest sprung from both the faithful and from those who for their own devices wished the next election to be held in Rome. They begged that the decision be reconsidered and the chorus of entreaty was swelled by the royal voices of Pedro of Arragon and the Swedish princess, St. Bridget. The latter warned the pontiff that he would die if he deserted Rome but it was all in vain. Urban was convinced France needed his presence and so he left Italy in the Autumn of 1370; but all that he accomplished in his native land was to give truth to the royal prophecy, for within three months of his return the monks of St. Victor's were making ready a tomb to receive the body of their ex-abbot and late pope. The memory of Urban V is held to be that of a good and saintly man and one writer, expressing the thoughts of his time, says of him: "He was a light of the world and a way of truth; a lover of righteousness." But another writer, the celebrated poet-philosopher Petrarch, could not forgive the return to France. "Urban would have been reckoned among the most glorious of men," he wrote, "if he had caused his dying bed to be laid before the altar of St. Peter's and had there fallen asleep with a good conscience, calling God and the world to witness that if ever the pope had left this spot it was not his fault but that of the originators of so shameful a flight."

The fifteenth century was nearing and the way was steadily being made the easier for a Luther. Despite the acts of saints and the sturdy faith of the zealous and the feats and good deeds of a vast army of churchmen who were sincerely serving their vocation, sure contempt for papal authority was increasing everywhere because of abuses persistently perpetuated by those in the clerical high places. In England an eloquent priest, John Wyclif, was cheered when he preached the subjection of Church to State and when later he attacked the doctrine of transubstantiation and called the Host "an effectual sign" there were neither riots nor drastic measures. He did not lose his life or his living but merely was forbidden to preach. There were constant signs of the spreading mood but the Sacred College seemed to pay little heed and the results of the conclave after the death of Urban provided sure ammunition for the cynics and apprehension on the part of believers. The new pope, GREGORY XI, was not a bad man but he was not remarkable for any talent and the best that could be said of him was that his nature was docile. He was the product of nepotism and he was to employ nepotism. As Peter Roger de Beaufort he had at eighteen years of age been created a cardinal by his uncle Pope Clement VI, though he was not ordained priest until his elevation to the apostolic throne twenty-two years later. Such a nature as his was easy prey to persuasion and influence and strangely enough it was this very weakness which was responsible for the return of the papacy to Rome.

Italy might be seething with unrest and disorder but all Italians were united in their intense dislike of everything French. Those papal properties, districts and cities, which had been, a few years earlier, pacified by the soldier-prelate Albornoz were once again in revolt and even the Republic of Florence, which for a long time had been a staunch ally of the Papal States, participated in the general antagonism. The Pope was forced to action and from Avignon went a stern and capable legate, the Cardinal Robert of Geneva, leading an army of Bretons. The papacy had turned to the sword and in an effort to stay it a woman's voice was suddenly heard. St. Catherine of Siena came to Avignon and the power of her goodness and courage proved sufficient to penetrate the morasses of court intrigue. Boldly she told Gregory his errors and weaknesses and with determination she stressed the fact that his presence in Rome was a dire necessity. His courtiers, both lay and clerical, were alarmed and showed their opposition; but the calm voice went on and with awe the impressionable Pope listened for he knew the advice was coming from one who since childhood had worn a reputation for saintliness and who had many times evidenced her closeness to the Holy State. Her words had effect and Gregory, to the disgust of his attendants, sailed from Marseilles soon after and arrived in Rome during the middle of January, 1377.

The Romans employed their fickle mood to give him a boisterous welcome but their ready noise was a hollow greeting in the great emptiness of the city's ruins. The number of the people had been reduced to 30,000 and most of them were in a state of abject poverty. The historic landscape had become a sad sight, for most of the famous monuments were broken and the majority of the basilicas, numbering over four hundred, were in disrepair. The streets were torn and dirty and the great edifices of ancient majesty and beauty were victims of a riotous and unopposed decay. It was an unhappy environment for the Pope and it became unhappier as the brightness of his welcome quickly faded; for unfortunately his occupancy did not bring tranquillity to the city or to any portion of Italy. The Florentines refused to make peace and other cities were quick to adopt the same bellicose attitude. And if possible even more odium was being attached to the French name because of the cruelties practiced in Northern Italy by those mercenaries who were there under the command of the legate, Cardinal Robert. In Rome the shelter of heavily armed escorts did not protect the French cardinals from insults and curses and in that city of many shadows every shadow seemed a threat to the satellites of the papal court. Under such conditions it is understandable Gregory should make the same decision as Urban. "I shall return to Avignon," he said. But he was wrong, for as preparations were made he became prey to a fatal sickness and died, one year and three months after his entrance.

For the first time in many a year a pope had died in Rome and the citizens were resolved his successor should be elected there. Six cardinals were at Avignon but there were sixteen in the city and the Romans, clanging shut the city gates, informed them with ferocity and tumult that the next to sit upon the pontifical throne should not be French and that, furthermore, he should be elected with rapidity. A great mob, many of whom were drunk, for the papal cellars had been looted, seethed outside the building where the electors had congregated and filled the air with demands and huzzas and threats. The majority of votes in the Sacred College was, of course, controlled by the French cardinals but this time and under such circumstances the ballot went to an Italian from Naples, Bartholomew Prignano, Archbishop of Bari. He was not of cardinal's rank and therefore had not attended the conclave: so while the news was sped to him an attempt to appease the increasingly noisy crowds was made by the announcement of his name. In the uproar the name *Bari* was mistaken by the people as being *Bar*, which was the name of a highly unpopular French prelate and such was the resulting fury that the cardinals decided to flee to their respective refuges. To cover escape they resorted to a ruse and vesting the aged Cardinal Teobaldeschi in the pontifical robes they hurriedly displayed him as proof that an Italian had been elected. The excited Romans thrust aside the guards and swept forward to kiss, despite his objections and explanations, the feet of the bogus pontiff. Their delight was boundless that an Italian should again be successor of Peter and so happy was their temper that when informed of the trick they bore no ill-feelings and with equal heartiness and joy cheered the arrival of the real pope who, after gathering twelve of his scattered electors, was installed with the name of URBAN VI.

He quickly showed he had little respect for those who had given him his position. The spirit of reform was strong within him and he regarded with horror clerical laxities which had been in large and flamboyant evidence during previous regimes. Unfortunately his measures against the abuses displayed neither tact nor understanding nor tolerance, and a nature that hitherto had borne a reputation for self confidence and austerity now became, with the omnipotence of his rank, harsh and arrogant. He was the Pope; and with his broad squat figure and his swarthy countenance set in rigid lines he imperiously summoned the Princes of the Church and rudely told them of their deficiencies and of his resolution to change such things. His choleric emphasis and blunt language bred disquietude among even the

Italian cardinals. The six of their colleagues who had remained at Avignon had at first accepted the calamity, for such it was from their viewpoint, of the Italian triumph at the conclave, but now as rumours reached them of the unpopular and uncouth methods of Urban they sent a representative, the Cardinal-Archbishop of Amiens, to investigate. When this prelate, with bold urbanity, gently suggested to the Pope that he should come to Avignon, Urban flew into an ungovernable rage and loudly swore that he would create a larger batch of Italian cardinals in order to subordinate the French influence. The Avignon emissary withdrew but from then on the dark business of intrigue rapidly gained momentum with a climax approaching when the impetuous pontiff, during one of his rages, gave substance to the growing suspicion of his sanity by attempting to strike a distinguished prelate. The whispers and secret meetings of the cardinals increased until there was a stealthy exodus of them from the city. Even the Chamberlain of the papal court deserted Rome taking with him, significantly, the tiara. The conspirators, for such was now their status, made rendezvous at Anagni and from there dramatically announced the selection of Urban to be invalid because it had been made under duress. It was a grave statement, coming as it did not from any heretical body but from the men who held the electoral privileges. Urban's answer, after one of his characteristic fits of anger, was to name twenty-nine new cardinals and two days later his antagonists calmly proclaimed a new pope, Clement VII. This was the formidable and powerful Cardinal Robert of Geneva, related to most of the royal houses of Europe and well known for his ruthlessness and indomitable energies, who, after an unsuccessful skirmish with troops loyal to Urban, journeyed on to Avignon.

The Great Western Schism, as it is called, had begun. There had been anti-popes before, twenty-seven in all, but never before had two claimants been elected by the same group. There is no doubt that Urban was the true pontiff but in the confusion of the time there was much dispute. St. Catherine of Siena and St. Bridget of Sweden unhesitatingly declared for Urban but equally sincere in the support of Clement were such men of unblemished character as St. Vincent Ferrer and Blessed Peter of Luxemburg. France, of course, supported the Avignon pope and by alliance and treaty it also gained for him the allegiance of Aragon, Castile, Savoy, Scotland and Wales, while Urban's legates secured the recognition of England, Brittany, Portugal, Germany, Hungary, Poland, Flanders, Sweden, Norway, the Catholic Orient, and most of Italy. A continued hurt to his own cause was the unfortunate bitterness of the Pope. The loyalty of Naples was lost because of his violent quarrel with its ruler and six of his cardinals he tortured and then executed because, it was alleged, they had sought to place him under the guardianship of a group of cardinals. "Accomplish your task with moderation," wrote the grieved St. Catherine. "For the love of Christ crucified, curb these sudden impulses prompted by your nature."

The advice went unheeded and to the end of his days Urban persisted in disastrous actions. The unhappy man died on October 15, 1389, after a reign of eleven distressful years and his death presented an opportunity to "Clement VII" and his supporters which was not neglected. The dark processes of intrigue and plot moved into action while the requiem for the late pope still echoed in St. Peter's. Bribes were attempted, promises made, and persuasion wielded, but to no avail and two weeks after Urban had breathed his last the conclave at Rome elected the Cardinal Peter Tomacelli to be Pope with the name of BONIFACE IX. He was from Naples and was to rule for fifteen years but not at any time was he to be popular. Never was he guilty of any grave error but neither can he be applauded for the invention or application of any outstanding reform. He lacked the genius of greatness and the magical quality which is charm; and because of his meticulous care in harvesting sorely needed revenues a stigma of avarice gradually enveloped his name. Throughout his entire time desperate but fruitless attempts were made to restore harmony again to the Church. The lamentable stage in its history had been reached where rival bishops were claiming authority to the same see and likewise abbots to monasteries and priests to churches, large and small. Temporal rulers could see the dangers of the unedifying situation and attempts on all sides were made to have Boniface and the Avignon pope resign and a new election held. In the fifth year of Boniface's reign, Clement died but the Avignon dynasty was rapidly assured by a quick replacement in the person of "Benedict XIII" who was the Cardinal Peter de Luna, a Spaniard by birth but pledged whole-heartedly to the French interest. Even his supporters were to disagree and eventually there was a party in France which re-fused to accept either claimant because both rejected a sugges-tion calling for arbitration and, in case of deadlock, resignation, put forth by the authorities of the University of Paris. It was laudable that the Parisian theologians should attempt to end the schism but their proposal, the danger of which was seen at both Avignon and Rome, and the measures they took after its rejec-tion, were manifestations of the increasing belief that the actions of a pope could be subjected to the opinions and judgments of Councils.

It was to a General Council that Boniface's successor, INNO-CENT VII, proposed to submit the entire vexatious question but he died before the project could be accomplished. His death could not have been a surprise to his electors for he had been almost seventy when he had won their votes. Most of his time and efforts were taken up with troubles in and about Rome, troubles that were well fertilized by the dreary curse, so familiar to the papal scene, of nepotism; for he enriched his family, hitherto neither wealthy nor ennobled, and in particular a favourite nephew who was given, along with many other fa-vours, a cardinal's hat. Before donning the tiara Innocent's name had been Cosimo de' Migliorati and he had been Archbishop of Ravenna and Cardinal-priest of Holy Cross.

His reign did not last two years. Following him was one even older than he. GREGORY XII, the former Cardinal Angelo Cor-rario, was about eighty years of age when he caught the favour of the Conclave and his solemn promise at that time was that he would end the schism even if it meant abdication on his part.

Perhaps he was sincere when he made the promise but his faction and his family, for he too had acquisitive nephews, were resolved that the great dignity should not leave their sphere. Consequently when negotiations were made with the Avignon pope and that dignitary said he would consider resignation providing Gregory would do the same there was procrastination in Rome. His cardinals were incensed at the development and when the Pope, prompted by his family, created four new and amenable cardinals the majority of the Sacred College left Rome and rebelliously convened at Pisa. Here they were joined by a group of Avignon prelates who were also discontented with the policies and stubbornness of their elected choice and who were resolved to end the schism. Such a meeting was a desperate measure and at Rome and at Avignon there were pronouncements, immediate and angry, against it. It was, indeed, itself a schismatical council for it acted upon the principle that its authority was superior to that of the Pope. This attitude was a reflection of the so-called "conciliar theory" exemplified principally in the writing of Marsiglio of Padua. This theory was inimical to the unity and to the very structure of the Church. It would have transformed it into a "limited monarchy" in which the ultimate power lay with the body of the faithful or with an Ecumenical Council acting as their mouthpiece. The Pope would have been merely an executive elected by the clergy for their own convenience. It is easy to see that, in the realm of ecclesiastical government, the Catholic Church could never accept these views either in theory or in practice.

Nevertheless the sympathy and hopes of the schism-fatigued peoples of all Europe were at Pisa and here the cardinals, twenty-four in number, were joined by one hundred and eighty-two bishops and hundreds of other distinguished churchmen or their representatives to form what became known as the Council of Pisa. Benedict and Gregory were summoned to appear before the determined group and when both ignored the unprecedented invitation, sentences of deposition, on the grounds of heresy and schism, were pronounced against them. An election was then held and at this stage the course of reform became diverted by contemporary guile and again we discover the wishes and schemes of one person dominating an entire assemblage. This time it was the will of the powerful Cardinal Balthazar Cossa from Naples which was imposed and thus his protégé, a learned and good but ineffectual Greek cardinal named Peter Philargos was given to Christendom as Pope Alexander V. Such an election was of course illegal and both Alexander and his successor were antipopes. His successor came soon, for Alexander only survived his election by ten months and "chosen" to follow him was his patron the Cardinal Cossa who took the name of John XXIII.

There now existed the sad spectacle, so tragic to Christendom, of three great prelates, each supported by a considerable party, claiming the papal honour. John, for a time, had the greatest following, although today, with the clouds of contemporary confusion and distortion and clamour removed, Pope Gregory stands as the validly elected pontiff. How then was the dilemma to be solved? Surely not by the entrance of John XXIII upon the historic stage for "of all the miserable consequences of the disastrous Synod of Pisa," states Pastor, "this election was the worst." John was not, indeed, the moral monster his enemies afterwards endeavoured to represent him, but he was utterly worldly-minded and completely engrossed by temporal interests. An astute politician and courtier, he was not scrupulously conscientious and was more of a soldier than a churchman. No help for the distracted Church was to be hoped from him. All eyes, therefore, turned to the powerful Sigismund, the King of the Romans, who was necessarily most deeply interested in the termination of the schism, inasmuch as his coronation as Emperor in Rome could not take place until Western Christendom was again united under one spiritual head. He did not disappoint the hopes which were fixed upon him, for the termination of the schism and the restoration of unity to the Church in the West were in a great measure his work.

Sigismund, on the basis of his imperial authority, planned and brought to actuality the sixteenth Ecumenical Council at Constance. Previously John, acting on a resolution formulated at Pisa, had held a council at Rome but the attendance, because of his hostile relations with the King of Naples and because of the waning respect for papal authority, was limited and the gathering had adjourned. The Council of Constance was probably the greatest assemblage of its kind ever yet convened. At the Imperial invitation came cardinals and prelates of the three obediences and significantly there also came ambassadors from seven kingdoms. The balloting was not the privilege alone of the great and care was taken to allow each nation an equitable share in the discussion. Indeed the convention can be said to have been conducted on democratic lines for to offset the schemes of a highly placed few, votes were given to parish priests and representative laymen and doctors of divinity as well as to ambassadors and prelates. The majority of the Council's members seem to have been imbued with a strong tinge of Conciliarism, but the approval given the assemblage clothed it with its necessary validity. John arrived with a great display of pomp to preside at the assembly but instead of a submissive flock he found an unfriendly throng, united in its intention to oppose him.

A long document, accusing him of almost every crime, had been drawn up by canonists, and realizing the campaign against him the second pope of Pisa accepted defeat: fearing for his personal safety he ignominiously fled the conference. However, at the behest of Sigismund, who gave him guarantee of safe conduct, he returned meekly to acknowledge the authority of the Council and to accept the sentence of deposition. He was at first imprisoned, but with dignity, and later he was made Cardinal-bishop of Frascati. There now remained only two claimants to the papal honour and the deadlock was soon broken by a magnanimous gesture from the true pontiff, Gregory XII, who abdicated and accepted the appointment of Cardinal-bishop of Porto, a position he occupied until his death during the autumn of 1417. His acceptance of the authority of this Council was a donation of legality to its judgments and decrees. The Avignon pope was not possessed of the same spirit of generosity and cooperation and even when his own cardinals withdrew their allegiance he stubbornly persisted in his pretensions. To his death, in the stern precincts of a lonely Spanish stronghold, he thus remained a pope without a church, pathetically and daily delivering interdicts and excommunications against an unheeding world.

One of the extra-curricular activities of the Council was its condemnation of the opinions of John Hus. The latter was a Bohemian heretic who had clamored for, among other things, the private interpretation of Scripture and the ministering of the Chalice to the laity . . . ideas which were to come to the fore again later in the most catastrophic manner. Even the Conciliarists were loud in their denunciation of Hus, for, it seems, they were anxious to prove their own orthodoxy. So in 1415 John Hus was burned for his heresy by decree of the Council. All this took place while the Church was still without a Pope.

For two more years the papal throne remained empty and while the electors slowly pondered, the ambassadors of the various nations and interests pressed forward the claims of their condidates with a multiplicity of devices. Finally, on November 11, 1417, a name was announced and the Cardinal Odo Colonna became Pope MARTIN V. His very name was a signal for the lowering of hopes and was a proof that his family had lost neither its ambitions nor its peculiar genius. Yet while he cannot be absolved of nepotism and he was certainly not the great reformer so urgently needed, he was, at least in the temporal sense, a good ruler and furthermore his private life was decent and empty of scandal; a circumstance not so rare as might be desired in the lives of other great prelates who had obtained their status in a similar way. To his credit he returned the papacy to Rome whereas a weaker man might have listened to the urgings of the Emperor who wished the Pope to dwell in Germany or to the French who offered Avignon. It took two years before he was able to enter his see and this was one occasion when the usually sinister system of family preferment had advantages: for with the help of the powerful Colonna clan he brought order to the horribly disordered and ruined city. Large projects, involving great expenditures, were embarked upon to bring beauty and cleanliness, discipline and prosperity, back to the ancient streets. Supported by the troops of his family he ruled with an iron hand and a contemporary writer describing the treatment of his cardinals states: "He has so crushed all the cardinals that they turn red and pale by turn when they speak in his presence."

That scientific and literary movement of the Renaissance which was called *Humanism,* which was illuminated at its beginning by the brilliance of Dante, and which endured until the sixteenth century received scant encouragement from Martin. "While we have Augustine," he said, "what care we for the sagacity of Aristotle, the eloquence of Plato, the prudence of Varro. We do not need these men. Augustine is enough for us." Extreme Humanists, in an effort to recapture the glories of the ancient culture, often rebelled against the authority and concepts of the Church but there rapidly came into being a school of philosophers, consisting of truly Catholic scholars who saw no reason why full appreciation of the treasures of the past should necessarily entail a denial of Christian principles.

A Council had been responsible for his elevation but Martin regarded such institutions with distaste; and although at Constance it had been agreed they should be convened with periodic regularity he displayed little enthusiasm or energy in that direction. That some semblance of sincerity should be given his promises he did, at Pavia in 1423, summon a Council. But when there was an outbreak of the plague at this city he transferred it to Siena and soon after, on the pretext of poor attendance, he dissolved it. But because of pressure from non-Italian interests he was forced to issue a summons for another to be held in 1431. The scene was to be Basle and that Martin suspected trouble is shown by the fact of his legate having authority to conclude the proceedings at any time he deemed it necessary. Before the prelates could be assembled an attack of apoplexy brought death to the Pope and in an honoured place before the High Altar of St. John Lateran were interred the remains of the man who has often been called the Second Founder of the Papal Monarchy.

The cardinals who met within the walls of a Roman convent to select his successor were of a generation which had witnessed the power and the presumptions of Councils and they were resolved that he who followed Martin should not be as dictatorial as that autocrat had been. Their votes went to the Cardinal Eugenius Gabriel Condolmieri, a nobleman of Venice and a nephew of Gregory XII, but only after he had promised that a major share of the government of both the Papal States and the Church should be controlled by the Sacred College. After making this bargain he was quickly made Pope Eugenius IV and almost as quickly he discovered that capitulation is a process that once begun is difficult to end. Five months after his installation found the Council of Basle in convention and although at its beginning there were only fifteen bishops the number gradually grew and soon was reinforced by several hundreds of earnest canonists and divines, eager for dispute and keenly alert for fancied infringements of fancied privileges, who came as representatives of the universities or absentee prelates. This gathering was strong with the tradition of Constance and the majority of its members were convinced that as a unity they were superior to the authority of a pope. Therefore when Eugenius saw the trend and ordered its dissolution he was met with defiance and contempt. Furthermore the rebellious attitude was endorsed by the Emperor Sigismund and almost every other ruling sovereign. This was not all. Even Rome turned against the Pope for he, on taking office, had tried to oust the Colonna from the position they had achieved during the reign of Martin. They were quick to rebel and to incite rebellion and soon there was the not unprecedented spectacle of the lawful head of all Christendom fleeing for his life from that place which should have been the sturdiest of his refuges. A Tiber boatman gave him the meagre shelter of a small river craft and with the humiliated but dauntless pontiff, disguised as a monk, crouching low in the flimsy sternsheets and with only the added protection of a leather shield given by a friendly soldier, an escape was made through a blockade established by ships filled with the unscrupulous henchmen of the vengeful Colonna.

It was Florence, so prosperous and powerful at this time, which gave him succour and protection and there came those of his cardinals who had remained loyal. The tide of the Renaissance was surging strong in this place which was to be the papal home for almost a decade and the spirit of the lovely city was gay and boisterous with the vitality of the new movement. It was a happy spirit which found a hearty patron in the person of the exiled Pope and it was this spirit and such patronage which fostered the genius of Michelangelo, Brunelleschi, Donatello, Fra Angelico, Botticelli, Lippi, Massalino, and Masaccio. But while there was gaiety in Florence the shadow of the Turk was falling closer to Constantinople and once again we witness a Byzantine Emperor appealing to a pope in an effort to enlist the aid of Latin Christendom. His representatives and those of the Eastern Patriarchs came to Florence and after much negotiation a reunion between the two Churches was announced although unfortunately the pact when attempted in practice proved to be but optimistic words. More than a decree, formulated in stress, was needed to heal the long schism and the reunion was never really accepted by the peoples of either the Eastern or Western Churches. However, the appeal and the entire affair illustrated the fact that Eugenius was regaining the authority that was rightfully his, and aiding him was a powerful friend, Cosimo di Medici, the ruler of Florence who was possessed of a host of allies. Against this happy friendship the rebellious divines at Basle, still convened in their obstinate Council, were gradually losing princely supporters and particularly so when they reached the climax of their impertinence by proclaiming a new pope, "Felix V." Europe, even those nations who had been against Eugenius, had nought but despair at the prospects of two claimants again contesting the papal throne. The anti-pope had been found in the person of the Duke Amadeus of Savoy who indisputably was an earnest minded and pious nobleman, specially ordained and consecrated for his dubious honour, and thoroughly convinced, thanks to the eloquence of his electors, that his pretensions were valid and just.

In the ninth year of his exile Eugenius was able to return to Rome with power and authority. The Colonna and Orsini were defeated and evicted and in a spirit of rejoicing he set out lavishly to endow the city with those arts he had enjoyed at Florence. A host of painters and sculptors and architects received his commands and while buildings grew and frescoes and statues and canvasses progressed he commissioned the famous Lorenzo Ghiberti to produce, among many objects of beauty, a magnificent tiara, heavily encrusted with precious stones. The magnificence which surrounded these undertakings was not reflected in his private life for as much as possible he lived with simplicity and austerity and always he was a determined opponent of nepotism. As the end of his reign neared he redoubled his efforts to bring back that unity which was his cherished dream and to achieve it he sacrificed many of the papal privileges in Germany. Thus peace was made with Sigismund and ambassadors came from the Emperor to make formal pledge of their master's allegiance. Eugenius received them gladly but instead of his pleasure being voiced from his throne the words of welcome were delivered from his deathbed.

Within a fortnight there was a new pope but the brevity of the Conclave did not prevent spirited argument and much intrigue, for the Colonna tried by every means they knew save direct force to secure the tiara for their own House. They failed however and far from being sprung of such exalted lineage the family of the Cardinal Thomas Parentucelli, who became NICHOLAS V, was not even possessed of the right to sport a coat-of-arms. This new pope was above all things a scholar and used to the company of scholars. The son of a country physician he had since childhood displayed a marked aptitude for learning and this appetite was never to leave him. He was fifty years old when made pope and his policies, it was soon evident, were modelled after those of his predecessor. He concluded the concordat with Germany and entered upon more harmonious relations with Scotland and France so that eventually it was only the stubborn prelates at Basle, rapidly dwindling in number and importance, who persisted in schism. But even they, and in this reign, were to admit mistake; and the good but misguided man whom they had called Felix V was magnanimously forgiven by Nicholas and given an honoured place in the College of Cardinals. This action marked the end of the Conciliar Movement.

In 1450, the third year of this Pope, a great Jubilee was held in Rome and crowds of pilgrims, drawn from all corners of Christendom, came to celebrate the unity of the Church. They found a busy and happy city for Nicholas, thoroughly imbued with the spirit of the Renaissance, was an even more avid patron of the arts than Eugenius had been and he was determined that Rome should not only be the religious centre of the world but that she should also lead in cultural enterprise. His particular fancy was the development of the Vatican library and, ardent book lover that he was, he collected and catalogued and preserved every manuscript of any value, ancient or contemporary, he could find. It was happy industry and one that kept him poring over books and bindings for long peaceful hours. But suddenly there came news which changed his mood and shocked him so that he sickened in body and soul. Constantinople, that place which, even if in schism, had been the Christian bulwark against the forces of Islam, had finally been conquered and occupied by the Turk. The Pope hurriedly and with desperation appealed to the various sovereigns and rulers for aid but there was no eager or quick response. It is true that when the news permeated throughout Europe of how the Sultan Mohammed II had with sacrilegious arrogance triumphantly ridden his horse through the splendid Church of Sancta Sophia there was some stirring of conscience and attempts were made to form a Crusade. Nicholas worked hard to organize and unite these attempts but before any perceptible progress was made he died, saddened and exhausted.

Both the Colonna and the Orsini fought desperately to control the next Conclave and perhaps to avert the deadlock so easily born of such maneuverings the cardinals quickly selected a non-Italian who was eighty years old. He was a Spaniard and he was the first pope from that family whose name on the written page seldom fails to quicken the interest of the reader. He was the Cardinal Alfonso Borgia and as Pope he was known as CAL-LISTUS III. Like Nicholas he tried to inaugurate a great and unified campaign against the Turk but his appeal had little response. Such Christian forays as there were remained independent and the victories were few. The Hungarians scored the greatest success against the Mohammedans in the field; and on the sea a papal fleet, commanded by an archbishop, captured twenty-five Turkish ships. At Rome, without shame or pretense, Callistus gave what he could to his family; two of his nephews, neither conspicuous for the excellence of his conduct, were made cardinals at a very early age. Indeed the unabashed preference shown to the Borgia clan was probably one of the reasons why the Sacred College should, after the end of his three year reign, once again turn to an Italian, the Cardinal Aeneas Piccolomini who was of a noble Siennese family and who was in every way a true and typical figure of the Renaissance.

The new Pope had been a courtier and he had been Poet Laureate to the Emperor Frederick. As a young man his talents as a writer, combined with that spirit of rebellious scepticism common to youthful intellectuals, had resulted in a document which questioned the papal authority. The existence of such a work was of course splendid ammunition for his critics when he became Pope Pius II. So much so that he was forced to make a formal repudiation and this he did in a communication to the University of Cologne. "Reject Aeneas," he wrote, "and accept Pius." His time was six years and although he tried valiantly his reign cannot be considered successful; for his attempts to bring reform in Church affairs met with as little response as did his appeals for a Crusade. Busy with their own troubles the leaders of nations had no wish to indulge in the costly luxury of distant adventures and the Pope's entreaties, like those of his predecessors, went for the most part unheeded. While he hopefully waited for favourable responses, he appointed a commission which was to devise a scheme for the contemplated ecclesiastical reform but the errors and laxities this commission found were of such magnitude and number, their report was so gloomy and pessimistic that it seemed as though a complete or honest eradication of such abuses would be impossible to achieve, at least in any one lifetime.

At last the Pope, stung by the impotence of his position and the futility of his pleas, determined on a dramatic course that would provide an example to the apathetic Princes of Christendom. If they would not resist the Turk then he, Pope though he was, would take to the field and assume their duty. Solemnly he pledged himself to the vows of a Crusader in the Vatican Basilica and the eighteenth day of June, 1464, saw him, despite his old age and frail health and lack of experience as a campaigner, beginning the militant journey, surrounded by a gay and undisciplined army which for the most part consisted of French and Spanish knights who had been attracted by the spectacular deed of the pontiff. "Farewell Rome," he cried as he left the city. "Never again will you see me alive." The cavalcade proceeded to Ancona and from there it was intended the journey should be continued on the sea, for Venice had promised to provide a fleet. The ships were long in coming and very quickly the sad history of previous crusades was given repetition. Mischief born of indolence and intrigue brought discord to the camps and Pius, now so weak from his illness that he could not leave his bed, was told that his army was melting away instead of growing stronger with those reinforcements which were his hope. Eventually the Venetian ships came and when their sails were raised on the horizon the Pope was carried to a window so he could see the long awaited sight. It was an attempt to revive him but it was an attempt doomed like his Crusade, to failure. The ships had come too late and, after exhorting his cardinals to continue with the expedition, Pius II breathed his last.

The cardinals sped to Rome where after sitting in a conclave which lasted only two days they elected the Venetian born cardinal of San Marco, Pietro Barbo, now to be PAUL II, a somewhat eccentric character who had been made a cardinal because of the fondness of his uncle, Pope Eugenius IV. Like his relative he was a devoted patron of the arts and was resolved that Rome should be made the most beautiful and cultured city of the world. His rich hospitality became famous and a familiar sight of his reign was to see him smiling benignly down from his palace window upon a throng banqueting at his expense. Carnivals and horse races and public games were other gifts he showered upon the populace in emulation of the ancient tradition. The new art of printing received his interest and encouragement and artists and sculptors and goldsmiths were familiar to his court. The famous tiara that Ghiberti had made for his uncle had cost thirty-eight thousand ducats but the one designed and made to meet his luxurious taste cost nearly four times as much. He was popular with the Roman mob and they cheered his extravagances and generosity; but with the intelligentsia it was another story for he frowned upon the pretensions and affectations of the extreme Humanists. When such members of the Roman Academy considered it fashionable to display pagan tendencies in their writings and discussions he caused the institution to be disbanded and imprisoned some of the leaders. The anger and resentment of these men found sympathy with most of the cardinals, who felt they had been deceived: for at the conclave which had given him the tiara Paul had glibly promised that if elected he would transfer fuller privileges and authority to the Sacred College. The promise was not fulfilled on the grounds that such an action would be invalid and contrary to canon law. Paul did not abandon the project of a Crusade and after the usual appeals had been made and received with the familiar lethargy of the temporal rulers he formulated a scheme whereby a general tax was to be levied and with the monies so derived mercenaries employed to carry on the campaign against the ever encroaching Turk who by now indeed was marching through Greece. His plan proved impracticable and the apathy of the nations, with the exception of Albania and Hungary (to whom the Pope sent financial assistance), remained unbroken; and although Charlemagne's title was still jealously claimed and used, the most powerful sovereign of the world was acknowledged to be the Moslem warrior, Mohammed II.

From the next conclave came Sixtus IV, the former Cardinal Francis della Rovere (a name which was not his by birth but gained by association with the noble family in the capacity of tutor). Born the son of a fisherman he had joined the Franciscans at a very early age and from that commencement his astuteness had won him promotion step by step until finally the supreme rank was his. Like most other popes of this era the acquisition of the tiara meant the enrichment of his family. Two of his nephews, unworthy in every respect, became cardinals and like the rest of their rejoicing relatives revelled in preferment and favour. He ruled thirteen years and, although he brought no improvement to his spiritual domain, the temporal power of the Papal States was regularized and strengthened —a process that could not apparently be accomplished without the accompaniment of intrigue, treachery, and bloodshed. A cathedral in Florence became the background of a particularly horrible crime when Giuliano Medici, one of the leaders of his family, now in disagreement with the Papal States, was brutally murdered whilst attending mass although his brother Lorenzo escaped to wreak a terrible revenge on the actual assassins and to declare war against their admitted ally, the Pope. The lack of saintliness in his own character did not prevent Sixtus from being a great friend of the monastic orders, whom he encouraged and protected by statutes and gifts; nor did his preoccupation with political affairs prevent him from sustaining that bright continuity of artistic patronage which was the happy legacy of a Renaissance pope to his successors. The Sistine Chapel owed its beauty to his generosity as do many other works of beauty

Sixtus IV (1471-1484)

still in existence. With less vigour perhaps, even though at one time he sold his silver plate to pay his mercenaries, he continued in the tradition of a Crusade. But in these years such efforts were reduced to a series of minor campaigns, even though at one time the Turks invaded Southern Italy, and the withdrawal of this capable foe was not due to any Christian victory but because of the opportune death of the Mohammedan leader. To the Inquisition in Spain Sixtus sent a message in which he stressed the need of moderation and the necessity of freedom from domination by political parties; with the latter purpose in mind he appointed the Cardinal Thomas de Torquemada as Grand Inquisitor.

The death of Sixtus was a signal for the Roman mob to demonstrate against his relatives. The family palace, rich with newly acquired treasures, was raided and plundered and the streets became noisy with maledictions and curses against the family name. But even violent proof of an intense unpopularity could not stifle the ambitions and designs of his favourite nephew, Cardinal Giuliano della Rovere. The opponent of this product of nepotism, in the elaborate intrigues which were set in motion with the gathering of the next conclave, was another favoured nephew, but of another pope. Rodrigo Borgia wished the tiara for himself but his promises and schemes were less effective, this time, than the persuasions of the unpopular but wily Della Rovere. For, after brief deliberation, the latter's candidate, the Cardinal John-Baptist Cibo, became INNOCENT VIII. Little could be expected of one elected under such auspices and indeed his reign was no interruption in what was now becoming a long and shameful record. Typical in all ways of the sad era was the move made by the new pope when, ungratefully wishing to free himself from the demanding and irksome friendship of his sponsor, he made peace with Florence by marrying his illegitimate son to the daughter of the enemy of the previous pontiff, Lorenzo de Medici. Such an alliance was not considered extraordinary at the time and the fact that a condition of the marriage contract made the sixteen-year-old brother of the bride a cardinal caused neither indignation nor protest save from such isolated personages as the eloquent Dominican friar, Girolamo Savonarola, who at this time was tramping throughout Italy and attracting large audiences by the fearless outspokenness and vigour of his sermons.

The summer of 1492 brought death to Innocent and once again the opposing interests of the Cardinals della Rovere and Borgia motivated the activities of the congregated electors. Twenty-three cardinals had assembled and after four days Rodrigo Borgia was able, by bribes and promises of future favours, to unite sixteen of his colleagues into a majority which proclaimed him to be Pope ALEXANDER VI, though he should have been Alexander V because the "pope" who bore the latter name was not a true pope. He was sixty years old when so honored and his is the unhappy distinction of being considered by many as having been the worst of the popes. There are historians who consider him to be maligned and question most of the charges brought against him, but whatever exaggeration there may have been, the fact remains that he was not in any way fitted for his high office. The best that can be said of him is that if the moral tone of his private life were no better than that of contemporary temporal princes it was certainly no worse, and the incidents which make his story seem outrageous in the cold light of today excited no great surprise in his own time. Actually such an election was to be expected and was but the product of a natural evolution for, save in a few instances, Rome had found the protection of foreign rulers to be either tyrannical or insufficient; for survival in the vicious anarchy which was keeping Italy in a condition of almost permanent disorder, the Papal States felt themselves forced to have a ruler, Peter's successor though he might be, whose employment of device and intrigue, threat and force, could thwart the avarice of those predatory princes who were the neighbors of the ancient city. It was then a temporal lord and not a spiritual leader that the Romans saw in his person and the news of his elevation was received by them with boisterous applause; for his popularity

Alexander VI (1492-1503)

was not only born of his singular grace of manner but of the knowledge that he was an extremely capable and resourceful leader and a generous patron of the arts. Prior to his acquisition of the tiara he had, as a rich and favored cardinal, lived with the splendor of a prince and like most great noblemen his existence was untouched by the rigors of celibacy.

He had had mistresses, in particular Vanozza Catanei, who bore him four children. These were his weakness and the cause of most of his troubles, and their names, wrongly or rightly, have persisted through the years as a synonym for all that can be evil in human form. One son he married to the daughter of Alphonso II, the King of Naples, but this alliance was marred by the actions of the French monarch, Charles VIII, who put forth a claim upon the Neapolitan throne. To him went the Cardinal della Rovere with a suggestion that the Pope be deposed on the grounds of a simoniacal election. Charles marched towards Rome and the fair weather friends of Alexander fled. But with adroit maneuvering the Borgia effected an arrangement whereby without actually acknowledging the claims upon Naples he permitted the unhindered transit of French soldiery through the papal territory which thus was spared the ravages of war. In return for this service and much to the disappointment of Della Rovere, Charles acknowledged Alexander as true pontiff. Meanwhile with characteristic guile Alexander was conducting negotiations with the holder of the Imperial title, Maximilian I, and the rulers of Spain and Venice who in a new unity became the formidable power which finally defeated the French.

One of the reasons which had prompted Charles to invade Italy was the encouragement he had received from the fiery tempered and vociferous Dominican, Savonarola, who hoped the French King would prove to be the instrument of punishment which would purge the papacy of iniquity. The hot blooded friar had, by the employment of high courage and brilliant oratory, effected the near miracle of bringing reform to the once riotously wicked Florence although, as wider territories invited his energies, there were accusations that his sermons were motivated by political reasons. Certainly there was insubordination in them for not only was the papal court a subject of his candor and ire but the person of the Pope was, with increasing repetition, becoming the target of his scorn and denunciation. Before heed is given to the tirades of the fanatical friar justice demands that some audience be allowed those men of that time who had no great need to indulge in sycophancy and yet apparently did not believe Alexander to be either incapable or despicable. It is now thirty-seven years," wrote Sigismundo Conti, who knew him well, "since his uncle Calixtus III (Callistus), made him a cardinal, and during that time he never missed a single Consistory unless prevented by illness from attending, which very seldom happened. Throughout the reigns of Pius II, Paul II, Sixtus IV and Innocent VIII, he was always an important personage; he had been Legate in Spain and in Italy. Few people understood etiquette so well as he did; he knew how to make the most of himself, and took pains to shine in conversation and to be dignified in his manners. In the latter point his majestic stature gave him an advantage. Also he was just at the age, about sixty, at which Aristotle says, men are wisest; robust in body and vigorous in mind, he was admirably equipped for his new position." From the pen of another writer who knew him, Hieronymus Portius, came the following description: "He is tall, in complexion neither fair or dark; his eyes are black; his mouth somewhat full. His health is splendid, and he has a marvellous power of enduring all sorts of fatigue. He is singularly eloquent in speech, and is gifted with an innate good breeding which never forsakes him." And in Germany the historian Hartman Schedel said that the Pope "is a large-minded man, gifted with great prudence, foresight, and knowledge of the world. In his youth he studied at the University of Bologna, and obtained there so great a reputation of virtue, learning and capability that his mother's brother, Pope Calixtus III, made him a cardinal; and it is further proof of his worth and talents that he was called at such an early age to a place in this honorable and illustrious assembly, and was also made Vice-Chancellor. Such things being known of him he was quickly elected to govern and steer the barque of St. Peter. Besides being a man of noble countenance and bearing, he has, in the first place, the merit of being a Spaniard; secondly he comes from Valencia, thirdly, he is of an illustrious family. In book-learning, appreciation of Art, and probity of life he is a worthy successor of his uncle Calixtus of blessed memory. He is affable, trustworthy, prudent, pious, and well versed in all things appertaining to his exalted position and dignity. Blessed indeed therefore is he adorned with so many virtues and raised to so high a dignity. . . ."

Far different was the judgment of Savonarola who in a letter to the rulers of the Christian nations urged that a Council be convoked and that Alexander be deposed because he was "guilty of simony, a heretic, and an unbeliever." "The hour of vengeance has arrived," he wrote in this intemperate document. "God desires me to reveal His secret counsels and to announce to all the world the dangers to which the barque of Peter is exposed . . . I assure you, *in verbo Domini*, that this Alexander is no Pope at all and should not be accounted as such for besides having attained to the Chair of St. Peter by the shameful sin of simony, and still daily selling Church benefices to the highest bidder, besides his other vices which are known to the world I affirm he is not a Christian and does not believe in the existence of God, which is the deepest depth of unbelief." Earlier, and it is but typical of many similar utterances, Savonarola told his congregations that in Rome the clergy "buy preferments and bestow them on their children or their brothers, who take possession of them by violence and all sorts of sinful means. Their greed is insatiable, they do all things for gold. They only ring their bells for coin and candles; only attend Vespers and Choir and Office when something is to be got by it. They sell their benefices, sell the Sacraments, traffic in masses; in short, money is the root of everything, and then they are afraid of excommunication. When the evening comes one goes to the gaming tables, another to his concubine. When they go to a funeral a banquet is given, and when they ought to be praying in silence for the soul of the departed they are eating and drinking and talking. They are steeped in shameful vices. There is no faith left, no charity, no virtue. It is considered a disgrace to live well. If a priest or canon leads an orderly life he is mocked and called a hypocrite. No one talks now of his nephew, but simply of his son or his daughter. Every priest has his concubine. The poison is so rank in Rome that it has infected France and Germany and all the world. It has come to such a pass that all are warned against Rome and people say, 'if you want to ruin your son make him a priest. . . .' O, prostitute Church, thou hast displayed thy foulness to the whole world, and stinkest up to Heaven."

The influence of Savonarola was mighty and his enmity was a grave threat to the position of the Pope, for not only was the Friar the real ruler of Florence at this time but his words carried weight throughout Europe. Alexander was well aware that, all circumstances considered, a Council was not impossible and indeed very probable. The ambitions of Della Rovere, the schemes of the various princes, his own deficiencies and excesses, were all ingredients that when brought together and touched by the flame of Savonarola's anger could easily ignite into a disaster terrible for the Borgia name and aims. Yet with a commendable display of restraint he took no hasty action against his voluble assailant and gradually the latter's position was weakened until it was made clearly evident to all that driven by his anti-papal obsessions he was repeatedly breaking the oath he had taken as a priest to obey his superiors. No matter how base his actions might be, Alexander was pope. After a considerable period had passed and the obstinate Friar had refused to abandon his campaign the sentence of excommunication was pronounced. There was no bitterness or malice in the Pope's action. "If the monk will prove his obedience," he told a Florentine official, "by abstaining from preaching for a reasonable time, I will absolve him. . . . If he persists in his disobedience we shall be obliged to proceed against him with the Interdict and all other lawful punishments to vindicate our own dignity and that of the Holy See."

The Friar persisted and his enemies, of whom there were many, including the powerful Medici family, were quick to seize the advantage when, even though excommunicated, he foolishly continued to preach and even administer the Sacraments. The Pope had threatened to put Florence under an Interdict if the Friar were not silenced and as he still had many supporters the city was faced with disorder and strife. Self-delusion made him believe he was the Voice of God and it was his habit to call dramatically upon the Divine Power to strike him dead if what he uttered was not of Divine origin. Repeatedly he offered to walk through flames in order to prove the righteousness of his teachings. Finally a Franciscan monk accepted the oft-repeated challenge saying, "I fully believe that I shall be burnt, but I am ready to sacrifice myself to free the people from this delusion. If Savonarola is not burnt with me then you may believe him to be a prophet."

Now that the time had come the Friar seemed not over anxious to engage in such a dangerous joust, but one of his zealous henchmen, a fellow Dominican, accepted on his behalf with alacrity and fervor. When the news reached Rome of the proposed carnival Alexander voiced displeasure but as the plan was endorsed by the secular power of Florence, the Signoria, it was beyond his power to prevent it. The day of the contest arrived and great crowds hungry for excitement assembled to witness a miracle or a tragedy; but their eagerness changed to disappointment and rage when Savonarola's champion refused to enter the flames unless he be allowed to carry the Host with him. The Franciscans indignantly cried that such an action would be sacrilege and as the blaze grew less and the mob took to jeers and insults there were long arguments and a deadlock, followed by the announcement that there would be no Ordeal by Fire. After this fiasco Savonarola's influence dwindled rapidly and soon his enemies had him arraigned before the secular authorities. Some alleged confessions were wrung from him by torture and he was sentenced to be hanged on the grounds of heresy. Heretic he was not and he went to his death with fortitude and grandeur, a man thought by many to be a saint, but in reality a pitiful victim of self-delusion and disobedience and obstinacy.

Alexander continued his vicious ways. The pursuit of sensual pleasures and the enrichment of his family seemed to be his main occupation. With shocking regularity treasures, revenues, and hereditary properties were looted from the church to aggrandize the House of Borgia and the most obscure members of that clan were certain of wealth and security if they came to Rome. It was an opportunity seldom neglected and as one writer put it: "Not ten papacies would suffice to support this swarm of cousins." Despite efforts from all directions there was only one time that Alexander gave serious thought to his errors and that was after his son, the dissolute Duke of Gandia, was murdered while engaged in some nocturnal adventure. The assassin was never discovered and rumor named his brother Caesar as being the criminal although reputable historians reject any theories of fratricide. The mutilated corpse was found in the Tiber and when the Pope was notified he became prostrated with grief, crying loudly that it was a punishment for his sins. Soon after he told the assembled Cardinals and Ambassadors that: "The blow which has fallen upon us is the heaviest we could possibly have sustained. We loved the Duke of Gandia more than anyone else in the world. We would give seven Tiaras to be able to recall him to life. God has done this in punishment for our sins, for the Duke had done nothing to deserve this mysterious and terrible death. . . . May God forgive the murderer. We, on our part, are resolved to amend our own life and reform the Church. The reform of the Church will be put into the hands of six Cardinals and two Auditors of the Rota. From henceforth benefices shall only be given to deserving persons, and in accordance with the votes of the cardinals. We renounce all nepotism. We will begin the reform with ourselves and so proceed through all ranks of the Church till the whole work is accomplished."

The promised Bill of Reform reached a draught stage but this was the limit of its progress and as the Pope quickly relapsed to his former ways even more affection and favors were lavished upon his surviving offspring. The dignity of the Cardinalate was not enough for his son Caesar, laden though it was with rich benefices and negotiable sinecures. He had even higher designs and the papacy became the channel through which flowed to him a rich stream of Dukedoms and Principalities. A tradition of the Church was broken when he was allowed to resign from the Sacred College and a policy of the Papal States was changed when, to permit of his marriage to a Princess of the French Royal family, an alliance was made with her country.

Suspicion and hostility and discontent, particularly in Spain and Germany, greeted these happenings but the doting father ensconced on his sullied throne would listen to no advice save from his son who more and more was acting the tyrant. Arrogance, cruelty, and ambition, were the main characteristics of this vain man who after his doffing of the Red Hat first took the title of Duke of Valentinois and later still caused himself to be addressed as Caesar Borgia of France, by the Grace of God Duke of the Romagna and of Valencia and Urbino, Prince of Andria, Lord of Piombino, Standard-bearer and General-in-Chief of the Church. To the detriment of ecclesiastical revenues he lived on a sumptuous scale, 100,000 ducats were spent to equip him for his journey to France and not only did he and his attendants wear the costliest of garments and rarest of gems and jewels but even the saddle cloths of his horses were embroidered with splendid pearls and the harness joined with gold and silver. His tempestuous nature kept the Papal States embroiled in wars and trouble and even brought bloodshed to the inner circles of the family. After quarreling with his brother-in-law, he caused him to be slain but not even for this crime could any law reach him or authority curb him; and Lucrezia was made to forget her sorrow by the donation of a new husband, the Duke d'Este of Ferrara, who was able to bring more riches into the family. For eleven years the loathsome regime existed and it seemed fated to endure much longer for the villains who sustained it seemed blessed with sturdy health; then suddenly both Alexander and

Caesar fell violently ill during the summer of 1503. The younger man managed to survive but the father perished and there were some who affirmed that both had sickened after mistakenly drinking poisoned wine they had destined for another. No great credence should be given this story for there was an epidemic of the dreaded Roman fever during that hot summer and it has been well established that the two had been contaminated by the malignant illness.

The dismal chronicle of this pontificate is relieved by a few bright chapters. Like most of the Renaissance popes Alexander gave lavish patronage to the arts and Rome gained greatly through his program of restoration and decoration. The swarm of poets and authors then thronging the city were allowed a wide scope in their efforts and this privilege was fully used and very often abused. A deluge of criticisms and lampoons and libels mocked and reviled the Pope but unlike his dark-tempered son he paid no heed, saying, "Rome is a free city, and here everyone has a right to write and say what he likes." With interest but without anger he had read to him a particularly savagely worded document which amongst other things said "There is no sort of outrage or vice that it is not openly practised in the palace of the Pope. The perfidy of the Scythians and Carthaginians, the bestiality and savagery of Nero and Caligula are surpassed. Rodrigo Borgia is an abyss of vice, a subverter of all justices, human or divine . . ."

No revenge was taken against the author of the venomous words and how lightly Alexander regarded them is shown by the fact that he afterwards received the author in audience. Personal attacks were treated far differently from attempted doctrinal innovations. The latter he would not suffer on any pretext and to prevent the new art of printing from spreading error he issued his Censorial Edict which stipulated that ecclesiastical opinion should be sought before the publication of a book. While profligacy and corruption flourished in Rome during his eleven years the machinery of Church administration continued to function without disturbance or hindrance. The voyages of

Christopher Columbus had provided new fields for the spreading of the Faith and brave men, armed only with faith, were resolutely preparing to face the unknown dangers of the New World. Under the seal of Alexander great support was given to the Orders and able measures taken to suppress heresy and to frustrate the ever belligerent Turk.

Evil though he was, he never attempted to challenge or change the doctrines of the Church. "Even his bitterest enemies are unable to formulate any accusation against him in this respect," states Pastor. "It seemed as though his reign was meant by Providence to demonstrate the truth that though men may hurt the Church they cannot harm her. In the Church there have always been unworthy priests as well as bad Christians and . . . just as the intrinsic worth of a jewel is not lessened by an inferior setting, so the sins of a priest cannot essentially affect his power of offering sacrifice or administering Sacraments or transmitting doctrine. The personal holiness of the priest is of course, of the highest importance for the lives of the faithful, inasmuch as he constitutes a living example for them to follow, and compels the respect and esteem of those who are outside. Still the goodness or badness of the temporary minister can exercise no substantial influence on the being, the divine character, or the holiness of the Church; on the word of revelation; on the graces and spiritual powers with which she is endowed. Thus even the supreme high priest can in no way diminish the value of that heavenly treasure which he controls and dispenses, but only as a steward. The gold remains gold in impure as in pure hands. 'The Papal office belongs to a higher sphere than the personality of its occupant for the time being, and can neither gain nor lose its essential dignity by saintliness on one side, or unworthiness on the other.' Even the first Pope, St. Peter, had sinned deeply in denying his Lord and Master; and yet the office of Supreme Pastor was given to him. In the words of the great St. Leo: *Petri dignitas etiam in indigno herede non deficit.*"

Italy and France and Spain struggled to control the next

conclave and the latter two powers did not hesitate to try and enlist the aid of Caesar Borgia. But happily the sinister creature was not as active at this important time as he could have been for he was yet weak from his illness. "I had counted on the death of my father and had made every preparation for it," he lamented, "but it never occurred to me that I should have at the same time to fight death myself." However he threw his influence to favor the candidate of the French king. But to thwart him there now returned to Rome, after an exile of nearly ten years, the antagonist of his father, the experienced and veteran Cardinal Giuliano della Rovere who, friendly though he himself had been with the French, warned the cardinals that if a Frenchman were elected the papacy faced the danger of being returned to Avignon. There seemed then every chance of a deadlock but this prospect was so distasteful to the Sacred College that a name hitherto not mentioned was quickly presented and acclaimed and a month after Alexander's death the Cardinal Francesco Piccolomini, nephew of Pius II, became Pope Pius III. He was sixty-four years old and was a hopeless invalid; this latter circumstance was probably the real reason that won for him the votes of the conclave for his tenure was expected to be short. Nor were the macabre expectations disappointed. He died in less than a month but during that brief time displayed much charity and kindness and announced reform to be his aim.

There was no deadlock at the next conclave for by bargain and by bribe Cardinal della Rovere secured for himself thirty-seven of the thirty-eight votes in proceedings that did not extend a full day. After long years he had finally won the tiara and triumphantly taking the name of JULIUS II he set out to restore the strength and possessions of the Papal States. This was no easy task, for Alexander had left a sad confusion of debts and trouble, and great properties rightfully belonging to the Church were in the clutches of his son. The Republic of Venice was noisily claiming Romagna, Spain was occupying Sicily and Naples, and the French, ever resolved to maintain a foothold in Italy, were willing to resort to arms against any who would

Julius II (1503-1513)

oppose them. Julius had been given a domain bankrupt in treasury and bereft of defence but not for nothing had he earned the description of *terrible*. He was possessed of enormous physical strength and had the courage of a lion, and his will and determination matched both these qualities. His abilities were those of a warrior statesman rather than those of an ecclesiastic but they were talents appreciated by the Romans at this time. He was not a saint and three daughters were testimony that his earlier life had been no better than that of other Renaissance prelates; but, although he had a few relations in high places, the charge of nepotism has never been levelled against him. He won, it is true, elevation to the chair of St. Peter by dubious tactics but once enthroned he acted only for the betterment, as he saw it, of that which had been placed in his care. In spite of his considerable years he was possessed of a driving energy. "No one has any influence over him," reported the Venetian Ambassador. "He consults few or none. Anything he has been thinking of overnight has to be carried out immediately the next morning, and he insists on doing everything himself. It is impossible to describe how headstrong and violent and difficult to manage he is. Everything about him is on a magnificent scale. There is nothing in him that is small or meanly selfish. Whatever is in his mind must be carried through, even if he himself were to perish in the attempt."

He despised the name of Borgia yet at the beginning of his reign there was no rupture with Caesar Borgia because of a pact made before his election. At that time he had made sure there would be no opposition from any quarter and Caesar Borgia might have possessed some influence with those cardinals who owed their preferment to his father. But when he became Pope the ill begotten territories of the wicked Duke were included in his program of independence via restoration. Venice had designs on these properties also and there was long disagreement with that Republic. "From the beginning of Our reign," the Doge of Venice was informed, "it has been Our steadfast purpose to restore to the Church the territories of which she has been despoiled; to this We hold fast, and shall ever do so . . . Nothing shall induce Us to desist from demanding the restitution of these places . . . Therefore We again admonish your Highness with all paternal kindness, and command you in the name of the Lord to do freely and at once that which in justice you are bound to do." The Venetians were obstinate but in the end Julius was victorious and the banner of the Papal States was unfurled again over the coveted places. Meanwhile the decline of Caesar Borgia was startlingly rapid and the man who had been so flamboyantly master of all Italy soon found himself without friends or troops. Julius placed him under a form of arrest and then he was released but only to be imprisoned again. After a captivity of two years he escaped and a few months later was killed whilst fighting with the army of his French brother-in-law.

The intrepid and impatient Pope would allow nothing to stand in the way of his plans and he marched with his troops and led them to victory at Orvieto and Perugia and Urbino. Other times the fortunes of war would turn but he was no poltroon and to the despair of less hardy members of his suite he would remain with the warriors, sharing their dangers and discomforts and inspiring them with example. To fit his policies he made and discarded allies as quickly as he made decisions and so the French were invited to assist him vanquish the Venetians and in turn, when the French became too demanding, he enlisted the support of other nations including the Venetians, to drive the French back to France. Before his election he had promised the cardinals that they should have some rights of consultation but any projected opposition from this body was made ineffectual by the creation at various times of twenty-seven new cardinals. A few discontented wearers of the Red Hat were induced by two irate monarchs, Louis XII of France and the Emperor Maximilian, to a foolish rebellion. Both rulers, with designs of their own upon Italy, were alarmed at the Pope's attempts at independence and at their instigation the renegade cardinals convoked a Council at Pisa. The scheme was a pitiful failure. A small number of churchmen did finally assemble but the townspeople were so hostile that the pseudo-Council was forced to adjourn and continue its futile mummery at another place. The world was weary of this brand of schism and the activities of the rebels never achieved importance save as a temporary annoyance to the Pope. It might have been otherwise if the French had gained the final victory and indeed for a gloomy time it appeared they would. A series of brilliant successes were achieved by the soldiers of Louis, aided by those of the Emperor, and there was strong likelihood that Rome would be sacked. Further gloom came when the strain imposed upon the overworked Pope had the expected result and he was stricken by an illness so grievous that the physicians pronounced his recovery impossible. Arrangements were made for his funeral and a panic descended upon the city when the news was known. "Never," wrote the Venetian Ambassador, "has there been such a clang of arms round the death-bed of any former Pope; never has the danger been greater than it is now. May God help us!"

To the amazement of all and to the dismay of his enemies the Pope recovered and quickly restored order to Rome with an iron hand. He was not yet discouraged and with typical determination he set out to win even at this apparently hopeless stage. And win he did for by extraordinary diplomatic skill he succeeded in inducing Maximilian to withdraw his support and separate his troops from the French army. Furthermore the Emperor, suddenly alarmed at the prospect of a French-controlled Italy, permitted Swiss soldiers to pass through his dominions. The Swiss had come in answer to the Pope's pleas and it was they who decisively routed the French. A wild joy prevailed in Rome and thunderous adulation was heard when Julius returned to the Vatican. "Never," reported the observant Venetian envoy, "was any Emperor or victorious general so honored on his entry into Rome as the Pope has been today."

No details seemed to miss the attention of this prodigious worker. The vexations and colossal labors of his martial campaigns and political efforts did not hinder a keen interest in the establishment of the bishoprics in the New World; a legate from an important court, a soldier with news from the army, a missionary returned from a remote place, all alike received his rapt interest. Laws and statutes were examined with meticulous care and the machinery of civil law was made less cumbersome. Roads and bridges were built or repaired throughout the Papal States and long needed measures were taken to protect the farmers and their crops from the avarice of the overlords and from the depredations of their soldiery. No matter how great the burden of his anxieties the Pope somehow in the interest of his subjects found the time to write such letters as he wrote to one of his governors: "A citizen of Bertinoro has complained to the Pope that the Castellan has taken wood from him and injured him in other ways. Let the Castellan and his abettors be punished without fail and take care that no harm comes to the complainant."

Nor did the realm of art escape the interest of the amazing man. Surpassed even were the examples of predecessors in this respect and his intense antipathy to all things connected with the Borgia name did not prevent him from continuing with projects commenced in Alexander's reign. Bramanti, the architect, was given the task of rebuilding St. Peter's basilica into a structure vast and magnificent and it was the beginning of the great edifice which stands today. Michelangelo was called to Rome and the world is aware of the splendid results produced by that inspired summons. The genius of Rafael and the prowess of his gifted colleagues flowered under the warmth of papal encouragement and subsidy. Julius had a rare sympathy for the artistic mind and he understood well, as he put it, "the humors of such men of genius." When Michelangelo had rushed from Rome in a rage swearing that he would leave his work uncompleted an astonished and shocked official in Florence told him, "You have behaved towards the Pope in a way that the King of France himself would not have ventured upon. There must be an end of this. We are not going to be dragged into a war, and risk the whole state for you. Go back to Rome." The obstinate artist took his time but finally returned and when he appeared before Julius a prelate thought to save him from the expected wrath by pleading, "Your Holiness should not be so hard on this fault of Michelangelo; he is a man who has never been taught good manners, these artists do not know how to behave, they understand nothing but their art." The Pope turned the full force of his anger upon the unfortunate cleric. "You venture," he roared, "to say to this man things I should not have dreamt of saying. It is you who have not manners. Get out of my sight, you miserable, ignorant clown." From this time on there were no great differences between the Pope and the great man of art, although there were many noisy arguments. Court attendants would marvel at the sight of their formidable master abandoning all dignity and clambering up the dusty scaffolding which festooned the Sistine Chapel. A grimy hand to help him would be extended by the busy genius, sometimes irritated at being interrupted, and there the two would discuss the details and progress of the superb frescoes.

After Julius had secured temporal strength and independence and brought order and prosperity to the States of the Church his restless mind became occupied with the gigantic problem of sorely needed Church reform. He had already issued a pungent bull against simony in papal elections and now he assembled in Rome, after a year of careful preparation, a heavily attended Council of the Church. By this time the exhausted and aged pontiff was nearing his end but what he wished to say was read by a cardinal. The congregated dignitaries of all nations were told frankly the critical time had come when drastic measures had to be taken to correct the dreadful state of Church discipline. Would that he had lived longer to employ the full force of his vigor on this project. But his time was run and he was soon on his death-bed. Even there the great, if imperfect Pope, weakened though he was, behaved as his usual self, calmly giving the necessary instructions for his funeral, uttering measured words of farewell to his weeping friends, and arranging prayers to be said for his soul. He then died and "Rome felt that the soul which had passed from her had been of royal mould," recorded a friend. "I have lived forty years in this city, but never yet have I seen such a vast throng at the funeral of any former Pope. The guards were overpowered by the crowds insisting on kissing the dead man's feet. Weeping they prayed for his soul, calling him a true Pope and Vicar of Christ, a pillar of justice, a zealous promoter of the Apostolic Church, an enemy and queller of tyrants."

The Bull against simony was read aloud at the next conclave and such elaborate precautions were taken to prevent the odious practice that no suspicion of this nature can darken the memory of the next pope, the thirty-eight year old Giovanni de Medici who became LEO X. Certainly a factor to contribute heavily to his winning the majority of the votes was his membership in the powerful Florentine family: although it is true that his life was without scandal and it is also true that to fit him for high ecclesiastical rank he had received a special and comprehensive education from a carefully selected group of distinguished tutors. He was the son of one of the most strong and colourful figures of the Renaissance, Lorenzo de Medici, the ruler of Florence who was called the Magnificent. At thirteen years of age he had been given the dignity of the cardinalate although up to the time of his elevation to the papacy the extent of his clerical progress was a deacon's orders. After receiving the acclaim of the conclave he was ordained priest, consecrated bishop two days later, and then solemnly and with splendor given the tiara on the steps of the now half demolished Basilica of St. Peter.

The debris of the broken structure was a strangely fitting background for his coronation because the rebuilding of this edifice provided the incident which in this reign was to bring unparalleled sorrow and disaster to the Catholic Church. To provide the funds for the erection of the new St. Peter's, indulgences were unfortunately offered for money and in Germany an outraged Augustinian friar protested vigorously by writing a series of ninety-five theses against such abuses and nailing his manuscript to the door of the castle church at Wittenberg. The name of the friar was Martin Luther, the fateful day was the

LEOX

Leo X (1513-1521)

31st of October 1517, and the historic and so tragically sym-
bolic wielding of hammer against church door occurred in the
fifth year of Leo's reign. And it was an event which, while
receiving instantaneous attention throughout Germany, failed
to cause alarm or immediate interest in Rome.

The storm had broken, the most critical time in the long
history of the Church had arrived, and there was nought but
apathy on the part of the Pope. Absorbed in the unsavory intrica-
cies of his politics and pleasures, Leo failed to recognize the
importance of Luther's initial deed and there can be little excuse
for his catastrophic lethargy. There was no lack of warning. For
years past the clamor for reform within the Church had been
steadily increasing throughout Europe and matching this spirit
in growth and volume was contempt for ecclesiastical authority.
At the council which his predecessor had inaugurated and which
had continued on into his own reign, lengthy and complicated
resolutions had been proposed and accepted; but, as a layman
who attended the Council complained, "We have heard a great
deal about the making of laws, but very little about their observance." In many ways the new Pope seemed to resemble Alexander VI rather than Julius. His family was enriched and given
favours whenever possible and his court, thronged by artists and
writers and frivolous noblemen, was that of a gay and youthful
prince rather than that of the Bishop of Rome. The delights of
the banqueting table, the amusements of dramatic pageants, the
mummery of buffoons, the thrill of the hunting field, all these
things occupied the time and interest of the man who was pope
when Luther began his attack and who, endowed with the tastes
and principles of his family, wove a mesh of political activities
which kept him continuously embroiled with the various rulers
of Europe.

Deceit and treachery were the habitual characteristics of this
dangerous game as played by him and consequently when he
tried to raise funds for the prosecution of a new crusade, the
response from the nations was mostly a cynical indifference. A
Florentine statesman who frequently served and advised him

was Niccolo Machiavelli whose name has endured as a synonym for subterfuge and intrigue of the basest type. So it was not unnatural that antipathy to Rome fattened upon the lavish duplicity which was presented as papal diplomacy. The unreal title of Emperor was still desired by kings and this vanity the Pope used freely in his schemes, openly supporting one aspirant for the historic but illusory honor while at the same time his legates would be whispering encouragement to another deluded prince. The intention behind Leo's ceaseless and complicated negotiations was to keep Spain and France and Germany from further encroachments in Italy. Once in his reign the French did attempt an invasion but they were driven back before the fury of the Swiss mercenaries. In the peace which followed it was agreed that the unsuccessful schism which had begun under French auspices at Pisa should now be abandoned and that, while the French monarch should possess the right of nomination in regard to benefices, canonical investiture could only be given by the pope.

Despite the resolutions of the recent Council clerical abuses continued and increased, and in Rome when thirty-one cardinals were made at one creation it was well known that although a few new wearers of the purple were indeed worthy men, the majority of their colleagues had openly purchased the honor. One of these was Ferdinando Ponzetti who had commenced life as a physician and who now was able to pay 30,000 ducats for his new rank. At least six wearers of the Red Hat certainly paid nothing, for this number of the Pope's relatives were so honored, and while his brother Giuliano paraded Rome with the title of Captain General of the Church, still another kinsman ruled Florence as temporal overlord. There was great discontent amongst certain of the younger cardinals who had voted for the Pope at the conclave and who felt that they had not been rewarded suitably. One of these unhappy prelates, the Cardinal Petrucci, brooding over supposed injustices, instigated a plot to murder the Pope and the condition and standard of the Sacred College at this time is shown by the dismal fact that four other of its members, including the Dean, gave their support to the proposed crime. A conscienceless physician was bribed to commit the murder while attending the pontiff but fortunately for the latter, who trusted few men, a letter was intercepted and the evil scheme revealed. Swift punishment came to the physician and to Petrucci. Both were executed along with a few accomplices, but the other guilty cardinals, perhaps because of the Pope's charity or, more probably, because of the influence of powerful friends, were neither hung nor strangled but merely fined heavily, deprived of their electoral privileges, and banished from the city.

Such conditions brought strong discontent everywhere and particularly in Germany where Luther found willing audiences, not because of the soundness of his theology, but because of the appalling abuses permitted and practised by those whom he attacked. The traffic in benefices, the ceaseless appeals from Rome for money, and the harsh fact that in Germany most of the great bishoprics were possessed by scions of royalty and nobility, overshadowed the efforts of those who were desperately working for reform from within the Church. Such men there were but, as is common, virtues and good deeds were submerged beneath the vices and wrongdoings of the spectacularly wicked; and despite the many examples of sincere vocations, the lamentable state of Church discipline was a fact acknowledged and deplored on all sides. More and more the cupidity of the Roman court was being resented and a steadily increasing spirit of nationalism was adding force to this feeling. "From his own dominion," went the words of a widely circulated pamphlet, "streams of wealth flow in to the Pope as to no other Christian prince; yet we have to pay for palliums, and send asses laden with gold to Rome, and exchange gold for corn, and rest content with blood-lettings —pardon me, I mean with indulgences! Woe to this monster of avarice which is never satisfied! The craftiness of the Florentine discovers a thousand devices, each one more execrable than the last. Let German freedom be mindful not to become tributary, and not to pay tithes." Such sentiments as these were echoed vigorously by the type of Humanists, extreme and violently anti-Christian, who at this time possessed great influence in the German universities. Their brand of philosophy frankly glorified paganism and of course viewed all activities of the Church with repugnance and contempt. "The Pope is a bandit," wrote one of the leaders of this movement, "and the Church is his army."

About this time a youthful but powerful prince in Holy Orders, the Elector Albert of Brandenburg, already Archbishop of Magdeburg and Administrator of the See of Halberstadt, was made Archbishop of Mayence. He wished to retain his former sees and after much negotiation with the papal representative he was allowed to do so but on the condition he pay a fee of fourteen thousand ducats besides a special tax of ten thousand of the same coin. It was a shameful transaction but not even yet complete. A banker, Jacob Fugger, advanced the over-beneficed prince the ready gold and then to enable settlement of the banker's loan, Albert was given the privilege of proclaiming the grant of St. Peter's Indulgence through his territories on the terms that he should share equally with Rome all funds so collected.

In an age when bribery and simony were to be found in high places, it is not surprising that the granting of indulgences should sometimes be tainted by mercenary consideration although the doctrine of the Church leaves no doubt as to the invalidity of any accepted with the knowledge of such an arrangement. The term Indulgence is derived from the Latin *indulgere* meaning *to be kind* and it is an excellent explanation for, as defined by the Church in the XIII century, an indulgence is the remission of temporal punishment due to sin after guilt has been forgiven. It is Catholic teaching that even after the guilt of a sin has been forgiven, there may still remain due to the justice of God some measure of punishment (called temporal to distinguish it from the eternal punishment of sin not forgiven because not repented). It is with this temporal punishment, and not with the sin or its guilt, that the Indulgence is concerned. To earn such a favor the suppliant must, in addition to possessing the habitual intention, be in that state of grace which is achieved by true repentance and sincere confession and by the performance of good works such as prayer and charitable undertakings. There are partial indulgences which remit, as the name implies, only in part and there are plenary indulgences which, given by the Pope alone, cancel all temporal punishment due to sin. There are indulgences for the living and those for the dead which actually, because departed souls are of course beyond the Church's jurisdiction, are nothing more than solemn requests for the divine mercy. An indulgence had been proclaimed in the reign of Pope Julius for those who, in addition to fulfilling the usual requirements of penance and contrition, should contribute to the rebuilding of St. Peter's. Because of the eager and none too scrupulous manner in which the monies were gathered and because of the intense and mounting anti-Roman feeling already strong in Germany, there were grave and spirited protests from that country when Leo X, upon becoming Pope, not only renewed the same indulgence but thought by means of it to gather even greater sums for his treasury.

The warnings were unheeded and after prolonged bickering the disgraceful arrangement with Albert of Mayence was concluded. The next step towards disaster came when the latter placed the responsibility of bringing the fateful Indulgence to the people in the hands of John Tetzel, a Dominican orator who had considerable experience in such enterprises and who was well known for his skill in gathering the lucre. It was a reputation not at all popular and even one of his brother Dominicans wrote angrily of him that he "devised unheard-of means of making money. He was far too liberal in conferring offices; he put up far too many public crosses in towns and villages, which causes scandal and breeds complaints among the people." This man now embarked upon the money raising campaign, for that is what it frankly was, with more zeal than doctrinal authority; for while he did not err in naming the requirements necessary to obtain indulgences for the living, he did make the mistake of declaring those for the dead could *be gained by money alone.* His statement was clearly contrary to the doctrines of the

Church and the leading theologian of the time, the Cardinal Cajetan, was vehemently positive on the subject of such erroneous teachings. "Preachers speak in the name of the Church," said he, "only so long as they proclaim the doctrine of Christ and His Church; but if, for purposes of their own, they teach that about which they know nothing, and which is only their own imagination they must not be accepted as mouth pieces of the Church. No one must be surprised if such as these fall into error."

Tetzel's route took him to Wittenberg where the district vicar and university lecturer, a thirty-four year old Augustinian priest named Martin Luther, impatiently awaited him with strong opinions and an able pen. Luther had once made a journey to Rome and although at that time he displayed no symptoms of displeasure he later claimed he had been disillusioned and angered at what he had seen. By nature he was deeply impressionable as well as self confident and strong willed. His adoption of the clerical state had not been the result of long and careful consideration but was because the sudden death of a close friend who had been destined for the priesthood convinced him he should take his place. This was done against the earnest pleas of his father, for the young Luther had studied for the law, a process involving hardship and sacrifice both to him and his family who were of humble circumstance. After his reception into monastic life the approval of his superiors encouraged his studies and conduct, and at the age of twenty-five he had become a professor at the new university of Wittenberg. Any measure of success is apt to be a hazard to the restraints of discipline and the academic triumphs of the young monk proved a dangerous stimulant to a proud and stubborn nature. In many ways he resembled Savonarola and even his vocabulary was marked by a similar bitter violence. "Knaves, dolts, pigs, asses, infernal blasphemers" were terms he hurled at his opponents with the harsh emphasis akin to that which had stirred the congregations of Florence. But where the Italian had been content to attack the *person* of a Pope and had not questioned the authority of the Church, the German was to take this fatal step and make denial and offer challenge to orthodox dogma. His "Ninety-five Theses" were nailed to the church door and soon all Germany rocked with the altercation which followed.

Tetzel, unlike many other churchmen, immediately realized the dangers underlying Luther's attack, and he countered with a carefully prepared work in which he emphasized that the affair was not a matter of indulgences alone but because of it "many will be led to despise the authority and supremacy of the Pope and the Holy Roman See." His apprehension did not disturb the equanimity of the Curia or bring any vigorous action from the hierarchy. Luther sent a copy of his theses to the Metropolitan who on the advice of his counsellors referred the matter to Rome with an accompanying letter which expressed the hope "that His Holiness would grasp the situation so as to meet the error at once, as occasion offers and as the exigency requires and not lay the responsibility on us."

The apparatus of correction and discipline moved slowly and ineffectually while the new movement, as yet not organized or recognized as such, spread with the rapidity of a fierce and sudden conflagration. The dislike held for Rome and the political and social state of Germany all made for the cause of Luther. The nobles coveted the properties of the Church. The intellectuals, dominated and excited by the Humanist movement, were delighted at an opportunity to destroy the conventional religion. And the peasantry, told of Roman iniquities in the most inflammatory terms, were given the chimerical hope that the new order would better their miserable lot. In the year following the gesture at Wittenberg, the Pope instructed the Vicar General of the Augustinians to silence the unruly monk; but Luther disregarded such measures and anticipating excommunication boldly preached that the sentence would be futile because "the real communion of the Church was invisible and that no one could be affected by it." A few months later the Emperor Maximilian, now thoroughly alarmed by the numbers and attitude of the priest's adherents, wrote to the Pope and declared serious measures should be immediately taken to quell him. Canonical processes commenced and Luther was summoned to Rome; but the only answer was the publication of a series of new pamphlets filled with heresy.

A Legate, the gentle and learned Cardinal Cajetan, went to Germany where after some difficulty Luther consented to meet him but would give no retractation. At intervals there were further negotiations with other emissaries and there were public debates with such skilled theologians as Johann Eck defending orthodoxy. Sometimes it seemed reconciliation might be possible, for often it was Luther's mood that he would not break with Rome and at these times he would profess obedience to the Pope. But never would he make retractation or express sorrow for his past actions; and as his words grew fiercer the hope became irretrievably lost and there remained only one road for his proud and stubborn nature to follow. Irrevocably he was committed to rebellion and with the full and powerful influence of the Humanists strong upon him politics gradually crowded theology to a lesser position in his sermons. Liberty and patriotism are the unfailing slogan of the revolutionary and to these inflammatory words was now added the name of the Gospel. *"Liberty! Fatherland! Gospel!"* The battlecry was made. "I have cast the die," he boasted, "I now despise the rage of the Romans as much as I do their favor. I will not reconcile myself to them for all eternity . . . If a thief is punished by a halter, a murderer by the sword, and a heretic by fire, why should not we, with all our weapons attack these teachers of corruption, these Popes, Cardinals, and all the rabble of the Roman Sodom, and wash our hands in their blood."

Thirty-two months after the incident at Wittenberg a Bull was issued by Leo condemning forty-one propositions extracted from the writings of Luther and excommunicating him unless he retracted within sixty days. But by now the Friar was firmly entrenched in Germany and had gained the protection of a powerful prince, the Elector of Saxony. Scornfully the claims of discipline were dismissed and with ceremony and to the cheers of the populace he publicly burned the Bull and told the students of Wittenberg that "It is now full time the Pope himself is burned. My meaning is that the Papal chair, its false teachings, and its abominations, should be given to the flames." The parchment burned brightly and the crowd roared lusty approval; and in the lurid glow of the noisy scene Protestantism thus became a fact although it was not until a decade later that the name came into use. This was at the Diet of Speyer where it was resolved that the new religion was established but that its adherents must not interfere with or hinder Catholic worship. The followers of Luther protested vigorously at the tolerant decree and hence the term, Protestant.

Leo died after a reign of eight years and before him the Emperor Maximilian had gone also. He was succeeded by his grandson, Charles of Spain. Henry VIII of England had been a candidate for the Imperial honor and at the long conclave which proceeded the election of the next Pope the name of Henry's counsellor, the great Cardinal Wolsey, received consideration. However, the Medici family was resolved that a cousin of Leo should secure the ballots and possibly to avert the evils of deadlock an unexpected name was finally announced, that of the Cardinal Adrian Dedel who in keeping his own name as Pope ADRIAN VI was to break a two hundred year old tradition. The fact that he possessed the friendship and respect of the new Emperor must have influenced the decision of the cardinals but it was a decision certainly not sought by the man whom it favored. He had not attended the conclave and it was with reluctance that he embarked upon the journey from Spain to accept the responsibilities of the tiara. Born at Utrecht in Holland he was the son of a shipwright and by ability and diligence had risen to the position of tutor to the young Charles who was impressed by his talents and his honesty and who never had reason to change the opinion. Successive and successful stages of advancement had eventually brought the Netherlander to the high position of Viceroy in Spain and now had come the Papacy. It was eight months before he was crowned in Rome and it was with coldness that the people of the City greeted him for he was in every way utterly unlike the great prince prelates to whom they were accustomed. Pomp he detested, flattery too, and those noisy and undisciplined crowds of artists and poets and merchants who had fattened on the generosity of former reigns quickly discovered that papal patronage had ceased to be. No lavish court or costly pageants or feasts and games or chances for easy or dubious riches could be expected during the time of this scrupulous northerner who earnestly desired reform and a united and tranquil Christendom. These were his aims, together with plans for a crusade against the Turks who had already won the island of Rhodes, but the obstacles he had inherited seemed insurmountable; he was too late and perhaps it was this realization that hastened his end. He died less than two years after his election.

The Romans received a pope more suited to their taste in the person of his successor for this time the plans of the Medici were triumphant. Giulio de Medici, cousin of Leo X, took his place as CLEMENT VII. It was not an easy victory, for the Emperor, the Kings of France and England, the Italian factions, all had their candidates and the conclave lasted fifty days. The struggle for ballots was most lively and for a while it again seemed as though the Englishman, Wolsey, might win; but the supporters of the Medici redoubled their efforts and enlarged their promises and so won the majority necessary for their candidate.

Unfortunately he was in no way equal to the responsibilities and burdens of the great position. He was a cultured and handsome man of fifty-six and was possessed of a grace of manner and ability expected of his birth and breeding. But these values were not sufficient to cope with the complex problems, both temporal and spiritual, which now confronted the papacy and disturbed the world. From the beginning misfortune attended his venturings in the intricate and dubious intrigues which constituted the diplomacy of his day. The Emperor

Clement VII (1523-1534)

Charles V and King Francis I of France were at war and the Pope adopted a faltering policy of pseudo-neutrality which under the existing circumstances was neither possible nor sincere and which quickly lost him the respect of both princes. Francis repelled a German invasion on his own soil and then marched to enforce his claims in Italy; but at Pavia the Imperial troops engaged again and this time the French were beaten and their monarch taken prisoner. Hopes for a united Christendom had been woefully shattered when, before this battle, the French king, made desperate by impending defeat, had tried unsuccessfully to make an alliance with the Turks. As a prisoner, he concluded a treaty of surrender with Charles but the terms were harsh and secretly he plotted to form a new combine. In an effort to escape Teutonic dominance the Milanese and Venetians were susceptible to the arguments of this would-be ally of the Turk and so unfortunately was the Pope.

When the Emperor learned of the covert negotiations his rage was kindled and soon his troops, a wild and long unpaid army of German and Spanish mercenaries, were unleashed upon the Papal States. Rome was defended with spirit and the commander of the attacking forces was killed but a breach was made in the walls and the city, so rich a prize, was open to a horde of ruffians savagely hungry for loot. All vestiges of discipline disappeared during orgies of killing, burning, sacrilege, and rape which followed. For centuries the sack of Rome had been the terror of those who feared the Turk. It was now a horrible fact but the despoilers of the churches and defilers of the altars did not carry the insignia of Islam. They called themselves Christians and their absent master proudly flaunted Charlemagne's grandiose title, Emperor of the Holy Roman Empire. The Pope and seven of his cardinals fled to a fortress at Orvieto and there remained for many long months; and when he did return to the city it was a ruined and broken landscape which saddened his eye and spirit. He was forced to a peace with Charles and on Imperial terms. Thus papal dignity was sacrificed when the Pope obeyed and travelled to Bologna where with the pomp of ancient ceremony he presided at the Imperial coronation. Another journey made at royal behest and destined to bear great and grave consequences was his voyage to France when his niece married the Duke of Orleans. It was an opportunity not neglected for the French monarch to discuss many momentous matters, including the historic demand from across the channel that the marriage of Henry VIII and his Queen be dissolved. Francis made plea for the English king and even hinted of the danger to the papacy of incurring a united French and English enmity. The Pope listened and was aware of the peril but he also remembered that the unwanted wife was the niece of the Emperor Charles.

Henry had married Catherine of Aragon, the young widow of his sickly elder brother, after special permission had been granted by Rome on the grounds that the first marriage had never been consummated. Five children had been born of this union between Spanish Princess and English King but only one survived, Mary, later to be Queen. That the popular and gifted Henry had no sympathy for Luther is a well known story for with a great flourish he banned the Reformer's books from England and composed, with the aid of his divines, the famous treatise in Latin, *A Defence of the Seven Sacraments against Martin Luther*. In return he received violent abuse from the monk but also the gratitude of the Pope in the form of a title, *Defender of the Faith*, an honor which was not relinquished for Henry never considered any deed of his to be Protestant in act or intent. Seventeen years he had lived with Catherine before he developed scruples regarding the validity of their marriage and these stirrings were not the product of a stern conscience or sincere canonical doubt but were born of an illicit if not obscure love affair. It would seem that all any man could desire on earth had been Henry's inheritance for not only did the favor of exalted birth give him rank and possessions but he was also superbly endowed in physique and mind. It was natural he should receive vast measure of adulation and flattery and perhaps it was equally natural he should fall prey to such subtle poisons. Maturity usually remedies the weaknesses of adolescence with that kind of sagacity which is born of time and pain, but on those occasions when the circumstances of life are made too easy the passing of years merely serves to ripen the young fruit to rot.

So it was with Henry, whose intelligence and body were subjected to temptation in numerous and elaborate forms of enticement and cunning. Self-discipline faded away and the noble ideals of youth became dim and distorted before the capricious demands of gluttony and sensual appetite. One of his mistresses had been Mary Boleyn and it was her sister Anne, who inflamed his fickle passion and distorted his judgment to such a degree that he became determined she should be his Queen. Eventually he made her so, but not with the sanction of the Pope and this fact stands out, cold and clear, from the morass of intrigue and procrastination which accompanied the royal folly. For six years the headstrong monarch tried by all means possible to win the necessary permission and the complicated negotiations which took place leave little credit to either side. Proceedings dragged on and papal and royal emissaries travelled busily to and fro, laden with the appurtenances of mystery and plot. Hopes were falsely kindled and threats rashly made. Universities were bribed to give opinions in favor of the divorce and crowds of servile courtiers masquerading as prelates eagerly and without shame prostituted their faith and their learning to assure the enamoured monarch that his conduct was correct. Counsellors of this mould even suggested that a solution of the problem would be for the Pope to grant a special dispensation allowing Henry to possess *two* wives! When the infatuated prince finally made Anne a Marchioness and took her to France where she was presented as the future Queen of England the Pope was forced to action. He threatened excommunication to both if they did not separate. The new Marchioness was pregnant but before her child was born a marriage ceremony was performed and the crown was placed atop her comely head amidst scenes of formal splendour.

The time, long dreaded by the timid and procrastinating Pope, had arrived and to his honour he remained firm and true to dignity and responsibility. The loss of allegiance to papal authority in Europe had been devastating and now England's loyalty could be kept at the cost of one divorce. Temptation must have been great but with clarity the final decision was pronounced in Rome; Catherine was the lawful wife of the English King. Persistent and contemptible attempts had been made upon the unfortunate woman by her deluded husband to have her resign her rights, but no argument or humiliation could wring from her an admission that the long years of her married life had been merely a term of concubinage and that their daughter, Mary, was illegitimate.

King and Queen met before the two papal legates, Wolsey and Campeggio, and Catherine spoke with the calm dignity of a faithful wife and good mother. "I take God and all the world to witness that I have been to you a true, humble, and obedient wife, ever comportable to your will and touch . . ." Only once did she pause and then her voice became lower. "This twenty years or more I have been your true wife, and by me ye have had divers children, although it hath pleased God to call them from this world . . . And when he had me at the first, I take God to be my judge, I was a true maid, without touch of man. And whether this be true or no, I put it to your conscience." Pressure was exerted to have her enter a convent and take vows but despite her great piety the cloisters were also rejected. Anne might occupy the royal bed but Catherine knew she was wife and Queen and no act of Henry could change the fact. This was the attitude firmly maintained to her death when with superb charity she wrote to her "Dear husband and King" and gave him her forgiveness. "For the rest, I commend unto you our daughter Mary, beseeching you to be a good father unto her, as I have heretofore desired. I entreat you also, on behalf of my maids, to give them marriage portions, which is not much, they being but three. For all my other servants I solicit the wages due them and a year more, lest they be improvided for.

Lastly, I make this vow, that my eyes desire you above all things."

Because of the failure of the divorce proceedings in Rome the mighty Wolsey lost the favor of his master and after a rapid series of degradations was charged with High Treason. A natural death intervened to save him from a shameful end and before he expired he uttered the pathetic words which were long to be remembered. "If I had served God as diligently as I have done my King, He would not now have given me over in my grey hairs." With the aid of evil Thomas Cromwell, master architect of terror, Henry made himself supreme head of the Church of England and with bloody prodigality the block and the gallows were invoked against the many who would not admit of this presumption. England's greatest Chancellor, the scholar who held the esteem of all Europe, joined the march to the scaffold. "I die," Thomas More said, "the King's good servant, but God's first." Monasteries were suppressed, churches and shrines robbed, yet the outward forms of religion were not changed in Henry's time: his rejection of papal authority brought no sympathy or tolerance for Protestantism or its author.

It was different on the continent. The Scandinavian countries were fast adopting Lutheranism, and Switzerland was falling under the influence of a similar-minded and equally eloquent ex-priest, Zwingli. In France the harsh and melancholy doctrines of Calvin were being given attention and in Hungary the prayers of the faithful were disturbed by the dreary wail of muezzins, calling to Allah, for the Turks had become masters of that country and a triumphant Mohammedan army even possessed Vienna.

After eleven unhappy years as Pope, Clement died unexpectedly, leaving both his spiritual and temporal domains in chaotic condition. His unfortunate pontificate had witnessed the birth of the so-called Reformation; but it also cradled the stirrings of a real reformation within the Church for great forces and good men were at work with a sincerity and zeal and genius which could not be denied success. The Lateran Council had been warned that "men must be transformed by religion, not religion by men" and these words typified the new spirit. A unity of belief might have been lost but the faith that remained was to be the sturdier because of surviving the storms of doubt and oppression. Spontaneously the new mood invigorated both the secular clergy and the ancient Orders and also caused the formation of other groups of devoted men and women who were moved to unselfish service of God and mankind. There were the Capuchins, the Oratorians, the Theatines, the Barnabites, the Somaschi, the Lazarists, the Sisters of Charity, the Ursulines, and others. And the same year that Pope Clement died, an ex-soldier of noble Spanish birth, Don Inigo Lopes Ricalda y Loyola, better known to history as Ignatius of Loyola, banded together a small number of similar-minded friends and communicated to them his enthusiasm and plans. Thus, in Paris, was commenced the disciplined organization which from then on has ever been an important influence in the story of the Church. The Society of Jesus was on the march.

An astonishingly rapid election brought success and fulfillment to the plans and ambitions of Alexander Farneses, PAUL III, who had been a cardinal for forty years. He was sixty-six years old and was of an ancient Roman family which, in adherence to the custom, was now to be deluged with riches and honors. His sons and daughters—for these, true child of the Renaissance that he was, he possessed—were favored in every way possible and two of his nephews, aged fourteen and sixteen, were promptly made cardinals at the commencement of his reign. He had been a cardinal during the reign of Alexander VI and in some respects his life followed the Borgia pattern; yet he often was to display a majesty of purpose akin to that possessed by Julius II and at other times it would seem as though he were moved by the same high motives which had guided the austere Adrian. That he had enjoyed the favour of these popes, so varying in character, and of the Medici too, is proof enough of his skill in diplomacy, apropos of which an ambassador to his court complained that an annoying and typical trait of the Pope was a "scrupulous avoidance" of ever uttering a positive "Yes" or "No." Save for his extravagant nepotism he was an extremely cautious and sagacious man and he embarked upon a policy of wily neutrality between the ever clashing schemes of the French king and the Emperor. It was a difficult policy to maintain but for the first years of his pontificate it was to have a certain if uneasy degree of success. It was unforgivable that he should have bestowed the Red Hat upon his young relatives but most other cardinals of his creation were noted for their worthiness. The English bishop, John Fisher, languishing in prison and soon to lose his head on the block was thus honored and so too was another deserving Englishman, Reginald Pole, a cousin of Henry VIII, who was in Italy and so safe from the ire of his vindictive kinsman.

The menace of Turkish attack was seldom absent from the cares of Paul III. Rakish craft, their lateen sails emblazoned with the Crescent, their decks crammed with blood-hungry warriors, had become a terror to shipping in the Mediterranean until the Emperor, at the behest of the Pope and with money and galleys from the same source, stormed the piratical stronghold at Tunis and administered a thorough and salutary defeat. But when war, despite the urgent entreaties of the pontiff, broke out again between France and Spain and the Emperor's troops became occupied in that direction, Barbarossa, daring chief of the Mohammedan buccaneers, recommenced his depredations upon the Italian coast and it became the boast of the Turkish Sultan that his seraglio would be moved to Rome. There were signs of panic in the Eternal City at this news for the potentate's announcement had strong chances of realization; but by the exercise of great and desperate ingenuity Paul caused an armistice to be declared between the Emperor and the French monarch and together they joined him in the formation of a Holy League. The Venetians, who held a treaty with the Turks, were persuaded that such a pact was wrong and they too became partners in the new alliance, and thus Rome remained unscarred by the scimitar.

Notwithstanding his own weaknesses Paul was acutely aware of other and less tangible evils which were besieging the papacy and with acrimony the more worldly of his cardinals were told "they should set an example to others by reforming themselves." To introduce peace and authority into the babel of contemporary theological dispute and to muster a united strength against the onslaughts of the papacy's antagonists Paul III made careful plans for the convocation of a General Council, for he was of the opinion that the voice of a Council was needed to reaffirm and clarify ancient dogma and to endorse authority. The scheme was commendable and simple in thought but in actual execution fraught with difficulty and danger. His own temporal strength was negligible and he had no wish, and there was the danger, for any one sovereign or nation to exert influence upon the decision of so important a body under the guise of patronage or protection. Prejudice and patronage must be avoided and the judgments of the Fathers left unhindered. With all the genius of his diplomatic talent he fought desperately to have it so. The idea of the Council was received with enthusiasm, even by some of the Protestant princes, but as the Pope had anticipated there were many who saw the convention as an avenue for their own designs and innovations.

The support of the Emperor was necessary, indeed the approval of all Christians was desired, and unwearyingly the Pope toiled to gain the good will of all, and the interference of none. The Emperor was sincerely enthusiastic for he readily perceived that under such auspices the Empire might be strengthened; but the Pope, with wider horizons beckoning, regarded the Imperial zeal with apprehension and even despair and many conflicts arose between the two regarding the policies, the procedure, and even the location of the Council. Usually it was the patient pontiff who was victorious but not without the penalties of strife. Charles was of the opinion that ecclesiastical discipline should be the first concern of the meeting but the Pope held to his plan that questions appertaining to doctrine should be settled before the discussion of a workable policy of discipline.

After many vexations and delays the Council assembled at Trent, in the Austrian Tyrol, on the 13 December, 1545, the eleventh year of Paul's reign. Ten times it was to meet during the remaining four years of his life and it was not to be formally dissolved, although on several occasions it suffered interruptions and a change of scene, until 1563. The decisions made and decrees issued, defining Catholic doctrine, provided splendid support for the champions of the Counter Reformation. By this time the Reformation was rapidly flowering to full development but the Council of Trent was, by a program of practical reform and definition, able to restore vigor to orthodoxy and bring strength and hope to the faithful again. The storms of altercation following Luther's outburst, the long theological arguments, the many and confusing interpretations of the Gospels, the admitted need for clerical reform, had brought perplexity to many a simple priest and layman. But now all was to be made clear and the road illuminated. The dogmas of original sin, justification, the sacraments, were explained with exactitude and so too were many other subjects of attack and dispute such as the veneration of saints and the granting of indulgences. Errors in clerical conduct were not merely censured but were exhaustively examined and practical measures for removing abuses were promulgated and adopted. A system of reform was founded which could survive and indeed grow in strength. Precise in its condemnations, constructive in its suggestions, grand in its scope, the Council of Trent can rightfully be regarded as one of the great bulwarks of Catholicity. "Thus the Council," wrote the Protestant historian Ranke, "that had been so vehemently demanded, and so long evaded, that had been twice dissolved, had been shaken by so many political storms, and whose third convocation, even, had been beset with danger, closed amid the general harmony of the Catholic world . . . Henceforth Catholicism confronted the Protestant world in renovated collected vigor."

Paul III lived with all the gaudy and benevolent luxury of a Renaissance prince and Rome benefited in many ways from his generosity and his appreciation of the arts. New streets were built, churches restored, great bastions were erected, engineers worked diligently on new schemes of fortifications, and scholars toiled over the long catalogues of the Vatican library. Titian, like many a lesser colleague, was subsidized and the classic beauty of St. Peter's dome, superb symbol of the supreme authority, was raised by Michelangelo. Paul III had done well and should have died content but the fruits of his nepotism made his end miserable and unhappy. An ungrateful and predatory grandson, with clamor and with violence, was claiming the duchy of Parma as his personal property. "My sin is ever before me," grieved the dying Pope. "If they had not the mastery over me, then I should have been without great offence."

It took the cardinals ten weeks to select a successor, Giovanni Ciocchi del Monte, who took the name of JULIUS III. For a time, at this conclave, it seemed as though the votes would go to Reginald Pole but the conscientious Englishman refused to bargain or make promises and his moment passed. Later, when Mary became Queen, Pope Julius sent him to his native country as Legate and there he officiated as Archbishop of Canterbury, the last of his faith to take that ancient title. The new Pope was friendly with the Emperor, soon to be fighting the French again, but neither alliance with that forceful ruler nor the great responsibilities of his own position gave him the confidence or strength of purpose which had characterized the previous reign. When the Protestant allies of France invaded the Tyrol and caused an adjournment of the Council of Trent, resignation to circumstances was the attitude of the Pope. He seemed overwhelmed by the number and magnitude of his problems, and frankly abandoning all pretence of active policy he retired to the peace of his gardens. Fortunately such indolence was not reflected in the toiling body of the Church for this was the time of such men as the indefatigable Jesuit, Francis Xavier, who before embarking for hostile and unknown shores cheerfully told his fellow adventurers, "The greatest trials you have until now endured are small in comparison with those you will experience in Japan. Prepare yourself for difficulties, by setting aside all consideration for your own interests." And later the pen of the same brave man inscribed: "I am journeying, deprived of all human protection, to the island of Canton, in the hope that a friendly heathen will take me over to the continent of China."

The pontificate of Julius III lasted five years. The next Pope was MARCELLUS II of whom much was expected, for as a cardinal and as a priest Marcello Cervino had earned an enviable reputation. Immediately after his enthronement he enthusiastically turned to the subject of reform and one of his first acts was to prohibit any member of his family from coming to Rome. Luxury was banned from his household and the customary elaborate ceremonies of coronation were avoided. In every way the hopes of the pious were fulfilled in the person of this pontiff but unfortunately their jubilance was brief for he was of delicate health and his reign ended abruptly, to the sorrow of all, after a mere twenty-two days. The name of Reginald Pole was mentioned again at the following conclave but he was absent in England and the Spanish influence which favored him was not strong enough to achieve its purpose. Elected instead, and after considerable balloting, was the seventy-nine-year-old Giovanni Pietro Caraffa whose advanced age showed no traces of senility—but neither had it brought that mellowness of thought and judgment which usually comes with the years.

PAUL IV was a severe and bad tempered old man, somewhat eccentric in manner, who often times affected the simplicity of a monk but on other occasions could formidably play the despot. He was of the reform school and was a founder of the first congregation of Clerks Regular yet he was not exempt from the disease of nepotism and one of his first actions as Pope was to bestow the Red Hat upon the head of his undeserving nephew, Carlo Caraffa. His support went to the French in the war with Spain; and guided by his nephew this policy brought matters to such a deplorable state that it was found necessary to employ Protestant mercenaries from Germany to protect the papal provinces from the invading army of the Duke of Alva. Meanwhile the French were defeated elsewhere and the Pope was forced to sue for peace, a costly and humiliating process for one so proud. His reign was characterized by the unbending severities of the true martinet and the punishments which came to those who crossed his will or broke the laws were as heavy as they were prompt. Eventually rumors came to him of the base conduct of his nephew and for once the ties of blood were spurned and the ungrateful and unfit wearer of the purple was expelled from Rome. Paul IV was an ardent supporter of the Inquisition, which as a cardinal he had reorganized, and wide use of its dreaded powers was made during his term. Even the Cardinal Morone, a highly respected member of the Sacred College, became enmeshed in the web of terrible accusation and to prison he went on the grounds of heresy. "Even if my own father were a heretic," said this Pope, refusing a petition for clemency, "I would gather the wood to burn him."

Reginald Pole was another object of his pessimism and suspicion but Pole was in England and had the wisdom to keep away from Rome. Clergy of lesser rank looked nervously to their conduct when at one sweep a hundred vagrant monks were despatched to the galleys or to the dungeons. Mercy was a quality lacking in this stern old man and when he died, after being pope four years, the mobs rioted to show their pleasure and to hurl hatred upon his memory. Down toppled his statue to be broken and defiled and with similar demonstrations of insult and delight the gates of the prison of the Inquisition were swept open and the inmates released.

Nearly four months dragged by before the next conclave was concluded and devious and ugly were the intrigues which hindered the cardinals from making a quick decision. "It is not of the least consequence," wrote the obnoxious Cardinal-nephew of Paul IV, "who will be Pope, the only thing of importance is that he who is chosen should realize that he owes the dignity to the Caraffa. This house does not enjoy any favor with the Spanish or French kings, and everything therefore depends on securing the favor of the future Pope, as otherwise the ruin of the family is assured." Other Italian clans had similar ideas and in addition to their dark activities there were the schemes of the various ambassadors, all determined to secure the election of a Pope who would favor their particular national interests. In such an atmosphere the most extravagant promises were made and cunning plots formulated; the audacious Ambassador of Spain even went so far as to gain, by window or secret door, access to the quarters of cardinals, supposedly shut off from the world, and there in the dim night hours whisper his bribes and subtly phrased threats. Finally, out of the tangle of discussion, the name of the Cardinal Giovanni Angelo Medici was proclaimed and this despite the fact that but a short time previously he had disturbed the conclave by remarking during a conversation with another cardinal that, "as regards the Germans, we should have to summon a Council to see if some concessions could not be made to them with regard to the marriage of priests and Communion under both kinds." That the startling statement did not prevent him from becoming Pius IV is indicative of the understanding his colleagues had of an expansive nature which was tolerant and easy going to a fault.

In all ways he was unlike his dour predecessor and he was famous for his disregard of formality and ceremony, and the conduct of his private life was continually marked by homely incidents which endeared him to the public. He was a fat man and long appreciation of the pleasures of the table had brought the gout. Thinking to reduce his corpulence and nullify the encroachments of his sickness it became his habit to take long walks. These perambulations, much to the disgust of his court, were conducted at a rapid pace and for considerable distances. "Exercise," he affirmed, "maintains good health and keeps away illness, and I do not wish to die in bed." The traditional geniality which is ascribed to rotundity was indisputably his and the clouds of gloom and suspicion which had hung over Rome during the previous pontificate now disappeared. He displayed no ill-will to the arrogant nephews of Paul IV after his reception of the tiara, but their crimes were many and foul and their enemies, so powerful and determined for revenge that retribution was inevitable. A particularly horrible murder within the hated family began the forces of its destruction.

The Duke of Paliano, brother of the Cardinal Carlo Caraffa, believed his wife unfaithful, and governed by extravagant ideas of honor he ordered her unfortunate supposed paramour dragged before him and then with shouts of rage he plunged his dagger again and again into the bound body of the wretch until he was dead. The drama became more horrible when the wretched Duchess, pregnant and crying her innocence, was strangled by her own brother, the Count d'Alife. That the Cardinal Carlo Caraffa was a party, by knowledge and condonement, to the bloody wickedness could not be denied and with no alternative possible the Pope reluctantly set the processes of accusation and judgment in motion. "If only to secure order," he said, "I have no choice but to bring the haughty nephews of Paul IV to submission." A long list of charges was prepared, varying from murder and high treason to heresy, and brought to justice was the Cardinal Carlo, his brother the Duke of Paliano, the brother-in-law the Count d'Alife, and a younger relative, the Cardinal Alphonso Caraffa. After a long trial the latter was pardoned but the others, despite their rank, were given the supreme penalty. All three faced the executioner with dignity, and a letter to his son by the fierce Duke—who was comforted by the Jesuits during his last hours—is a missive to remember because of its faith and beauty: "This paper contains, I believe, the last words and advice I shall be able to address you in this life," he wrote. "I pray God that they may be such as a father should address his only son. . . . Flee from sin and have compassion on the misery of others; practice works of piety, and flee from idleness, and conversations and pursuits which are not fitting for you; take pains to acquire some knowledge of science and letters, for these are very necessary for a true nobleman, especially for one who has power and vassals, as well as to be able to enjoy the sweet fruits of the Holy Scriptures, which are so precious for both soul and body. If you savour such fruits, then you will despise the things of this sorrowful world, and find no small consolation in the present life. I wish you to show indomitable courage at my death, not behaving like a child, but as a reasonable man, and not listening to the promptings of the flesh, or to the love of your father, or to the talk of the world. For your consolation ponder well the fact that whatever happens is ordained by the decrees of the great God, Who rules the universe with infinite wisdom, and, as it appears to me, shows me great mercy by taking me hence in this manner, rather than in any other way, for which I always thank Him, as you also must do. May it only please Him to exchange this my life for that other, the false and deceitful for the true. Do not be troubled by whatever people may say or write; say to everyone: My father is dead, because God has shown him great grace, *and* I hope He has saved him, and granted him a better existence. Therewith I die, but you shall live, bear no one ill-will of my death."

Conciliatory measures were employed with the rulers of Europe by Pius IV, and ably representing him in many important conferences north of the Alps was the Cardinal Morone who had suffered imprisonment because of the delusions of the late pope. Nepotism was not absent from Rome for this Pope had his nephews too, but for once the custom brought glory instead of disgrace: one of these relatives was the Cardinal Charles Borromeo, a truly devout and talented character devoted to reform and good works who was, under the dispassionate scrutiny of a later generation, to be judged worthy of canonization. The goodness and ability of the young Cardinal was responsible for the resumption of the labors of the Council of Trent and in several sessions many important and historic decrees were formulated and in turn confirmed and strengthened by papal Bull. The influence of Cardinal Borromeo did not wane with the death of his uncle for happily the next pope, Pius V, a true and zealous churchman, was of a similar mind and purpose and the work of reform swept on. The new pope was the former Cardinal Michele Ghislieri. He was born of poor parents and had been a member of the Dominican Order since his early youth. As a friar he had taught and preached for twenty-eight years, then episcopal responsibilities had been given him and later had come the Red Hat and the stern duties of Inquisitor General under Paul IV. He had been well liked by that severe ruler and when he was given the supreme honor the people feared a return to the harsh discipline of the hated regime. There was, it is true, an immediate tightening of the laws, and justice was to move more swiftly than hitherto, but unlike his patron Pius V tempered strictness with mercy and understanding. He was determined Rome should be the model Capital of Christendom and a courtier, sighing for the riotous-ness of former days, complained that the entire city was taking on the air of a monastery. The courts were purged of bribery, the streets of prostitutes and thieves, and a ruthless war was made on corrupt officials and unjust taxes. The finances of the Papal States were subjected to critical and profound examination and many changes were made. When an enthusiastic official suggested a new scheme for bringing added revenues to the treasury, the Pope chided him and remarked that instead of amassing monies more thought should be given to collecting the allegiance of those nations which had broken away from the church. The papal army was reduced to a few companies, for he was averse to becoming embroiled in martial adventures; although his belief in the wide authority of the Holy See over the conduct of secular princes was unwavering.

This belief was responsible for the issuance of a Bull which excommunicated Elizabeth of England and released her subjects from their allegiance to her. The pronouncement was a mistake which only served to bring further resentment against Rome and misery to the English Catholics for the power of England was mounting, new triumphs were being won on and across the seas, and the Queen's name was tightly woven into the cloth of national honor and patriotism. A few years after the papal sen-tence sturdy seamen, Protestant and Catholic alike, cheered for their good Queen Bess and merry England when they turned their small craft to meet the Armada. The vast array of great ships was laden with the flower of Spanish chivalry and carried the papal benediction but was doomed to an utter and terrible destruction.

Ambition had not brought the tiara to Pius V and he had wept when informed of the decision of the cardinals. But once elected he worked at the great duties with unflagging energy and scrupulous honesty. It was fortunate that such a man should occupy the papacy so soon after the conclusion of the Council of Trent. The value of his administration to the decrees and decisions of the Council can be likened to the worth of a good cannon to the proper ammunition. Drastic changes were made in Rome. The Curia was reformed, the conduct of the cardinals examined and criticized, and stern measures were undertaken to make bishops reside in their sees. Such important works as the Catechism and the New Breviary and the New Missal were published, the value of seminaries was emphasized, and a vigilant eye was turned upon both the secular clergy and the Orders. One cardinal, an irresponsible creature who owed his Hat to the laxity of a previous reign, was confined in a monastery and placed under the conscientious care of Jesuit chaplains. Indeed no great fondness was held for the majority of the cardinals and once when the Pope was ill he was heard to remark that he was sorry death was approaching, not because he was afraid to face his Maker, but because he was leaving on earth a Sacred College filled with conniving and undeserving men. The acquisition of his high rank had brought no great change in the lowly circumstances of his family, most of whom were forbidden to enter Rome. "God has called me to be what I am, in order that I may serve the Church," he said, "and not that the Church might serve me." It is true that two nephews received his favor, if such a word can be applied to his austere patronage, but this was only because of his mistrust of the cardinals and the ceaseless intrigues kept in motion by the various ambassadors and faction leaders. In order to find a confidential secretary whose loyalty was beyond all doubt he turned to his family and thus his nephew Michele Bonelli who was also a Dominican became a cardinal. The Pope never quite forgave himself for this action and consequently made life miserable for his relative by a constant inquisitiveness as to his way of living and an equally constant criticism. The unfortunate prelate was seldom at ease and at any hour his larder, his table, his conduct, was liable to a surprise inspection from his uncle. His income was kept at a minimum, he was not allowed silver on his table, and he was even denied the consolation of his parents visiting him. His cousin, a soldier by profession, was made a Captain of the Papal Guard but from the beginning of his service he was in trouble with the Pope who expected his soldiery to live like monks. Finally the warrior, who had far different ideas, was arrested and hauled before the civil court where in the presence of his forbidding kinsman he heard that he was "to forfeit all his goods and revenues, and under pain of death to leave the Vatican within two days, the Borgo within three, and the Papal States within ten." It was a drastic sentence and nothing could induce the Pontiff to extend leniency.

Little escaped his stern eye, and the devotees of the bull fight learnt that "these spectacles, where bulls and wild beasts are baited in a circus or amphitheatre, are contrary to Christian mercy and charity, suitable to demons rather than men. We forbid all clerics, regular and secular, to be present. . . ." His dislike of war did not prevent him from sending ships and men to Malta where the Knights were besieged by the Turks and later his encouragement helped mould a Christian Alliance which was able to inflict a shattering and decisive defeat upon the Turkish fleet at Lepanto. Throughout his entire reign he suffered from a painful disease which was finally the cause of his death. Pain was seldom absent from his tortured body but he never complained. "Increase, O Lord, my pains," he once cried, "so long as Thou wilt increase my patience also." He was not the kind of man to court popularity and when he had been elected there had been little rejoicing. But when he died there were true tears and the streets of Rome were silent with respect. It was as he would have wished, and so passed Pius V, the last of the popes whose memory has been honored by canonization.

In less than two weeks his successor was named, the seventy-year-old Cardinal Ugo Buoncompagni, Pope GREGORY XIII, who as a youth had fully enjoyed Renaissance pleasures but who had with the progress of time turned to the sterner delights of duty and reform. As prelate and papal official he had served for many years with distinction and had won considerable renown as a jurist, but neither the course of righteousness nor the possession of judicial talent prevented him on becoming pope from lavishing favors upon two nephews and a son whom he frankly acknowledged. This son was made Governor of St. Angelo while his cousins were invested with the purple. Easy-going to a fault Gregory was inferior to his predecessor; nevertheless the good works begun in the earlier reign did not cease and they continued before an impetus steadily supplied by individual churchmen and the Orders. The great and main attack of Protestantism had been halted and a vigorous and purified Catholicism was on the increase. Gregory's chief accomplishments were in the field of education and no fewer than twenty-three new colleges opened their doors during his pontificate. Over two million Roman *scudi* were expended to help deserving but needy students and besides founding the English, German, Greek, and Maronite colleges in Rome the institution, later to be called the Gregorian College, which owed its existence to St. Ignatius was enlarged to accommodate scholars of all nations. Another inauguration to carry his name through the centuries was the calendar which supplanted the Julian calendar. Neither his relations with other sovereigns nor his temporal rule of the Papal States were blessed by good fortune and when he died after a reign of thirteen years there were difficult problems of government and diplomacy both within and without the papal boundaries to greet his successor, SIXTUS V.

The former Cardinal Felice Peretti, who as a boy had been a swineherd, was the son of a vineyard laborer and had entered the Franciscan Order in his early adolescence. In nature and bent he resembled his patrons Paul IV and Pius V rather than his immediate predecessor and from the beginning of his reign these stern traits were revealed. The brigandage and disorder which were disturbing the papal territories at the close of the former reign were stamped out by ruthless methods and by the end of his rule his temporal domain had become the most orderly in Europe and an empty treasury had become filled with gold. Imposition of new taxes accomplished this latter feat and it was not a way for him to win the cheers of either the nobles or the merchants; but he cared little for the applause of men and his only interest was his mission. The former swineherd was Pope and he was resolved to exercise without fear and with dignity the majesty and authority of his office in all spheres. In support of the Catholic League he excommunicated the King of Navarre, heir presumptive to the French throne, in order to prevent a Protestant from ruling a Catholic nation. It was not a popular decision in France and later the monarch, after becoming a Catholic, was as Henry IV, to make peace with another pope. Sixtus also supported Spain in that country's disastrous war with England, but despite the utmost pressure he would not endorse the Spanish King's designs upon France. Grandiose schemes were propounded by him for the complete overthrow of the Turkish Empire and he dreamed of joining the Red Sea with the Mediterranean and "thus restoring the commerce of the ancient world." Preservation of the historic beauty of Rome and additional architectural projects were tasks he assumed with enthusiasm and an ingenious system, both practical and ornamental, of nobler and wider avenues in the city was devised and commenced.

The important decree was issued in this reign which limited the membership of the Sacred College to a maximum number of seventy cardinals and these were ranked in three divisions, six bishops, fifty priests, and fourteen deacons. The rule was to stand and equalling it in importance was the bull *Immensa* issued by the same pope which systemized the centralized government of the Church by forming fifteen Congregations, each consisting of churchmen and officials of varying rank, to assume in specialized departments the burden of detailed administration. Thus, with no diminution of his authority, an immense amount of routine work was lifted from the person of the pope.

The five years in which Sixtus occupied the throne of St. Peter were crowded with wise and good works but there were some blemishes to mar the record—his severity and his nepotism. For he too succumbed to what by this time appeared to be a papal tradition and a fourteen year old relative was elevated to the cardinalate. There can be no justification for such an act; but the contemporary mind was neither surprised nor shocked, and as with former and later reigns the hateful practice was accepted by the majority of both clergy and people with that equanimity which is the due of precedent and tradition. After the death of Sixtus three worthy but ancient prelates in rapid succession and within sixteen months were elected to the papal throne. No grave mistake or scandal can assault their reputations but neither can any of the three be credited with the deeds that are born of exceptional leadership or great initiative. The same pope, Gregory XIII, had made them cardinals on the same day and they were all of an equal age, past seventy. The first to follow Sixtus was Giovanni Batista Castagna, URBAN VII, noted for his charities and diplomatic skill. He reigned thirteen days and then came Nicolo Sfondrato of Cremona who in honor of his patron took the name of GREGORY XIV. The policies of preceding pontificates remained unchanged during his term which did not last a year and then called was the Cardinal Giovanni Facchinetti who became INNOCENT IX. Within a few months he too was in his tomb and the Sacred College, after great discussion, decided that the Cardinal Ippolito Aldobrandini should be Pope. He took the name of CLEMENT VIII.

The choice was a bitter blow to Spanish hopes and indeed the far seeing policies of the new pontiff were to effect a tremendous change in the destiny of that country which was now at the peak of its glory. Clement "by peaceful means, little by little, without disturbance or excitement, but with all the more security," was to strengthen the independence of the papacy by effecting happier relations with France and this circumstance was one of the factors which halted the expansion of Spanish power and made way for the decline of a proud and great nation. During the preceding pontificates Spanish influence upon the diplomatic course of the papacy had gradually become so strong that when Clement took his throne he felt Rome was almost the vassal of Madrid. This meant that the enemies of Spain were automatically on ill terms with the Holy See and no great perception was needed by the pontiff to realize the danger of a permanent rupture with France, the most hated foe of Spain. Henry IV, master of France, had been excommunicated; but now, seeking the united allegiance of his subjects he was imploring to be readmitted to the communion of the Church. Was it the gesture of one who was alleged to have remarked "Paris is well worth a mass," or was the prince truly sincere in his repentance? It was a delicate problem for the Pope. If he were over-severe, schism would be assured and France surely would go the way of England; but if he were foolishly lenient then contempt for papal authority would grow everywhere. A constant clamor of both plea and threat came from the nations involved but the cautious and conscientious Pope trod the difficult and torturous path of negotiation with extraordinary diplomatic skill and never once was principle or scruple sacrificed. He well realized that independence of the Holy See demanded relief from the ever growing dominance of Spain and that relief was possible only with France active as a counter balance; yet the sentence of excommunication could not be lifted lightly, and often the French envoys were in despair. "Would to God," the Pope told an official, "that we could trust Henry. But what has he done to deserve absolution? . . . Is it enough that he now once makes the Sign of the Cross?"

At length repeated argument and evidence convinced him that the prince indeed was truly penitent and with a great and solemn ceremony, and much to the consternation of Spain, the dreaded sentence was lifted. "I have no words to praise the kindness of Your Holiness as it deserves," Henry wrote with gratitude. "My life henceforth shall have no other purpose than to glorify God by meritorious obedience. . . ." The extravagant promise was never to be completely fulfilled but an alliance had been made which brought advantages to both Pope and King. France remained a Catholic country and the papacy was no longer at the mercy of the pretentious dictates of Philip II of Spain who was an absolutist and harbored ambitions of functioning as a kind of Pope-Emperor. When the Duchy of Ferrara was left empty of a legitimate heir the Spanish king presented a candidate to contest the claims of the Pope; but supported by the new friendship of France, Clement was able to remain firm and in the end the Duchy was returned to the Papal States. In pursuance of the papal dream of a united and tranquil Christendom the Pope was able on several occasions to act as a peacemaker between the nations: products of his diplomacy were the *Peace of Vervins* between Spain and France and the *Treaty of Lyons* between the latter nation and Savoy.

In 1600, the eighth year of his reign, Pope Clement proclaimed a grand Jubilee in Rome. Over three million pilgrims responded to the invitation and their devotion and presence was gladdening evidence of the success which was attending Catholic revival. Throughout all Europe the Jesuits, the Franciscans, the Benedictines, the Dominicans, in fact all the Orders, old and new, were carrying the fight with example and zeal. "Thanks be to God," reported a nuncio from Vienna "the number of Catholics is on the increase." The same could be said of other places which were strong-holds of Protestantism. Because of men who patently had but one purpose, the salvation of souls, who were afraid of nothing on earth, and who indeed were prepared to welcome martyrdom, great numbers of men and women were being regained to the ancient faith in Germany and the Netherlands. And from Switzerland a German doctor wrote to a friend: "Truly moving, and reminiscent of the most beautiful days of the past are the life and the works of the Capuchins, whom I have known in Switzerland and the Tyrol. They are poor and humble and filled with true charity. During their missions their confessionals are besieged, stolen property is given back, and conjugal peace restored." Saintly endeavours were not restricted to distant regions. In Rome the Pope listened respectfully to such men as the eminent Jesuit St. Robert Bellarmine and St. Philip Neri, founder of the Oratorians, while at the same time St. Francis of Sales was providing the world with an immortal example of episcopal perfection. In France the same pope exhorted the bishops to be true leaders of their flocks. "Do honor to your ministry," he instructed them, "help your country, drive away heresy, preach and convert those who have gone astray. God, and the authority of the king and the Pope, will be kind to you in this work."

An example of the persistence and patience which marked the diplomacy of the cautious Clement was provided in the lengthy developments attending the return of the Jesuits to France. That strange antipathy, that special mixture of repugnance and strenuous hostility, of suspicion and apprehension of the sinister, which the Jesuit name seems periodically and peculiarly to invoke in the minds of parliaments and princes and even prelates, had been responsible for the expulsion of the Order from France a few years earlier. "Slaves of Spain" Henry had called the followers of St. Ignatius of Loyola and his parliament had gone even further, terming them: "Corrupters of youth, disturbers of the peace, and enemies of King and State." Anxious though he had been for the lifting of the ban of excommunication Henry would not consent to the return of the Jesuits as being one of the conditions. A less sage negotiator might have halted in rash deadlock at such an attitude but the patient Pope resolved to wait and work and after five years of ceaseless effort his will triumphed. The Society of Jesus went back to France and the great change which had been wrought in the King's opinion is shown in his address to those of his subjects who remained more stubborn in their prejudices.

"How can you," he asked, "accuse of ambition men who renounce the honors and benefices which are offered to them, and who even vowed to God never to accept them, and who ask for nothing else on earth than to be allowed, without reward, to serve those who wish to avail themselves of their services? . . . The university is opposed to them, but only because they do better than others, which is shown by the crowds that attend their lectures. If men did not learn more and better from them than elsewhere, how is it that, because of their skill, your universities have nothing to show against them but empty benches and that in spite of your prohibitions, the students follow them everywhere, even beyond the frontiers of the kingdom? You complain that they attract to themselves all the clever children, and choose the best. For this reason I esteem them highly . . . Do we not ourselves choose the best soldiers to lead the battle . . . It must be admitted that their patience is great, and for my part I admire them, because it is by patience and virtue that they obtain their ends. With regard to the authority of the Pope, their teaching is no different from that of other Catholics, and if you would put them on trial for that, you would have to do the same to the Catholic Church. I do not believe they withdrew the clergy from my authority, or teach regicide. Therefore leave me alone to deal with this Society."

The thirteen years that Clement held the papacy were remarkably fruitful. Nevertheless neither his piety nor his wisdom nor his caution prevented him from indulging in outrageous and flagrantly open nepotism. Fortunes were given and nephews and great-nephews received both secular and ecclesiastical office of the highest rank. It was thus thought that the family was firmly ensconced in a rich and permanent security; but less than fifty years after the death of Pope Clement an aged cardinal was asking, "Where today is the greatness of the Aldobrandini? Where are those fine nephews that I so often saw in the antecameras of the Pope? They are dead, as is Clement VIII and Cardinal Aldobrandini. The male line is quite extinct; how vain are the hopes of men, and how frail the happiness of this world."

The next conclave was divided into two parties and the rulers of Spain and France, employing all devices and resources in the cloistered struggle, awaited the outcome of the balloting with eagerness and anxiety. The French deemed it a victory when a kinsman of their Queen, the Cardinal Alessandro Ottaviono de Medici, was chosen. But the sweetness of the triumph turned abruptly to the uncertainties of suspense again when the new pontiff sickened and died after a reign of twenty-seven days. He was seventy-one years old and on his tomb was inscribed the name of LEO XI. The same parties which had struggled to control the previous conclave now maneuvered again and finally compromised in the selection of the Cardinal Camillo Borghese who became PAUL V. He was a Roman and the conduct of his reign could be anticipated from the name he chose; for like Paul IV he was a stern and haughty nepotist whose harsh pronouncements were seldom softened by mercy. He was but fifty-five years old and most of his career had been spent in the study and application of canon law. Thus, save in the matter of enriching his family, his policies and viewpoint were those of an academically correct lawyer rather than the adaptable ways of the professional diplomatist. Perhaps it was fortunate that such a man should now supervise the Curia for the decrees of the Council of Trent were still new and stern discipline was needed to make sure of unhindered observance and to keep clear the channels of interpretation.

The unyielding and uncompromising nature of the Pope brought him into conflict with the Venetians who for a century past had been a source of various troubles to the papacy. When insolence from that quarter was carried into his reign Paul V made little endeavour to parley but unhesitatingly put the Republic under interdict. The actual incident which brought the drastic sentence concerned the seizure and imprisonment of two Venetian ecclesiastics without attention to the existing law of clerical immunity. Great indignation was manifested in Venice at the papal action and the Doge, supported by local theologians, ordered the clergy to disregard the Interdict. His command was obeyed except by the Jesuits, the Theatines, and the Capuchins, all of whom were forced to vacate their pulpits and their properties in the city of canals. It then appeared as though the next stage of the conflict would, much to the delight of Protestant observers, result in bloodshed. But as both armies prepared the French King intervened and by the efforts of his representative a species of reconciliation was effected although with little good will on either side.

In this reign began an incident which was to be magnified and distorted in the telling by anti-papal writers of later generations. Living then was the celebrated Galileo Galilei of Pisa who mingled his great talents in the realms of physics, astronomy, and philosophy. His firm belief in the heliocentric planetary theory which had first been formulated but not completely proved by the priest Copernicus led him into conflict with those of his colleagues who supported the Ptolemaic or geocentric system and as was the noisy habit of the day invective and insult were invoked to support argument. The noisy argument as to whether the sun revolved around the earth or vice versa was heard beyond the academies because both sides rashly invoked scriptural allusion to support their beliefs; and as the possession of high talent is usually escorted by the malice and envy of those less favored, it was only to be expected that complaints against the scientists' unorthodoxy should reach the alert ears of the Inquisition. It was known that certain astronomers mixed their science with more mysterious practices and so the doctor was summoned to Rome where a court of *theologians*, ever supersensitive in their fears that scientific innovations might be but subtle disguises for novelties in doctrine, pronounced the opinion, after consultation with men of science, that the Copernican theory was erroneous and contrary to scriptural teaching. Galileo, displaying a discretion rare in a man of genius, promised not to spread his beliefs any further and so was released. But as time passed the complacency of his erstwhile critics presented a temptation too great to resist and once again he was called to Rome where he was tried, *not* for his theories, but for breaking his former promise. Considering that the shadow of heresy had rested on him the terms of his punishment were lenient and in all he only spent twenty-two days in the buildings of the Holy Office. Another pope now ruled and it was he, Urban VIII, who afterwards gave the distinguished scientist a pension while he lived and his blessing when he died. Charges have been made that this was a case where the Church clearly tried with all authority to obstruct the enlightenment of scientific progress. The facts are that while certain theologians did disagree with Galileo, the Pope, as the Voice of the Church, never pronounced against the views of the scientist nor was such opposition incorporated into the doctrinal belief of the Church. And as for the mistake of the ecclesiastics it should be remembered their attitude was fortified by established belief and the profound opinion of almost every contemporary scholar, Catholic or Protestant. "Even such a great man as Bacon," says Macaulay, "rejected with scorn the theory of Galileo."

Paul V was Pope for sixteen years and when he died the conflict known as the Thirty Years War had commenced. Although it was supposedly a religious quarrel the Pope did his best to remain neutral for he realized that political differences were the real reasons: they were to extend the hostilities for three decades. A revolt in Bohemia started the campaign, which is divided by the historians into four periods, Palatine, Danish, Swedish, and French. The battles were many and so were the shifts of fortune and by the time conclusion had been reached Catholics had fought shoulder to shoulder with Protestants against similarly assorted opponents. Opposing national interests fed the fires of the conflict and in the last years the aim of France, under the leadership of Cardinal Richelieu, was to overcome the Catholic House of Austria, and the Treaty which marked the cessation of the long hostilities was indeed a bitter and humiliating blow to the latter power.

After the death of Paul a clever canonist and diplomatist, the Cardinal Alessandro Ludovisi, was quickly chosen. GREGORY XV was the name he selected. He was a silent and sickly man with the wan appearance of an aged scholar whose health had been broken in over-study. He was able to support his new and great burdens only for two years, but short though the time was his accomplishments were many and permanent. New rules were made to govern the procedure of future conclaves, and the methods of choice were limited to three processes; that of *scrutiny* which is the employment of secret ballot and the method most commonly used; that of *compromise,* which delegates by general consent the elective power to a small committee of cardinals; and *acclamation* which is a contingency to provide for those rare occasions when by an unanimous agreement the hopes and approval of the Sacred College unite in the person of an unopposed candidate.

To meet the problems involved in the complex administration of the great missionary activities which were now in full and noble motion in the Americas and the Indies and Africa as well as the remote places of the Orient, the Congregation of the Propaganda was established. And new names were added to the calendar of Saints, including those of Ignatius Loyola, Francis Xavier, Philip Neri and the mystic Teresa of Avila. The difficult business of guarding the Papal dignity through the vicissitudes and treacheries of the current war was accomplished with tact and dexterity. That combination of Princes who determined the Imperial succession numbered seven, and Gregory by his astute diplomacy increased the Catholic influence so that five of the votes became pledged to Catholic policy. While friendship was maintained with Spain, the city of Paris was elevated from the status of an episcopal see to metropolitan dignity; and to gain further support from France, which was already protecting the missionaries in Turkish territory, an eloquent young prelate with powerful friends was sent the Red Hat. His name was Armand Jean du Plessis, Duc de Richelieu.

Assisting the ailing pontiff in most of his enterprises was a nephew who had been elevated to the purple and the accession of the next Pope, URBAN VIII, certainly brought no halt to what now seemed an established custom. On the contrary several relatives were made Eminences, others were given lucrative positions, and it has been estimated that during a pontificate which extended twenty-one years this Pope's family was enriched by one hundred and five million scudi. As the Cardinal Maffeo Barberini he had served the Church well, and particularly in his capacity as Nuncio to the French court he had won distinction, although from this association was formed a policy which brought him criticism and trouble. The delicate position which his predecessor had adroitly managed to keep during the ever changing fortunes of the Thirty Years War was abandoned by Urban VIII; and to the disgust and rage of the Catholic Princes he openly supported Richelieu who with his Protestant allies was determined to crush Catholic Austria. Manifestations of chagrin and bitterness only induced the Pope to open wide his treasury for the defence of Rome and elaborate fortifications were built and the ancient walls repaired. For the glory of his name and the vanity of his kin artisans and artists were also kept busy on such famous structures as the Barberini Palace and the villa of Castel Gandolfo which is the present summer residence of the Pope. The Quirinal gardens were designed for his approval and so great and constant was the building activity that when lead was stripped from the roof of the Pantheon to provide material for new projects a typical Roman sarcasm was born. "What the barbarians spared, the Barberini have taken."

Infected by the same greedy ambitions which had already intoxicated his nephews the Pope sent his troops to occupy the Duchy of Castro, property of the Farnese family, but the unjust encroachment alarmed and angered the other great clans and principalities to such an extent that with their ready assistance the Farnese duke enlisted a capable band of experienced warriors, well equipped with the tools of war. The Papal States were invaded with cries of revenge and promises of destruction to the Barberini and a catastrophic campaign was only averted by the timely intervention of the French king, who forced the Pope to deliver the usurped domain back to its duke. Because, in Italy, his covetous conduct was frankly that of the head of an aggressively ambitious family rather than the example expected of the leader of Christendom, and because, across the Alps, his unwise and shifty abandonment of neutrality had dissipated the aloofness which should have earned him the respect of the nations, Urban VIII can be blamed for the fact that at the close of his considerable reign the attention shown a papal pronounce- ment was rapidly achieving the same small degree of importance as might be accorded the voice of a temporal sovereign whose territories and armies were neither large nor important. A decree of Urban thus received was his solemn condemnation of the book *Augustinus* written by Cornelius Jansenius, Bishop of Ypres, which purported to interpret the teachings of St. Augus- tine and which among opinions of Calvinistic tinge declared the will of man was not free and that Christ had not died for all. The bishop died soon after the publication of his work but there rapidly, despite the Papal ban, sprang into existence the tena- cious sect of Jansenism which was to bring much trouble during the coming century.

If the prestige which Urban had lost was to be regained in the next reign, it was necessary that his successor should be a man of energy and strong will, yet the sad truth is that these were the very characteristics missing in the nature of INNO- CENT X. The cardinals had pondered weeks before agreeing on their pleasant-tempered and nobly born colleague, Giovanni Battista Pamfili, who as a prelate had lived correctly and offici- ated with discretion but who was now past his three score and ten and who was distinctly not one of those ancients whose vigor excites the wonder of lesser men. In fact he was shame- lessly content that his family should guide his will; and defeating a cardinal nephew for this privilege was his brother's widow Olimpia Maidalchini, an extraordinary and resolute woman well able to dominate the actions of a tired old man. Even in an age when nepotism was the accepted custom the arrogance of this presumptuous shrew excited scandal and dismay. She ruled the papal household from the kitchens to the reception cham- bers and her anger was feared alike by cooks and cardinals. A bare and looted treasury aroused the ire of this formidable character and steps were taken to make the Barberini disgorge their ill-gotten wealth. But the nephews of the previous Pope wisely fled to France where, with the hope of securing their favor at a future conclave, protection was given them and influence brought to bear so that they were able eventually, with fortunes unimpaired, to return to Italy.

The ornamentation of Rome was continued in this reign with generous patronage and was appreciated by the citizens; but a gauge of the dwindling papal prestige outside the Papal States is best illustrated by the hearty indifference which was accorded the Pope's objection to the Treaty of Westphalia. Historic rights and properties of the Church were arbitrarily given to Protestant rulers in this agreement between the nations and it was in vain that Innocent declared "all articles of the Treaty prejudicial to the Catholic religion, to divine worship, to the Apostolic See or to subordinate Churches . . . are to be null and void, invalid, iniquitous, rejected, without force or effect in law." The Treaty was supposed to mark the end of the Thirty Years War although in fact Spain and France continued hostilities for another decade; but Austria accepted humiliating terms and the actual break-up of the so-called Empire was assured.

Innocent X was eighty-two years old when he died and so wretched and confused was his household that his corpse lay unattended for three days. It had been thought that the Donna Olimpia, hitherto the governing spirit of the Lateran, would arrange the funeral but the remarkably practical dowager, well aware her time was over, did naught but announce that such action was impossible for "a poor widow."

The next conclave was not a hasty conference. The responsibilities confronting this assemblage were particularly grave. It was the middle of the seventeenth century, the end of that period which historians have allotted to the Reformation, and all Europe was writhing in a disunity and exhaustion from which France had emerged, thanks to the genius of Richelieu, holding the balance of power. France had remained a Catholic

INNOCENT X

Innocent X (1644-1655)

nation but it was the plan of the great Cardinal, followed by his successor, Mazarin, to bring all things ecclesiastical under the absolute control of the State, and to pay what in effect would be *Gallicanism* but lip service to the Pope. Catholic revival in France had been earnest and successful and as proof there were at this very time living and spreading their good works such men as the saintly Vincent de Paul and the famous theologian and historian Bossuet; but many a good churchman, sincere in intention but intoxicated by patriotism, had diverted his allegiance and given his support to the proposed alliance of Church and State which was to be known as *Gallicanism*. Across the English Channel Puritan passions were in full fury. King Charles had lost his head, altars had been overturned throughout the country and Catholic blood was shed freely. But these outrages seemed almost inconsequental when compared to the crowded massacres which were the awful work of Cromwell's men in Ireland. Protestant princes held sway in Holland and the north countries but the story of Hungary, because of the efforts of one of her own sons, the Archbishop Pazman, was a triumph of the counter-reformation.

The people of Spain had held their faith too but her prelates and her sovereign were uneasy and fearful that the papacy would become a permanent instrument of French policy; and the King, Philip IV, who had not resigned himself to the painful lessons of the Thirty Years War, still cherished hopes that once again Spain would become the foremost nation of Europe. A like mirage dazzled the minds of the Turks and at Constantinople modern implements of battle were made ready, ancient scimitars sharpened, and a fleet of fast feluccas outfitted in preparation for the wild joys of a Holy War. In that minaretted city where the great church of the Christians had become the premier mosque of the Moslems, the Patriarch of the Eastern Church still dwelt under the sufferance and capricious protection of the Caliphs, clinging to an ill heeded authority, contemptuously spurning the advances of Protestant theologians but always, true to the ancient and miserable tradition, stubbornly refusing union with Rome. The Russias were rumbling with the approach of a new era and there was a chance that the Church might gain opportunities, hitherto denied, to propagate throughout the wider regions. The popes had long tried to draw the Muscovite Christians into the fold but the Orthodox metropolitans with a persistence, equal in duration and tenacity, had consistently met such advances with spirited opposition. Pope Gregory XIII had earned the esteem and had received the envoys of Ivan the Terrible with the result that the Jesuits had been allowed to cross the long boundaries and they were now achieving success among the people, but they were also incurring the wrath and hatred of the native clergy. Formidable this hatred proved to be, for the time of Peter the Great was approaching and after many vicissitudes the followers of Ignatius were, at the beginning of the next century, to receive the order of expulsion.

For three months after the death of Innocent X the cardinals deliberated and argued and at one time decided that the good and well qualified Cardinal Sacchetti should be their choice. But the ring of the Fisherman was denied him because the representative of the Spanish King presented the solemn objection of Spain. Thus was exercised the "Right of Exclusion," in virtue of which the head of a nation claimed to veto the election of a candidate on the grounds that such an elevation would be incompatible with the interests of his country. This privilege is now explicitly rejected by the Church but up until recently it was claimed at various times by the Governments of France, Austria, Spain and Germany. After the Spanish objection to Cardinal Sacchetti had been recognized the votes were cast again and this time the majority went to Fabio Chigi, a cardinal who had spoken for the Church at the negotiations leading to the Treaty of Westphalia and who had consequently incurred the dislike of the French. This antipathy was now manifested when that nation objected to the possibility of his being Pope. Sacchetti was the candidate preferred in Paris but as a hopeless deadlock seemed likely the worthy prelate magnanimously persuaded the French to withdraw their opposition to the other candidate. Chigi was then proclaimed pontiff and the Borgia reputation did not prevent him from taking the name of ALEX-ANDER VII.

He was fifty-six years old and was a grandnephew of Paul V. He had been an important legate and in an age which produced such illustrious names in the realms of science and scholarship as Bacon, Galileo, Descartes, Napier, Leibnitz, Isaac Newton, Bellarmine and many others of like genius and learning he was reckoned to be a scholar of repute. Much could be and much was expected of him but he proved to be an indifferent adminis-trator. Indolence was his weakness and many hours were spent each day enjoying the warmth of the sun, coining epigrams and quoting Latin verse amidst the pleasant chatter of friends who were of similar taste. When this languorous routine palled there were long vacations in the country where life was even less irk-some. The burdens of Government and even important decisions involving policy were left to the wisdom of either the Secretariate of State or the Congregations; and in a sense this was but a reflection of a change in government that was then taking place in every land. Monarchs, formerly so absolute in their authority, were yielding ground to the growing and accumulated power of the higher aristocracy and as the great families of the Papal States, their ranks augmented from time to time by the kin of reigning popes, were as alert and as effective as their noble equals elsewhere in claiming and occupying offices of the State, many important positions in the Congregations were now held by bearers of familiar names. Alexander VII was pope twelve years and most of the time he was on bad terms with France. There were numerous disagreements which finally resulted in the troops of the young King Louis XIV occupying Avignon. The circumstance which brought this belligerent action had begun in a dark corner of a Roman street when a drunken serv-ant of the French Embassy received a fatal thrust from the sword of an equally drunken soldier of the Papal Guards. For this crime the minister of the foremost nation of Europe demanded reparations, including a long and full apology from the Pope.

The lackadaisical Alexander had allowed many of his most vexatious cares to fall upon the shoulders of the papal Secretary of State, Cardinal Giulio Rospigliosi, and it was this distinguished and hard-working prelate who became his successor as CLEMENT IX. It was a popular choice and there was rejoicing among good men for though the new pope was famous for his sweet temper and devotion to high ideals he was also an administrator whose experience would not allow him to be the easy dupe of villains. The enthusiasm of his admirers was never betrayed; and if his rule, parental rather than regal, was renowned for kindness it was never despised for weakness. In Rome Clement IX was accessible to all and twice a week he could be found in St. Peter's with attendants dismissed, assuming the duties of a humble confessor. No nephews came to wear the purple or fatten their purses and when buildings were erected the new walls, in defiance of the established custom, remained bare of his name or heraldry. Taxes were reduced, the evils of the grain monopolies abolished, and so earnest were his charities that the citizens cheered at the mention of his name. Nor did his popularity cease at the walls of Rome. Across the boundaries of nations it flourished and over the thresholds of courts. Though his policies with the powers were conciliatory they were also characterized by the firmness of will and unswerving adherence to principles of a true priest. Trouble with the Jansenist movement was averted in his reign because of his gentle and understanding treatment of those who were so inclined, and when Spain and France decided to end hostilities the same peace-loving mind was credited with having played a considerable part in the preliminary negotiations. It was his wish that these powerful nations should form an alliance that would awe and prevent Turkish aggression but before his plans could be realized the audacious Mohammedans landed at Crete and conquered Candia. The calamitous news was a bitter blow to the anxious and fatigued pontiff and when informed he was felled by a shock and grief from which he never fully recovered. Soon the pontificate of but two years and a few months was at an end and there were tears and gloom.

The Sacred College, assembling with haste but already subjected to the heavy intrigues of France and Spain, met with confusion and dismay in a conclave that was long and miserable. The weeks dragged by and the fifth month was almost concluded before the honor was given to the Cardinal Emilio Altieri who fervently wished to assume the name of his friend and predecessor and so became Pope CLEMENT X. That he had held the esteem of Clement IX was sufficient endorsement of his character; but he was eighty years old and his election cannot be regarded as being other than a device of compromise on the part of the cardinals. It was an escape from deadlock and the opposing parties of the conclave each thought to increase their strength during a pontificate that could not be long, although in fact their venerable choice lived for six more years. He brought no great change to the policies of Clement IX but neither did he bring the vigor of the inspired leadership of that good man. Most of the papal authority was put into the hands of a young adopted *I* nephew, the Cardinal Paoluzzi-Altieri who tried, but in vain, to create a league of the Christian nations which for all time would end the Turkish threat. Savage battles were already being *II* fought by the Hungarians under the command of gallant John Sobieski; but it was the French strategy, always inimical to Austria, to keep trouble on the eastern borders of that country so instead of opposing the Turks the envoys of the most Christian King actually made pact with Mohammed IV.

Little heed was given to any word of the Pope in France for Gallicanism was on the increase in the kingdom of Louis XIV. *III* Revenues of vacant bishoprics were arbitrarily claimed in the *regalia* royal name and under the seal of the same authority elevations were, without reference to Rome, made to the episcopacy. But if little respect was shown by France to Clement X, the Czar Alexis of Russia, a bitter enemy of the Turks, despatched an embassy to Rome. His envoy bore the name of Menzies and was the son of a Catholic Scotsman who had fled from Cromwell's soldiers; but unfortunately he was a poor diplomat and making no effort to disguise his dislike of Rome and the Romans he accomplished little save to draw upon himself an enormous unpopularity.

Death came to Clement in his eighty-sixth year and there was determined resistance on the part of those cardinals who were under French influence to prevent the election of the Cardinal Benedetto Odescalchi. Opposition from the same quarter had denied him the honors six years earlier but this time his supporters were stronger and more than ever convinced he should reign. Their persistence succeeded and at the end of two months their unassuming but capable candidate was hailed as Pope INNOCENT XI. The hostile presumptions of Louis XIV were met without fear or weakness by the new pontiff and he remained unintimidated when the monarch commanded the French clergy to meet in a formal assemblage for the purpose of defining the rights of the Church in France. Most of these churchmen had the Erastian bias of their king and the shadow of schism loomed terribly near when their deliberation resulted in the *Four Gallican Articles* which declared that Kings and princes in temporal things were not to be subjected to ecclesiastical power, the decrees of the Council of Constance were to be upheld, the use of papal power was to be moderated by the Canons, and the decision of the Pope could not be final without the consent of the Church.

The response of Innocent to the violation of his authority was a swift condemnation of the assemblage and its declarations, and this measure was followed by an announcement that henceforth canonical investiture would be denied ecclesiastics possessed of such views. Thirty-six French bishoprics thus became vacant and although royal nominees were able to usurp revenues of certain sees they remained devoid of spiritual jurisdiction and were denied by the Curia. The rage of Louis mounted and in retaliation there was further trespass by his troops at Avignon. Rome showed no fear and the quarrel took an even more violent course when the French envoy refused to surrender certain diplomatic privileges, involving extra-territoriality, which had been withdrawn by the papal government because of abuse. Louis sent soldiers to bolster the ambassadorial attitude and when his haughty representative was excommunicated the nuncio in France was arrested. Relations between this Pope and King were never to be happy, yet the grievous altercation brought no aid to Protestantism in France: in fact the continual harsh treatment given to the Huguenots awakened the compassion of the pontiff to such a degree that he appealed on their behalf to James II of England, hoping that words of the English king would have weight with his brother monarch and thus lessen their miserable lot. "As the French government became severer towards the Protestants," one writer recorded, "so the Pope became milder, while remaining immovable, however, on matters of faith." His strict and unbending orthodoxy on the subject of moral theology brought his displeasure upon that flexible school of moral theory known as *Casuistry*, which supposedly was enjoying favor amongst those French Jesuits who were fighting the dour and severe teachings of the Jansenists. The Casuist sought to explain moral principle through practical example and as it was a method which could easily lead to error and misunderstanding the stern Pope condemned a series of propositions which had been taken from the writings of moral theologians considered to be possessed of too lax leanings. This action against their enemies naturally pleased the Jansenists and their dangerous applause drew a suspicion of Jansenism upon the reputation of Innocent XI which was to linger long after his death.

But certainly nobody could deny that his was a model reign. He lived simply and humbly and though he reduced taxes a sizable balance grew in the papal treasury. Thus he was able to send financial assistance to the Austrians and Poles who were still carrying on their bitter struggle against the hordes of the Crescent. He sought to impose his own decorous way of life upon the Romans, the citizens were deprived of their gambling dens, and their wives were forbidden to wear immodest clothing.

Like many of his predecessors he deplored usury and comprehensive legislation was made in an effort to control and limit the
disastrous practice. Wisdom and moderation characterized his
relationship with England and it was without his support and
against his counsel that the Catholic King James II employed
the violent and imprudent measures which cost him his throne
and so dealt a crushing blow to Catholic hopes in that kingdom.

The difference between Innocent XI and Louis XIV always
remained unbridged and when the former died the royal representative once again labored strenuously to secure the election
of a candidate who would be more sympathetic to their sovereign. They were not entirely successful but neither were their
intrigues a complete failure. After a struggle of two months the
opposing factions within the conclave agreed to a compromise
in the person of the eighty-year-old Pietro Ottoboni who was a
Venetian. He took the name of ALEXANDER VIII. He had had
wide administrative experience but he was now an old man and
with indulgence and relief he allowed his aristocratic but greedy
family to participate in many of his decisions. He only reigned
sixteen months and no great changes were made in the broader
policies which he had inherited except for the establishment
of a more amicable relationship with France. Louis reciprocated
the good will and as a grand gesture removed his troops from
Avignon; but further steps toward a complete reconciliation were
halted by the sudden although not unexpected death of Alexander. The rivalries of national intrigues kept the cardinals
imprisoned for five months before they could tell the world that
there was a pope again. The Archbishop of Naples, the Cardinal
Antonio Pignatelli del Rastrello, was proclaimed Pope INNO-
CENT XII and quickly illustrated the high standard of his reign
by providing a permanent and heavy check to nepotism in the
form of the Bull *Romanum decet Pontificem*. With canonical
authority carefully exercised the decree left scant opportunity
for abuses on the part of future papal kinsmen. A pope, if the
circumstances so demanded, might raise one relation to the
Sacred College, but no more than one, and similar limitations

INNOCENT XII

Innocent XII (1691-1700)

regulated the appointment of other officers, ecclesiastical or civil or military, which were under papal patronage. Adherence to the enactment by the cardinals, as well as future popes, was assured by the institution of an obligatory declaration under oath. "If the head of the Church," declared Innocent XII, "has poor relations, let him give them the same charity as he gives other needy people."

The conciliatory mood which Louis XIV had shown towards the previous pontiff did not lessen with the new reign. Perhaps the increasing strength and unity of the anti-French nations, Austria, Spain, Sweden and later England and Holland, made him more appreciative of papal friendship; but whatever the cause his former extravagant claims were gradually abandoned and in time the Declaration of the Four Articles was supplanted by a more reasonable edict which without any radical departure from canon law redefined the rights of the ecclesiastical and temporal powers in France. The enemies of Louis regarded these happenings with suspicion and alarm and soon the current holder of the Imperial title, Leopold I, was making angry accusations against the pope. As a pretext for quarrel his ambassador in Rome claimed those diplomatic privileges of immunity and asylum which had been denied the French envoy during the reign of Innocent XI. The Pope rejected the claims, the quarrel grew, and when Charles I of Spain looked for an heir the papal advice was that his territories should be pledged to a French prince, Philip of Anjou. The decision brought glory and power to the House of Bourbon but it also brought the cruel War of the Spanish Succession and before Philip could enjoy his throne the martial genius of John Churchill, first Duke of Marlborough, had inflicted defeat after defeat upon the French armies during the campaigns of Blenheim, Ramillies, Oudenarde, and Malplaquet. But these battles were fought after the time of Innocent XII and his last days were bright with the hopes that the approaching century would be an era of peace. There was a lull in the European struggles, the Crescent seemed subdued, and with dreams based upon such fragile foundation the Holy Year of the Jubilee of the year 1700 was celebrated with happiness and success. Great crowds of pilgrims pressed forward to receive the tremulous blessing of a worthy old man who was awaiting his end without fear or regret, content that he had done his best in all things. He had ruled with justice and wisdom and charity and when he died the memory of this pope —whom the poet Browning was to salute as being "simple, sagacious, mild yet resolute"—was honored even by those who had incurred his censure.

The eighteenth century had arrived and eight popes were to make their entrances and their exits during its crowded span, this hundred years which saw such formidable opponents of the papacy as the philosophers Voltaire and Jean Jacques Rousseau, the statesmen Duc de Choiseul and the Marquis Pombal, the sovereigns Louis XV of France and Joseph II of Austria. It was the hundred years which was to be rent by the bitter miseries of the French Revolution, which was to witness the fantastic successes of Napoleon Bonaparte, and which, as it ebbed, was to provide the depressing drama of a pope imprisoned and his properties garrisoned by alien troops. It was a century when the rights of the Holy See were entirely ignored by the nations and the protests of the popes were received with contempt, their praise with indifference.

The successor of Innocent XII was the handsome clever Giovanni Francesco Albani who became CLEMENT XI on November 23, 1700, and who held the tiara for twenty-one years, the longest reign since the twelfth century. He was young for a pope, being in his early fifties; but he looked even younger, perhaps because he wore no beard, an oddity which astonished and often shocked visitors to Rome. He owned an enviable reputation for charity and piety and his work as Secretary of Briefs had been marked by diligence and brilliance. When he came to the throne there was no lessening of ideals or slackening of energy. Yet his reign cannot be considered successful. It seemed as though no barricade could be erected, no scheme devised in one man's time to stem the rushing stream of event and movement, the mad current of history. Tranquillity and order Pope Clement XI managed to preserve in the Papal States and this was no mean feat in itself, but the general turmoil of Europe and in particular the war of the Spanish Succession made activities outside his boundaries precarious and fruitless. Neutrality was impractical, nor would it be permitted or even believed by either side; and seeing no reason to change the policy of his predecessor he chose to maintain amicable relations with France, a path which automatically brought to him the ill-will of the Emperor and the Imperial allies.

A very dangerous ill-will this was, for the armies of Marlborough and the Prince Eugene were heaping a series of bloody disasters upon the French who could do little to help the Pope, even when Italy was invaded. A terrible price was paid for French sympathies and heavy blows at the political prestige of the papacy were struck from all sides with bewildering rapidity. Hopes for unity among the Catholic nations, always the dream of a pope, were woefully shattered when the Emperor made alliance with that stronghold of Protestantism, the Kingdom of Prussia. The Papal protests were ignored and they were ignored again when the Imperial banners were unfurled over Milan and Naples. A constant flow of humiliation and trouble enveloped the Curia with sorrow. In Sicily a triumphant usurper persecuted the clergy. The papal nuncio was driven from Madrid. And the French Ambassador left Rome contemptuously, declaring that it was no longer the seat of the Church. Yet the City itself seemed untouched by disorder or panic and in fact grew richer by the addition of new academies and works of art. The missions were not neglected, the intricate business of the Congregations continued, and the Pope found time to deal with the Jansenists who once again were disturbing France. So great was the controversy this time that the French king razed the walls of Port Royal, an abbey which housed many of the movement's most fanatical adherents who satisfied their vows and their consciences by paying but an outward obedience to past edicts. In his first bull, *Vineam Domini,* the Pope declared that this form of "respectful silence" was not enough; his second, *Unigenitus,* was a severe condemnation of their theology. These measures were sufficient to halt the movement and although traces lingered on for some time within the Church most of the extremists went into schism and found refuge in Holland.

The reign of the next pope, INNOCENT XIII, did not last three years and little glory was brought to the papacy by the Cardinal Michele Angelo Conti, a scion of one of the great Roman families. One of his first actions was to make the wily and un-principled French statesman, the Abbé Dubois, a member of the Sacred College; and this deed plainly indicated the trend of his sympathies and provided foundation for the accusations which declared him to be governed by French influence. The dwindling respect for the papal office became the more sharply accentuated in his time when, because of the machinations of the Emperor, Don Carlos of Spain was made heir to the childless Prince Francesco Farnese, ruler of the Grand Duchy of Parma and Piacenza. The Duchy was a fief of the Holy See but the Pope's protests were overridden and the Imperial will was triumphant. The raising of the notoriously vocationless Dubois to the purple brought criticism and troubles in abundance to Innocent XIII but his successor, BENEDICT XIII, was to give the honor to a far worse creature, a villain whose crimes clouded the Holy See with grief and shame.

The conclave which elected this pope had been divided into three parties, the Imperial, the French, and those cardinals who fought for the Italian interest. The last were successful and in the final scrutiny the majority of the ballots were for the Cardinal Pietro Francesco Orsini. He was an Orsini but he had no wish to be pope and earnestly tried to avoid the distinction. He was seventy-five years old and for five decades had worn the purple with honor and humility. All his life he had lived like a monk and as Pope he made no change in a worthy routine. Perhaps it was a mistake; for the long hours spent lingering over his rosary or meditating in the peaceful shadows of his chapel left him with small time for the grander duties. He heard confessions in St. Peter's, he visited and comforted the sick, and as the appearance of the Roman clergy affronted his monastic standards he took measures to enforce somberness in clerical attire. But the really important problems and decisions were left to the judgment of his friend and adviser, Nicholas Coscia, who was given the Red Hat along with the complete confidence and trust of his benefactor. Coscia had also been a monk but neither Carmelite vows nor discipline prevented him from being a hypocritical rogue of the first rank. Once secure in high position he proceeded to loot the papal treasury and revenues with speed and efficiency. His avarice and treachery were perceptible to all except his patron, and when after six years the regime was ended by the death of Benedict it was to the Coscia palace that the mobs rushed with cries of vengeance and threats of burning.

The right to veto was invoked freely by the Imperial representative at the following conclave and it was not until four months had passed that the Cardinal Lorenzo Corsini was presented to the world as Pope CLEMENT XII. He was a Florentine, a friend of the Medici, and born of a family which had given many sons, including the illustrious St. Andrew Corsini, to the service of the Church. A suspicion of compromise could well fall upon those who had chosen him, for he was nearly eighty years old and soon was to be completely bedridden and blind too. Yet the surprising fact is that his policies and decisions were not devoid of a certain vigor and initiative. Coscia had been given asylum in Naples by the Emperor's Viceroy, but Clement was unyielding in his insistence that the unworthy cardinal should be returned to Rome and justice. Eventually this was done and the villain was imprisoned and made to disgorge what could be found of his ill-gotten wealth. Because of his dishonesty and bad management the papal treasury had become woefully bare and the new pope was forced to replenish it from his private fortune, an act that he was able to do without great hardship or regret for his family was enormously rich and he had been long celebrated for the grand scale of his charities. Amongst the recipients of his special patronage were the Maronite Catholics, for he had always been an eager student of the Eastern rites; indeed all Catholics holding the faith in remote places attracted his concern and prayers. Not always could he send advice or assistance for this was a time when the ships of Protestant England, with prize-hungry crews eagerly sniffing the horizons, were prowling the oceans and severing communication with the colonies of the countries she happened to be warring against. Many missions across the seas were thus deprived of guidance and help, but there was little the pope could do: for the steady deprivation of temporal power continued in his reign and he had as little success in his dealings with the kings as had his immediate predecessors.

The Papal territories were invaded periodically during the interminable operations of the nations at war and the noise of guns and the clash of steel against steel were heard again in Naples and Sicily as Charles of Bourbon disputed the Imperial claims and took possession by force of arms. The Pope's advice was ignored and it was ignored again when he offered to adjust the disagreement between Genoa and Corsica. Rejection of the papal guidance brought no prosperity or great success to the Catholic governments or princes and in fact their power was decreasing while the importance of the Protestant nations was mounting steadily. But no lesson was learned and the old quarrels and presumptions continued. In Spain the voice of a woman was suddenly lifted to challenge the papal authority. It was that of the Queen Elizabeth, whose Farnese blood and an unfortunate propensity for meddling in clerical affairs gave her the eloquence to convince her husband, Philip V, that he should make the episcopal appointments and control the benefices of Spain. She also demanded that canonical investiture to the Archbishopric of Toledo should be given her third son who was not yet nine years old.

It was this Clement who in his bull *In Eminenti* was the first pope to frown upon Freemasonry, a papal condemnation not always understood by non-Catholics in Great Britain and North America: for the Masonry they know, mild and charitable in activity but nevertheless a secret society, does not, like the brand often practiced in Europe, exist to carry on questionable political activities or to attack both civil and ecclesiastical authority. Up to this reign the devotion of the Way of the Cross, a meditation upon the tragic procession to Calvary, was only to be witnessed in the churches of the Franciscans who had adopted the practice some time in the fourteenth century; but Clement's encouragement and wish spread the custom and today all Catholic churches are equipped with fourteen Stations of the Cross, either in the form of wooden crosses, pictures, groups of statuary or other constructions of art, depicting the sorrowful last journey of Christ on earth.

Clement XII died at the age of eighty-eight but the Sacred College was slow in assembling and nearly three months passed before a conclave was mustered. Three more wearisome months dragged by and despair mounted as each fresh count of the ballots failed to produce a majority. After one of these disappointments the Archbishop of Bologna, the Cardinal Prospero Lambertini was heard to say: "If you want a saint choose Gatti, if a statesman Aldobrandini, if a plain honest man then take me." The words had been spoken in jest but they were taken seriously and it is well they were: for their author as BENEDICT XIV made an illustrious pope. His own words, "a plain honest man," were hardly an adequate description of his values. He was honest but he was also the most famous ecclesiastical scholar of his time and his talents had not been confined to the library or harnessed to academic obscurity. A long apprenticeship in the Roman courts and congregations had sharpened his wits and then had come the pastoral responsibilities of the mitre, first at Ancona and then at Bologna, where fittingly enough, for it was his native city, his reputation as an administrator gathered fame and commendation. He was a tremendously popular man both before and after his election and if his pontificate brought no temporal restoration at least a greater respect was earned for his office and the conclusion of his reign found the Holy See enjoying extraordinarily amicable relations with most of the governments, both

Catholic and Protestant. His charm and ability conquered big-
otry and opposition and in England the usually acrid pen of
Horace Walpole reported that here was "a man whom neither
wit nor power could spoil." Even Voltaire whose superb prose
usually mocked the priesthood was impressed; and he paid tribute and showed his admiration by dedicating his tragedy *Mahomet* to the pontiff whom he described as being "the pride of
Rome and father of the world, who taught mankind by his
writings and honored it by his virtues." Voltaire's martial friend,
Frederick the Great, succumbed to the prevailing mood and
saluted the pontiff in his correspondence; and the Sultan of
Turkey likewise expressed admiration in high terms. Such com-
pliments made some of the cardinals draw long faces and they
were gloomy too when Benedict made concessions to the Catholic nations with what indeed seemed a very prodigal hand. The
King of Portugal was granted certain privileges of episcopal
nomination and allowed to call himself the most Faithful King.
The King of Sardinia became the Vicar of the Holy See and he
too was given the right of nomination, and similar concessions
delighted the ruler of Spain.

The policies of Benedict were certainly most conciliatory
yet they were not weak. He well understood the weakness and
dangers of his temporal position and so realized the futility of
stern decrees or unreasonable demands. Shortly after his election
he remarked: "The pope gives orders, the cardinals do not obey,
and the people do as they like." There was no force to back his
decisions nor did he seem to need force: it was by moderation
and good will that his ends were achieved. By such graceful
means the loyalty of Eastern Catholics to the Holy See was
strengthened, and rebuke went to overzealous Roman ecclesiastics who had proselytized too vigorously on behalf of their own
rite. "We desire most intensely," he declared, "that all should be
Catholics but not that all should be Latins." He ordered that no
changes should be made in the ancient Eastern practices, including the right of their clergy to marry before ordination.

Tolerance truly marked his every activity. The extreme

Jansenists, the campaigning Protestants, the cynical atheists, were not the targets of his rage but were benefited by his understanding and gentleness, and those officials who were in charge of the Index of Prohibited Books were instructed to be less severe. When there was need he spoke with strength and authority, and the decree of the preceding pope which condemned Freemasonry was endorsed with a vigorous clarity. Without hesitation two books written by his admirer Voltaire were forbidden to the faithful.

Like many of his predecessors Benedict XIV was aware of the dangers of a financial system which utilized usury and a grave and paternal warning was delivered against the evil. But the advice again fell on unheeding ears. Indeed the system was too far developed, the banker too necessary a figure in the affairs of men and nations, for any one man to effect a change at this stage. He had better success with the problem, growing large in his reign, of marriages between Catholics and non-Catholics and his rulings, with but a few changes, form the law on the subject as it stands today. He was a prolific author and his great theological and historical works have survived the test of time. He was always cheerful and his court sparkled with epigram and humor. The bright mood stayed with him even when death, a very painful death, approached. He died in his eighty-third year, cheerful in spirit to the end, and for once the satirists and scandal-mongers common to the time were silent. So much so that an amazed observer recorded: "Marvel of marvels! The people speak no evil of the dead Pope!"

Sixty-two days later the world was informed that the Cardinal Carlos Rezzonico had become Pope CLEMENT XIII. He was sixty-five years old and was born of a noble Venetian family. His election marked a triumph for the Italian faction. The noisy Romans were delighted and the ranks of a less boisterous group, the Jesuits, were stirred with a great hope for the new Clement was their friend and the time had come when the followers of St. Ignatius sorely needed a protector. The work of the Order had been a too aggressive and too successful thing in a human world to escape hostility and resistance; and the elements against them at this time, the too absolute pretensions of the sovereigns, the free thinking brand of philosophy as expounded by such capable men as Rousseau and Voltaire, and the bitter enmity of Jansenist sympathizers, made, when united, a formidable foe indeed. The amiable genius of Benedict XIV had stayed the storm but he was now dead and the attack began.

It was easy to bring the rulers to action. Regalism had reached its pinnacle but the great princes and in particular the Bourbons were becoming fretful and suspicious of an intangible something that was in the air. They did not recognize or understand the elements that were making for the terrible and significant tragedy of the French Revolution but they were conscious that unseen and dangerous forces were at work. Their fears and agitations made them susceptible and willing listeners to the most preposterous stories; and at every court there was a statesman ready with the mischief, ready to produce victims for the wrath of their royal masters. "When we have destroyed the Jesuits we shall have short work," Voltaire had said and the idea raced and spread to the courts with the spluttering fury of a quick fuse. The Prime Minister of Portugal, the villainous Marquis de Pombal, pointed a finger at the Jesuits and swore he had evidence that they conspired to murder the King. In France the Duc de Choiseul frightened his monarch with a similar tale and the royal nights were made miserable by a softer but more dangerous voice repeating the charges: for the King's mistress, Madame de Pompadour, was an ally of the duke. The Spanish king, Charles III, was persuaded that Father Ricci, the General of the Society of Jesus, had declared him to be a bastard and thus not entitled to his throne. The rulers of Parma and Malta and Naples were told of odious intentions directed at them and the basest calumnies, a long calendar of crimes ranging from the weaknesses of the flesh to ghastliest use of dagger and poison, flooded Europe with an organized persistence that was strangely effective. A touch of the mysterious, a hint of the sinister, had always hovered about the activities of these men in unadorned black, these learned and disciplined men who professed to spurn for themselves all wealth and privilege, even the benefices and titles of the Church.

The first blow was struck in Portugal. By royal edict the Society of Jesus was suppressed in both the mother country and the colonies and all property was confiscated. Three of the Fathers were condemned to death and the rest either imprisoned or loaded aboard ships which were despatched to the Papal States. "A present for the Pope," declared the infamous Pombal who was in great humor because of his triumph. In France similar measures were adopted and four thousand Fathers, deprived of their churches and colleges, were banished from the country. The fever spread to Spain and her colonies, where the number of those victimized exceeded six thousand, and the smaller powers of Parma, Naples, and Malta, joined the procession of injustice. But even yet the enemies of the Society were not satisfied. Acting in concert the Ambassadors of France, Spain, and Naples waited upon the Pope and demanded a *total* suppression of the Order. He refused. French troops then marched upon the papal territories of Avignon and Venaissin and Neapolitan soldiery occupied Benevento, but even more disturbing to the aged pontiff was the frightening threat of schism which the envoys swore would be a fact unless the Jesuits were dissolved. Clement was distressed and frantic but death intervened to solve the problem for him. Before he expired he made a desperate appeal to the Empress Maria Theresa of Austria; but her ministers coldly stated that interference was impossible since, in their opinion, the affair of the Jesuits did not involve religion but was a temporal matter. Clement XIII died broken hearted and the conclave which followed his death was stormy and ridden with the intrigues of the determined ambassadors.

The policy to be followed by the next pope sharply divided the Sacred College into two parties. Should their choice bow to the will of the nations and so preserve peace and a species of allegiance, or should they elect one who would pursue the stubborn course, the way that would lead to disaster and schism?

Passionate speeches were made, subtle arguments were employed, complicated compromises attempted. The right of veto was invoked abundantly. After three months of such conduct a majority was found and it was thus that Lorenzo Ganganelli became Pope CLEMENT XIV. He was a cardinal and a Franciscan of unblemished reputation and he had been a pupil of the Jesuits; yet there is good cause to believe that at the conclave he promised the Spanish representative that if elected he would be agreeable to the Bourbon wishes. The transaction is supposed to have been put in writing and signed by the future pope but extensive searches have failed to produce such a document. Great pomp and ceremony surrounded his coronation but underlying the pageantry there was the nervous ache of suspense and worry for the Jesuits who could not but feel that a bargain had been made and that the doom of the Order was assured. No sooner was Clement enthroned than the Spanish and French Ambassadors pressed forward and arrogantly demanded immediate action. They were disappointed if they expected abject and quick obedience: for by every device of conciliation and procrastination at his disposal the pontiff tried to dispose of the problem without actual compliance to the drastic demands.

For four harassed years he avoided positive decision by pleas and the showering of honors and the granting of concessions; but finally, after the threat of schism was again made, the inglorious day arrived when he was forced to issue the cruel Brief of Suppression, *Dominus ac Redemptor noster.* The charges against the Society were repeated in the brief but it is significant that no judgment was passed. "Impelled by the duty of restoring harmony in the church," the pope said, "convinced that the Society of Jesus can no longer fulfil the purposes for which it was founded and moved by other reasons of prudence and governmental policy which we keep to ourselves, we abolish and annul the Society of Jesus, with its offices, houses and institutions." With a splendid exhibition of obedience the twenty-two thousand members of the Society bowed to the will of the pope, and their General, Father Ricci, submitted to imprisonment in the

PIUS VI

Pius VI (1775-1799)

Castle of Saint Angelo without trouble or any show of rancor or revolt. But two monarchs, the Protestant Frederick II of Prussia and one who professed the Greek Orthodox faith, Catherine II of the Russias, received the Edict with indignation and protest and both proclaimed that it would have no force within their domains.

The Jesuits were vanquished. Or so thought their delighted enemies, who celebrated their victory with wild and self congratulory enthusiasm. The Jesuits were gone and Avignon and the rest of the occupied papal properties were returned to the Holy See. But no happiness came to ease the hours of Clement XIV. He had probably acted with all sincerity but he seemed conscious that he had made a grievous mistake and a great melancholy and misery descended upon him and stayed with him until he died, fourteen months after the issuance of the ignoble Brief.

Four months marked by conclave activities of the usual sorry kind went by and then the Cardinal Giovanni Angelo Braschi, who enjoyed the support of the French interests, was elected as Pope Pius VI. He was not yet sixty and he was so strikingly handsome that the Romans called him *Il Papa bello*. His tastes and ways of life fitted the golden days of the Renaissance rather than his own anxious days. Indeed the Renaissance tradition provided the pattern for his ambitions and standards. A great palace was erected to house a nephew whom he enriched and married to an heiress, and another nephew was given the purple and the means to wear it with princely dignity. He desired to be a patron of the arts in the grand manner and he wished his name to be remembered in the Roman story because of splendid buildings and because of such great projects as the draining of the Pontine marshes which in their swampy condition were a perpetual menace to the health of the city. But his attention was soon drawn from such schemes because it was rapidly becoming evident that the conciliatory policies of the late pope had ushered in an even greater contempt for the ancient rights of the papacy. And the affair of the Jesuits lingered on. The French and

Spanish ambassadors had supported Pius at his election but the astute Pombal of Portugal had suspected him of harboring sympathies for the Society and the suspicion proved correct; for when a commission in Rome after extensive investigation acquitted the Fathers and pronounced the accusations against them to be groundless, Pius permitted their schools and institutions to continue in Prussia and Russia where, under the protection of friendly rulers, continuity was assured the great Order. But he did not repeal the harsh brief because he was a realist and thought that as yet reinstatement was impossible in those countries where the ruling cliques held such a violent antipathy to the Society. Therefore justice was postponed and as the pontiff gloomily meditated over this matter a new storm broke, this time in Austria.

Maria Theresa had been dead for about three years and her son, Joseph II, was now the Emperor. He was a man who determinedly and aggressively believed that the sovereign head of a State should be an absolute ruler in all things, and this exalted idea naturally meant conflict with the Holy See. So once again there was to be a repetition of the old story, the unfortunate and familiar story of a presumptuous prince attempting to exercise temporal authority over spiritual affairs and ecclesiastical properties. What had been called Gallicanism in France now blossomed in full strength in Austria. The Emperor claimed complete jurisdiction over the Church in his territories and ordered the bishops to cease direct communication with Rome. Several hundred religious institutions had their doors closed by Imperial edict and it was forbidden that monies or alms of any kind should be conveyed to the Holy See. Clerics who showed any trace of opposition received prompt and severe punishment and the Imperial interference was so extensive that laws were issued regulating the size and number of candles and images to be used in the churches. The ordinary channels and resources of diplomacy seemed inadequate to the pontiff and he conceived the bold idea of abandoning the usual practice of negotiating through representatives and proceeding to Vienna in person. This he did and there were splendid processions and majestic receptions and great cheering crowds and the complicated etiquette of the Imperial court paid the requisite respect and deference to the handsome pope. But no jubilance gladdened his heart for he could detect an insolent spark in the eyes of the Prime Minister who bent his knee with little grace, and the Imperial words of salute and greeting were noticeably devoid of enthusiasm or true friendliness. Two Red Hats were left in Vienna but nothing was gained and the disappointed Pius returned to Rome saddened and wiser. Any further or stronger degree of opposition from him would mean schism and this calamity he had no wish to invite. So all he could do was to wait and hope for a better day.

The Imperial measures were too hastily contrived and too stringent and unpopular to be assured of permanence and when Joseph died in 1790, and was succeeded by his brother Leopold II, most of the innovations were abandoned; but not until there had been further anxiety for the Pope. His inability to enforce his authority and his reluctance to risk schism had not escaped the notice of some of the powerful prelates of Germany and Italy who, prompted and encouraged by Imperial intrigues, had proposed to make themselves virtually independent of the Holy See. Their outrageous resolution and plan was expressed in a document known as the *Punctation of Ems,* and later the *Synod of Pistoja* professed a similar insubordination; but Pius proved himself capable of dealing with both emergencies and neither movement survived a decade. Far greater troubles were in store for this pontiff but before they came there were two agreeable incidents. The King of Sweden visited Rome whilst travelling incognito and finding much to please and nothing to frighten him gave his consent to the institution of a Vicariate Apostolic in his country. And across the wide waters of the Atlantic, in the second year of this remarkable pontificate, the North American colonies of Great Britain decided to break with the mother country. Several years of bitter fighting brought success to the decision and the famous Declaration of Independence was assured the devotion of a great nation and the respect of all peoples. Freedom of worship was the guaranteed privilege of each citizen in the new commonwealth and the Holy See was not slow to commence the hierarchy which since has been blessed by exceptional vigor and success. In 1790 a former Jesuit, John Carroll, born of Irish parentage in Maryland, was consecrated Bishop of Baltimore.

But while these gains were being made, Europe was startled by the sudden violence of a greater and more tragic revolt. The Bastille had been stormed and freedom and equality for all Frenchmen proclaimed. The Terror had begun and events were moving swiftly and bloodily to the monotonous and never ceasing accompaniment of the guillotine's dull thud. The Church had suffered in France because of the absolute pretensions of the Kings, but now she was to share with the monarch the wrath of the mob-inciters, for disorder was incompatible with an unhindered and officiating clergy, and disorder, particularly wild and savage, was the irresistible pace of these mad times. The reasons for the Revolution were understandable enough. Unsuccessful wars had brought the financial condition of the country to a chaotic state and the lot of the majority of the people was terribly wretched and miserable; yet the aristocracy with a limitless apathy had chosen to blind themselves to the surrounding tragedy and to live within their own unnatural circles of fashion and caste. The crime of their stupidity was paid by their blood and sorrow and those who did not die suffered the torments of concealment or the hardships of exile.

The evils and the weaknesses caused by the trends of Gallicanism and Jansenism had made the French Church vulnerable to the attack of those who were possessed by the wild madness to destroy all the ancient things. There were nobly born bishops whose only qualification for the mitre was the endorsement of the Crown, and fresh in the memory of many a revolutionary were the unreasonable severities which had been taught and practiced by clerics of Jansenist tinge. But the bulk of the serving clergy were neither high born nor given to theological innovations. They were from the people and served the people well; but, as opposers of violence and defenders of order, they too went to the scaffold in crowds. The heads of the King and Queen also fell to the gory baskets and many a revolutionary leader was to meet a similar grim fate before normalcy came to the country again. Policies and decisions changed with dizzy rapidity before the fickle moods of mobs and the whims of opportunists, and it often seemed as though the ceaseless rise and drop of the guillotine's sharp edge would be the only institution of the new régime to enjoy survival and achieve permanence. The Republic's attitude towards religion veered sharply at varying times from the project of a state-controlled non-celibate clergy to plans that called for the complete dechristianization of France. Rupture with the Holy See came at an early stage and Avignon and the district of Comte Venaissin were quickly annexed. Events moved at a torrential speed and there was little the anguished Pope could do but offer his prayers and give hope and hospitality to refugees. All the nations regarded the Republic with repugnance, hostility, and with a mounting fear that the wide conflagration would not be held at the French frontiers. There were councils and alliances and hasty plans were made to hold the flanks.

To the south the armies of Austria and Piedmont gathered on the Lombard Plain and to meet them Paris despatched an Army whose General was young and confident that he would add his name and exploits to those of Hannibal and Charlemagne. His bold genius was equal to his large confidence and soon the courts of Europe were aghast at the lightning speed with which the victories of Napoleon Bonaparte were accomplished. Austria was vanquished and most of Italy quickly succumbed before the astounding triumphs of the young General. The Pope was forced to pay two indemnities. The first was in the amount of two million francs and some works of art; but the second demand was for thirty million seven hundred thousand francs and car-loads of famous paintings, statues, tapestries, and precious manuscripts. The papal army was disbanded and territories were stripped from the papal sovereignty.

Joseph Bonaparte, brother of the general, was made French Ambassador to Rome and promptly set out to further Republican ideas and sympathy. Victories always kindle a certain admiration and enthusiasm for the victor and now in the city Republicanism became fashionable and popular. The ancient days when Rome had been the model Republic were recalled and lamented by conspirators who rapidly grew in number. There were treasonable speeches and brawls in the streets and when a French General was killed in a skirmish between malcontents and papal guards, Joseph Bonaparte immediately demanded his passports and soon a French army was advancing upon Rome. The Pope gave the order that there should be no resistance or fighting and then retired to his quarters as street orators with much noise and no little absurdity proclaimed the glorious days of the Republic and the Senate to have arrived again. During the darkness of the night two French officers burst in upon the Pope and rudely told him that his temporal power was gone; and to emphasize the humiliation and helplessness of his position his ring of office was stripped from his finger. Pius VI was now in his eighty-second year and he was ill and tired. Earnestly he pleaded that he should be allowed to die where he had lived but the request was ignored and that same night a strange cavalcade clattered heavily-armed from the city. There was a brief stay at Siena and for a month the place of imprisonment was a monastery near Florence. But even then the dying man was not allowed to rest fully. Commands came to take him across the Alps and it was at Valence, some six weeks later on the 29th August 1799, that the captive pontiff breathed his last.

The death of a pope in such humiliating circumstances caused high glee amongst the aggressively anti-religious. At last that thing against which their fury and malice had been directed was vanquished and finished. There would be no more popes, the pontifical story was at an end, the long dynasty of St. Peter had been concluded with the miserable exit of the 248th pope.

So it seemed. But elation based on such belief was as short lived as the new Roman Republic, for the fickle fortunes of war sent Napoleon to Egypt, the Austrians and Russians pressed forward again, and the French evacuated Rome shortly after the death of Pius.

In Venice, which was garrisoned by Austrian troops, the cardinals, each with a tale of adventure and peril to relate, congregated to perform their traditional duty. They enjoyed the protection of the Emperor, Francis II, but from him also was suffered a constant interference during the entire session of the conclave. It was a nervous assemblage, this gathering of thirty-five aged and harassed men, all bewildered by the quick events which had changed and which still were changing the world as they knew it, and all acutely conscious of the awful responsibility linked to their judgment at this critical movement. On their decision might rest the fate of the Church. They knew they should produce a champion and with considerable anguish they realized that a mistake on their part would easily, so easily, bring further ruin to the papacy. Feverish appraisal and an anxious scrutiny went to each of their company but what was seen gave little hope. There were not lacking good men, able and pious, but there was no superman standing above his fellows, no sign of the genius that was urgently needed. Should they accept the candidate of Francis and thus join the destiny of the Church to the fortunes of the Austrian throne? The idea was not attractive but, as the practical ones asked, could an independent pope survive? The French Republic was an active foe of religion and already the world appreciated the fearsome capabilities of the Republican armies.

A note of hysteria and desperation crept into the discussions but one voice remained calm and unafraid, a persuasive and persistent voice, but of the background: for its owner Monsignor Ercole Consalvi was not yet a member of the Sacred College, merely an attending official. He was an exceptionally brilliant young churchman and gradually it was his opinions which gained the confidence of the assembly. He thought that the Cardinal Barnabo Chiaramonti, able Bishop of Imola and a distinguished member of the Benedictine Order, should be pope and finally the majority of the ballots was given this prelate who became Pius VII.

The Austrian monarch desired that the new pontiff should come to Vienna but Pius, flanked and fortified by his friend Consalvi, was determined he should take possession of his rightful capital, which at this time was garrisoned by the soldiery of the King of Naples and under the command of Sir John Acton, a Catholic Englishman. The pope arrived in Rome during the hot summer of 1800 and as usual the citizens were profuse with their cheers and noisy acclamations. They thought this new sovereign a fine-looking fellow. He was handsome and did not look his sixty years. He had a reputation for generosity and tolerance and it seemed as though a happy reign might be commencing. A treaty was made with the Neapolitans and quickly the pontiff set about putting the affairs of his small territory in order although at the same time an anxious eye was turned to the North; for once again Bonaparte, audaciously dragging his cannon across the Alps, had defeated the Austrians, this time at Marengo. What would be the outcome of these continual French victories? Would there be a vaster and more terrible persecution of the Church? The pious trembled and all men wondered. Happily the answer was not long in coming. Bonaparte became First Consul, the supreme director of the French destiny, and in surveying his position his keen vision detected the plain fact that the structure of a tranquil and successful State is incomplete without religion. "I am aware that in no state," he said to the amazement of the Parisians, "can a man be truly virtuous and upright unless he knows whence he comes and whither he is going. Unaided reason cannot tell us these things. Without religion, we grope in the dark. But the Catholic faith throws a clear light upon the origin and the destiny of human beings."

The astonishment of Paris at the words of its Master can be readily imagined. The streets, the cafés, the salons, were agog, for this was the city which so recently had spawned the crimes and the obscenities of the Terror. Its churches still carried the stains of defilement and plunder and the great and ribald feasts which had celebrated the triumph of Reason over Superstition were a close memory even to the youngest citizens. The Voltairian tradition set the conduct and moulded the standards of its schools, and did not the God haters of the world regard the city by the Seine as their capital? Now had come the shock. The Church was to return. The Mass was to go on. And it was the command of a man who was supreme, whose will could not be thwarted.

The new attitude was not a simple matter of faith. By now the grand ambitions held the Corsican, and Charlemagne's majestic pattern gave the size to his dreams. Superb strategist and soldier that he was he knew the value of the weapons at his disposal. And that was the meaning of the papacy to him, a weapon at his disposal, an instrument to be used when and how he pleased. "Catholicism kept the pope in being for me," he declared later, "and in view of my grip upon Italy, I continued to hope that sooner or later I should be able to bend him to my will. What immense influence I should then wield! What a means to have at my disposal in my dealings with Europe!"

No time was to be lost. The whole affair, plan and execution, was conducted with the usual speed of a Bonaparte campaign. The invitation was sent to Rome, a Legate hurried back and then it was Consalvi who came. He was ushered to the great man's presence by the limping apostate bishop Talleyrand, and there was much rattling of drums and clanging of arms by the Guards. Bonaparte had surrounded himself with a glittering array of uniformed councillors and functionaries and it was thus, already an Emperor in manner and bearing, that he received the cardinal. This man who had intimidated all Europe had made elaborate preparations to impress his scarlet-clad guest but as Emil Ludwig remarks of the occasion: "The shrewdest of worldly sages can find his master in the Vatican. When the consul wishes to browbeat him, the prince of the Church smilingly stands his ground. What a spectacle for Talleyrand, who looks on in silence!"

After the first meeting an agreement gradually took shape and the grand attempt to achieve harmony between the Church and the Bonaparte regime resulted in the Concordat of 1802. Concessions had to be made by the Holy See but much was also gained. The seals were affixed and the signatures inscribed and a great ceremony of thanksgiving was arranged to be held in Notre Dame. The First Consul ordered his court, for it was that already, to attend. "We are going to Mass today," he said to his brother with a chuckle. "What will Paris say to that!"

Discord with the Holy See was not long in developing. It could not be otherwise with such a man, who insisted on being the Dictator in all things and who would not admit that the authority or office of any man or institution could counter his will. There were violations of the recent concordat and encroachments of privilege and protests. But before the final rupture the Pope, at the earnest behest of the warrior, came to Paris to officiate at the coronation service; for Napoleon now wished to wear the Imperial title. In Rome there had been a spirited discussion amongst the members of the Sacred College as to whether the invitation should be accepted or not and when, in the interests of peace, it was decided he should go several cardinals registered vigorous protests.

"*Tu es Petrus*" sung a large and superbly trained choir as the Pope went to his throne in the Cathedral of Notre Dame. A splendid sight of massed brilliance met his eye and outside the tall walls of the great edifice a light snowfall touched the usually grimy gargoyles with a glistening whiteness. An ocean of densely packed citizens darkened the boulevards and impatiently fidgeted and grumbled as they waited to glimpse Napoleon and his Josephine. The Pope, the Ambassadors, the high functionaries of State, they waited and fidgeted too and it was a part of the proud Corsican's plan that they should do so. Everything was as he wished and timed to his plan; but it had very nearly not been so for soon after his arrival in Paris the pontiff, rather bewildered

Pius VII (1800-1823)

and half convinced already that he was being duped, had heard from Josephine herself that her marriage was invalid and that she had not been married by a priest. Pius listened gravely and saw that here was his chance to escape further indignity. He could not be expected to preside at the Coronation of such a pair.

So the Pope voiced his objection and waited the fury but from that man whose actions were so unpredictable there was merely a shrug and smile. The matter could easily be rectified. Candles were lit in the palace chapel. The Emperor's uncle, Cardinal Fesch, was summoned and a marriage enacted. The Coronation itself followed an elaborate plan and one bold piece of the glittering scheme was to startle the world. The solemn moment had come when the Emperor was to receive the Crown but instead of bending his knee before the Pope the audacious creature seized the anointed circle and turning to the congregation and standing erect placed it firmly on his head. He had crowned himself. There was a murmur and excitement even amongst his puppets and all eyes turned to the Pontiff who said nothing and whose sad eyes showed no surprise. There was no movement or protest from his throne. Silent and pale and aloof his was the role of an onlooker of a masquerade but there came the time when he had to give the kiss of peace. *"Vivat Imperator in Eternum,"* he said softly as he followed the ritual and his blessing was a gesture of compassion. In a loud voice the Emperor recited the oath of his office, swearing to protect the State and respect Religion. But there was little hope in the heart of the Pope.

His apprehensions were soon fulfilled for next year Napoleon had a request to make and a story to tell of his brother, Jerome, later to be King of Westphalia, whom he had put in a ship to acquire the benefits of discipline and to learn the art of sextant and sail. Midshipman Jerome had crossed the seas and landing at Baltimore had immediately struck his flag to a local Miss Patterson. There was a quick marriage, there were hopes of a family, and when the Emperor heard of the alliance there was anger and trouble. He had loftier plans for his kin and the bride was not allowed to land in France. Once ashore her husband, set to calculation by his brother's bright promises, was ungallantly content that the separation should be permanent. The next step was to have the Pope dissolve the union by declaring it invalid; but Pius, after a careful scrutiny of the facts, was of the opinion that the marriage was indisputably correct and in a polite but firm epistle so informed the Emperor.

The breach was to widen still further when Pius refused to cooperate in Napoleon's Continental System, which aimed to close all European ports to English ships and trade. This was too much opposition for the despot who had already written "Your Holiness is sovereign of Rome, but I am its Emperor. All my enemies must be yours." In the bivouac on the outskirts of Vienna it was decided to annex the Papal States. The maps were consulted and the instructions given. The bugles sounded, troops marched to a schedule arranged by undeniable genius, and on the sixth of July, 1809, the Pope was informed by a French general that his dominion had been taken and that he was no longer free. It was as simple as that. Soldiers rushed him to a carriage, he was whirled away from Rome and conveyed to Savona in a manner painful to his age and health. The long way was made easier by the inhabitants of the countryside who tendered impromptu demonstrations of respect and devotion. But to these spontaneous displays the illustrious captive had but one message. *Peace.* There must be no bloodshed over his fate or person, that was his chief concern, and it was his victory.

There now commenced an ingenious campaign to bend the will of the Pope and to win him to the wishes of the Emperor. Continually it was emphasized that the measures taken against him had been levelled at his status as a temporal sovereign and then only because emergency had so demanded. Naught but reverence would ever be accorded the true Holy Father was the Imperial promise. An annuity of two million francs was settled upon him and a great show of respect to his rank and person was made by all in attendance, although no deference in speech or manner could disguise the fact that they were guards and he a prisoner. From the waking hours until the depths of the night there was always a persuasive voice ready to extol the Emperor's wisdom, to tell of his incomparable martial abilities, and to dwell on the great benefits that would gladden the world if Pope and Emperor would work together. This kind of propaganda was ceaseless but perhaps the most dangerous aspect of the papal captivity was his ignorance of what was happening in Rome. He was shut off from his counsellors and from his documents and any information that came to him was passed through the censor and flavored by the filter of his captor's opinion. Some prelates and churchmen were allowed to see him but they were all creatures of the Regime and to a man they pleaded the cause and talents of their master.

Twenty-seven French bishoprics were now vacant and the ecclesiastical henchmen of Napoleon strenuously endeavored to receive from Pius his approval of the Imperial nominees and thus assure them of canonical investiture. But the old man remained firm in his refusal. Napoleon then convened a National Council and ordered the attending bishops to pass a resolution which would pronounce the papal approval unnecessary; but there were demurs and resistance to the proposal and because of unconcealed indignation and opposition some wearers of the mitre were arrested. It was not the way of the Emperor to let matters rest at such a stage. The churchmen were ordered to meet again and this time it was proposed that a metropolitan or senior bishop of a province could bestow *in the name of the Pope* canonical investiture after a see had been vacant for six months. The assemblage passed the measure but only on condition that it be approved by the Pope. Eight prelates of Napoleon's choosing waited on Pius and begged him in the interests of the Church in France to give his endorsement. Long and persistent persuasion had its effect this time and finally, after making a few changes, the Pope, now a very ill man, succumbed to the entreaties and gave his seal. But the proud and impatient nature of the Dictator was not satisfied. The victory was neither clear cut nor quick enough for him. And with his talent for sensing the thoughts and sympathies of the people he was conscious of a growing distaste on all sides at the treatment accorded the pontiff. He determined to settle the affair himself and he ordered that the Pope be brought to Fontainebleau.

But by the time the ailing old man arrived the exigencies of war demanded the Emperor should be with the Army. This time the march was to Moscow and the tragedy of that vain campaign with its long and corpse-strewn retreat was soon to startle the world. But the terrible energies of its author were not yet stemmed nor had his ambitions dwindled. A new army must be trained. New battles must be fought. The Empire must and should survive. And while a fresh crop of lads were hurriedly bent to martial ways and more cannon beaten into shape the Emperor came to Fontainebleau to achieve a victory of a different kind. A great lethargy, the inevitable penalty of a long illness combined with the toll of age and despair, enveloped the Pope at this time and it was with but little interest or spirit of any kind that he received his visitor.

Napoleon made a great display of devotion and respect, talked in excited tones of the glory of a united Christendom, swore that his sword was at the service of the papacy. At first the old man heard these things without emotion or understanding but gradually the more extravagant phrases seemed to penetrate his torpor. A faint spark lit his weary eyes when the Emperor artfully talked of peace between State and Church, a peace that would be translated everywhere. The magnetic voice went on, painting in pleasing words great schemes of justice and charity and there came the time when a document appeared before the pontiff and a pen was held to his trembling fingers. His signature was traced while the jubilant voice of the Dictator filled the room with majestic promises. Napoleon could well afford to rejoice for by that tremulous scrawl Pius VII had agreed the papacy should henceforth be resident in France and that the Papal States should remain the property of his captors.

But it was a victory too preposterous ever to achieve the status of fact. Many of the restrictions surrounding the person of the pontiff were now removed and fortunately he was permitted to receive his cardinals. They emerged from their various places of detention with melancholy faces and lost no time in telling him what he had done. A great anguish was his reaction to their woeful recital and the pangs of this emotion imbued him with the fire of a new spirit of opposition. Quickly the Emperor was informed that the papal signature was withdrawn and that an agreement made under such dubious conditions must be considered null and void. The reply to the pronouncement was awaited with calmness but also with apprehension. Tempestuous measures were certainly to be expected but they were never realized, for fortune was forsaking the Corsican on all sides now, and there were more desperate and bloodier combats to engage his energies and presence. Calamity was clouding his every horizon and his genius was being challenged as never before. There was no purpose to be gained in keeping the Pope a prisoner any longer and in fact the presence of so august a captive in his territories might make circumstances even more adverse. Gloomily he decided to allow Pius to return to Rome and in his letter to Prince Eugene telling him of the decision, he pathetically clings to the pompous magnanimity and dignity of his fast ebbing power. "I have given orders," he wrote, "that the Pope be sent to the Austrian outposts by way of Piacenza and Parma. I have made known to the Pope that, having asked, as Bishop of Rome, that he return to his diocese, I have permitted him to do so. Be careful, then not to pledge yourself to anything relative to the Pope, either as to recognizing him or as to not recognizing him."

After nearly five years of absence the Pope entered Rome and both he and the cardinals received a tremendous welcome. There were many things to do and the tangled reins of government and administration had to be gathered in order; but there could be little stability to any enterprises of a civic or national character until it was certain that the era of Napoleon had definitely ended. His abdication had been proclaimed and he had gone to little Elba, apparently resigned to the emptiness of the title which he had been allowed to retain. But who could be confident that the proud and restless spirit was really broken? There were rumors and conjectures and within ten months the world was electrified but hardly surprised by the news that the Emperor was making another grasp at glory. The restored Bourbon monarch, Louis XVIII, ensconced in the Tuileries, was handed a sealed dispatch. He read it and calmly said, "Napoleon Bonaparte has disembarked on the coast of Provence!" His calmness was admirable but it soon vanished along with his royal person and once again it was Napoleon who occupied the Tuileries. A splendid and happy moment it was for the great soldier but it was only a moment, fleeting and brief. His destiny was not to be revealed in the halls of palaces but on the battlefield. This time the baton pointed at Waterloo and this time he was to hear the cry that he had boasted no man would ever hear. "The Guard is breaking!" Those proud veterans did break and there was rout and massacre and Waterloo was over. Napoleon's day was over too, utterly and inexorably, and there remained for him only the bitter and dismal end at St. Helena.

All Europe rejoiced and prepared for the comforts of long denied tranquillity as an English frigate carried the forlorn and beaten Emperor south to the lonely island. But much havoc had been done and many boundaries had been changed and these things demanded immediate adjustment and reparation. Could there be a complete return to the status quo of yesterday? The men who were given this complicated problem were a shrewd and brilliant company. There was Metternich of the Austrian Empire. There was Hardenburg of Prussia. Nesselrode represented the idealistic Czar of Russia, Alexander I, when that monarch did not act for himself, and the wily Talleyrand served the new French sovereign with the same glib fidelity he had given to Napoleon. England had the ability of Castlereagh and the reputation of the Duke of Wellington to serve her interest and there were men of equal wit to speak for the smaller nations. Representing the Holy See in the long and complicated negotiations was the long standing friend of the Pope the Cardinal

Consalvi, and all things considered, he did well. Except for Avignon which remained under the French flag and a small strip of land retained by Austria, the Papal States were restored to their pre-Napoleonic size.

The rapid changing of fortune had brought Pope Pius better health and an increased vigour and well it was for there was much for him to do both within and without his frontiers. One of his first deeds was an act of long awaited justice. By formal announcement the Suppression of the Society of Jesus was revoked. Separate Concordats were made with the various nations and each of these processes demanded long discussion and study. The national Colleges in Rome were restored and the Congregations were set in full motion again. Institutions and laws which had been established by the Napoleonic regime and which had proven successful were wisely retained and with superb charity it was the Pope who gave a gracious and dignified asylum to the mother of the Corsican and to other members of his family. He bore no malice towards Napoleon and in fact pleaded with the British Government that gentler treatment should be given the famous prisoner. He bore no malice and proved his forgiveness but he never forgot the dark days of his own captivity. When he died at the age of eighty-four during the late summer of 1823 his last words, ejaculated in the accents of the final agony, were *Savona! Fontainebleau!*

The great and significant changes in society which were taking shape during the American and French Revolutions were a disturbing factor in the thoughts of this generation. Men, whether they were aristocrat or peasant, merchant or intellectual, when gathered for discussion were usually sharply divided into two opinions. Either sympathy for the new ideas as in some form or a determined rejection of liberalism under any guise. So it was with the Cardinals when they met in the Sistine Chapel to select a successor to Pius, and it was the conservatives who were in the majority. After three weeks their candidate, the Cardinal Severoli, was about to be declared pontiff, but a veto from the Austrian monarch prevented his elevation. Acting quickly before another such missive could be received he and his party produced the necessary ballots in favor of Annibale della Genga, the Cardinal-Vicar of Rome, who was genuinely horrified at the swift swing of circumstances which thrust the honor to him. He protested his inadequacy and pleaded his ill-health with tears but to no avail. He was made Pope and with reluctance and apprehension he took the name of LEO XII.

There was cause for his honestly expressed lack of confidence, for his health was indeed bad and while he was a good man his record as prelate and diplomat was devoid of outstanding achievement or success in any form. He was one of those correct characters who all their lives eschew gaiety of any kind: even in adolescence they adopt the more sombre moods of their seniors and studiously avoid the light hearted joys, however innocent, of their comrades. At sixty-three, his age at his election, he seemed much more ancient, and in place of the alert and progressive Consalvi, he installed an eighty-year-old crony as the Secretary of State. The two dour and sickly old men held conference and decided that the best way to fight the evils of liberalism would be the imposition of austerity and severity. The most stringent and extraordinary regulations were put into effect and spies were set to report their observance. The sale of wine was restricted in the Papal States and a great gloom descended upon the traditionally festive taverns of Rome. The strictness of the Pope even disapproved of the realism of historic works of art and much to the general indignation he caused some of the ancient ornaments to be removed from the public gaze and in others ordered a covering to be put over the anatomical portions he deemed offensive. An intense unpopularity was of course the result of such harsh tactics but Leo XII cared little for the opinion of his subjects as long as he was convinced duty was being followed.

Unrest and dissatisfaction became prevalent throughout his domain and membership rapidly increased in the forbidden secret societies whose aims were revolutionary in character even though anarchy might be the sinister cost. He expired, this unloved Pope, in the sixth year of his reign because of clumsy surgery and this time the liberal cardinals succeeded in winning the tiara for their candidate, the popular Cardinal-Bishop of Frascati, Francis-Xavier Castiglione. The new pope had enjoyed the favor of Pius VII and in his honor he chose to be called Pius VIII. He was popular and with his accession a more gentle and sensible application of the laws was immediately perceptible, but he was also seventy years old and his health was no better than that of his predecessor. Most of his problems and decisions were therefore passed to the jurisdiction of his Secretary of State. The Holy See, so desperately in need of a vigorous and energetic leadership, had once again been failed by the cardinals.

The happiest news of this reign, and certainly not of the Pope's making, was the Catholic Emancipation Act of Great Britain which brought a newer and wider freedom in the practice of their religion to the Catholics of that kingdom who hitherto had been harassed by unjust legal restrictions. Less gratifying and significant of the current mood everywhere was the report from France that once again the forces of Revolution had triumphed in that country and although the disorder was less bloody than before, the *legitimist* king, Charles X, was replaced by a *constitutional* monarch, Louis Philippe. This news was encouragement to radicals in the Papal States and through the well-organized activities of their secret societies a violent campaign of noisy objection and resistance to legitimate authority now began. There were open skirmishes with the police. There were loud demands for a united Italy and a new form of government, and of course there were the usual cries and promises of Liberty and Equality. In 1830, Pius VIII died. But even though the poison and violence of rebellion seethed on their every side it took the cardinals seven weeks before they could name a successor to Pius VIII. He was a cardinal but not yet a bishop and he was from the ranks of the ancient congregation known as Camaldolese monks. His name as a cardinal and a monk was Dom Mauro Cappellari and as pontiff, GREGORY XVI. He was sixty-three years of age and had been a successful abbot and canonist. He had won considerable renown as a scholar and theologian but proportionate distinction was not to be his as a pope. The situation to greet him was alarming and the future was a promise of even worse. Active revolution broke out as he took his throne and he was forced to accept the help of Austria. Regiments came and steel was bared until there was a semblance of order; but the parade of a foreign soldiery within a state is no healthy antidote for trouble and faces remained sullen and conspirators continued to meet and plot. The obnoxious doctrines of the extremists found audiences of increased size because there were undoubtedly some reasons for grievances amongst the people. They were exasperated at being ruled by the priesthood in all things, for in the papal territories few laymen held important offices or were allowed to sit in the grand councils. Rule of the most absolute type prevailed although almost every other nation had seen fit to make concessions of some form to the advancing spirit, diluted and perverted though it might be, of what was called democracy. The Pope, who once had written a work entitled *The triumph of the Church against the Assaults of Innovators,* and the old men around him refused to bow in any way to the popular and prevailing trend. It was their opinion that chaos and confusion would result in changing the methods of yesterday and modern tendencies were regarded with horror as having been born of the violence of the French Terror and the irreligious teachings of Voltaire.

But this was a time when the bulk of the people everywhere considered the idea of parliaments and such bodies from the ecstatic viewpoint of idealism. Romans of a later generation might cheer lustily at the appearance of a Dictator but in the second quarter of the XIX Century the same precincts had echoed just as loudly with enthusiastic shouts for the liberal way. The Pope, while wishing to be charitable, resolutely set his face against Liberalism with the result that revolt flared for a second time and again the Austrians, fearful of a general insurrection, marched to the rescue. This ready assistance alarmed the French who suspected the Austrian garrisons might be in

Italy for other purposes than suppressing rebellion. So they too despatched regiments to the papal property of Ancona and neither power withdrew until several years later.

Prince von Metternich, the great Austrian statesman, convinced Pope Gregory that many of his troubles could be rectified by the appointment of a new Secretary of State and thus the stern and haughty Cardinal Lambruschini was given the position. His remedy for social unrest was severity and so matters grew worse instead of better in the temporal territories of the Church. It must not be thought that the struggle for wider political freedom was confined to laymen alone. Many a churchman was sympathetic to the new ideas and the journal *Avenir,* edited by the brilliant and enterprising Abbé de Lamennais, earned the particular disapproval of the Pope because of the support it gave liberalism and in fact it resulted in the encyclical *Mirari vos* which was a hearty condemnation of the new trend. It would seem indeed that Gregory XVI had little use for anything of the coming age and that his appreciation in all things was confined to the past. Under his patronage scholarship was given impetus in Rome but his doctors and students must survey only what had been. He founded a rich museum which exhibited the ancient Etruscan and Egyptian glories, but with thunder in his voice he forbade the building of a railroad within his domain.

But while there might be trouble in Rome and discontent in Italy and change throughout Europe the great machinery of Church organization, lubricated by devotion and fueled by the fires of faith, continued to function smoothly and progressively. A new hierarchy on a new continent was being established in Australia and vicariates were springing into existence throughout the wide areas of the South Seas. The Mass was being sung by missionaries in the distant corners of most of the dimly known places, China, Tibet, Africa. The trudge of the persevering priest, the glitter of his upraised chalice, was known in all these lands, and in both South and North America the ancient faith,

long established, was flourishing with mounting energy and
assured permanency.

Death came to Gregory XVI on the first day of June, 1846,
and a fortnight later the cardinals met with the knowledge that
the grave conditions of the time demanded a speedy election.
And yet, to their own surprise and not quite according to plans
of the various parties, there was a pope within the next forty-
eight hours. This was because the Austrian faction had pressed
immediately and heavily for their candidate, the stern ex-Secre-
tary of State, Cardinal Lambruschini, and in a quick move to
thwart the unpopular design the other cardinals, actually not
yet fixed on their own choice, cast their ballots for the cardinal
Bishop of Imola not thinking that a decisive majority would be
forthcoming. But the result was a heavy majority in his favor
and though the Viennese court made haste to send a veto it
was too late. By the time it arrived the name of the new Pope,
Pius IX, had been recorded and proclaimed.

In most ways the new pontiff differed from his predecessors.
He was much younger, being only fifty-four, and he had travelled extensively, even to South America where he had served
on the staff of the Delegate to Chile. He had enjoyed a distinguished career as a diplomat and as an administrative prelate
and he had made no mistakes. His family was proud of its
quarterings and in his youth it was intended he should wear
the impressive uniform of the Noble Guard; but ill-health killed
these hopes and later had come a vocation and the cassock. His
full name was Giovanni-Maria Mastai-Ferretti and he was a man
of imposing and handsome presence who was not alarmed at the
new order and as a sovereign was willing to negotiate and indeed
quite anxious to make concessions to liberalism. Only thirty days
after his installation he was given the salutes and plaudits of a
popular ruler as a series of wise actions made for the public good
will. A general amnesty was proclaimed for all political exiles
and prisoners of whom there were about two thousand from the
previous reign. It was announced that railroads, noisy symbols
of progress, would be permitted within the papal territories and

that henceforth there would be few or no restrictions to prevent the publication of newspapers. A layman, Count de Rossi, was made Prime Minister. Plans were put in motion to have representative non-clerics form a Government Council and other laymen were given posts hitherto occupied by churchmen. But while there were easy cheers on the Roman streets for these measures they failed to win the favor of the more dangerous and stubborn of the plotters who were firmly resolved not to make peace with any wearer of the tiara. It was their idea that the temporal power must be vested in secular hands, and circumstances were so shaping that this objective seemed not unobtainable: for revolution was flaring again in those countries which were bound to the Papal States by geography and treaty. In Paris there was high excitement in the streets, the bourgeois Louis Philippe hastily abandoned his sceptre, and soon the Second Republic, from which was to emerge the unimpressive figure of another claimant to the Imperial title, Louis Napoleon, nephew of the great warrior, was in existence. The contagion of change spread to Austria and the Emperor Ferdinand raced from the throne accompanied by his minister, the haughty Metternich. Later the young Francis Joseph was given the crown and order was restored but meanwhile there were gunfire and cries for liberty in all directions. The Hungarians rose in revolt but lost their strength because of fierce dissension between Magyar and Slav. The Milanese and Venetians took to arms and were aided by the King of Sardinia who, like the rulers of Tuscany and Naples, had been forced to grant his people a constitution amidst tumult and clamor.

The Papal States did not remain exempt from the prevailing fever. Pius met the mood with an offer of constitutional government but he refused to sanction war against Austria and this refusal provided the alert insurrectionists with a weapon to destroy his popularity. The inciters and rumor-mongers went to work and from obscure corners the whisper of "traitor" grew to hysterical shouts and accusations outside the Quirinal. The Prime Minister, Count Rossi, was assassinated, the Pope's secretary shot by his side, and in the uncertain darkness of an autumn night Pope Pius IX was forced to flee his city. He went to Gaeta and there was given the protection of the King of Naples whilst great disorder and confusion prevailed in Rome. Pius appealed for assistance to the Catholic nations and in Paris the shrewd Louis Napoleon, as yet wearing only the title of President, reacted favorably, not so much from motives of charity or pity, but because he saw that in occupying the Papal States with French troops he would gain strategic advantage against Austria. So French soldiers invaded Italy and were engaged by the Army of Garibaldi who had some success until reinforcements arrived from France. Rome was besieged and won and Garibaldi retreated while the other leader of the Italian nationalists, Mazzini, fled to Switzerland. A triumphant flourish of French trumpets declared the Roman Republic to be at an end and the Pope was invited to return. He displayed no great haste in doing so and, disillusioned by the results of his overtures and concessions to the liberals, he put, for the time being, the affairs of his temporal government in the hands of three cardinals who gained notoriety as the "Red Triumvirate." These three were of a breed and viewpoint which would have earned the approval of the stern Leo XII. They acted swiftly and with little mercy and soon the courts were filled and the gaols crowded. The Pope made Cardinal Antonelli his Secretary of State and this man, the last cardinal not to be a priest—for he was only possessed of deacon's orders—proved as severe as his three colleagues. Indeed his ruthlessness and domineering character quickly earned him a high unpopularity with both clergy and laity.

The Pope turned to his ecclesiastical tasks and found much to do. The Catholics of England, who up to this time like a missionary province were under the care of vicars apostolic, were given back their bishops. Westminster was created the Metropolitan See, twelve suffragan dioceses were designated, and thus the dignity of the hierarchy, the hierarchy which was so illustriously studded with the names of martyrs and saints and scholars, was restored. Nicholas Wiseman was made a cardinal and became Archbishop of Westminster. There was great rejoicing in Catholic circles but a howl of protest and alarm was heard from that unfortunate element of the English population which scents a sinister purpose every time the name of their country is inscribed by the papal pen. "I agree with you," Lord John Russell wrote from Downing Street to the Anglican Bishop of Durham, "in considering the late aggression of the Pope upon our Protestantism as insolent and insidious . . ." A member of the Upper House of Parliament declared that war should be made upon the Pope and from his pulpit an Anglican clergyman stated: "I would make it a capital offence to administer the Confession in this country. Transportation would not satisfy me. Death alone would prevent the evil. This is my sober conviction."

Despite such sentiments a great revival of the old religion was taking place in the island kingdom. The hierarchy was restored in 1850 and during the year following among the large number of converts there were no fewer than thirty-three Anglican ministers, including Edward Manning who was to be the successor of Cardinal Wiseman. The hierarchy was also re-established in Holland and once again to the sweet thunder of the ancient chant an Archbishop stepped to his throne in the historic see of Utrecht. In every direction Pius IX showed how seriously he regarded his title as Father of the Universal Church. Great efforts were made to win the loyalty of the Eastern schismatics and success of this kind was had at Goa. In Jerusalem the Latin Patriarchate was re-established and the long fidelity of the Irish acknowledged by the bestowal of the Red Hat upon the Archbishop of Dublin, Dr. Cullen, the first time that an Irish prelate was so honored. The New World was not ignored or neglected and in the United States alone, despite the ravages of a terrible civil war in which brother fought against brother and religion proved no better cement than the ties of blood, there was the erection of forty-six new dioceses or vicariates, and a North American College was approved for Rome. A few years later Archbishop McCloskey of New York was raised to the scarlet and before this event full and comprehensive concordats had been made with the Central and South American nations. New treaties were also made with Spain and Portugal and Austria, although there were fresh anxieties and long vexations to the Catholic interest in Germany and Switzerland and in Russian-dominated Poland which required delicate negotiation and manipulation. All these things and many more, so different and so full of detail and problem, received the attention and the direction of the Pope during the thirty-two years of his pontificate, but they dwindled to littleness in comparison with the importance of two great dogmatic pronouncements which were made in this reign. After profound consultation with hundreds of theologians and wise men of the Church he provided another beacon to light the way for the faithful amidst the storms of cynicism and rejection and doubt which were characterizing his era. Just before the Christmas of 1854 the doctrine of the Immaculate Conception was defined as an article of Catholic belief and in the majestic confines of St. Peter's an audience of over two hundred bishops and many other dignitaries heard the solemn words. "We declare, pronounce, and define that the doctrine which holds that the most Blessed Virgin Mary was, in the first instant of her conception, by a singular grace and privilege of Almighty God, in virtue of the merits of Christ Jesus, the Saviour of the human race, preserved free from all stain of original sin, is revealed by God, and on that account is to be firmly and constantly believed by the faithful."

Fourteen years later Pope Pius was to summon a General Council of the Vatican, an event which demanded and received immense preparation and care. Such a call had not been heard in the Church for three centuries and when the Fathers, at one time to number nearly eight hundred prelates, did assemble it was with the painful knowledge that the temporal power of the papacy had again suffered a severe setback. After the return of the Pope to Rome from his flight to Gaeta the security of his State had depended upon the presence of French troops but eventually Count Cavour, the Piedmontese premier, whose ambition it was to mould Italy into one nation under a constitutional and monarchical form of government, had struck a bargain with Napoleon III. A Franco-Italian war against Austria followed in which the latter power was vanquished. Then the spoils were shared and, regardless of mutual accusations of treachery amongst the allies, Nice and Savoy went to France and four-fifths of the Papal domains were annexed to Sardinia while the protests of the Pope were lost in the clamor of the new Italian nationalism and patriotism. All that remained to the pontiff now was one province and his temporal rule of the small strip of land was only guaranteed by a French garrison which the French Emperor had the grace to leave in Rome. Once indeed these troops were withdrawn and immediately an army, under the command of the audacious Garibaldi, attacked Rome. It was beaten off and the Frenchmen, because of Catholic sympathy in France, were then returned.

On the eighth day of December, 1869, the Twentieth General Council gathered in the Basilica of St. Peter. It was the largest-attended synod in the history of the Church and an almost complete unanimity was to mark its decisions although in the preliminary discussions there were periods of hot dispute and bitter words. There were important matters of doctrine and faith and discipline to be discussed but the main subject, the thing that was on all lips and in all thoughts, was the proposed definition of Papal Infallibility. Violent controversy raged both within and without the Council over this question and the newspapers of the world became filled with the noise of the argument. The Pope kept aloof from the debate and so too, surprisingly enough, did most of the national rulers who, although there was powerful influence to provoke their intervention, preferred to follow the example of Bismarck who wisely declared that the affairs of the Council were affairs of religion alone and that there would be no interference, diplomatic or otherwise, from him. An aggressive leader of the non-Infallibilists was another German and one of the Church's most learned historians,

Dr. Döllinger of Munich, and because of his fierce opinions he chose the road of schism rather than bow to the will of the majority. It is difficult to understand his attitude. Sincere Catholics had always accepted the dogmatic pronouncements of a pope without question and such obedience was acknowledgement of infallibility. But now that it was proposed to make it a formal article of faith the very meaning of the word itself became confused and was challenged. *Infallibility* was mistaken for *impeccability* and it was erroneously assumed and widely believed that if the definition were adopted infallibility would be claimed for the conduct and actions of the Pope at all times. Nothing could be clearer than the graceful prose of Cardinal Manning's translation. "We teach and define that it is a dogma divinely revealed: That the Roman Pontiff when he speaks 'ex cathedra,' that is, when in discharge of his office of Pastor and Doctor of all Christians, by virtue of his supreme Apostolic authority, he defines a doctrine regarding faith or morals to be held by the Universal Church, by the divine assistance promised to him in blessed Peter, is possessed of that infallibility with which the divine Redeemer willed that His Church should be endowed for defining doctrine regarding faith or morals: and that therefore such definitions of the Roman Pontiff are irreformable of themselves and not from the consent of the Church."

There existed a party of prelates who while not doubting the truth of Infallibility were of the opinion that the time was inopportune to declare the definition and because of this fifty-five bishops remained absent on the day of the final vote, which was July 18th, 1870. Five hundred and thirty-five of their brethren did attend and of this number five hundred and thirty-three voted their favor and only two, Bishop Riccio of Sicily and Bishop Fitzgerald of Little Rock in the U.S.A., gave the answer of objection, *non placet*. But after the doctrine of Infallibility had been officially promulgated the two bishops along with their absent colleagues withdrew their dissent and with admirable and prompt docility made submission of obedience and agreement.

In all corners of the world the decision of the Council had

been awaited with eagerness but now another excitement, the
explosion of cannon, intervened to occupy the popular attention.
For on the day following the promulgation Napoleon III chose
at last to challenge the growing military strength of Germany.
War was declared and the armies marched; and finally, after
the terrible meeting at Sedan, Napoleon glumly offered his
sword in the traditional gesture of defeat and surrender. Defeat
in Paris was no less a disaster in Rome for the French garrison
was hurriedly evacuated and the city became destitute of defence
except for a small corps of brave but inadequate volunteers and
guards. King Victor Emmanuel II of the new kingdom of Italy
sent an envoy to Pius who begged that the pontiff should bow
to the inevitable, but he steadfastly refused to make terms and
a few months later, after but a brief display of resistance on the
part of the Papal troops, the Italian army took possession of
Rome. Much to their dismay Pius had ordered his soldiery to
put down their arms and as the invaders entered the city he
addressed some diplomats who had come to his side, anxious
for his safety. He was serenely unafraid. "I have written to the
King," he told them calmly, "I do not know whether my letter
has reached him. But, whether it has or not, I have now no hope
of touching his heart, or of arresting his ungracious proceedings
. . . Bixio, the notorious Bixio, is here at our doors, supported
by the Italian army. He is now a Royal General. Years ago, when
he was a simple Republican, he made promise, that should he
ever get within the walls of Rome, he would throw me in the
Tiber . . . Only yesterday I received a communication from
the young gentlemen of the American College, begging, I should
say demanding, permission to arm themselves and to constitute
themselves the defenders of my person. Though there are few in
Rome in whose hands I should feel more secure than in the
hands of these young Americans, I declined their generous offer
with thanks . . . I would be glad, gentlemen, to say that I rely
upon you and upon the countries you have the honor to represent . . . But times are changed. The poor old Pope has now

no one on earth upon whom he can rely. Relief must come from heaven."

There was a deep and solemn silence after this pathetic speech for the diplomats knew well that the pontiff had spoken truly. No help could be expected from the Governments they represented. As though reading their thoughts the Pope suddenly spoke again: "Still, gentlemen, remember the Catholic Church is immortal!"

No objection to the seizure of Rome came from any of the nations save a solitary protest from the small and distant Republic of Ecuador. The Italian Government, in a legislation known as the Law of Guarantees, promised to safeguard the independence of the Holy See and to give extra-territorial privileges to such premises as the Vatican Palace and the Basilica and to provide an annual payment to the pontiff of three and a quarter million lire but he ignored all such overtures and refused to countenance or accept in any way the usurpation of his temporal power. He retired in full dignity to the confines of the Vatican Palace and its gardens and remained there, a voluntary prisoner, until his death some eight years later and it was an example which was followed by his successors until the signing of the Lateran Treaty in 1929. But though Pius chose to be a prisoner he was no hermit nor did idleness eat his time. Great numbers of pilgrims came yearly to present their professions of respect and devotion and to his end he was occupied with administrative duties and problems.

Further trouble came to sadden his remaining days when Germany was disturbed by the struggle between Church and State which was known as the *Kulturkampf* movement. Prince Bismarck was imbued with the fear that the strength and influence of Catholicism within his country constituted a menace to that Teutonic unity which was his dream, so a highly organized attack to obliterate the influence of the Church was commenced. Antagonistic Protestant officials were appointed to supervise Catholic ecclesiastical and educational affairs. The Jesuits and then many of the other religious Orders were expelled and laws were made to regulate the training of the clergy and to limit the powers of the episcopacy. Severe restrictions of different varieties but all with the one purpose, the crushing of the Church, were imposed and enforced but it was all in vain. Their sees and parishes might become vacant, their bishops and priests could be slandered and sent to exile or prison, but German Catholics remained true to their pledge of baptism and faith. The inglorious campaign of their Government was a failure and eventually Bismarck was convinced of his mistake; but such news never came to gladden the heart of Pius for by this time he had been carried to his grave. And even during this last sad journey, which by request of the Italian Government was made under cover of the night darkness, his name and dignity were not spared insult and humiliation. Gangs of ruffians, hired by those whose interest it was that there should be no demonstrations of papal popularity, accompanied the mourners and intruded upon their sorrow with jeers and threats to hurl the corpse into the Tiber. Their ferocious promises were not fulfilled and Pope Pius IX was honorably buried amidst the echoes of sincere lamentations in the church of San Lorenzo, outside the Walls. He had lived eighty-six years and his pontificate of thirty-two years was the longest on the long roll.

One of the many burdens carried by the successor of St. Peter is the fact that the many centuries have accumulated a legacy of significant and traditional ceremonial which haunts every major and most of his minor acts. Even when death approaches there are prescribed rites and, no matter how great his agony or torture, witnesses within sight of his deathbed; and when finally his spirit leaves his frame there is again no escape from the rules of the tradition. That high official who is called the Camerlengo (or Chamberlain) of the Church has to verify the death of the Pontiff according to an historic formula, for this, in addition to supervising the property and revenues of the Holy See and managing the convention of a Conclave, is one of his traditional duties. He advances to the corpse and addresses the dead man three times, calling him by his baptismal name, and three times also he taps him gently on the forehead with a silver hammer. Then, after the sad and solemn silence, he makes the official announcement that the pontiff is dead. The prelate who so officiated over the remains of Pius IX was a thin and pale faced cardinal of aristocratic and ascetic appearance named Vincenzo Gioacchino Pecci. The next time it would be his head that would receive the touch of the silver hammer for a few days later a conclave of sixty-one cardinals, after three quick sessions of voting, chose him to be Pope.

He took the name of Leo XIII and one of his first gestures was a display of initiative and independence: to show that he was of the same mind as his predecessor towards the Italian Government he broke with tradition and instead of giving his first blessing, *Urbi et Orbi,* to the City and the World, from the outside of St. Peter's, the famous words were uttered from the inner loggia. That friendly relations were never to be restored with the Italian Government during his reign was not due to any stubborn hostility or sullen resentment on the part of Leo XIII. He was not that kind of man. It is true he adhered to the policy he had inherited, remained within the Vatican, and at certain times forbade Catholics to participate in the municipal and parliamentary elections; but he also let it be known that agreement was not impossible. It was the continued anti-papal actions of various Italian officials which prevented any formation of a reasonable and tranquil arrangement. There were anti-clerical legislations and even the Pope's seclusion within the Vatican was at times violated by the noise of coarse demonstrations, celebrating the end of the temporal power of the papacy, which were permitted and indeed encouraged by the secular authority.

Because of his vigorous championship of the rights of the working man Leo XIII was to be called the Socialist Pontiff in an age when the majority of society scented anarchy in any attempt to foster social justice. Yet he was no product of the oppressed but was from the nobility. His father was Count Ludovico Pecci and his mother was born of an ancient and illustrious line. From his early years the young Pecci had seemed marked for the great things. At the age of eight along with his elder brother, he was entrusted for education to the Jesuits, first at Viterbo and then at the Roman College, and at both places he displayed an astonishing aptitude for scholarship, taking honors in all subjects. Experience in government came to him early, for after his reception into the priesthood Rome saw fit, after a brief apprenticeship, to employ him as an administrator in the provinces. He gained both distinction and popularity in this role and then, in his early thirties, he was made an Archbishop and despatched to Belgium as Nuncio, a highly important diplomatic assignment, for the King of that country, Leopold of Coburg and uncle of Queen Victoria of England, was considered to be one of the most astute of Europe's sovereigns. The youthful Nuncio remained in Belgium for three years and then was called back to Italy and given the ancient See of Perugia which he occupied with distinction and grace for the following thirty-two years. During this period he established all manner of charitable institutions and colleges and hospitals but he seldom ventured to Rome for, although he possessed the favor of Pius IX, the Papal Secretary of State, Cardinal Antonelli, held little liking for him. But after the death of Antonelli the Pope summoned him and soon he was given the important office of Camerlengo.

With the donning of the tiara this man, who was destitute of temporal power, found himself involved in the great struggle with Bismarck who already had declared he would "never follow the road to Canossa" and that the Church in Germany would be forced to his terms. Leo inherited the problems of the *Kulturkampf* and he dealt with them not only with courage and principle but with a masterful and tactful diplomacy which amounted to genius and which attracted the attention and admiration of the chancelleries of Europe. A passive resistance on the part of the Catholics in Germany was the answer to Bismarck's schemes and he countered with ruthless methods. Hundreds of priests were imprisoned and so too were the bishops and archbishops, but the principle of "Render unto Caesar" was given a rigid obedience. The Catholics of Germany would suffer no intrusion upon their spiritual rights but neither would they offer disloyalty to the State. "We appeal to Your Majesty's magnanimity in the hope of obtaining a restoration of peace and repose of conscience for a great number of your subjects," wrote the Pope to Emperor Wilhelm, "and the Catholic subjects of your Majesty will never fail to show themselves, as the faith which they profess ordains that they should do, with the most conscientious devotion, respectful and faithful towards your Majesty . . ." The royal hand was guided by Prince Bismarck in reply. "The cordial words of Your Holiness lead me to hope that you will be disposed to put in operation the powerful influence that the constitution of your Church gives you over its ministers, in order that those among them who have refused to follow the example of the population confided to their care may submit themselves to the laws of the country which they inhabit."

Leo answered courteously but suddenly another element intervened to change the policy of the German Government. A small anti-monarchial party, wild and radical and atheistic, was growing within the country and two attempts were made to assassinate the Emperor. He escaped and his answer to congratulations upon doing so was significant. "This only shows," he said, "how we must take care that the people shall not lose their religious scruples." A great number of Catholic clergy were either in exile or gaol at this time but soon Bismarck was telling Parliament: "It is the part of a brave man to fight when the conditions demand it, but no real statesman desires to make combat a permanent institution." It was an admission of defeat and gradually the laws against the Catholics were relaxed. Diplomatic relations were resumed between the Holy See and Berlin, and the German Prince Imperial paid a cordial visit to the Pope. Then to astonish the world came a request from the German Government, petitioning Leo to act as arbitrator in a dispute with Spain over the possession of the Caroline Islands. It was a return to the ancient respect and a gracious and splendid acknowledgment of papal impartiality and Leo did not fail the trust. He refused to arbitrate but he would mediate and his scheme of settlement, an example of justice, was accepted cheerfully and with gratitude by both States.

A crisis also confronted the Church in France where the Government was markedly anti-clerical and where all those in opposition to the Republic, the Monarchist and Conservative elements, persisted in identifying their political activities with the interests of the Church. Leo, with his splendid detachment from prejudice, perceived that such a state of affairs was wrong. Continental Republicanism, particularly in France, had hitherto been antagonistic to the Church: but that was in the past and the present, and the Pope, with far seeing vision, was thinking of the future. He summoned and conferred with his friend Cardinal Lavigerie, and shortly afterwards this prelate, who was the influential Archbishop of Algiers, upon welcoming a group of French naval officers to his See, made a speech in which it was emphasized that the Catholics of France should resign themselves to the existing Government. His declaration excited all France and threw the conservatives into consternation. One bishop wrote to the Papal Secretary of State, at this time the capable Cardinal Rampolla, asking for definition and guidance. Which form of rule did the papacy endorse? Republic or Monarchy? The reply came quickly and to the effect that the Church "whose mission is divine, and embraces all times and places" was against no system of government and that the Vatican was aloof from the struggles of dynastic and political factions. Later, in 1892, the Pope addressed an Encyclical to the French people in which the same principle was reiterated. "The Catholic, like every other citizen, has full liberty to prefer one form of government to another, where none of those political or social forms is opposed by its very nature to the teachings of sound reason or maxims of Christian doctrine." But, explained the Pope, "Governments must change. No one can consider any form of civil government as so definite that it must remain for ever immutable. In societies purely human, all history shows that time works great changes in their political institutions. These changes may modify partly or totally the form of government; these changes often come as the result of a violent crisis to which succeeds anarchy and the breaking up of laws. In such conditions a social necessity is imposed on a nation. It must without delay provide for its own security. That social necessity justifies the creation and the existence of new governments whatever form they take, if these new governments are necessary to public order, all public order being impossible without some recognized form of government. . . In practice the character of the laws depends more on the character of the men in power, than on the mere form of that power. The laws will be good or bad, according as the lawmakers have minds inspired by good or bad principles, and allow themselves to be guided by political prudence, or by partisan passion."

A representative of the *Petit Journal* of Paris was received by Leo who, unlike many contemporary sovereigns and statesmen, well realized the power and the wide audience accorded the Press in a modern world. The journalist was told: "My conviction is that all French citizens ought to re-unite on constitutional grounds. Each one, of course, can keep his personal preferences, but when it comes to political action, there is only the government which France has given herself. The Republic is a form of Government as legitimate as any other. . . The United States, in the republican form of government, despite the dangers of a liberty almost boundless, grow greater and greater every day, and the Catholic Church has developed itself there without having any struggles to sustain against the State . . ." With the same clarity further instruction and advice came in a later Encyclical: "Accept the Republic, that is to say, the power constituted and existing amongst you; respect it, and be submitted to it, as representing the power that comes from God. All political history furnishes, without cessation, examples of unexpected changes in form of government. These changes are far from being always legitimate in their origin. It would be vain to expect that it should be so. Nevertheless, the supreme advantage of the common welfare and of public tranquillity imposes on us the acceptance of those new governments established *de facto* in place of former governments, which *de facto* are no more."

Leo XIII might be a sovereign without cannon or fleets but the impact of his influence was felt everywhere. In Africa an infamous commerce was being renewed. The savage crack of the slave driver's whip was becoming louder and more audacious and the pitiful processions, the self-propelled freight, fettered and handcuffed, of the desert caravans, were becoming longer and commoner. The misunderstanding and jealousy which had marked the relations of the European powers in their intrusion and exploitation of Africa's wide regions and fabulous riches had resulted in a stimulation of the slave trade which was conducted by Arabs but which was protected by profit-sharing scoundrels of all races and creeds. The suspicion with which each nation regarded the activities of a rival power on the so-called Dark Continent prevented any effective action against the vile traffic and so it flourished without hindrance and with increasing boldness. In Brazil slavery, although under far more humane conditions, existed also, and to the hierarchy of that country the Pope sent instructions, exhorting them to work for *immediate* abolition rather than the gradual process of liberation which had been suggested in other quarters. To the credit of the Brazilians, the Pope's suggestion was adopted very quickly. Meanwhile, acting with his friend Cardinal Lavigerie, Leo embarked upon a campaign to break the abominable power of the Arab traders. "Since Africa," he said, "is the principal theatre of this traffic . . . we recommend to all missionaries . . . to consecrate their strength, and even their lives, to that sublime work of redemption. We recommend them also to ransom as many slaves as it may be possible for them to do. . ." A gift of 300,000 francs accompanied these words while Cardinal Lavigerie preached a crusade throughout all Europe and the nations bestirred themselves to a Conference on the subject. In England, which had produced such champions of human liberty as Wilberforce and

Clarkson, a great movement was already under way and publicly the Pope complimented the country "which had so well and for so long a time proved her interest in the cause of negroes." The slave traffic was gradually abolished but the lot of the negroes was to remain hard and unjust in many countries. With the vision that he exhibited in all matters, Leo foresaw and deplored such conditions and in an attempt to change them he stressed the age old fact that color and racial prejudices were no part of Catholic dogma and he urged that vocations should be encouraged amongst the liberated slaves and their sons and that they should be given every facility to train for the priesthood.

As the years of his pontificate mounted the justice and philanthropy of Leo XIII was universally acknowledged and the result was an enormous popularity. Many of the old prejudices and antagonisms, hitherto existing in the Protestant countries, were lessened. In him the Uniate Catholics of the East found an intelligent and zealous patron and as a consequence there was a great revival of religion and scholarship in their ranks. The non-Catholics of the East were impressed by a spirit of cooperation and understanding which was neither clumsy nor presumptuous and which did much to efface long-standing feuds and enmities. During his reign two hundred and forty-eight episcopal or metropolitan sees and forty-eight vicariates were established and a new respect was given the Nuncios and Apostolic Delegates whom he sent to the capitals of the world. In England the stream of conversions which had begun in the previous reign continued and High Church circles, in which the first Viscount Halifax was a predominant figure, were stirred by hopes and agitation for a return to Rome. Leo acknowledged and encouraged such aims by a special letter, *Ad Anglos,* in which he stated: "The time cannot be far distant when We must appear to render an account of Our stewardship to the Prince of Pastors, and how happy, how blessed should We be if We could bring to Him some fruit, some realization of these, Our wishes. . . Difficulties there may be for us all to face, but these are not of a nature which should delay. . . No doubt the many changes that have come about, and time itself, have caused the existing divisions to take deeper root. But is that a reason to give up all hope of remedy, reconciliation, and peace?" The appeal caused no anger in England even amongst those who were always on guard against the devices of "Papistry," for it was patently no haughty summons or subtle enticement but merely a sincere and gently worded prayer. But despite such a tolerant reception and despite the strong yearnings of the High Churchmen the time had not yet arrived for the Return and this was made plain by the Archbishop of Canterbury who in a letter to his clergy displayed no resentment but nevertheless was firmly of the opinion that as yet there was no chance of a practical agreement.

Strong differences existed within the Church of England regarding ritual and rite. In some parishes the sight of candlesticks on an altar was sufficient to incite cries of "Popery" but other churches were ornamented with the Stations of the Cross, and in such premises the Confessional functioned and a fully vested clergy, to the swing of thurible and drift of incense, followed the forms of the old practice. Amongst Anglicans of this liking there were often qualms, invoked by the memory of Cranmer and Cromwell, as to the sacramental powers of their clergy. Cleavage with the Holy See does not necessarily mean invalidity of clerical orders and Rome acknowledges that the Apostolic succession is carried on by the schismatic Churches of the East. Leo XIII appointed a commission to examine the complicated and delicate question as to whether the succession was possessed by the Church of England. After a dispassionate and thorough scrutiny the commission gave judgment that the sacred community had been broken during the reign of Queen Elizabeth. The adverse decision, even if not accepted by many whom it concerned, was received peacefully enough in England and so too was the establishment of hierarchies in Scotland and Wales. A few years earlier the latter procedure in England had been greeted by excessive alarm and storm but now, thanks to the charm and graceful diplomacy of Leo XIII, there was but little objection and between Queen Victoria, who was supposed to have shown great anger when Pius IX named an Archbishop of Westminster, and the Pope there were nought but messages of esteem and good wishes.

This amity was regarded with little enthusiasm in unhappy Ireland where a long suffering tenantry was showing signs of organized revolt against an intolerable system which amongst other evils permitted absentee and uncaring landlords to put their affairs in the hands of agents whose methods were often terribly brutal and notoriously unscrupulous. An organization known as the Land League was formed to combat unjust conditions. Its leaders were promptly gaoled by the English but to the amazement and indignation of Irish Nationalism the Land League Plan of campaign was also condemned by the Vatican as being illegal opposition to constituted authority and thus contrary to the principles of social law. To many it seemed as though the influence of Whitehall had formed the opinions of the Pope's advisers and for a time there was excitement and extravagant talk among a minority of rebellious spirits. But the cloud passed by. Dr. Walsh, a cleric noted for his courageous efforts to secure justice for the Irish peasant, was appointed Archbishop of Dublin, and the papal blessing went to gladden the nuptials of a Land League leader who had suffered imprisonment. These, and many similar acts, soon convinced the most ardent of Irish Nationalists that the Vatican had not fallen victim to English guile. The strength of Irish Catholicism was proven again, and the sturdy faith that had endured for nigh on fifteen centuries, the faith that was the pride and glory of a race, flowed on with unabated strength and undimmed lustre.

Leo XIII was keenly aware of the rapid growth of Catholicism in the United States and his interest and observance of the affairs of the Republic was unflagging and thorough. Upon despatching the young ex-Rector of the American College, Bishop, later to be Cardinal, O'Connell, to his new See he advised him that: "There is no room today in the bishop's chair for a mere mystic. The bishop of today, in America in particular, must be a man of high and keen intellectual vision, thoroughly in touch with conditions that affect the public and spiritual welfare of his diocese and his nation. . . He must be a man of action. That is his particular duty as a bishop . . ." When it was proposed to Leo that a Catholic University be founded in Washington his approval came quickly for, in addition to his other talents, he was a scholar and a patron of scholars. Indeed his enthusiasm and direction brought revival of Scholasticism and in a special Bull he urged that the philosophy of St. Thomas Aquinas be stressed in the schools. With his consent for the erection of the institution in Washington went the wise admonition that it should be: "directed by American intelligence, and if, for the moment, you have to ask for your faculties the help of foreign professors, it must be done with the intention of developing the national talent, and training professors capable of forming, by degrees, native faculties worthy of the name that is borne by your university." Between the hierarchy of the United States and the Pope there always existed an extraordinary sympathy and understanding, and the dangers that so easily could have been products of the phenomenally rapid spread of the Church in the wide expanses of the young Republic never materialized. Once indeed, a French author in writing of the activities of the zealous founder of the Paulist Order, Father Hecker, penned a picture in which Rome detected a theological concept which could be construed as error and innovation. A letter went to the American episcopate and promptly there was returned a model reply of filial agreement and assurance. Orthodoxy was in no danger in the United States. The Pope had bestowed the red hat upon the popular and distinguished Archbishop of Baltimore, Cardinal Gibbons, and this prelate was given earnest attention when he vigorously upheld the rights of the "Knights of Labour" which was in reality a trades union and not, as its high flown title had led some churchmen of lesser perception to believe, a secret society of the continental type, dominated by anarchistic aims.

Of all the triumphs, and there were many, which gave fame

to the memory of Leo XIII, the greatest was achieved in the field of sociology. For he was, in advance of his generation, acutely aware of the hardships and injustices inflicted upon the working man by the capitalistic system. Always a protector of human dignity he deplored the humiliating serfdom which had grown with the industrial age, the base system in which labor was just a commodity to be bought cheaply, used and abused until exhaustion, and then discarded abruptly, the ignoble system in which the employer was all powerful and his laborer without voice or right. It is the passing of time which either dissipates or endorses a claim to greatness and as the years go by it is significant that the pronouncements of Leo XIII on social justice loom with increasing importance. Not only did he lament and protest against the condition of his day, but he foresaw the dangers that such evils were forming for the future. In his famous encyclical, Rerum Novarum, *On the condition of the Working Classes,* he offered a plan which while it received attention and applause was not given practical support. The established system was too firmly established for an immediate change. Trial of the proposed plan meant smaller profits, the risk of being overwhelmed by competitors. It was all very well for the Pope to be idealistic and talk of justice but in the world of cold fact who wished to think of future and problematical troubles at the cost of smaller dividends? So reasoned those who had it within their power to give trial to the papal ideas.

Leo XIII was considered to be an old man when he was elected for he could already count sixty-eight years to his life, but he ruled until he was ninety-four and to the end he was active in thought and constant in achievement. His encyclicals and pronouncements form the lengthiest series in the long story of the papacy and always they were clear and easily understood by the humblest of his flock. Typical of the force and simplicity of his prose is his explanation of the Church's objection to divorce: "Because of divorce, the nuptial contract becomes subject to fickle whim; affection is weakened; pernicious incentives are given to conjugal infidelity; the care and education of offspring are harmed; easy opportunity is afforded for the breaking up of homes; the seeds of discord are sown among families; the dignity of woman is lessened and brought down and she runs the risk of being deserted after she has served her husband as an instrument of pleasure. And since it is true that for the ruination of the family and the undermining of the State nothing is so powerful as the corruption of morals, it is easy to see that divorce is of the greatest harm to the prosperity of families and of State."

He wrote continuously and even when the final weakness came he called for pen and paper and composed a Latin sonnet on the death that was surely approaching. His illness lasted two weeks and then, on July 30th, 1903, after receiving the Sacraments he died with serenity. As he expired there arose a spontaneous chorus of mourning and tribute from a world which already was aware of the prestige and lustre he had brought to his office.

For sixteen years Cardinal Rampolla had shared the confidences and had executed the policies of Leo XIII in his capacity as Secretary of State. "We have worked well together, you and I," Leo had told him before he had died: and indeed it had been a collaboration so marked by success and tranquillity that it was thought, on all sides, that the next pope would surely be Rampolla. The conclave assembled, the doors were locked, and the first three ballots were in his favor but suddenly to prevent his election the solemn proceedings were dramatically halted by Cardinal Puzyna who rose and, white-faced and tremulous of voice for his was a disagreeable task, informed his startled colleagues that on behalf of the Emperor Franz Josef of Austria he was forced to exercise the right of veto. There was consternation amongst the scarlet clad voters but after a formal protest the candidature of the former Secretary of State was withdrawn with dignity and with manifestations of relief on his part. There were four more ballots and each time more votes were counted for Cardinal Giuseppe Sarto, the Patriarch of Venice. The fourth scrutiny revealed that he had acquired the necessary majority and, accepting his fate, he received the homage of his electors as Pope Pius X.

Unlike the aristocratic Leo and unlike Rampolla whose family were of princely rank the new Pius was peasant-born, the second of a large family that knew well the sting and anxiety of poverty. While he was still a child, an aptitude for scholarship had attracted the attention and favor of the local schoolmaster and the village priest, and both had helped with encouragement and tutoring. The vocation had come and at twenty-three the young Sarto was a priest and before him were eighteen years of work as curate, parish priest, and canon. Then had come the great moment when he was made a bishop. With pardonable pride it is related he displayed the episcopal ring to his mother and in answer the old peasant woman held up her left hand and smilingly reminded him that without the simple gold band the miracle would not have been possible. He was given the See of Mantua which because of the resistance of the Italian Government had been without a bishop for ten years and which as a consequence was in wretched circumstance. In the next ten years Bishop Sarto accomplished wonders and gained the praise and attention of the alert Pope, who rewarded him with the Patriarchate of Venice. This was an ancient and exalted office but it made no difference in the simple and frugal habits of the future Pius whose unmarried sisters continued to attend to his domestic wants. The Red Hat came, his administration was a conspicuous success. Then arrived the fateful day when, grieving for his late patron, he left to join the conclave. A great crowd accompanied him to the railway station where, it was noticed, he bought a return ticket.

On becoming Pope he continued to avoid pomp and ceremony as much as it was possible to do so, and when asked by a court official what distinctions he intended to bestow upon his sisters Pius, who could now scatter titles and rank as lavishly as his inclinations so desired, answered gravely that *Sisters of the Pope* would suffice for his kin. His earnest humility and sincere simplicity did not prevent him from being firm of will and determined in action when necessity demanded. For his Secretary of State he made a wise choice in the person of Raphael Merry del Val who was of Irish-Spanish ancestry and whose brother, a grandee of Spain, was the Ambassador of that country to the court of St. James. The combination of peasant Pope and nobly born Secretary of State proved to be a happy one and for the entire pontificate of eleven years, it worked with a rare harmony and with fruitful results. Pius remained more aloof in his diplomatic relations with the temporal rulers than had Leo XIII and to make sure there would be no more unseemly intrusions on their part to change the decisions of future conclaves, his *Commissum nobis* constitutionally abolished the right of veto. Although the policy inaugurated by his predecessors toward the Italian Government was followed he relaxed some of the restrictions of previous reigns, and thus made it possible for Catholics to participate in all the elections and to accept office as deputies in the national parliament. It was the cautious and friendly commencement of a slow and difficult road to reconciliation.

Fresh troubles came from France for the government of that republic had become even more anti-clerical in its opinions and finally, after a series of discreditable and carefully calculated incidents, the Concordat which had been in existence for a century was declared to be at an end and the Law of Separation between Church and State put into force. This meant confiscation of ecclesiastical properties and revenues and persecution and insult to the clergy. It also meant violence and demonstrations and often the unfortunate officials who were the instruments of the law were forced to call for protection or run from the ire of angry parishioners. The action of the French government was distinctly not popular with the French people and considerable dissatisfaction was voiced, particularly in the provinces, when the protest of the Pope was received with contempt and indifference by the President and the so-called Liberal group which surrounded him. In one respect the new and unjust law was beneficial to the Church for although it brought suffering and sudden poverty to the French clergy it also brought them a greater freedom from secular control and interference. There were now no rich benefices to excite the cupidity and invite the plots of the worldly-ambitious.

The same brand of Liberalism which held sway in France was also gaining ground in Spain and Portugal and in both countries there were anti-clerical outbreaks. A king and his son had been murdered in Portugal, the next king had abdicated, a Republic was proclaimed, and in the separation of Church and State which followed, numerous outrages in the name of Liberalism were perpetrated against the clergy. The doctrine of the mistitled and inflammatory creed was aptly described by Leo XIII as being "every man a law unto himself," and as a political force in practice its aims and methods, violent, revolutionary, subversive, and often atheistic, were antipathetic to Christian principles and vastly different to the tolerance and generosity that its benign label implied. Like Freemasonry the continental species of Liberalism held nothing in common with the movement of the same name which exists among the English speaking peoples and this is a fact which is often not understood in Great Britain and North America and which too often has caused bewilderment and anxiety in those countries as well as a misdirection of sympathies. Another movement to incur the alarm of the pontiff was that which went by the name of Modernism, an attempt by some misguided clerics and others to adjust religion to the prevailing fads of science and the current fancies of pseudohistorians. Pius saw the danger to orthodoxy, the threat to dogma, and by decree and encyclical the insidious propaganda was condemned. To leave no doubts as to the subject of his prohibition an encyclical, condemning major errors in the writings of the modernists, was issued from the Vatican. A storm of indignant and verbose protest greeted the papal action and, as he expected, the Pope was accused of being reactionary and narrow minded, but the heat of the crisis passed quickly and the cult of Modernism dissolved quietly into oblivion.

Pius X was the author of several reforms and innovations within the ecclesiastical structure and as the fiftieth anniversary of his ordination approached he declared: "Reform of the priesthood is the most beautiful gift that the clergy can offer us." Thorough examination and constructive criticism was given to the training of priests and to the operation of seminaries. A decree banished non-liturgical music from the churches and an Academy of Music was founded to encourage the study of the Gregorian chant. Church music, it was his firm opinion, should be marked by three qualities. "It should be holy; it should be a work of art; and it should have a universal appeal." The stupendous task of arranging and cataloguing the formless mass of Canon Law, the complicated accumulation of many centuries of continuous law-making, was a duty that appealed as a necessity to his orderly mind and a Commission of Cardinals, headed by Cardinal Gasparri and armed with powers to mobilize a corps of theologians, historians, and lawyers, was formed to vanquish the problem. Pius did not live to see the completion of this project but it was finished after fourteen arduous years and his successor paid him well deserved tribute for having commenced and made possible the success of the colossal undertaking. It was the wish of Pius that the people should partake of the Sacrament more often and because of his pleas there was a Eucharistic revival and Catholics everywhere, young and old, pressed forward in greater numbers and with increasing frequency to receive Holy Communion.

The fateful year of 1914 was the last year of Pius X. He was acutely conscious of the gathering clouds of war. The weight of his grief was perceptible to all and by every means within his power he attempted to avert the crisis; but his advice and pleas fell on empty ears. Many a responsible statesman belonging to the nations which were to be involved in the approaching disaster refused to believe up to the last minute that there would be war: but three months before the terrible hostilities began, the Pope quietly told a citizen of a South American republic: "How fortunate you are that you will not be here when war breaks out." When the fatal shots were fired at Sarajevo Pius was not surprised but, realizing the awful consequences, cried out in anguish, "Willingly would I sacrifice my life to ward off the terrible scourge!" Twice the Austrian Ambassador, in answer to a request that the papal blessing should be given to the armies of his country, was bluntly told: "I bless peace." But peace was not to be. Austria declared war on Serbia, Russia moved her great armies, and Germany, France and England joined the fray. Weakened by the strain of his anxiety the Pope sickened and was ordered to bed by his doctors. It was not a serious illness, they said, and there was nothing to fear for the Pope had inherited the sturdy physique of his peasant forebears. But in a few days, on the 20th of August, he was dead and although the attending physicians wrote bronchitis on their last bulletin his friends knew it was heart-break. The will that he left was typical of his humility. He asked that his funeral should have the minimum of ceremony and he humbly requested that a monthly allowance, "not to exceed 300 lire" should be given to his two sisters. For he had no money to leave, this Pope who had once said: "I was born poor; I have lived poor; and I wish to die poor."

The difficulty of travelling in wartime did not prevent the next conclave from functioning two weeks after the death of Pius. Cardinals from the warring nations arrived and faced each other in an atmosphere of tension as the ballots were given. The proceedings lasted three days and then the world was told that again there was a Pope, the Cardinal Jacopo della Chiesa, Archbishop of Bologna, who became BENEDICT XV. The education and training of the new pontiff differed greatly from the pastoral career of his predecessor for he was the son of a marquis and his studies at the Academy of Noble Ecclesiastics had been followed by long service in the Curia both as a diplomatist and economist. He had lived abroad as the secretary to a Nuncio and his abilities had won the confidence and esteem of the great Cardinal Rampolla. He had been an able Under-Secretary of State and, as Archbishop of Bologna, a successful administrative prelate; and it was believed by the Sacred College that he, more than anyone else, was fitted to deal with the involved diplomacy of a chaotic era. He was sixty years old and a man of diminutive

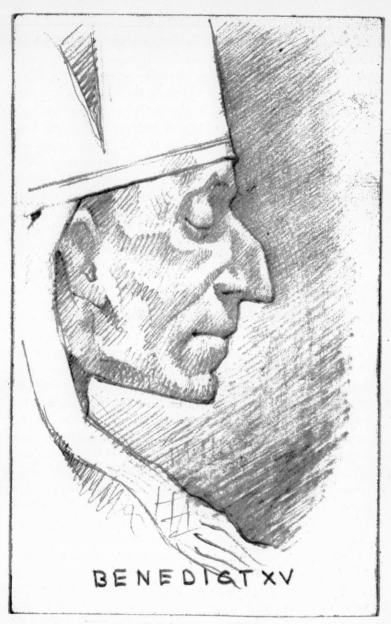

Benedict XV (1914-1922)

stature; and when, in adherence to traditional procedure, he was taken after the decisive scrutiny of the conclave to be garbed in the garment of his new rank it was found there was none to fit him. There were white cassocks of various sizes and to fit most men but all were too large for the new pope. "Caro," he remarked with a smile to the attending tailor, "you had quite forgotten me!"

Benedict donned the white cassock with a smile but from that moment there were few opportunities for him to indulge in pleasantries, for sorrow and disappointment and frustration were to be the dark mood of his reign. Before he became Pope he had told the priests of his archdiocese that "I should regret it if any of my clergy should take sides in this conflict. It is desirable that we pray for the cessation of the war without dictating to Almighty God in what way it should end." His opinions did not change when he was given the tiara. Throughout the long war he successfully pursued the difficult course of true neutrality and very soon after his election he announced he would "leave nothing undone to hasten the end of this calamity." Untiringly and heedless of rebuff and insult he worked to bring back peace to the world; but with sad and disheartening repetition his efforts were rejected or ignored and often received with misunderstanding and suspicion. In ancient times warring armies had sometimes suspended hostilities on Christmas day in observance of a charitable custom which was called the Truce of God. Benedict tried to revive this truce on the first Christmas of the war but although Great Britain, Germany and Belgium were not unsympathetic to the idea the rulers of France and Russia strongly opposed it, so there was no interruption to the thunder of the guns or to the flow of blood. The strict neutrality of the Vatican was questioned and criticized by zealous nationalists everywhere. The fiery patriot, inflamed by prejudice and passion and sincerely convinced of the justice of his country's cause, could not understand the impartiality of the Pope. In every nation voices were raised, the same voices that would be so quick to resent "papal interference" in normal secular affairs, the same voices that would angrily reject a decision adverse to their interest, now in critical and continual chorus demanding of Catholics why Benedict did not pronounce against the crimes of the enemy and uphold the true champions of righteousness. To such questions the Pope had given an answer early in 1915. "The Roman Pontiff," he declared, "must embrace all the combatants in one sentiment of charity; and as the Father of all Catholics he has among the belligerents large numbers of children for whose salvation he must be equally and without distinction solicitous. It is necessary, therefore, that in them he must consider not the special interests that divide them, but the common bond of faith which makes them brothers."

Rigidly observing the rules of neutrality himself, the Pope was courageously outspoken when those rules were broken by others. Even the German Chancellor had publicly admitted, in an address to his Parliament, that the bloody crossing of the Belgian frontiers by the German army was contrary to international law and justified only by the demands of military strategy, yet the only protest to come from a neutral source came from the Vatican. "The invasion of Belgium," wrote the Papal Secretary of State, Cardinal Gasparri, in a letter to the Belgian Minister to the Holy See, "is directly included in the words used by the Holy Father when he condemned openly every injustice by whatever side and for whatever motive committed."

The first year of the war passed and there were no signs of peace. Great armies were interlocked in gigantic battles over vast areas, the fight was carried to the seas with equal bitterness, and for the first time men fought in the skies. The terrible weapon of blockade had been invoked and while the British fleet severed the commerce of Germany, the latter's submarines were sinking allied merchant ships at sight and in mounting numbers. Never before had there been destruction on such an appalling scale but unheeded was the agonized plea from the Vatican. "May this cry be heard above the terrible tumult of arms by the stricken people and their leaders and dispose them to make peace with one another . . . Let all participants quench their lust for destruction . . . Why not even now examine the rights and wishes of the people with conscientious impartiality? Why not inaugurate, directly or indirectly, an exchange of views in order to end the terrible conflict?"

By this time Italy had been drawn into the struggle, in partnership with the Allies, and a shameful condition was secretly included in the new pact. Fearful that a restoration of the Papal States might be included in post war settlements the Italian Ministers had demanded and had received assurance that the Pope would be excluded from peace negotiations. Solemnly the pledge was given that the advice of the Vatican, a sure influence for impartiality and unprejudiced decision, would be banned from the councils which were to shape the destiny of Europe. The second year of the conflict came and went, the slaughter went on with increasing fury, more nations became involved, and an end of the conflagration, either by negotiation or force of arms, seemed more remote than ever. But although his efforts to achieve peace remained fruitless, one organization erected by the Pope met with a singular success and was given cooperation by the governments. Through agencies in Switzerland, and because of the labour of neutral priests and bureaus established within the belligerent nations, vast numbers of prisoners of war were exchanged, the wounded given succour and better hospitalization, and tens of thousands of families who were grieving for missing sons and husbands were informed of the safety and whereabouts of their kin.

As the third sad year approached Benedict informed his Vicar-General that "We must again raise our voice against this war, which appears to us as the suicide of civilized Europe." Carefully he prepared a plan, a workable basis for negotiation, a practical scheme which could be received by all the warring powers without affront, which could still the gunfire without loss of prestige or national honour to either side. On August 1st of 1917 a peace note was despatched from Rome. Once again the evils of the war and the dangers of the future were emphasized and then the carefully pondered words went on to state that "We desire now to put forward some more concrete and practical propositions and invite the Governments of the belligerents to come to some agreement on the following points, which seem to offer the basis of a just and lasting peace, though leaving to them the duty of adjusting and completing them . . . First of all, the fundamental point must be that the moral force of right shall be substituted for the material force of arms; thence must follow a just agreement of all for the simultaneous and reciprocal diminution of armaments, in accordance with rules, and guarantees to be established hereafter, in a measure sufficient and necessary for the maintenance of public order in each State; next, as a substitute for arms, the institution of arbitration with its exalted peacemaking function, subject to regulations to be agreed upon, and sanctions to be determined against the State which should refuse either to submit international questions to arbitration or to accept its decision. Once the supremacy of right is thus established—let all obstacles to the free intercourse of peoples be swept aside, in assuring by means of rules to be fixed in the same way, the true liberty of and common rights over the sea . . . As to the damage to be made good, and the cost of the war, we see no other way of solving the question but to lay down, as a general principle an entire and reciprocal condonation . . ." But, insisted the Pope, there should be a return of the conquered areas by both sides, "restitution of Belgium by Germany, with guarantees; similar restitution of French territory; restitution of the German colonies by the Allies." And territorial disputes and minority problems should be solved with due respect to the aspirations of the populations.

The Note was given serious attention by the governments but although in the beginning there was a faint gleam of hope in some quarters, notably in Germany where the efforts of the Papal Nuncio, Monsignor Pacelli, were given a certain amount of encouragement, the final answers amounted to the same inexorable result. The war went on and it was not to cease until the Armistice of 1918. Even then the thunder of cannon was not quieted nor violence ended, for in the next few years there were continued the terrible ravages of the Russian civil war, in which the losing side was half heartedly supported by the Allies who, in such a spirit, aided with contingents instead of armies. There was the brave struggle of Poland against the newly established Bolshevists, and there was the equally bitter conflict between the Greeks and the Turks. There was bloody strife in Ireland; and in Lithuania, Syria, Morocco, and Hungary, men killed and maimed each other with a similar and unrelenting hatred. Nor was it men alone who were dying. The grim companions of war, pestilence and famine, had appeared and were reaping a terrible harvest. Millions had been killed. Whole populations were starving. Cities and countryside alike were exhausted and ravaged, for the new methods and great machineries of modern warfare had obliterated the sharp difference which formerly had separated the lot of civilian and combatant. The commerce of the world was disrupted and impoverished.

Benedict had foreseen and had warned and had tried to avert the catastrophe with practical advice. He had been ignored and he was still to be ignored. Peace, as he had proved by his unremitting toil, was the great aim of the Papacy and it is remarkable that in the postwar mood of bitterness and cynicism not one voice was raised to accuse him of partisanship. The intricate and far flung organization of the Church, the international and *catholic* nature of the Church, brought to the Vatican a wide knowledge and understanding of the problems, national, economic, and racial, which confronted the world. The spiritual subjects of the Pope dwelt within all the frontiers and there was nothing to be gained by him in favouring either the victor or the vanquished. Yet the secret promise made by the Allies to the Italian Government was given strict adherence, and when the representatives of the nations gathered at Versailles elaborate precautions were taken that no emissary from the Vatican should be there, either for counsel or for participation. The glittering Hall of Mirrors echoed with lofty phrases and idealistic speeches as penalties were imposed and frontiers were changed and measures adopted which, however nobly put, resulted in people being ordered to change their native languages, to forget and discard the traditions of their fathers, and to swear allegiance to new masters and new flags. Idealism and sincerity were undoubtedly the property of some of the assembled statesmen but it was greed and revenge and stupidity too that dominated the terms of the doomed Treaty. "Remember," cried the unhappy and unheeded Pontiff, "nations do not die; in humiliation and revenge, they pass from generation to generation the sorrowful heritage of hatred and retaliation."

One country at least appreciated the labours of Benedict and while he still lived a statue to honour his name was erected by the Mohammedans of Turkey; and though the rulers of the Christian nations had chosen to spurn his peace plans the high standard of papal statesmanship and the conduct and ability of the papal nuncios and delegates had commanded admiration and had earned an increased respect in the Chancellories and Foreign Offices. New Embassies and Legations became accredited to the Holy See and even the government of France, so recently anti-clerical, saw fit, when the canonization of Joan of Arc was proclaimed, to adopt a more amicable attitude and to send an envoy to the papal court.

Thirty-three new dioceses, twenty-eight vicariates, and nine missionary prefectures were established during Benedict's reign and in a masterful encyclical he charged the missionary priests to encourage and foster vocations in their territories. It was a significant instruction, for that policy of the Church which encouraged each race and country to provide its own clergy had been given added emphasis since the time of Leo XIII and it was the intention of Benedict that the wise practice should not suffer because of the prejudices and hatreds which were following in the wake of the Great War. The awareness of these passions, the knowledge of the dark events which they inevitably would breed, were thoughts seldom absent from the mind of the Pope whether he addressed missionary or cardinal, ambassador or simple pilgrim, or meditated alone. He was now sixty-seven years old and the continual strain, the constant anxiety, the spectre of future disasters, the long succession of disappointment and sorrow, did not fail to exact the usual penalty. Thus, when his exhausted body was attacked by influenza there was little resistance to the sickness. He died on the 22nd of January 1922, and typical were his last words, "We offer our life to God on behalf of the peace of the world."

Four years before his death Benedict summoned the Prefect of the Vatican Library, Monsignor Ratti, from his books and surprised the sixty year old scholar by appointing him Apostolic Visitor to the devastated regions of Poland. Monsignor Ratti was a doctor of both canon law and philosophy and in academic circles he bore a distinguished reputation as a historian and theologian but he had had no experience in the realm of professional diplomacy. For thirty years his life had been the tranquil lot of the librarian and before that, in a brief span that followed his studies, he had served as a professor in a seminary. But long years spent in exploring the secrets and treasures of rare manuscripts had not confined Monsignor Ratti's vision and interest to the villainies and glories of the past. He was a keen observer of the ever changing drama of modern history and during his twenty-two years at the Ambrosian Library in Milan he became noted for his wide knowledge of contemporary events. This reputation followed him when, in 1910, he was summoned to Rome and appointed assistant to the Librarian of the Vatican. Four years later he was promoted to the Librarianship and during the anxious years of the war the Cardinal Secretary of State would often discuss with the alert scholar the problems of Europe. He found the conversations to be useful and instructive and so it was that Cardinal Gasparri recommended to the Pope that the Monsignor should leave the peaceful precincts of the great library and be the papal representative to a nation which had been sorely lashed by war and oppression and which was at this moment confronted with one of the most critical periods in its long and troubled history. After many years of servitude and division territory had been regained from Russia by the Poles, and although the Germans still occupied important regions, including Warsaw, national independence and unity seemed assured a brave people. Great excitement and confusion attended the birth of the new Republic as treaties were made and plebiscites undertaken and the complicated structure of government erected. There was poverty and disease and hunger too and there was to be the sharp misery of war again when the newly won independence was savagely assailed by the Soviet armies.

It was a stormy environment for the ex-librarian but he greeted it with calmness and initiative and from the moment he arrived at Warsaw and established his headquarters in the modest residence of a parish priest his labours were conspicuously successful. Ecclesiastical affairs were in as sorry a tangle as the prevailing political conditions. Important sees were vacant and without administration, others were under the control of German or Austrian prelates, and often even parish priests were of a different nationality than their parishioners. There were numerous scandals and much violence, and grave and bitter were the quarrels between Catholics of the Eastern and Latin rites. Revenues had ceased and hospitals and schools were in a critical state. All these troubles and the multitudinous problems they caused received the careful attention of the papal envoy and gradually, because of his work, order and organization grew out of the chaos. His jurisdiction was extended to the new countries of Finland, Esthonia, and Lithuania, and again and again it was his difficult duty to settle complicated disputes which were infected by the dangerous and obstinate fevers of national rivalries. In Russia the campaign to eradicate religion had commenced and to Rome Monsignor Ratti reported that "in order to accomplish the salvation of this country sacrifice as well as prayer will be necessary. The shedding of Catholic blood, the shedding of the blood of priests." He asked permission to cross the frontier and persistently he applied for a Soviet visa but he was never allowed his wish and such a possibility ended with the outbreak of the Russian Polish war. Before the Bolshevists commenced their onslaught the Pope increased the diplomatic rank of his representative to that of Nuncio and the mitre soon followed. The Nuncio was made titular Archbishop of Lepanto and the ceremony of his consecration was held in the Cathedral of Warsaw.

Most of the foreign diplomats who were accredited to the newly formed State left Warsaw when the Russian army approached the capital. Once indeed, the Boshevists fought their way to within six miles of the city and the plight of the Poles was desperate. The fighting was singularly bitter and little quarter was given or asked by either side. The inhabitants of Warsaw knew well that if the Russians were victorious their city would be sacked without mercy or restraint. Archbishop Ratti could hear the sounds of the great battle, the thunder of the guns shook the walls of his residence, but he remained at his post, doing works of charity with his accustomed calmness and helping with counsel and example. The Poles never forgot his courage and from then on greeted him as a hero and a true friend of their country. But plaudits did not alter his nature and on one occasion, after a particularly enthusiastic crowd had saluted him with cheers then knelt for his blessing, he told his secretary: "Now I realize better what the Pope is. Although only a poor librarian, I see crowds bend the knee before me solely because the shadow of the Pope follows me."

Early in 1921 he was created a cardinal and made Archbishop of Milan but before assuming his new duties he went to Rome where he received the Red Hat from the hands of the Pope, then there was a pilgrimage to Lourdes, and a month of meditation and prayer at the Monastery of Monte Cassino. When he entered Milan he received a tumultuous welcome. An aeroplane showered flowers from the air, bands played, soldiers paraded, and thirty thousand cheering citizens crowded before the Cathedral to greet him. Even the so called radical elements and anticlericals joined their voices to the general acclamation for during his long residence in their city he had won the respect of all classes. "Long live the Cardinal of Youth!" cried a group of young men as his carriage passed. "Long live the Cardinal's young friends!" was his quick reply. He had been accessible to everybody when he was librarian and his occupancy of the archiepiscopal palace was to bring no change. "The house of your Father will be always open," he declared in a public address. "However young, however poor, however humble you may be, do not imagine that the steps of my house are too high or that you cannot easily climb them. If you are young, humble, poor, weighted down by the burden of life, then my invitation is but the echo of that of our Redeemer: "Come to me all you who labor and who are in suffering. You have an especial right to demand that your Father should open his arms to welcome you."

Five months passed and Cardinal Ratti left his diocese to participate in the conclave which followed the death of Pope Benedict. His person attracted considerable interest on the journey for in the fever of speculation and rumor which always precedes a papal election his name had received conspicuous mention in the press. He joined fifty-two other members of the Sacred College in the Sistine Chapel and after solemn preliminaries had been enacted the voting began. There was no long deadlock or procrastination of any kind and a majority was quickly achieved although it was not the name of the Archbishop of Milan which was read to their eminences. Cardinal Laurenti, head of the Propagation of the Faith, had received the necessary votes but the decision appalled him and firmly he refused to accept it, declaring it was his wish "that this exalted office be given to another who is stronger and better able to carry the heavy burden." The balloting commenced again and the fourteenth scrutiny revealed forty-two votes in favour of Achilles Ambrogio Damiano Ratti. He accepted the honour and when he was asked what name he wished to adopt he answered "In the pontificate of Pius IX I was initiated into the body of the Church, and made my early studies for the ecclesiastical state. Pius X called me to Rome. Pius is a name of peace. Desirous of devoting my efforts to attainment of that world peace which was the aim too, of my predecessor, Benedict XV, I choose to be called Pius XI. I wish to add, and I proclaim the fact before all the members of the Sacred College, that I have at heart the preservation and defence of all the rights of the Church and of all the prerogatives of the Holy See, but I desire that my first blessing, as an earnest of that peace for which humanity longs, should go forth not only to Rome and to Italy, but to the furthest limits of the earth. I shall impart my blessing from the exterior of St. Peter's."

With great interest the newspapers of the world emblazoned the message on their front pages and with emphasis also readers of every race and nationality were informed that the academic triumphs and diplomatic achievements of the ex-librarian were not due to any accident or favour of high birth. Indeed the new pope was the fourth son of a silk weaver and the story of a rise from such circumstances made for dramatic reading. Adding further color to the romantic tale was the fact he had also gained some renown as an athlete for he was a skilled and courageous Alpinist. "There are few recreations," he had written, "which are more wholesome for body and mind and more to be recommended than a little mountain climbing." The lover of the tall peaks and great spaces had become the "prisoner" in the Vatican but was the imprisonment to endure? That he chose to give his blessing from the external balcony of St. Peter's provided instant fuel for speculation and an immense crowd swirled into being on that historic day. Rumor said at last peace would be made between the Vatican and the Government of Italy.

Diplomats and priests, soldiers and tradesmen, peasants and citizens, joined close together in an enormous assemblage to receive his first benediction. No pope had thus appeared on the balcony for fifty-two years and there was great enthusiasm and much cheering. But one man who had speeded across the Atlantic to participate in the conclave arrived too late either for the election or the happy first blessing. At the moment that Pius XI was appearing on the high loggia of St. Peter's the Archbishop of Boston, Cardinal O'Connell, still confident that his vote would help elect a new pope, was on a train that was bearing him from Naples to Rome. A Vatican official met him at the station and told him the election was concluded. Frankly disappointed that his four-thousand mile journey should thus end the American prelate recalled that at the previous conclave Cardinal Gibbons and he had suffered a similar experience. When he was received in audience by the new pontiff he courageously gave voice to his chagrin. "We feel so sorry for you," replied Pius, "that after making the long journey you could not be here in time for the election. We wished at least one representative of the American hierarchy. And, sorry as We are, We will so arange things from now on that this through which you have passed shall not happen again. It shall not happen again. We will change the Apostolic Constitution." In a few days time it was announced that *fifteen* days, instead of the customary ten, should elapse before the inauguration of a conclave. And if, even then, further time be needed to permit the attendance of American Cardinals this period could be extended another three days.

Although thirty-five states now deemed it necessary to maintain diplomatic representation at the Vatican the policy of the Italian Government was apparently to remain unchanged. By now such an attitude found scant sympathy with many of the Italian people. Before Benedict had died there had been spirited argument in the Italian Parliament and one deputy was heard to cry: "I say that the Latin and Imperial tradition of Rome is today represented by Catholicism . . . The development of Catholicism throughout the world, the fact that four hundred million men, from every country under the sun, have their eyes fixed on Rome, there is a thing that must interest us who are Italians and should fill us with pride." The speaker of these words was Benito Mussolini, the ex-socialist and anti-clerical, who soon was to grasp power and to forge, with the nationalistic doctrine of Fascism, the unity of a despondent and disrupted Italy. There can be no denial that Fascism brought order to a nation which had been terribly torn by the tragedy and injustice of the First World War. Confusion and inability characterized the futile efforts of a weak government and anarchy was erupting with startling and bloody rapidity. Mussolini and his Black-shirts brought some degree of stability and hope but it was at the cost of violence and intolerance and the employment of such measures meant an inevitable incompatibility with the teachings of the Church.

From the beginning there was conflict between the Church and Fascism but there were attempts at peace too. Priests might be assaulted and Catholic institutions attacked, but the Crucifix was restored to Government buildings and religious instruction was proclaimed necessary in the schools: for Mussolini, like Napoleon and unlike the rulers of Bolshevist Russia, held the opinion that religion is necessary for the well being of the State. And on one subject the Vatican and Fascism were in complete agreement. Both opposed Communism. Pius XI had given deep attention to the tragic events of Russia and both his scholarship and his close experience with the practitioners and propagandists of Communism in Poland had brought him a keen realization of a danger which was rising to menace Christian civilization. A government which proposed to obliterate God from the structure of human society necessarily must find itself in opposition to the Catholic Church. But the fact that Communism was also the target for Nazi and Fascist antipathy created much misunderstanding amongst opponents of the latter philosophies. The fervor of his enthusiasm and hope has caused many a "liberal" to hold the opinion that political belief must arbitrarily take direction either to Right or Left. Disciples of this school of thought have at certain times accused the Church of pro-Fascist leanings because of anti-Communist policy. With an equally dark suspicion the ardent Fascist has affirmed that the Vatican looks too favorably upon the Communist. But the inheritor of St. Peter's mantle has no need for new political ideologies and Pope Pius XI lost no time in informing the world that he regarded the greed of the capitalist and the obsessions of the communist with an equal dislike. Adherents of the latter persuasion would deny a free man the right to own private property. The capitalistic system permits an unjust man or group of men to divert and distort that right with the wiles and resources of avarice and selfishness. Elaborating on the splendid *Rerum Novarum* of Leo XIII Pope Pius issued a comprehensive and constructive encyclical *Quadragesimo Anno* which stressed the evils of modern economic and sociological trends. After a clear analysis of existing dangers he made practical suggestions and a strong plea for a reorganization of the state which would permit all men to enjoy life with freedom and without fear.

On the day of his election Pius XI had indicated he would make peace with the Italian Government. No announcement was made but secret negotiations were commenced during the autumn of 1926. Signor Barome, an Italian Privy Councillor, represented the Government and the Marquis Pacelli, brother of Cardinal Pacelli, spoke for the Vatican. Many and complicated were the problems to be settled but with both sides anxious to end the dispute a settlement was gradually achieved. The Pope gave up his claims to the properties which had formerly constituted the Papal States and in return he was given a cash indemnity and the temporal sovereignty of a tiny state which embraced the buildings and gardens of the Vatican, the Lateran, the College of the Propaganda, and the papal summer residence, Castel Gandolfo. Temporal power might only be held over about one hundred and twenty acres but it meant that at last the papacy was to be free, yet unburdened by the responsibilities and demands of a larger territory. It was also agreed that the papal treasury be enriched by a cash payment of seven hundred and fifty million lire and that another billion, guaranteed by government bonds, be paid over a period of years. Once again Catholicism was to become the official religion of the Italian people, civil law was to be in accord with canon law, and Christian education was to be obligatory in the schools. The Papacy was to enjoy all the rights of an independent State such as the privilege of possessing an "Army," of maintaining its own postal and customs service, and of operating a radio and telegraph station. There were numerous other points of agreement and compromise but these constituted the body of the treaty. The negotiations lasted about two and a half years and although there were rumors during that time there was no statement or admission from either the Pope or Mussolini, now head of the Italian Government, until February 11th, 1929. On this day Pius had occasion to be addressing the parish priests of Rome and when the bells tolled the noon hour he glanced at the clock and calmly told his astounded audience that at that very minute Mussolini and the papal Secretary of State, Cardinal Gasparri, were affixing their signatures to the Treaty of the Lateran.

Congratulations poured in from all parts of the globe. With photogenic triumph Mussolini beamed at millions of readers and the Pope accepted plaudits with dignity and grace. The design for peace had been sealed with all the gestures of protocol but was it to endure the test of reality? Could the demands and aims of a totalitarian form of government be reconciled with the policies of the Church? Apparently not, for soon there was trouble, the age old trouble of Caesar's due. Sponsored by the Church throughout Italy was the movement known as Catholic Action which embraced the activities of Youth Clubs, Boy Scouts, Student Societies, Educational Boards and a Public Morals Federation. Special classes were organized in each parish to receive instruction in the theory of social justice as explained by Leo XIII and the reigning pope. The Fascist Party regarded these groups with a suspicion which soon flared into open antagonism. There were hostile street scenes and a series of disagreeable incidents which culminated in the Pope issuing an Encyclical, *non abbiamo bisogno.* The encyclical was not issued in the usual way at the Vatican for normal procedure would have almost certainly invited delay or interference from Italian censorship. Instead the Pope summoned an American priest in whom he placed great confidence, Monsignor Francis J. Spellman, later to be Cardinal and Archbishop of New York, but then attached to the Vatican Secretariat of State, and instructed him to smuggle the document from Italy. Monsignor Spellman displayed the same courage and initiative that the world later was to recognize as being so characteristic of him. He successfully ran the gauntlet of the Fascist police and their elaborate system of inspection and surveillance and crossed the border into France. The spirited words of protest were dramatically given to the world in Paris. "A conception of the State," wrote the Pope, "which makes the rising generations belong to it entirely without any exception, from the tenderest years up to adult life, cannot be reconciled by a Catholic either with Catholic doctrine or with the natural rights of the family. It is not possible for a Catholic to accept the claim that the Church and the Pope must limit themselves to the external practices of religion (such as Mass and the Sacraments) and that all the rest of education belongs to the State."

The Pope had spoken, to use his own words, with "profound bitterness" and the sympathetic reception which the encyclical was given in foreign countries was not lost upon the Italian government. Mussolini apparently saw the folly of repeating Bismarck's mistake of engaging in an open war with the Church. Overtures were made and once again envoys of the Vatican and the government met and conferred. Out of their talks came the agreement that Government antagonism towards Catholic Action would cease and on its side the Church guaranteed that religious clubs or organizations would not mark anti-government activities. Once again friendship between State and Church was announced with fanfare and amidst scenes of pomp and splendor Mussolini, in the full uniform of his rank, came to pay his respects to the pontiff. His King and Queen had already made their visit but this was the first time for the Prime Minister. A violet-robed prelate met and conducted him through the frescoed chambers and historic halls, the gaily dressed Swiss Guards swung glittering halberds to the Present Arms, and finally the Dictator of Italy was in the presence of the Pope. For one hour the two men talked and then after a brief call upon the Papal Secretary of State Mussolini was ceremoniously conducted to the basilica of St. Peter's. Here, before the tomb of the Fisherman, a prie-dieu had been placed and it was here that the man who once had so ardently preached anti-clericalism and who had written heresy now kneeled and bent his head.

Significant and gratifying though the historical meeting was it could not result in absolute harmony. The course of Fascism was bound to conflict with the way of the Church at many points. That veil which shrouds all contemporary history does not permit of a true perspective of the situation as it has existed since Pius XI gave audience to Mussolini. But repeatedly since that date the voice of the Pope has been raised against doctrines which exalt Stateism or Racism. When Italy was making ready to invade Abyssinia and when all the fiery ingredients of patriotism were being invoked to stir popular enthusiasm amongst the Italian people Pius XI made known his alarm and disapproval. "We long for peace," he told an audience of nurses, "and We pray God that We may be spared from war. The mere thought of war is a terror to Us. And now We understand that, abroad, there is talk of a war for conquest, a war of aggression. That is a hypothesis that We do not wish even to consider, a supposition which is truly disconcerting. Any war which is a war only of conquest would be an unjust war, obviously—a thing which routs imagination, something sad beyond words and horrible. We cannot think about an unjust war; We cannot envisage its possibility, and We deliberately turn our mind from it; We do not believe, We do not wish to believe there can be an unjust war. On the other hand, in Italy, they are saying that the war of which there is question will be a just war, because it is a war of defence, to make the frontier safe against the continual, the incessant dangers to which it is exposed; that it is a war necessary now by reason of the expansion of the population which is increasing from day to day; that it is a war undertaken to defend or to make certain the country's material security; that such a war justifies itself. It is however true, and We cannot but reflect on this truth, that if there is this need for expansion, if there is this need to defend the frontier and make it secure, We can only wish that some other means may be found than war. What is this other means? Obviously it is not easy to say. We do not

believe it is impossible to find another means. All the possibilities must be studied. One thing there is which seems to Us
beyond all doubt, this namely that if the need for expansion is
a fact with which We must reckon, the right of defence has its
limits and qualifications, and these must be observed if the
defence is to be free from blame."

The Pope spoke in vain. The Italian armies invaded Abyssinia
on the 2nd of October, 1935. Six weeks later the League of
Nations imposed sanctions against Italy and thus a further step
was made towards the Second World War. The United States
was not a member of the League but the press of that republic
left no doubts as to where sympathies were. But neither the
sentence of the League nor North American opinion prevented
the eviction of Haile Selassie and the annexation of his country
to Italy. The economic power, and behind that power the martial
strength, of the democracies proved incapable of stopping
Mussolini's grandiose schemes, yet within these countries there
were critics who upbraided the Vatican for not accomplishing
that which their governments would not, or could not, do. The
insignificant temporal power of the tiny Vatican State, so completely devoid of defence, was ignored by such critics and they
cried that the Pope should invoke the resources of spiritual authority, such as the imposition of an interdict, to end the imperial
direction of Fascist policy. The employment of such an extravagant measure would have had only one result, further
bloodshed and chaos and the *catholic* nature of the Church has
for a goal the achievement of universal peace, not the castigation
or exaltation of a particular party or nation. The Pope can de-
plore and condemn the actions of a government but he cannot
force men to accept his decrees or wishes. The very voices in
the democracies that called upon him to take more aggressive
action against Mussolini would be the first to resent "papal
interference" in the affairs of their own countries and few are
the nations without ignoble episodes in their story, recent or
past.

On January 30th, 1933, Adolf Hitler became Chancellor of

Germany. Six months later a Concordat between the Vatican and the Reich was signed but disagreement was not long in coming. Since its beginning certain actions of the National Socialist party had drawn the criticism of German bishops and the Concordat brought no ease to a situation which gradually developed into persecution. Catholic societies were dissolved and ecclesiastical properties and schools were confiscated. Attacks, physical and oral, were made upon the clergy and they were accused of immorality and disloyalty to the state. A return to ancient German paganism was advocated by leading members of the Nazi party and the Judaic origins of Christianity were held up to ridicule. Catholic newspapers were suppressed and a law was passed which decreed that all young people must be educated "in the Hitler Youth, educated physically, spiritually and morally, in the spirit of National Socialism, for the service of the people and the commonwealth."

With sorrow and anxiety Pius XI gave his close attention to the developments in Germany and made known his concern several times. Then on March 14, 1937, he issued the encyclical, *On the Present Position of the Catholic Church in Germany.* Because of the antagonistic attitude of the government great secrecy attended the publication of the encyclical and parish priests did not receive it until the early hours of the day on which it was intended it should be read in the churches. "It is with deep anxiety and growing surprise," said the pontiff, "that We have long been following the painful trials of the Church and the increasing vexations which afflict those who have remained loyal in heart and action . . . The experiences of these last years have fixed responsibilities and laid bare intrigues, which from the outset only aimed at a war of extermination. In the furrows, where We tried to sow the seed of a sincere peace, other men—the 'enemy' of Holy Scripture—oversowed the cockle of distrust, unrest, hatred, defamation, of a determined hostility, overt or veiled, fed from many sources and wielding many tools, against Christ and His Church. They, and they alone, with their accomplices, silent or vociferous, are today responsible, should the storm of religious war, instead of the rainbow of peace, blacken the German skies . . . Whoever exalts race, or the people, or the State, or a particular form of State, or the depositories of power, or any other fundamental value of the human community—however necessary and honorable be their function in worldly things—whoever raises these notions above their standard value and divinizes them to an idolatrous level, distorts and perverts an order of the world planned and created by God: he is far from the true faith in God and from the concept of life which that faith upholds . . . None but superficial minds could stumble into concepts of a national God, of a national religion . . . Whoever wishes to see banished from church and school the Biblical history and the wise doctrines of the Old Testament, blasphemes the name of God, blasphemes the Almighty's plan of salvation, and makes limited and narrow human thought the judge of God's designs over the history of the world . . . It is on faith in God, preserved pure and stainless, that man's morality is based. All efforts to remove from under morality and the moral order the granite foundation of faith and to substitute for it the shifting sands of human regulations, sooner or later lead these individuals or societies to moral degradation. The fool who has said in his heart 'there is no God' goes straight to moral corruption (Psalms XIII, I), and the number of these fools who today are out to sever morality from religion, is legion. They either do not see or refuse to see that the banishment of confessional Christianity, i.e., the clear and precise notion of Christianity, from teaching and education, from the organization of social and political life, spells spiritual spoliation and degradation. No coercive power of the State, no purely human ideal, however noble and lofty it be, will ever be able to make shift for the supreme and decisive impulses generated by faith in God and in Christ . . . To hand over the moral law to man's subjective opinion, which changes with the times, instead of anchoring it in the holy will of the eternal God and His commandments, is to open wide every door to the forces of destruction . . . Thousands of voices ring into your ears a Gospel which has not been revealed by the Father of Heaven. Thousands of pens are wielded in the service of a Christianity which is not of Christ. Press and wireless daily force on you productions hostile to the Faith and to the Church, impudently aggressive against whatever you should hold venerable and sacred. Many of you, clinging to your Faith and to your Church, as a result of your affiliation with religious associations guaranteed by the Concordat, have often to face the tragic trial of seeing your loyalty to your country misunderstood, suspected, or even denied, and of being hurt in your professional and social life . . . Today, as We see you threatened with new dangers and new molestations, We say to you: If anyone should preach to you a Gospel other than the one you received on the knees of a pious mother, from the lips of a believing father, or through teaching faithful to God and His Church, *let him be anathema* (Gal. i,9). If the State organizes a national youth, and makes this organization obligatory to all, then, without prejudice to rights of religious associations, it is the absolute right of youths as well as parents to see to it that this organization is purged of all manifestations hostile to the Church and Christianity. These manifestations are even today placing Christian parents in a painful alternative, as they cannot give to the State what they owe to God alone. No one would think of preventing young Germans establishing a true ethnical community in a noble love of freedom and loyalty to their country. What we object to is the willed and systematic antagonism raised between national education and religious duty. That is why We tell the young: Sing your hymns to freedom, but do not forget the freedom of the children of God. Do not drag the nobility of that freedom in the mud of sin and sensuality. He who sings hymns of loyalty to his terrestrial country should not, for that reason, become unfaithful to God and His Church, or a deserter and traitor to His heavenly country. You are often told about heroic greatness, in lying opposition to evangelical humility and patience. Why conceal the fact that there are heroisms in moral life? That the preservation of baptismal innocence is an act of heroism which deserves credit? You are often told about the human deficiencies which mar the history of the Church: why ignore the exploits which fill her history, the saints she begot, the blessing that came upon Western civilization from the union between that Church and your people?"

The anti-clerical parties in Spain and Mexico were of the extreme Left variety and bitter and bloody were the attacks on the Church in both countries. In 1931 Spain ceased to be a monarchy and with Republican government came a separation of Church and State, a difficult and cruel process for a nation whose traditions and spirit had been Catholic for so long. Ecclesiastical properties, hospitals and schools as well as churches, were ruthlessly confiscated and stringent anti-clerical laws were decreed. The Society of Jesus was dissolved outright; harsh restrictions were placed upon other religious orders. The Pope protested against this in his encyclical, *Dilectissima Nobis,* but the oppression continued to grow more savage. Radical elements, bolstered by foreign aid, sought to form a Communist State of the Russian pattern and to prevent such a project General Franco led the military revolt of July, 1936. The horrors of the civil war which followed were particularly devastating and tragic and it is estimated that because of their religious belief more than six thousand priests were killed and in the fury of the conflict some twenty thousand churches were sacked and pillaged. Even the graves of churchmen and nuns were not exempt from insult and violation. "It appears clear from its beginnings," declared the Spanish bishops in a joint letter to all the bishops of the Catholic world, "that one of the belligerent parties was aiming directly at the abolition of the Catholic religion in Spain." Violent though the attempts had been to eradicate religion the bishops, in the same letter, stressed that: "We have not tied ourselves to anybody—persons, power or institutions—even though we thank for their protection those who have been able to preserve us from the enemy who wished to ruin us . . . As regards the future we cannot tell what will happen . . . We would be the first to regret that the irresponsible autocracy of a parliament should be replaced by the yet more terrible power of a dictatorship, without roots in the nation."

In 1914 Mexican churches had been burnt and their pastors slaughtered with a ferocity which equalled the violence of the Spanish and Russian revolutionaries. Fifty years previously the properties of the Mexican Church had been confiscated yet the clergy always remained a favourite target for the accusations and plots of dishonest politicians. When Plutarco Elias Calles became President in 1924 there was a vigorous renewal of persecution. "Whole chapters of canons, old men amongst them who had to be transported in their beds, were hauled to prison," wrote the Pope in his encyclical *On the most bitter state of the Catholic Church in Mexico.* "Priests and laymen, too, were pitilessly slain, at the cross-roads, in the public squares, before their very churches." The brave cry of "Long Live Christ the King" was heard in all corners of the large and rich country as scenes of martyrdom were enacted time and time again. The Apostolic Delegate was expelled from the country and the number of clergy permitted to officiate among a Catholic population of 17,000,000 was reduced to such a pathetically low figure that by the end of 1936 their total did not exceed two hundred. The severest restrictions, often grotesque and absurd, hindered the activities of these priests and although national law required them to be of Mexican birth they were, with ordination, automatically deprived of civil or political rights. Their churches, their residences, their schools and seminaries, had been confiscated and the wearing of clerical dress was banned. Religious instruction was forbidden and the performance of all religious functions needed police permission. The passing of Calles from the presidency brought a lessening of the persecution but although his regime had been one of outrage and terror there was little indignation or emotion in the foreign press. Pius XI deplored such "a conspiracy of silence" yet he did not allow his sorrow to bring further grief to the Catholics of Mexico. Revolution is a familiar process in their country and there were many who would have followed the banners of a Holy War with eagerness and despatch. But from the Vatican came no rash counsel. The faithful in Mexico were advised to practice patience at the cost even of heroism. They were instructed to give the lie to the accusations of their tormentors and to abstain from organizing a Catholic political party. Catholic Action should not take the form of insurrection. The Church must not assume the direction of purely temporal affairs but must keep to its own domain. The bishops must not "be preoccupied more with the numbers than the quality of collaborations" and as for the formation and exercise of Catholic Action "publicity and the method of the circus have no place in it. It looks upon noisy methods as an enemy." Time has proven the wisdom of the Pope's advice and gradually and peacefully Catholicism is returning to its rightful place in the life of the Mexican people.

The chant of the anti-clerical in both Spain and Mexico was a recitation of familiar accusation. All priests were either ignorant fools or rich knaves, covering their misdeeds with the dark cloak of superstition and hypocrisy. No admission was made of clerical charity or vocation. Priests, and nuns too, were always the villainous allies of the landlord, the employer, and the capitalist. They were never the dispensers of alms, the friends of the poor, hosts to the sick, teachers of the young. There are knaves and fools in the ranks of the clergy everywhere and undoubtedly there will always be so as long as priests are men and not creatures of another world. There were ecclesiastical conditions in Spain and Mexico which called for change and correction but it was conveniently forgotten by the Communist propagandists that these conditions were the product of centuries of lay intrusion upon Church affairs, the continuous determination of successive governments and rulers to control investitures and benefices and to confine Catholicism within the boundaries of nationalism.

The constant exhortation from the Vatican to the practice of social justice was ignored by those who pointed at the priest as being the tool of the oppressor. The words of Christ were forgotten, as were the profound teachings of St. Thomas Aquinas and Leo XIII and all the intervening Doctors of the Church. It was even forgotten that earlier in the century a Spanish archbishop had been murdered because he championed the rights of the working man to form trade-unions. The great cathedrals, the glorious works of art, the richly adorned altars, all these historic accumulations of piety were pointed at as visible evidences of the Church's wealth. Little was said about the long years of confiscation which had made them "national property." Little was said of the miserable pittance which, by statute, served as salary for the average priest. Little was said of his sacrifices and good deeds. The sins and weaknesses of an occasional rascal provided the sole pattern of his detractor's calumnies.

Opinion or prejudice on the part of those hostile to Catholicism was not needed to persuade Pius XI that clerical standards could be strengthened and elevated. The learning and conduct of the clergy of today compare well with that of any age but he never ceased to stress the necessity of rigorous discipline and the advantages of thorough training and education. The possession of a pious nature, the consciousness of a religious sense, these factors alone were not sufficient to make a good priest for he was of the same opinion as St. Jerome that "uninformed holiness profits only its possessor, and whatever the service his merits render the Church of Christ, he does it just as much harm when he is unable to throw back the enemy . . ." Pius XI was a stern man and from the moment he took the tiara the Vatican felt the strong hand of an autocratic master. As a man's years are usually reckoned he was old but like Leo XIII he was driven by energy that would have been remarkable even in a far younger person. He lived in difficult and distressing times and with the clear discernment of the trained historian he was aware of the dangers of the future. Yet he never displayed confusion or fear nor did he ever hesitate to do that which he considered his duty or responsibility. The extreme Leftists of Mexico and Spain received his condemnation but equally severe was his attitude towards the extreme Rightists of France who supported the *Action Française*. This movement was growing rapidly in num-

bers and influence and many priests and bishops as well as laymen had been deluded by its leaders. Ostensibly it was Christian
in principle and it was definitely a reaction to the mistakes of
liberalism but the keen eye of the Pope detected "a new religious,
moral and social system . . . the traces of a renaissance of
paganism" that would, he thought, lead to the deification of the
state. Here were the beginnings of a totalitarian power which
proposed to operate under the cloak of Christianity. The books
and newspapers of the *Action Française* had been in ill repute
at the Vatican since 1914 but because of the war no disciplinary
measures had been taken. Pius XI was definite in his condemnation and alarm and invoking the drastic threat of excommunication he forbade Catholics to support the movement.

Pius XI was a realist and while he appreciated the treasures
of the past he faced with comprehension the uncharted seas
of tomorrow. The harsh litter of modern civilization, the vast
clatter and confusion of a mechanical age, these all made for
materialism in its basest forms. Yet the Pope saw no reason why
the Mystery of the Altar should not continue to give the same
hope and comfort as it had in those days when fervent men had
translated their prayers into Gothic glories. His days were full
and no corner of the world was too distant to escape his attention. Visitors of every nationality and race and class crowded
his ante-chamber and those with something to say would be
given a keen interest. But he had little use and certainly no
time for the superficial courtesies and for that reason he has
been accused of irascibility, this busy man who in one year alone
and in deference to custom turned from his many tasks to allow
one million, two hundred thousand pilgrims to kiss his ring.

Every sphere of ecclesiastical influence was carefully examined by him and the thorough scrutiny resulted in many and
far reaching decisions. His dislike of Bolshevism did not prevent
him from taking two and a half million lire from the Vatican
treasury and sending a relief mission to Russia and from appealing to the world for further assistance when a terrible famine
blighted that country in 1922. The rulers of the Kremlin per-

mitted his charity on this occasion but their attitude towards religion remained unchanged. However, Pius was too great an historian to believe that a whole people could be abruptly deprived of their faith by decree or proclamation so looking beyond the tragedy of his own time he made preparations for that day when the men and women of Russia could bring their children before their altars and ikons without fear or restriction. The organization of the Orthodox Church had been previously controlled by the Czarist government and had grievously suffered because of the revolution, and in the revival of religion that the Pope was confident would eventually and surely come he saw a chance for the reunion of the Eastern and Western churches which for so long had stirred the hopes and haunted the dreams of the popes. He appointed a special commission to study Russian ecclesiastical affairs and he opened a college in Rome for the purpose of training clergy in the Slav-Byzantine rite. These priests were not only to work amongst refugee populations but were to prepare for the time when they would be allowed entrance to Russia.

Aware of the growing consciousness of nationalism and race which was dominating political life everywhere Pius sought to avoid future problems by encouraging and preparing, wherever possible, a native clergy and hierarchy amongst those peoples whose spiritual needs had hitherto been administered by foreigners. It was an ancient policy of the Church to do so but no pope gave it stronger emphasis than he. In 1936 six Chinese bishops were personally consecrated by him before the tomb of St. Peter and an Apostolic Delegate was appointed to deal directly with the government of their country. No great enthusiasm was evinced in France at this action for formerly, because of the preponderance of French missionaries in China, the discussion of Chinese ecclesiastical affairs had been negotiated through the offices of the French diplomatic service. European priests serving in China and other missionary fields were emphatically reminded that in their work they must shed allegiances to the country of their birth and must act only as Catholic priests.

Catholicism, stressed the Pope, must be "understood in a truly Catholic spirit and not as an occidental importation." He issued orders that ecclesiastical architecture and art in China should utilize the native tradition rather than copying Western styles. Similar messages went to Japan and Indo-China and India where native clergies and hierarchies were already functioning. In every way possible he made his theories of *catholicism* practical. A school was established at the Vatican for Ethiopians, a Catholic University was founded in Pekin, seminaries were built in Central Africa, a Syrian prelate was elevated to the cardinalate, and in 1937 a Japanese archbishop presided for the first time in Tokio. There was an enormous increase of missionary activity in the time of this pope and further expression of his energy was reflected in the many names which, after the required processes of scrutiny and announcement, were added to the Calendar of Saints. He created fifty-two cardinals and during the seventeen years of his pontificate thirty-seven encyclicals were issued. They form a fitting monument to his industry and his learning and their varying titles give evidence of the universality of his interest.

During the latter part of 1936 the Pope was taken ill and the world was told he was dying. He was nearly eighty-one years old yet the news came as a shock, for his strength and customary freedom from illness had made most men forget his age. His retirement to the sick-bed had not been accomplished without a struggle for he had insisted upon working until he collapsed and repeatedly he had refused medical attention. "The Pope cannot be ill," he told one doctor with firmness. "The Pope is in the hands of God who will call him from his labours in His own good time. We shall continue to work until called." When Christmas Eve arrived he insisted upon rising to broadcast a message to the world. "The pains are atrocious," he admitted on this occasion, "yes, most atrocious. But we are here to labour. Our vocabulary does not find words to express the torment which we are now suffering. Nevertheless, we shall continue to labor. We are desirous of delivering the message as we have planned."

He spoke as he desired and the effort resulted in a confirmation of the doctor's fear. There was collapse and worse and soon his physician was making the sorrowful statement that "Pius XI is slowly passing away."

In the shadow of the Vatican walls a group of journalists gathered to keep the "Death Watch." The obituary of the dying pope was written and complete save for the hour of his death. It only remained for the journalists to wait and report that actual moment by the clock. But this time the macabre expectation was not fulfilled. The Pope did not die. He willed that he should live and he did. By Easter, to the astonishment of the awed physicians, he was able to preside from his throne in St. Peter's and soon after his activities resumed their previous full tempo. He had so much to do. The spectre of another world war was looming. The Pope knew it, he had always feared it, and throughout his pontificate he had struggled to avert it. Now, after his illness, crisis was succeeding crisis in the national capitals with frightening rapidity and desperation and hopelessness had become the mood of envoys. The machinery of diplomacy was breaking down and the generals and admirals were looking to their maps. These were the melancholy facts to distress the last years of the man who had taken the name of Pius because it was a name of peace. But he did not despair and to the end he employed every resource at his disposal to stave off the catastrophe. The full story of what he did cannot yet be told. There are rumours and whispers of remarkable things. But the facts are not yet gathered or revealed. They remain locked in the archives of the chancelleries and in the memories of living man. Pius XI lived until his eighty-second year and then during the early hours of a February morning he died and his last words were an echo of the purpose which had dominated his pontificate. "Peace. . . . Peace of Jesus. . . ."

The official period of mourning prescribed to honor his memory came to an end and on the first day of March 1939 the Sacred College assembled to elect his successor. There were sixty-two cardinals present, including those from North and

South America. Thirty-five of their Eminences were Italian born. On the second day of the conclave the violet canopied chairs which lined the historic walls of the Sistine Chapel, traditional scene of the papal election, were occupied early and at ten o'clock the first ballot had been collected and counted. By four thirty that same afternoon the third ballot had been taken and a majority had been found in favour of the Cardinal Eugenio Mario Giuseppe Giovanni Pacelli. It was a unanimous decision and the quickest of any conclave. A thin column of white smoke rising from a chimney atop the Sistine told the multitude outside that a pope had been elected and soon, clad in white and gold and scarlet, he appeared on the high balcony of St. Peter's to give his benediction to the world. Cannons shook the air with salvo after salvo and the great crowd cheered and all the bells of Rome made song when it was announced that in honor of his predecessor the new pope would take the name of Pius XII.

It was a popular choice, this selection of the sixty-three year-old former Papal Secretary of State, who in every way seemed qualified for the exalted office which was now his. He came of a family which had served the Vatican well. His father had been Dean of the Vatican Bar and his elder brother, the Marquis Francisco Pacelli, who was also a lawyer, had represented the Church in the negotiations which led to the Vatican Treaty. It had been the plan of his parents that the future pontiff should follow the family profession but a steadfast vocation led him to the seminary and then to the altar. He was a brilliant pupil, excelling particularly in foreign languages, but delicate health forced him to abandon community life and special permission was given for him to continue his clerical training as a day student. The favour did not weaken his diligence and in 1899 he was ordained and said his first Mass. He wished to assume parochial duties but his reputation as a scholar had attracted attention and he was attached to the staff of Cardinal Gasparri. Success continued to attend every step of his career and when Cardinal Gasparri was appointed Papal Secretary of State it was his friend and protégé, now Monsignor Pacelli, who succeeded him as Secretary of the Congregation for Extraordinary Ecclesiastical Affairs. In this position he was responsible for the execution of the papal scheme to exchange prisoners of war and so successful was he that in 1917 the Pope, Benedict XV, made him titular Archbishop of Sardes and sent him as his nuncio to the Catholic Kingdom of Bavaria. In the turbulent and shifting scenes of war and defeat and revolution which was the sad story of Germany for the next decade the name of Pacelli became noted for ability and courage and honesty. It was he who presented the papal peace plans to the Kaiser. It was he who, during the revolutionary disorders of Munich, felt the cold steel of a looter's pistol pressed against his breast. He was unafraid. "What good," he calmly asked the ruffian, "would it do to shoot me?" In 1929 he was recalled to Rome but before leaving Germany he received the publicly expressed gratitude of President von Hindenburg and thousands of workers and students escorted him to his train. A Red Hat awaited him at the Vatican and when in 1930 Cardinal Gasparri, because of his advanced age, resigned the Secretariat of State the appointment went to his friend Pacelli.

From then on his life was attuned to the rapid tempo of the many activities of Pius XI. It was always a harmonious relationship and as the years passed by it was believed by many that the Pope hoped his Secretary of State would be his successor and thus the continuity of his policies be assured. It certainly seemed as though Cardinal Pacelli was receiving a special training for the great position. Not only was he the Pope's confidant and responsible for the execution of the papal decisions but acting as Papal Legate he journeyed to France and to Hungary and even across the oceans to North and South America. The United States he explored by air, visiting many cities from the Eastern to the Western coasts, meeting all types of citizen from President to working man and winning the esteem of everybody, including the journalists of the Republic. Superb diplomat though he showed himself to be, he was first and foremost the priest and this fact impressed itself upon all who saw him. He claimed no privileges of rank and there never was the slackening of even the minor disciplinary observances because of the exigencies of travel. Those who had the privilege of witnessing him at his daily devotions, who saw his tall figure bowed before the Tabernacle, who saw his ascetic face raised to the uplifted chalice, these fortunate ones carry the vivid memory of an unusual sincerity, of unshakable faith.

The death of Pius XI was a grievous personal loss to the new Pope and he had wept bitterly. A friend had gone and so too had a guide. The great responsibilities were now his and he was alone. With the death of his predecessor there had seemed to come everywhere a greater realization of the significance of the papacy. Non-Catholics and even non-Christians, as well as Catholics, were looking to the Vatican as an influence which might halt the onward sweep to war. Woven with hope and desperation a surge of worldwide acclamation saluted the election of the new pontiff but he knew well the instability of applause. Custom decrees that the pomp of papal coronation should be halted by a priest who displays a wisp of burning oakum and in Latin cries to the pope: "Holy Father, so passes away the glory of the world." To the new Pius, carried high in a golden chair and flanked by a glittering procession of prelates and chamberlains and gold helmeted soldiers, the admonition must have seemed particularly significant. The gigantic interior of St. Peter's was ablaze with light and warm with enthusiasm and a great congregation bent knee to him as he passed. Outside, in the warm sun, a multitude waited patiently for his benediction and beyond the precincts of Rome men everywhere sent assurances of devotion. The most extravagant gestures of respect were shown to his name and person but surely there must have been gloom in his heart. Men saluted him, men hoped fervently that he would find the formula for peace, but it was terribly certain that these same men would ignore or reject his guidance and advice.

In his first message to the world and in his Easter sermon he revealed that the policies of Pius XI would also be his concern. There would be the same zealous pursuit of peace and social justice, the same insistence on a moral code which would govern not only the conduct of individuals but governments as well. "How can there be real and solid peace," he asked, "while even men with a common nationality, heedless of their common stock or their common fatherland, are torn apart and kept asunder by intrigues and dissensions and the interests of factions? How can there be peace, We repeat, while hundreds of thousands of men, millions even, lack work? For work is not only, for every man, a means of decent livelihood, but it is the means through which all those manifold powers and faculties with which nature, training and art have endowed the dignity of the human personality, find their necessary expression, and this with a certain natural comeliness. Who is there, then, who cannot see how, in such crises of unemployment as those our own time experiences, huge multitudes are created, through this very lack of work, of men utterly wretched, whose unhappy condition is worsened by the bitter contrast it presents with the pleasures and luxurious living of others altogether unconcerned about these armies of the needy? Who does not see how these poor men fall an easy prey to others whose minds are deceived by a specious semblance of truth, and who spread their corrupting teaching with ensnaring attractions?

"Moreover, how can there be peace, if there be lacking between the different States that common, equitable judgment of reason and consent of minds, which have been the power guiding the nations of the world along the shining road of civil progress? When, on the contrary, solemnly sanctioned treaties and pledged faith are stripped of that force and security which plighted faithfulness implies and by which it is strengthened, if this force and security be taken away, it becomes every day more difficult to lessen the increase of armaments and to pacify the minds of men, twin desires today of all men everywhere. . . . Let men seek once more that road by which they may journey back to friendly alliances in which the convenience and the profit of each are carefully considered in a just and kindly system; in which the sacrifices of individuals shall not be made an excuse for the acquisition of the more valuable properties of the human family; in which, finally, faith publicly given shall flourish as an example to all men of goodwill."

In an Encyclical Letter *To the American Hierarchy* the Pope gave voice to the pleasure he felt at the growth of the Church in the United States, then he touched upon other subjects close to his heart. "And here We have a complaint to make, although in a most fatherly spirit, about many of the schools in your country. They despise or ignore Christ's Person, and are content to explain the whole of nature and of history without reference to religion, with science and reason for their guides. New educational methods and systems are being tried, which can only develop lamentable consequences for your people, as far as the training of mind and character is concerned. In the same way the life of the home, so fruitful in happiness where Christ's commandments are kept, falls sadly into decay and is ruined by sinful habits when once the Gospel is thrust on one side: *He who seeks guidance in the law will find contentment therein; he who deals craftily with it will find it a stumbling-block to his feet.*

"Is there any institution in the world more happy, more contented than the Christian family? It begins before God's altar, where love has been hailed as a holy bond that can never be dissolved, and by that love, which is fed in its turn by heavenly grace, it takes root and grows. Here you see *marriage held in all honor, and its bed unsullied.* Those peaceful walls do not echo with quarrels, do not witness the secret tragedies that spring from the discovery of the adulterer's treachery. Utter confidence leaves no room for aching suspicion; an exchange of loving goodwill tempers grief and redoubles joy. Children are looked upon as the welcome gauge of love, not as a burden to be borne; no mean calculation, no frustrated enjoyment of pleasure is there to withhold the gift of life, and abolish the endearing titles of 'brother' and 'sister.' It is the chief ambition of such parents, that a family of sturdy children should follow the oft-called examples of their ancestors, and grow up faithful and honorable men and women. Their gratitude engaged by so many titles, the children consider it the first of duties to reverence their parents; falling in with their wishes, giving due support to them in old age, and comforting their gray hairs with an affection that will not die with their death, but will be restored, with a new brightness and a new fullness, in heaven. Cheerful in adversity, grateful in prosperity, the Christian family trusts in God at all times, obeying His commandments, reposing in His will, hoping, not vainly, for His assistance.

"Consequently, all those who hold governing or teaching positions in the churches under your charge, if they are making a genuine effort to bring God's people to perfection, must be constantly urging on the faithful this duty of founding and maintaining the family according to Gospel principles. For this purpose, no pains must be spared to ensure that those who contract marriages both firmly hold and faithfully cherish the Christian doctrine on the subject; namely that matrimony is by divine law an indissoluble and permanent tie. Many who are far from professing our faith, but have a deserved reputation for political wisdom, recognize that this tenet of Catholic theology is of the utmost importance if the family is to be held together, if the social life of the community is to flourish, if the nation is to keep sane, if we are to deserve the name of civilized people. Would that your country had been able to learn from the experience of others, not from its own, what a mass of unfortunate consequences must arise where divorce is tolerated! It is to be hoped that veneration for religion, and love of the great American people, will remedy and extirpate the disease which has taken so terrible a hold. The ill-effects of it have been described, poignantly but with unmistakable truth, by Pope Leo XIII: 'Legal recognition of divorce makes all the ties between husband and wife precarious; it wears down their goodwill for each other; it offers a dangerous temptation to infidelity; it interferes with the maintenance and education of the children; it undoes all the bonds of home life; it sows the seeds of enmity between one family and another; it worsens and degrades the position of women, who are in danger of finding themselves deserted when the passions of their husbands have been sufficiently gratified. And since corruption of manners is the most powerful of all influences which work for the breakdown of families and for the decay of kingdoms, it is easy to see that divorce is the worst enemy to the welfare of either.'

"We feel certain that the regulations laid down by Canon law for the celebration of marriages in which one party is a non-Catholic, or in which one party is unbaptized, are carefully observed in your country. You yourselves know, from frequent experience of their effects, that such marriages often fail to produce a happy wedded life, and that the Church is apt to suffer loss from them. These inconveniences can be best avoided, if the fullness of God's truth is brought home to all minds, and the way of salvation is made known to the nations of the world in its entirety. To this end, We would seriously urge upon priests the duty of acquiring proficiency, both in sacred and in profane learning. They must not be content with the knowledge they have made their own in youth; they must study the law of the Lord, with its utterances that are more pure than silver, with due attention; they must be tasting and relishing at all times the sweetness of Holy Scripture; they must be acquainting themselves with the history of the Church, her doctrines, her sacraments, her privileges, her laws, her ceremonies, her literature, ever more deeply as the years pass over them, thus growing at once in virtue and in accurate knowledge of the truth. But they should also cultivate letters and the secular sciences generally, those more especially which are directly germane to the subject of religion; thus they will be able to preach the way of salvation with eloquence and with grace; they will be able to subdue, under the light-burdened yoke of Christ, the brilliant intellects of our time. Happy is the state of the Church when she is thus *founded on sapphire*. The needs of our age demand that the laity too should be able to give assistance to the clergy; and that, not on a small and grudging scale; they should equip themselves with a generous grounding in theology, by reading, by discussion, by circles that meet for study. It will be of advantage to themselves, and it will enable them to instruct the ignorant, to refute the objector, to help their right-minded friends with advice.

"We are very glad to learn that the Catholic cause is ably defended in your country by newspaper articles, and that the microphone, whose voice echoes at once all over the world, as if to typify the Catholic faith, with its universality of appeal, is often used to good purpose, to give as wide publicity as possible to what concerns the Church. We congratulate you on these achievements. At the same time, those who undertake duties of this kind must be careful to follow closely the Church's teaching, just as much when they are discussing or defending social doctrines as at any other time. They must forget self-interest, they must not aspire to cheap publicity, they must not throw themselves into any merely partisan appeal. . . ."

Through the summer of 1939 papal nuncios and representatives strove desperately to convince the heads of governments that war could be averted by negotiation. There were rumors that the Pope had suggested the convention of a Five Power conference at the Vatican but this was officially denied although there is no doubt that many appeals were made to the various rulers. In June the Regent of Hungary, Admiral Horthy, told his parliament that: "The time has certainly come for the Powers finally to meet and find a solution which, if just, must be adhered to by all and it would probably be best if this call came from some high personage like the Pope." A great diplomatic activity was evident in Rome and speculation was rife as the interested journalists watched important visitors hurrying to and from the Vatican. There were schemes afoot but what happened or what was proposed is yet unrevealed. That a great war was inevitable few could doubt and in those anxious days pessimism was the mood as suspicion and obstinacy and hostility triumphed over reason. With terrible acceleration the fever of violence was spreading but the Pope persisted in his efforts and a fervent message went *To Those in Power and Their*

Peoples who were told that: "Conquests and empires not founded on justice cannot be blessed by God. The danger is enormous, but not desperate. Nothing is lost by peace, but everything may be lost by war. Men often retrace their steps and yield to negotiation. Once they begin discussing with goodwill and respect for mutual rights, they will discover that peaceful negotiations never stood in the way of a creditable issue. . . . We know that the heart of every mother beats in response to ours. The fathers who would have to leave their homes, the humble who work and care not, the innocent who will bend under the threat, the young who are inspired by the noblest ideals, are all with Us. With Us also is the very spirit of old Europe which has preserved the faith and the genius of Christianity: With Us the whole human race which hungers for bread and liberty, not for steel; which has turned maternal love into a fundamental principle, and made it part of its religion as a promise of salvation to men and nations." . . . These words came from the Vatican on the 24th of August, the very day that Poland informed Germany that the annexation of Danzig would not be tolerated. Polish troops moved to stations of combat and England and France made ready for mobilization. Declaring that his only way was to "meet force with force" Adolph Hitler a week later unleashed the German army and without a formal declaration of war German batteries opened fire and German bombers poured destruction and death upon Polish cities.

The Second World War had begun and the Pope's part in it, for the first few years at least, parallels the sad story of Benedict XV and his relations with the warring countries during the conflict of 1914-1918. There is the same noble record of constant plea and negotiation and suggestion and there is, alas, the same melancholy record of rejection and obstinacy on the part of those to whom he has appealed. A little more courtesy is perhaps paid to the present pontiff, polite audience is given to his voice, the niceties of protocol are suitably observed but actually the same bitter failure seems to be his. Nevertheless he continues his efforts. Shortly after the outbreak of hostilities he issued his aptly named encyclical *Darkness over the Earth* and then, on Christmas Eve, came his Five Point Plan for Peace.

"The unspeakable calamity of war," said the Pope, "which Pius XI foresaw with deep misgiving, and which with all the energy of his noble spirit he strove to avert from the comity of nations, is now upon us as a tragic reality. Our soul is flooded with bitter affliction when We think that this holy festival of Christ, the Prince of Peace, must today be celebrated amidst the deadly roll of cannon, under the menace of warlike missiles and the attacks of armed vessels of war. Moreover, since the world seems to have forgotten the peaceful message of Christ, the voice of reason and Christian brotherhood, we have been forced to witness a series of acts irreconcilable alike with the precepts of positive international law and those of the law of nature, as well as with the elementary sentiments of humanity; acts which show in what a vicious circle the juridical sense becomes involved when it is led simply by considerations of expediency. Among such crimes We must include a calculated act of aggression against a small, industrious, and peaceful nation, on the pretext of a threat which was neither real nor intended, nor even possible; atrocities (by whichever side committed) and the unlawful use of destructive weapons against non-combatants and refugees, against old men and women and children; a disregard for the dignity, liberty, and life of man, showing itself in actions which cry to heaven for vengeance: *The voice of thy brother's blood crieth to me from the earth;* and finally an ever-growing and increasingly methodical antiChristian and atheistic propaganda, especially among the young.

"It is Our duty, as well as Our sacred desire and purpose, to preserve the Church and its mission from all contact with this anti-Christian spirit, and therefore We warmly and insistently urge especially the ministers of the altar and the 'dispensers of the mysteries of God' to be ever more assiduous and exemplary in the teaching and the practice of charity, bearing always in mind that in the kingdom of Christ there is no precept more inviolable or more fundamental than the service of truth and the strengthening of the bond of love.

"With deep distress We contemplate the manifest and growing damage to souls caused by the spread of ideas which, more or less purposely and openly, are distorting and obscuring the truth in the minds of individuals and nations, whether belligerent or not; and We are overwhelmed with the thought of the immense labor which will be necessary, when the world has tired of war and turns to thoughts of peace, in order to break down the gigantic walls of hatred and hostility which have been built up in the heat of conflict.

"Aware of the excesses to which the way is opened and an impulse provided by a policy which takes no account of God's law, We used every endeavor, when war threatened, to avert the supreme catastrophe and to persuade those in power, upon whose shoulders rested the heavy responsibility of decision, to withdraw from an armed conflict and to spare the world a tragedy beyond all foreseeing. But Our efforts, as well as those of other parties enjoying influence and respect, failed to produce the desired effect, chiefly because it appeared impossible to remove the deep feeling of distrust which during recent years had been steadily growing and had placed insurmountable spiritual barriers between one nation and another.

"The international problems involved were by no means insoluble, but that lack of confidence, due to a series of particular circumstances, presented an almost insuperable obstacle to faith in the efficacy of any promises or in the lasting character of possible agreements. The recollection of the short and troubled duration of similar pacts and agreements in the past finally paralyzed all efforts to promote a peaceful solution.

"It remained for Us, Worshipful Brethren and beloved sons, only to repeat the words of the Prophet: *We have looked for peace and there is no good; and for the time of healing and behold trouble,* and to use every possible endeavor meanwhile to alleviate the misfortunes arising out of the war, endeavors which are not a little obstructed by the impossibility, not yet overcome, of bringing the aid of Christian charity to those regions where the need of it is most urgently felt. For four months now, and with anguish beyond all words, We have gazed upon the ruins which this war, begun under such unusual circumstances, has been piling up. And even though hitherto, if we except the bloodstained soil of Poland and Finland, the number of victims may be considered to be smaller than had been expected, nevertheless the sum-total of calamities and sacrifices has already reached proportions which cannot but cause grave anxiety for the economic, social, and spiritual future of Europe, and not of Europe alone. As the war-monster progressively acquires, swallows, and demands more and more of the materials available, all of which are inexorably put at the disposal of its ever-increasing requirements, the greater becomes the danger that the nations directly or indirectly affected by the conflict will become victims of a sort of pernicious anemia—and the inevitable question arises: How will an exhausted or attenuated economy contrive to find the means necessary for economic and social reconstruction at a time when difficulties of every kind will be multiplied, difficulties of which the disruptive and revolutionary forces now holding themselves in readiness will not fail to take advantage, in the hope of striking a decisive blow at Christian Europe?

"Even the fever of conflict should not prevent nations and their rulers from giving due weight to considerations such as these, which ought to cause them to examine the likely consequences and reflect upon the aims and justifiable purposes of the war.

"Those who keep a watchful eye upon these future consequences and calmly consider the symptoms in many parts of the world already pointing to such a development of events, will, We think, in spite of the war and its hard necessities, keep their minds open to the prospect of defining clearly, at an opportune moment and so far as it lies with them to do so, the fundamental points of a just and honorable peace; nor will they categorically refuse negotiations for such a peace in the event of a suitable occasion, with the needful guarantees and safeguards, presenting itself.

"I. A fundamental postulate of any just and honorable peace is an assurance for all nations great or small, powerful or weak, of their right to life and independence. The will of one nation to live must never mean the sentence of death passed upon another. When this equality of rights has been destroyed, attacked, or threatened, order demands that reparation is determined, not by the sword nor by the arbitrary decision of self-interest, but by the rules of justice and reciprocal equity.

"II. The order thus established, if it is to continue undisturbed and ensure true peace, requires that the nations be delivered from the slavery imposed upon them by the race for armaments, and from the danger that material force, instead of serving to protect the right, may become an overbearing and tyrannical master. Any peaceful settlement which fails to give fundamental importance to a mutually agreed, organic, and progressive disarmament, spiritual as well as material, or which neglects to ensure the effective and loyal implementing of such an agreement, will sooner or later show itself to be lacking in coherence and vitality.

"III. The maxims of human wisdom require that in any reorganization of international life all parties should learn a lesson from the failures and deficiencies of the past. Hence in creating or reconstructing international institutions which have so high a mission and such difficult and grave responsibilities, it is important to bear in mind the experience gained from the ineffectiveness or imperfections of previous institutions of the kind. Human frailty renders it difficult, not to say impossible, to foresee every contingency and guard against every danger at the moment in which treaties are signed; passion and bitter feeling are apt to be still rife. Hence in order that a peace may be honorably accepted and in order to avoid arbitrary breaches and unilateral interpretations of treaties, it is of the first importance to erect some juridical institution which shall guarantee the loyal and faithful fulfillment of the conditions agreed upon, and which shall, in case of recognized need, revise and correct them.

"IV. If a better European settlement is to be reached there is one point in particular which should receive special attention: it is the real needs and the just demands of nations and populations, and of racial minorities. It may be that, in consequence of existing treaties incompatible with them, these demands are unable to establish a strictly legal right. Even so, they deserve to be examined in a friendly spirit with a view to meeting them by peaceful methods, and even, where it appears necessary, by means of an equitable and covenanted revision of the treaties themselves. If the balance between nations is thus adjusted and the foundation of mutual confidence thus laid many incentives to violent action will be removed.

"V. But even the best and most detailed regulations will be imperfect and foredoomed to failure unless the peoples and those who govern them submit willingly to the influence of that spirit which alone can give life, authority, and binding force to the dead letter of international agreements. They must develop that sense of deep and keen responsibility which measures and weighs human statutes according to the sacred and inviolable standards of the law of God; they must cultivate that hunger and thirst after justice which is proclaimed as a beatitude in the Sermon on the Mount and which supposes as its natural foundation the moral virtue of justice; they must be guided by that universal love which is the compendium and most general expression of the Christian ideal, and which therefore may serve as a common ground also for those who have not the blessing of sharing the same faith with us.

"We are not insensible of the grave difficulties which lie in the way of the achievement of these ends which We have described as needful for establishing and preserving a just peace between nations. But if ever there was an objective deserving the collaboration of all noble and generous minds, if there was ever a spiritual crusade which might assume with a new truth as its motto, 'God wills it,' then it is this high purpose, it is this crusade, enlisting all unselfish and greathearted men in an endeavor to lead the nations back from the broken cisterns of material and selfish interests to the living fountain of divine justice, which alone is able to provide that morality, nobility, and stability of which the need has been so long experienced, to the great detriment of nations and of humanity.

"To these ideals, which are at the same time the real objectives of a true peace established in justice and love, We hope and trust that all those united with Us in the bond of faith will keep open their minds and hearts; so that when the storm of war shows signs of abating there may arise in every nation men of foresight and goodwill, inspired with the courage which can suppress the base instinct of revenge and set up in its stead the grave and noble majesty of justice, sister of love and consort of true wisdom. . . ."

For a while there was a glimmer of hope and the headlines flared when special emissaries from the United States came to Rome and then flew to other capitals. But the hope died and despair deepened as the conflict instead of diminishing spread on to newer territories. The conflict truly and terribly was becoming a world war. On every ocean, in every sky, death was petitioned as never before. In all the continents all the ingeniousness and all the resources of modern civilization were mustered in the service of calamity.

The Pope was "beyond every rivalry and outside every party" but when neutrality was violated he did not hesitate to lift his voice and to Poland, Norway, Denmark, Holland, Belgium, and Luxembourg, went messages of profound sympathy. "The territorial neutrality of two more countries has been violated," stated the *Osservatore Romano,* journal of the Holy See, at the time of the invasion of Norway and Denmark. "Those who have defended the sacred rights of neutral countries against all and any cannot but regard with the deepest pain this sudden and dramatic extension of the theater of war." "The life of one nation or people," said the Pope, "does not mean the death of any weaker neighbor." His concern for neutrality and the absolute necessity for his own neutrality did not prevent the usual carping from those men in all countries who without offering the slightest token of allegiance to the Pope in any form give grieved tongue to accusations of partisanship or timidity when the Vatican does not endorse their views or actions. As in the First World War the organization of the Church was utilized for works of mercy and charity. The Vatican Information Service for War Prisoners was formed and made into a free service for anybody. Consolation was thus brought to hundreds of thousands and because of its merciful efficiency many a family was given the first and often only news of their loved ones. When Allied troops arrived in Rome they found four hundred thousand persons were receiving a daily meal in the soup kitchens at the Vatican and Castel Gandolfo. The needy of many countries, on both opposing sides, also received aid. There was also a special service for the transmission of correspondence and the seeking out of information about missing persons; both combatant and non-combatant. Of the hard-oppressed Jews, who were among the objects of the Holy Father's tenderest care, an innumerable multitude were given sanctuary in the Vatican and in churches and monasteries throughout Italy. Assistance was also generously given to refugee Jews from other countries. Perhaps it was this true example of pure Christianity which prompted Professor Israel Anton Zolli, former Grand Rabbi of Rome, to ask for baptism.

Shortly after the outbreak of hostilities President Roosevelt sent a distinguished Protestant gentleman, Mr. Myron C. Taylor, as "personal Representative of the President of the United States of America to His Holiness Pope Pius XII." Such action, of course, brought immediate protest from bigots but during the bitter years of war an extraordinary valuable and harmonious relationship between the Holy See and Washington was thus developed. For five years the Pope and the President exchanged views and aims in a series of historic letters. "It is in the American tradition of open diplomacy," said President Truman when this correspondence was published after the war, "that the world should be given the texts of the messages . . . they constitute a record of incalculable value."

Time and time again the Pope made his plea for peace and justice. In his address on Easter Sunday, 1940 he said: ". . . It is not only the private lives of individual citizens and their private welfare that depend on this course of action, it is the highest interest of the whole confederacy of mankind. And not least in these times, when all eyes are fixed upon events so lamentable, all hearts are daunted by the fear of worse to come. You can see for yourselves what an age it is we have been born into. Peace between nations lies hopelessly shattered; pacts solemnly confirmed by agreement on both sides are continually being revised, or violated outright, at the discretion of one party, without any attempt at discussion and clear adjustment of mutual relations; the voice of brotherly love and brotherly goodwill is silenced. All the fruits of research and experiment, all men's energies, all their wealth and property, are now being devoted to the conduct of war, or to the ever-increasing production of armaments. What was designed to promote the prosperity of nations and the growth of civilization, is now, by a preposterous change of direction, being used for its downfall and its ruin. The commerce of peace-time, held up by every possible device, is at a standstill; and this means a want of supply which falls most heavily upon the poorer classes. More than this, and worse than this; in many parts of the world, where men's hearts are blinded by hatred and ill-will, the earth, the seas, and even the sky, noble image of our heavenly country, are being polluted with fratricidal massacre. More than once, to Our great distress, the laws which bind civilized peoples together have been violated; most lamentably, undefended cities, country towns and villages, have been terrorized by bombing, destroyed by fire, and thrown down in ruins; unarmed citizens, even sickness, helpless old age, and innocent childhood have been turned out of their homes, and often visited with death.

"As these evils crowd in upon us, what hope of remedy is left to us, except that which comes from Christ, from His inspirations, and from His teaching, a healing stream flowing through every vein of our society? Only Christ's law, only Christ's grace can renew and restore private and public life, redressing the true balance of rights and duties, checking unbridled self-interest, controlling passion, implementing and perfecting the course of strict justice with His overflowing charity. He who only could give His commands to wind and storm, who could allay the waves of an angry sea and reduce them to calm, He it is who alone can turn men's hearts to peace and brotherly love: He alone can bid the nations settle their disputes, freely and successfully, not by violence but by the law of truth, of justice, and of charity: He alone can strike the swords from their hands, and join those hands at last in a treaty of friendship. . . ."

Despite his continuous and insistent declarations of neutrality, Pius XII found much to say against frequent vexations suffered at the hands of the Nazis and Fascists who refused to respect that neutrality. In Italy anti-Fascist priests were arrested for "defeatism" and the semi-official Vatican newspaper, the *Osservatore Romano,* was forced by the authorities to limit its circulation. There was a systematic persecution of the Church in Poland in both the German and Russian occupied zones. Cardinal Suhard's condemnation of the deportation of Jews from Vichy France met approval from the Pontiff despite the fact that the Vatican had maintained diplomatic relations with Vichy. The Nazi propaganda machine went so far as to blame the Pope for the war because he had rejected racism. Early in 1942, Pius declared that, no matter how much it might irk certain powers, "the Catholic Church will continue to express its determination to defend the rights of people to liberty which it considers one of the fundamental conditions of equitable peace. Liberty, moreover, is considered by the Church to be a natural law without which there can be neither personality nor responsibility." Nor could the Holy Father be convinced that the Church in Germany was in a reassuring status.

There was a violent protest from Germany when New York's

Archbishop Spellman, in the early part of 1943, landed at an airport near Rome and was given diplomatic immunity in his transit to the neutral precincts of the Vatican State. Persistent denials from the Vatican could not suppress the belief that the prolonged visit of Archbishop Spellman was more than religious in character. There were continuous rumors of plans for a negotiated peace between Italy and the Allies in which the Pope was to have a hand. Though Pius XII refused any open endorsement to the Allied cause, and put in a complaint against the Allied bombing of Rome on July 20th, it was considered a strange coincidence that Mussolini was ousted by an interim government under Badoglio shortly after the Spellman sojourn. Unfortunately, peace did not follow in Italy. The Germans did not surrender and, in September, the Vatican suffered the supreme indignity of being occupied by Nazi troops who placed the Supreme Pontiff under their "protection." Protests from Pius XII brought nothing but an increase in the guard around the tiny papal state and the world press pictured the pontiff as the new "prisoner in the Vatican." To all the repeated offers of the German command for "haven" in Germany, the successor of Peter replied with a resolute "no."

Although for a long time there was widespread fear of the bombing of Rome, the Pope still would not hear of leaving the city. He said in 1942: "I have ordered all my bishops throughout the world to remain at their posts as good shepherds among their flocks. . . . The Bishop of Rome does not wish to be the first to disobey the order which he himself has given." Rome was indeed bombed on two occasions. The first time, in an Allied raid, the church of St. Lawrence-outside-the-Walls was damaged. Though embittered by this act, the Pope ventured to correct exaggerated reports made by German broadcasts concerning the amount of destruction which had resulted. The second bombing came from planes of an unidentified nationality and brought damage to the Vatican itself—a neutral state. As anxiety mounted Pius XII finally labelled all plans to bomb Rome as "matricide," calling attention to its sacred character and historical and artistic importance. But the Eternal City was not bombed again and when, in June of 1944, the Allies marched into the City the Pontiff joyfully thanked both sides for having spared it.

The major concern of Pius XII was the restoration of peace. His fondest dream was that a peace might be negotiated without reference to *unconditional surrender,* and he implored the victors to be just, generous, merciful and forgiving. The world in general paid him little heed and the Moscow press branded his pleas as a defense of "Hitlerite robbers." When surveying the chances for peace the Holy Father's outlook must have been somewhat gloomy. Such, at least, is the impression one gets from his Christmas speeches of 1942 and 1943. He declared that men had placed all their faith in material things, in the expansion of economic life, in a science and culture divorced from God, in bodily comforts and pleasures. He called for a recognition of the spiritual side of man, of the sacredness of the family, of the nobility and prerogatives of labor, and of the need for Christian morality in law, politics, and government. Marxian Socialism, with its materialistic and atheistic collectivism and regimentation was, of course, the very opposite of a solution. Said the Pontiff in his Christmas discourse of 1943: "The progress of mankind in the present confusion of ideas has been a progress without God and even against God, without Christ and even against Christ."

The secular press gave indulgent lip service to these ideas but publicized highly the Pope's Christmas address of 1944 which explained the benefits, right and duties of democracies. Reminding his hearers that the Church supported no one form of government over another, he set forth as the two rights democracies guaranteed their citizens, that "they shall have full freedom to set forth their own views of the duties and sacrifices imposed upon them, and that they will not be compelled to obey without being heard. . . . Hence follows a first conclusion with its practical consequence. The State is not a distinct entity which mechanically gathers together a shapeless mass of indi-

viduals and confines them within a specified territory. It is and
should be in practice the organic and organizing unity of a
real people. The people and a shapeless multitude (or, as it is
called, 'the masses') are two distinct concepts. The people
lives and moves by its own life energy; the masses are inert
of themselves and can only be moved from the outside. . . .
Hence follows clearly another conclusion: the masses—as we
have just defined them—are the capital enemy of true democracy and its ideal of liberty and equality." According to Pius
XII, under the rule of "the masses," liberty, which is really a
moral duty of the individual, becomes a tyrannous claim of freedom to give free rein to one's impulses and appetites at whatever cost or detriment to others. Equality degenerates to a
mechanical level, and becomes a colorless uniformity in which
the sense of true honor, of personal activity, of respect for tradition, of dignity—in a word, of all that gives life its worth—
gradually fades away and disappears. As for the government,
"the democratic state, whether monarchical or republican, must
have the power to command, with a real and effective authority.
The divinely established order of beings and purposes . . . calls
also for the existence of the State as a necessary society, and
gives it authority, without which it could neither exist nor live.
If men in using their personal liberty, were to deny all depend-
ence on a superior authority possessed of a coercive power, they
would by this very fact cut the ground from under their own
dignity and liberty. . . . No form of state can avoid taking
cognizance of this intimate and indissoluble connection between itself and the divine order—least of all a democracy. If
those in power do not see it, or discount it in any degree, their
own authority is shaken." On the other hand, "State absolutism,
which ·is not to be confused, as such, with an absolute monarchy, which is not now under discussion, consists in fact in the
false principle that the authority of the State is unlimited and
that even when it gives free rein to despotic aims, and goes
beyond the confines between good and evil, there is no right
of appeal against it to a higher law which binds in conscience."

As corollaries of these principles the Pontiff called for the banning of wars of aggression and of wholesale punishment of peoples, the establishment of a supra-national organization of nations, the protection of the rights of all nations, "victor, vanquished, and neutral," and the subjection of States to moral principles. The speech was widely acclaimed as a change of heart on the part of the Catholic Church in favor of democracy. It was not a change of heart at all. It was a mere reaffirmation of the principles of Aquinas, Bellarmine, and Suarez in the light of modern conditions, the principles that authority in a State comes from God through the consent of the governed and that the people have the right to resist the encroachments of an unjust government. The theory of the Divine Right of Kings, though used by Catholic monarchs, was in origin and content, essentially non-Catholic and the very negation of Medieval political theory.

Peace finally came to the world. A strange and uncertain peace, ushered in by the use of a terrible new weapon, the atomic bomb. This fearful instrument of titanic destruction was dropped on the Japanese cities of Hiroshima and Nagasaki and a quarter of a million people—men, women, and children—were killed or wounded. Hostilities ceased. The vanquished countries were prostrate. Forty-one of Germany's principal cities had been destroyed by bombings. Forty per cent of Japan's sixty-six cities had suffered the same fate. Millions were homeless and hungry. "If we contrast the principles for which the struggle was started," said the *Osservatore Romano,* "the aims that were set, and the promises that were made to people with what has been accomplished, then the victors may doubt the victory." Before the end of the war the Pope had informed the world that he looked forward to a society in which an international organization would prevent further aggression. Once again he deplored the evils of revenge and warned of the folly of trying to punish whole countries for starting the war.

On February 18th, 1946, at a secret consistory in the Vatican, the Red Hat was given to thirty-two prelates. It was the largest number of Cardinals ever to receive the honor at the same time and it was the first time since the middle of the 14th century that a non-Italian majority was established in the Sacred College. Africa, Australia, Chile, China, Cuba, and Peru were represented for the first time, the cardinal from China being the first in the history of the Church who was not of the white race. Canada had its first English-speaking cardinal. There were four new princes of the Church added to the American hierarchy, among them Francis J. Spellman, whose elevation had, however, been expected. The Armenian Patriarch of Cilicia took his place beside the Syrian Patriarch of Antioch as another representative of the Oriental Rites in the College. The most outstanding fact about the new nominees was that they came from all five continents, thus giving the Sacred College an international aspect. The Pope, by his choices, seemed to wish to manifest and give concrete expression to the universality of the Church and also to acknowledge the moral reduction of the size of the globe through modern invention.

The wartime Pope had not neglected projects of a peaceful and lasting nature. Perceiving the scholarly dissatisfaction with the old Vulgate version of the Bible, he gave his approval for a new Latin translation which was to be based on critical editions of the original Hebrew and Greek texts and under the supervision of the best modern scholarship available. Furthermore, among a multitude of encyclicals, he published two which stand out for their permanent significance. One, known as *Mediator Dei*, which came out in 1947, is on the Sacred Liturgy and, reflecting the contemporary revival of interest in things liturgical which had been stimulated by his immediate predecessors, concerns itself with evaluating the traditional liturgical practices of the Latin Church, and integrating them with the exigencies of modern life. The other encyclical, *Mystici Corporis Christi*, was written in 1943, during the war, and serves to explain and clarify a most important but somewhat neglected doctrine of the Church—that of the Mystical Body of Christ. The Mystical Body is the Church, with Christ as its head, the Holy

Spirit as its soul, and the faithful as its members. It is not our purpose to go deeply into the dogmatic ramifications of this teaching; suffice it to say that it has important social and moral implications. "But a body calls also for a multiplicity of members, which are linked together in such a way as to help one another. And, as in our mortal composite being, when one member suffers, all other members share its pain, and the healthy members come to the assistance of those ailing, so in the Church the individual members do not live for themselves alone, but also help their fellows, and all work in mutual collaboration for their common comfort and for the more perfect building up of the whole body . . . every man must rise to this supernatural charity, so that by the combined efforts of all good men—We have in mind especially those who are active in any kind of relief organization—the gigantic needs of mankind, spiritual and corporal, may be alleviated." Although "only those are really to be included as members of the Church who have been baptized and profess the true faith and who have not unhappily withdrawn from Body-unity or for grave faults been excluded by legitimate authority" the Pope also made the admonition that "we must also recognize as brothers of Christ according to the flesh, destined together with us to eternal salvation, those others who have not yet joined us in the body of the Church." His special devotion to this doctrine was probably an influential factor in prompting Pius to advocate constantly the formation of an international federation of nations and to give his heartiest support to the UNO and the Marshall Plan. The doctrine of the Mystical Body is also the basis and foundation of the lay apostolate to which Pius gave steadfast encouragement. "We desire that all who claim the Church as their mother, seriously consider that not only the sacred ministers but the other members as well of the Mystical Body of Jesus Christ have the obligation of working hard and constantly for the up-building and increase of this Body. We wish this to be remembered especially by members of Catholic Action who assist the bishops and priests in their apostolic labors . . . and by those associations of pious unions who contribute their work to the same end." This declaration was reminiscent of an earlier one made in 1939: "At a moment when one is forced to note with sorrow the disproportion between the number of priests and the calls upon them . . . the collaboration of the laity in the Apostolate of the Hierarchy . . . stands out as a precious aid to the work of priests and shows possibilities of development which justify the highest hopes."

Events closer to home led Pius XII to make a clear pronouncement on an issue long beclouded and muddled by sentiment or interest. In Italy the first free elections were to be held since the beginning of Mussolini's regime and there was a new provision for woman's suffrage. The Supreme Pontiff thought the time ripe to make a public statement on woman's rights and duties in social and political life. "In their personal dignity as children of God," he said, "man and woman are absolutely equal, as they are in relation to the last end of human life which is everlasting union with God in the Happiness of heaven. . . . But a man and woman cannot maintain and perfect this equal dignity of theirs, unless by respecting and activating qualities which nature has given each of them, physical and spiritual qualities which cannot be eliminated, which cannot be reversed without nature itself stepping in to restore the balance. . . . The two sexes, by the very qualities that distinguish them, are mutually complementary to such an extent that their coordination makes itself felt in every phase of man's social life." He then outlined the various benefits of the married, single, and religious states and recalled the diverse functions and missions of man and woman. He spoke of the loss of feminine dignity which ensued from woman's "abandonment of the home where she reigned as queen and her subjection to the same work strain and working hours." But, "Shall we conclude then that you Catholic women and girls must show yourselves averse to a movement which willy-nilly carried you with it into social and political life? Certainly not. . . . A woman is, in fact, kept out of the home not only by her so-called emancipation but often too by the necessities of life, by the continuous anxiety about daily bread. It would be useless to preach to her to return to the home while conditions prevail which constrain her to remain away from it. . . . Your entry into public life came about suddenly as a result of social upheavals which we see around us. It does not matter. You are called upon to take part. . . . The fate of the family, the fate of human relations are at stake. They are in your hands. . . . Every woman has then, mark it well, the obligation, the strict obligation in conscience, not to absent herself but to go into action in a manner and way suitable to the conditions of each so as to hold back those currents which threaten the home, so as to oppose those doctrines which undermine its foundations, so as to prepare, organize, and achieve its restoration. . . . This direct participation, this effective collaboration in social and political activity does not at all change the normal activity of woman. Associated with men in civil institutions, she will apply herself especially to those matters which call for tact, delicacy, and maternal instinct rather than administrative rigidity. Who better than she can understand what is needed for the dignity of woman, the integrity and honor of the young girl, and the protection and education of the child? . . . no wise woman favors a policy of class struggle and war. Her vote is a vote for peace. Hence in the interest and for the good of the family she will hold to that norm, and she will always refuse her vote to any tendency, from whatever quarter it hails, to the selfish desires of domination, internal or external, of the peace of the nation."

The concern of the papacy over the Italian elections was chiefly with the progress of the Communist Party. In the elections both of 1945 and 1948, the Reds in Italy were checked in great part through the opposition of the Catholic Church. But these events were merely local indications of the growing tension between Catholics and Communists throughout the world. For a brief time it looked as if a *modus vivendi* might be reached between Rome and Moscow—a compromise of a purely political nature of course, for both sides were adamant on the question of basic principles. In May of 1946 the Holy Father applauded

Stalin's promise to support the UNO and to work for peace. It was a gesture that was not reciprocated. In fact, the Moscow Communist organs, *Pravda* and *Izvetsia* were unabating in their stabs at the Vatican, accusing it of wanting a soft peace for Germany and being allied with Fascism. At the same time, the Pope continued his warnings against the dangers of a "new tyranny," and the reference was obvious.

The real conflict, however, was not so much in the press or on the pulpit as it was on the steps of churches and rectories in those territories occupied or controlled by the Soviet Union (behind the "Iron Curtain" to use Winston Churchill's masterly phrase). For reports were to be had in abundance about the suppression, both insidious and open, of the liberties of the Church in those countries—the closing of places of worship, the confiscation of ecclesiastical property, the slaughter of priests and religious. With the exception of those in Yugoslavia and, to some extent, Hungary, it was mainly the clergy of the Byzantine Rite who bore the brunt of the persecution. The reason is not hard to find. If the people of the Orthodox countries come into the Catholic Church it will be through the Byzantine Rite. But it is to the interest of the Soviet government to maintain the Orthodox Churches in those countries because they are of a national, rather than an international, character, thus facilitating State control that much more. Should the supra-national Catholic Church replace them, it would be harder to manipulate its policies. Hence the Red attempt to eradicate the Catholic Byzantine Church which is the bridge of reunion with the East. It was thus that, just a few days before Stalin's protestations of peace, the Pope received the painful news of the Ruthenian Church's "return to freedom." Actually only forty-two priests out of two thousand seven hundred—and not one bishop—signed the document precipitating the schism, but this gave the Red authorities an excellent excuse to liquidate the Church in Gallicia and the Ukraine (or "protect its liberties" as they may have euphemistically termed the operation). The Catholic Byzantine bishops were either jailed, driven from their sees, or made to disappear mysteriously. In the Eastern Rite Churches of Rumania and Hungary similar events occurred, often with the approval of the Orthodox Churches, whose offices, however, had, in general, first been filled by the Communist chiefs with their own creatures. In Yugoslavia the Tito government was equally vehement against the clergy of the Roman Rite. There the martyrdom of ecclesiastics found its chief symbol in the person of Archbishop Stepinac of Zagreb, who, in the fall of 1946, was tried on charges of collaboration with the Nazis. After a vigorous denial of the accusation and a brave defense he was sentenced to a long term of imprisonment. The Pope retaliated by excommunicating Tito, who was a nominal Catholic, but the persecution of the Church in Yugoslavia went right on.

Among the cardinals recently created was Joseph Mindszenty, Archbishop of Esztergom and Primate of Hungary. In 1946, when he was to come to Rome to receive the scarlet, he had had some difficulty in getting out of his Communist-dominated country and arrived in the Holy City later than most of his confreres. It was probably in view of this delay that Pope Pius XII foresaw that the Hungarian prelate might be the first of the new cardinals to be asked to suffer for his faith. This prediction was remembered two years later when the government of Hungary made history by arresting a Prince of the Church—something never before dared by anyone. The Supreme Pontiff proceeded therefore to excommunicate all who had had a hand in Mindszenty's arrest. The latter was brought to trial on several charges, the chief of which was treason and, under circumstances which are still looked upon as equivocal, confessed his guilt although he had, at first, denied all accusations and rejected beforehand any admission he might make through human frailty. A startled world, hearing the news, refused to believe it, and its suspicions seemed confirmed when this conviction was followed by that of fifteen Protestant clergymen in Communist Bulgaria, who were tried for similar transgressions and made similar confessions.

It was now apparent to the world that the struggle between

Catholicism and Communism had overstepped the bounds of the intellectual sphere and had descended to the physical plane. But in the midst of rising hysteria and the clamor for war with Russia, the *Osservatore Romano,* on Holy Saturday of 1949 spoke in a more sober vein: "It is impossible to paralyze an idea with violence, destroy it by force, drown it in blood . . . Communism one defeats by prayer and demonstration with works that social justice has no need to deny God in order to activate it. . . . If one should think by a war with Russia . . . if one should think by a Soviet liquidation to liquidate Communism, he would fall into unpardonable equivocation."

In the historic and splendid confines of the Sistine Chapel Pius XII, on the 12th of March, 1949, presided at a Pontifical Mass which marked his tenth year in the Chair of Peter. In many ways it had been a decade of anguish for him who as Vicar of Christ had labored indefatigably for Christian principles. He was now in his seventy-third year and had been a priest for nearly fifty years but there were no signs of a lessening in that tremendous vigor which characterized his continual struggle for justice and truth. A few months after the celebration of his tenth anniversary as Pope one of the most sweeping decrees in the history of the Church was issued at the Vatican. Catholics everywhere were solemnly forbidden to collaborate with, or take part in, the activities of the Communist Party. Violation of this pronouncement would automatically ban the offender from the Catholic Church and its Sacraments. The Pontiff later explained why he had invoked the power of excommunication. In a radio speech delivered on September 5th, 1949 he addressed a rally of 300,000 workers at Bashum, Germany, and for the first time he spoke of Communism by name. "If recently there has been traced a line of separation, obligatory for all Catholics, between the Catholic faith and atheist Communism, it has been done . . . to construct a barrier which aims at saving not only the workers but everyone without exception from Marxism which denies God and religion. The excommunication decree has nothing to do with the contrast between poor and rich, between capitalists and proletarians, between proprietors and propertyless. It concerns the conservation and purity of religion and the Christian faith, the liberty of the action and, with these, the well-being and dignity and the rights and liberty of workers."

On the same day that he spoke to the German workers the Papal voice was again heard on the radio. A congress of Swiss Catholics listened in Lucerne while the Pope spoke to them in the three official languages of their country, German, French, and Italian. They were told to resist, "religious negligence" and they were warned that "materialism contradicts all manifestatation of the spirit." But against this latter evil was ranged an even more powerful force: "Catholic force with all its riches, all the energy of its convictions, and all grandness of the divine way. This potent force is equipped to dominate victoriously over materialism."

Pope Pius XII had since 1944 been contemplating the proclamation of a Holy Year of prayer and penance for the expiation of crimes committed during the war. After a number of informal, but explicit, announcements in this regard, the Holy Father, in May of 1949, solemnly designated 1950 as the Holy Year. He has attached four main intentions to this observance. They are the sanctification of the soul through prayer, penance and acts of faith, the realization of social justice, especially through works of assistance to those in need, the protection and defense of the Church against attacks from the godless, and the achievement of peace and the safety of the Holy Places in Palestine, which are endangered because of the intransigient attitude of both Arabs and Jews in the turbulence accompanying the formation of the new state of Israel.

The Papacy now faces another of the critical periods in its history. It is beset by many dangers and problems. But the Papacy is no stranger to peril, and from the long pattern of history the Pope draws confidence for the future. "Whilst in fact, with the passing of years," he stated in the early years of his pontificate, "and with the alternate vicissitudes of events, in·

numerable things rise, grow and fall, and then, changed and renewed again, emerge or, quite consumed, precipitate and perish, the Catholic Church is not shaken by the waves of times, is not overcome by difficulties, is not changed by pressing vicissitudes. Instead the Church advances with firm and sure step, and still today, through her vocation and divine mission, accomplishes for the good of mankind what she already accomplished twenty centuries ago. And while desires for earthly things, internal hatreds and jealousies too often split and divide the souls of men, the Church of God, beloved mother of all peoples, embraces wtih immense charity the whole human family, without distinction of race or rank, and provides, either with prayer or with external works, for the salvation and the true felicity of all. . . . The Church of today holds her head high and maintains unchanged in her members the vigor of her youth; she remains necessarily what she was at her birth. Always the same, she does not change in her dogma or in her strength. She is impregnable, indestructible, invincible; she is immovable, changeless in the writ of her foundation; sealed with the blood of the Son of God, yet she moves, she takes new forms with the age in which she goes forward on her way—progressing, yes, but not changing. . . . No, there cannot be for the church whose steps God directs and accompanies through the ages—there cannot be for the human soul who studies history in the spirit of Christ—any going back, but only desire to go forward toward the future and to mount upward. . . ."

So speaks Pope Pius XII.

LIST OF POPES

There is uncertainty about the dates of some of the earlier Popes

St. Peter .... died 67	St. Julius I 337-352
St. Linus 67-76	St. Liberius 352-366
St. Cletus 76-88	St. Damasus I ... 366-384
St. Clement I 88-97	St. Siricius 384-399
St. Evaristus 97-105	St. Anastasius I 399-401
St. Alexander I 105-115	St. Innocent I 401-417
St. Sixtus I 115-125	St. Zosimus 417-418
St. Telesphorus 125-136	St. Boniface I 418-422
St. Hyginus 136-140	St. Celestine I 422-432
St. Pius I 140-155	St. Sixtus III 432-440
St. Anicetus 155-166	St. Leo I (the Great) ... 440-461
St. Soter 166-175	St. Hilary 461-468
St. Eleutherius 175-189	St. Simplicius 468-483
St. Victor I 189-199	St. Felix III (II) 483-492
St. Zephyrinus 199-217	St. Gelasius I 492-496
St. Callistus I 217-222	Anastasius II 496-498
St. Urban I 222-230	St. Symmachus 498-514
St. Pontian 230-235	St. Hormisdas 514-523
St. Anterus 235-236	St. John I 523-526
St. Fabian 236-250	St. Felix IV 526-530
St. Cornelius 251-253	Boniface II 530-532
St. Lucius I 253-254	John II 533-535
St. Stephen I 254-257	St. Agapitus I 535-536
St. Sixtus II 257-258	St. Silverius 536-537
St. Dionysius 259-268	Vigilius 537-555
St. Felix I 269-274	Pelagius I 556-561
St. Eutychian 275-283	John III 561-574
St. Caius 283-296	Benedict I 575-579
St. Marcellinus 296-304	Pelagius II 579-590
St. Marcellus I 308-309	St. Gregory I (the Great) 590-604
St. Eusebius 309	Sabinian 604-606
St. Melchiades 311-314	Boniface III 607
St. Sylvester I 314-335	St. Boniface IV 608-615
St. Mark 336	St. Deusdedit I 615-618

Stephen X 1057-1058
Nicholas II 1059-1061
Alexander II 1061-1073
St. Gregory VII 1073-1085
B. Victor III 1086-1087
B. Urban II 1088-1099
Paschal II 1099-1118
Gelasius II 1118-1119
Callistus II 1119-1124
Honorius II 1124-1130
Innocent II 1130-1143
Celestine II 1143-1144
Lucius II 1144-1145
B. Eugene III 1145-1153
Anastasius IV 1153-1154
Adrian IV 1154-1159
Alexander III 1159-1181
Lucius III 1181-1185
Urban III 1185-1187
Gregory VIII 1187
Clement III 1187-1191
Celestine III 1191-1198
Innocent III 1198-1216
Honorius III 1216-1227
Gregory IX 1227-1241
Celestine IV 1241
Innocent IV 1243-1254
Alexander IV 1254-1261
Urban IV 1261-1264
Clement IV 1265-1268
B. Gregory X 1271-1276
B. Innocent V 1276
Adrian V 1276
John XXI 1276-1277
Nicholas III 1277-1280
Martin IV 1281-1285
Honorius IV 1285-1287
Nicholas IV 1288-1292
St. Celestine V 1294
Boniface VIII 1294-1303
B. Benedict XI 1303-1304
Clement V 1305-1314

John XXII 1316-1334
Benedict XII 1334-1342
Clement VI 1342-1352
Innocent VI 1352-1362
B. Urban V 1362-1370
Gregory XI 1370-1378
Urban VI 1378-1389
Boniface IX 1389-1404
Innocent VII 1404-1406
Gregory XII 1406-1415
Martin V 1417-1431
Eugene IV 1431-1447
Nicholas V 1447-1455
Callistus III 1455-1458
Pius II 1458-1464
Paul II 1464-1471
Sixtus IV 1471-1484
Innocent VIII 1484-1492
Alexander VI 1492-1503
Pius III 1503
Julius II 1503-1513
Leo X 1513-1521
Adrian VI 1522-1523
Clement VII 1523-1534
Paul III 1534-1549
Julius III 1550-1555
Marcellus II 1555
Paul IV 1555-1559
Pius IV 1559-1565
St. Pius V 1566-1572
Gregory XIII 1572-1585
Sixtus V 1585-1590
Urban VII 1590
Gregory XIV 1590-1591
Innocent IX 1591
Clement VIII 1592-1605
Leo XI 1605
Paul V 1605-1621
Gregory XV 1621-1623
Urban VIII 1623-1644
Innocent X 1644-1655
Alexander VII 1655-1667

Clement IX	1667-1669	Pius VI	1775-1799
Clement X	1670-1676	Pius VII	1800-1823
Innocent XI	1676-1689	Leo XII	1823-1829
Alexander VIII	1689-1691	Pius VIII	1829-1830
Innocent XII	1691-1700	Gregory XVI	1831-1846
Clement XI	1700-1721	Pius IX	1846-1878
Innocent XIII	1721-1724	Leo XIII	1878-1903
Benedict XIII	1724-1730	Pius X	1903-1914
Clement XII	1730-1740	Benedict XV	1914-1922
Benedict XIV	1740-1758	Pius XI	1922-1939
Clement XIII	1758-1769	Pius XII	1939-....
Clement XIV	1769-1774		

BIBLIOGRAPHY

Acta Apostolici Sedis. Rome: Typis Polyglottis Vaticana, 1908, *seq.*

Acta Sanctae Sedis. Rome: Typis Polyglottis Vaticana, 1865-1908.

Acta Sanctorum. Paris: V. Palmé, 1863, *seq.*

Baldwin, M. W. *The Medieval Papacy in Action.* New York: Macmillan, 1940.

Barry, W. F. *The Papacy and Modern Times; a Political Sketch, 1303-1870.* London: Williams & Norgate, 1911.

—— *The Papal Monarchy from St. Gregory the Great to Boniface VIII.* New York: G. P. Putnam's Sons, 1902.

Bell, M. I. *A Short History of the Papacy.* London: Methuen, 1921.

Bettenson, H. S. (ed.). *Documents of the Christian Church.* New York: Oxford University Press, 1947.

Cambridge Medieval History. New York: Macmillan, 1911-36.

Cambridge Modern History. New York: Macmillan, 1907-25.

Catholic Encyclopedia. New York: Gilmary Society, 1936.

Creighton, M. *History of the Popes from the Great Schism to the Sack of Rome.* London: Longmans, Green, 1899-1901.

Dawson, Christopher. *The Making of Europe.* New York: Sheed & Ward, 1945.

Funk, F. X. *A Manual of Church History.* St. Louis: Herder, 1910.

Gregorovius, F. *History of the City of Rome in the Middle Ages.* London: Bell & Sons, 1894-1912.

Grisar, H. *History of Rome and the Popes in the Middle Ages.* London: Paul, 1911-12.

Holsapple, Lloyd B. *Constantine the Great.* New York: Sheed & Ward, 1942.

Howells, T. B. *The Men of the Vatican.* London: Independent Press, 1936.

Hughes, Philip. *A History of the Church.* New York: Sheed & Ward, 1935-47.

Mann, H. K. *The Lives of the Popes in the Middle Ages.* London: Paul, Trench Trükner & Company, 1902-32.

Mansi, G. D. *Sacrorum Conciliorum Nova et Amplissima, Collectio.* Florence-Venice: 1759-1927.

Migne, J. P. *Patrologiae Cursus Completus. Series Graeca.* Paris: 1854-66.

—— *Patrologiae Cursus Completus. Series Latina.* Paris: 1844-80.

Mourret, F. *La Papauté.* Paris: Bloud et Gay, 1929.

von Pastor, L. *History of the Popes from the Close of the Middle Ages.* London: J. Hodges, 1891-1941.

Taylor, H. O. *The Medieval Mind.* London: Macmillan, 1930.

NAME INDEX

Adalbert, 82, 83
Adeodatus II, 43
Adolph (of Nassau), 156
Adrian I, 55-7
Adrian II, 71
Adrian III, 73
Adrian IV, 124-26
Adrian V, 149
Adrian VI, 215, 222
Aethelred, 87
Agapitus I, 35, 37
Agapitus II, 80
Agatho, 43
Agiltrude, 75
Agrippa, 5
Aistulf, 52
Alberic, 80, 81
Albert (of Austria), 156
Albert (of Brandenburg), 210, 211
Alexander I, 8
Alexander II, 102-04
Alexander III, 128-30
Alexander IV, 144, 145
Alexander V (Anti-Pope), 177, 190
Alexander VI (Borgia), 190-200,
    204, 207, 222
Alexander VII, 251, 252
Alexander VIII, 256
Alexander (of Russia), 284
Alexis (Czar of Russia), 253
Alfred (the Great), 66, 73
Alphonse IV (of Leon), 136
Alphonso II (of Naples), 191
Alva (Duke of), 228
Ambrose, 26
Anacletus II, 119, 120
Anastasius, 67, 71
Anastasius (emperor), 33
Anastasius I, 26
Anastasius II, 32
Anastasius III, 78
Anastasius IV, 124, 125
Andronicus II, 152

Angelico (Fra), 182
Anicetus, 10
Anscar, St., 64
Anterus, 13
Anthimos, 36
Antonelli (Cardinal), 292, 301
Aquinas, See Thomas Aquinas, St.
Aristotle, 135, 180
Arius, 20
Arnold (of Brescia), 123-26
Arnulf, 74, 75
Athalaric, 34
Athanasius, 22
Attila, 29
Augustine, St., 28, 180, 247

Bacon, 251
Bandinelli (Cardinal), 127, 128
Bardas, Caesar, 69, 70
Barome, 330
Basil, St., 44
Basil II, 92, 93
Becket (Thomas à), 128, 129
Belisarius, 37
Bellarmine, 251, 367
Benedict, St., 44
Benedict I, 39
Benedict II, St., 43
Benedict III, 67, 68
Benedict IV, 77, 78
Benedict V, 84
Benedict VI, 85
Benedict VII, 85
Benedict VIII, 91, 92
Benedict IX, 93-95, 155
Benedict X, 100, 104
Benedict XI, 159, 160
Benedict XII, 164
Benedict XIII (Anti-Pope), 175, 176
Benedict XIII, 260, 261
Benedict XIV, 263-66
Benedict XV, 316-26, 328, 347, 354
Berengar, 77, 79, 82, 83

382

SUBJECT INDEX